D1564188

PUBLICATIONS OF THE
DEPARTMENT OF SOCIAL AND ECONOMIC RESEARCH
UNIVERSITY OF GLASGOW

GENERAL EDITOR: A. K. CAIRNCROSS

SOCIAL AND ECONOMIC STUDIES

4

JOHN MILLAR
OF GLASGOW
1735-1801

JOHN MILLAR OF GLASGOW

1735–1801

*His Life and Thought and his Contributions
to Sociological Analysis*

BY

WILLIAM C. LEHMANN

Ph.D. (Columbia)

*Emeritus Professor of Sociology
Syracuse University*

CAMBRIDGE
AT THE UNIVERSITY PRESS
1960

PUBLISHED BY
THE SYNDICS OF THE CAMBRIDGE UNIVERSITY PRESS
London Office : Bentley House, N.W. 1
American Branch : New York
Agents for Canada, India, and Pakistan : Macmillan

Printed in Great Britain at the Villafield Press, Bishopbriggs, Glasgow

To
WILLIAM LEONARDO
AND
SHIRLEY JEANNE

'The most celebrated and most successful teacher of his time.'

David Murray, *Memories of the Old College of Glasgow*

'The most effective and influential apostle of liberalism in Scotland in that age.'

John Rae, *Life of Adam Smith*

'Among the most instructive things that ever were offered to the minds of youth.'

James Mill, on his lectures and writings

'. . . an astonishing book containing one of the best and most complete sociologies we possess. . . . The technological-economic theory of society already present in embryo in many eighteenth-century thinkers was brought to its final consummation by John Millar. To his ideas the nineteenth century was unable to add anything but details. . . . One must admit that Millar's formulation of the economic theory of society is superior to Marx's in completeness and clarity.'

Werner Sombart, speaking of the *Ranks*, in *Die Anfänge der Soziologie*

'Millar's classes were . . . the great training school for the lawyers and statesmen of the next generation; and many of them in after life owned that Millar's prelections had first given the impulse that stimulated them through life. . . . There can be no question that the bold lines of thought on which the *Edinburgh Review* was afterwards constructed, were first laid down by his masterly hand.'

A reviewer in the *Edinburgh Review* of a later date

*   *   *

'The lives of men of letters seldom abound with incidents. A reader of sense and taste, therefore, never expects to find, in the memoirs of a philosopher or poet, the same species of entertainment or information which he receives from those of a statesman or general. He expects however, to be either informed or entertained. Nor will he be disappointed, did the writer take care to dwell principally on such topics as characterize the man, and distinguish the peculiar part which he acted in the varied drama of society.'

Mason, *Life and Writings of Gray*, Preface

TABLE OF CONTENTS

Table of Contents

PART IV. SELECTIONS FROM OTHER WRITINGS

APPENDICES

The frontispiece, a Tassie medallion of John Millar (1796), is reproduced by permission of the Board of Trustees for the National Galleries of Scotland

x

FOREWORD

In the history of modern civilization one country after another has been in the van, for a time, giving a lead to the others and leaving behind imperishable monuments in letters and the arts, as well as great advances in the sciences. For the little country of Scotland that time began around the middle of the eighteenth century, and after a further effervescence in the early nineteenth century, ended about 1830. During that period David Hume and Adam Smith gave a new direction especially to philosophy and economics, and around them were significant figures such as Adam Ferguson, Thomas Reid, Francis Hutcheson, and William Robertson. There was James Watt in applied science, the man who more than any other developed the steam engine, and among other scientists James Hutton, who revolutionized the study of geology. In literature three leading poets were Allan Ramsay, Robert Burns, and Robert Ferguson, and the great literary series culminated in Walter Scott.

Among the remarkable men of this period, one distinctive figure has suffered considerable neglect. He may receive casual mention when an account is given of the new ferment of learning that characterized the Scottish universities in his time, but rather as a great teacher than as a leading scholar. And yet a strong case can be made for the claim that this man was a seminal thinker who did more than any of the others to advance the area of knowledge we now call sociology.

Dr Lehmann deserves the gratitude of social scientists generally in that he has at length brought John Millar out of obscurity and through the devoted labour of many years has revealed the lineaments of this sociological pioneer, assessing his contribution and characterizing his place in the group of distinguished men who centred around the universities of Glasgow and Edinburgh. They were nearly all interested in broad inquiries into the nature of society, frequently with ethical overtones. Millar's interest led him to give particular attention to the sociological aspects of human relationships, to the inter-relations of institutions and the impact on institutions of customs, *mores*, and traditions, and in especial to the class structure.

It is that emphasis and the way he developed it that well entitles him to a place in the history of sociology. We cannot call him a sociologist *pur sang*. The title did not then exist. Politics, economics, sociology, jurisprudence were all merged in some inclusive doctrine of society. But as Adam Smith gave distinctive consideration to the economic aspects of the 'progress of society', so, in degree, did Millar to the sociological aspects. Earlier thinkers had of course discoursed on the class structure—men like Harrington, for example—but essentially in the light of its particular role in the body politic, while Millar is interested not only in power-relationships but also in the particular usages and ways of life characteristic of different classes, and he is aware of certain changes in the structure of the class system that the development of the manufacturing or capitalist class had already brought about.

The temper of the age in Scotland provided the necessary intellectual background for the characteristic achievements of its leading thinkers. The theological dogmatism of an earlier period gave place to a liberalistic trend of thought. As Dr Lehmann well puts it, a peculiarly 'Scottish realism' took hold in the middle eighteenth century. It was quietly anti-ecclesiastical and limitedly rationalistic. The nature of human society was a subject to be inquired into, not one to be moralized about. This inquiry was kept within or bounded by an accepted framework of social ethics, which included a belief in 'the natural progress of mankind' and a general acceptance of the established social order aside from its abuses. The farthest reach of scepticism was represented by David Hume, with his rejection of causal knowledge and his mechanistic explanation of the 'passions'. But this form of scepticism had little application to the social order. Millar shared to the full the spirit of the times. In accordance with its realistic trend he sees, for example, in property and the mode of its transmission the corner-stone of the social structure, and he views the church in its aspects as a power-agency and instrument of social control.

Dr Lehmann brings the reader very close to this eighteenth-century sociologist. He shows the interplay of Millar's life and his thought. He traces the influences on him of his contemporaries and Millar's own influence on others. And finally, he makes accessible Millar's major sociological work as well as apt selections from his other writings. In short, the author presents us with a comprehensive and definitive study of a forgotten pioneer.

ROBERT M. MacIVER

PREFACE

John Millar was Professor of Civil Law at the University of Glasgow from 1761 to 1801. The essay that follows, together with a reprint of portions of his published works, represents an attempt to rescue him from oblivion, and make available to the student of the history of ideas and of the liberal tradition in Western thought the record of his life and work and thought. Although named in his lifetime alongside such men as David Hume, Adam Smith, Adam Ferguson, Thomas Reid, William Robertson, Lord Kames and Dugald Stewart, by a strange quirk of fate his very memory suffered, after a brief generation or two, all but complete eclipse. It is my belief that, both as a matter of historical justice to the man and because of the permanent contribution to thought of some of his ideas, he deserves to be restored to a place among the creative thinkers of his time.

A number of features of this book are accounted for by the somewhat unusual historical position of its subject. In the first place, this is not an attempt merely to round out and bring up to date a story that has already been told. A brief obituary sketch by a colleague has long since been lost, and another by his nephew, John Craig, is very sketchy indeed. Apart from *An Account of his Life and Writings* by the same author, still somewhat obituary in character (see below, p. 7), no life of Millar exists. We can therefore make no assumption of a previous knowledge of Millar's life and work on the part of any but a very few of our readers, and have included many details that under other circumstances might have been omitted.

Since his memory has so completely faded out, and his published works are all but forgotten, I have sought to convey the impression left by Millar through direct quotation from contemporary testimony, even though this meant more frequent and often lengthier quotations than might otherwise have seemed desirable. For the same reason, and because, to the American reader at least, his works are accessible only in a few outstanding libraries, I have included in this volume as much of Millar's writings as limits of space would allow, including the full text (some footnotes excepted) of the *Origin of the Distinction of Ranks*. This may serve to give the reader a fair impression of his style, an indication of his leading ideas and material from which to judge his contributions to social and political thought. Full details of Millar's works are contained in the Bibliography at the end of this book.

Partly because of the same set of circumstances, I have found myself

Preface

trying to address three or four different audiences at the same time. The general reader in Scotland might be expected to have one kind of interest in Millar, the English reader another, and the American still another. The student of social and political theory, of the beginnings of modern sociology, and of the history of legal education, will, regardless of country, each be interested in a different aspect of his life and thought. For the informed Scottish reader, some matters could have been omitted that were indispensable for other readers. How far the compromise here struck will satisfy any or all readers, I am in no position to judge.

One purpose of any publication of this kind must be to aid in the uncovering of further materials that may have escaped one's search. The author and the editors of this series will be grateful for any information brought to their attention regarding any letters or other manuscript materials relating to Millar and for any references to him in personal memoirs and newspaper or other periodical accounts.

ACKNOWLEDGEMENTS

It would be impossible to name here all who have contributed, in one way or another, toward making this study possible. My first and very special obligations are to Dr Ronald L. Meek and Dr John Highet, both of the University of Glasgow, the former chiefly for many suggestions coming out of his intimate knowledge of Millar's work, the latter chiefly for constructive suggestions on inclusions, exclusions, arrangement and style, both for painstaking reading of the manuscript in various stages of its development and for encouragement along the way. Going back even farther I am under very considerable obligation to Dr Howard Becker of the University of Wisconsin for encouragement and constructive suggestions in my entire eighteenth-century Scottish study and for a critical reading of the whole manuscript in its near-final stage, with a number of suggestions for its improvement.

For early encouragement to continue with the work begun with my *Adam Ferguson and the Beginnings of Modern Sociology* many years ago I am under obligation to Professors MacIver of Columbia University and Sorokin of Harvard University and to Dr Harry Elmer Barnes.

It would be ungrateful of me not to acknowledge here the kindly interest taken in my work by the late Dr Henry Meikle, Historiographer Royal to her Majesty the Queen and formerly head librarian of the National Library at Edinburgh, and the many helpful leads he gave me early in the study; and the many courtesies extended me by

Preface

Professor Mackie of the University of Glasgow, with useful hints on early university history and organization.

Mr Shepperson of Edinburgh University read the entire manuscript in the middle stage of its development and offered useful suggestions. Mr Nobbs of the same university gave me helpful comments on Millar's political theory. Without the encouragement of Professor A. K. Cairncross and Dr T. T. Paterson of Glasgow, this book could not be appearing in its present form.

The research entering into the present study and its background was carried out chiefly in the following libraries: The National Library of Scotland at Edinburgh, the University of Glasgow Library, the Edinburgh University Library, with also some use of the Public Library and the Signet Library at Edinburgh and the Mitchell Library at Glasgow, particularly for the contemporary newspaper files; the British Museum in London, the Library of Congress at Washington and the Widener Library and other libraries at Harvard University. It would be impossible to make individual acknowledgement of help received at these libraries, but special mention must be made of Mr Weir at Glasgow for many helpful leads on local matters and repeated access to the Murray Collection of student-notes and also the Bannerman MSS., and to Mr Sharp and Mr Finlayson at the Edinburgh University Library for many courtesies extended me. I am in great debt to my wife Jane and to my daughter Shirley Jeanne both for their encouragement and for their assistance in the preparation of this volume.

None of these persons should, of course, be held responsible for any of the shortcomings of this study.

W. C. L.

ABBREVIATED TITLES

H.V.   John Millar, *Historical View of the English Government*. 4-volume edition, London, 1803, unless otherwise indicated.

Ranks   John Millar, *The Origin of the Distinction of Ranks*, 3rd edition (Edinburgh, 1779), reprinted in this volume.

Life   John Craig, 'An Account of John Millar's Life and Writings', in the fourth edition of *The Origin of the Distinction of Ranks*.

Crito   John Millar, *Letters of Crito* (Edinburgh and London, 1796).

GENERAL INTRODUCTION

The distinguished author of *The Origin of the Distinction of Ranks* and of *An Historical View of the English Government* was in many ways a remarkable figure on the late eighteenth-century educational and political scene in Scotland. He was a man, first of all, of striking personality and of great vigour and daring, both in and out of the classroom. His rise, in a few short years and when still barely thirty years of age, to a reputation that brought students to his law classes from far and wide and in unprecedented numbers was phenomenal. In a time of rapid change in social and religious outlook, and of sharp political controversy, he was as bitterly attacked by the reactionary elements in the community as he was idolized by his students and highly regarded by other young liberals who came under his influence.

Three elements of abiding significance stand out in Millar's life to justify an attempt to remedy the neglect of a century and a half. The first of these is his role as a teacher of youth, and his influence as an educator in a time of great educational revival in Scotland. The elder Mill rated his lectures as probably 'among the most instructive things that ever were offered to the minds of youth', so that 'to have been a pupil of Millar's must have been an advantage of no ordinary sort'.* Francis Jeffrey, the distinguished Edinburgh Reviewer, who had known him as a student, considered his instruction in the classroom to be in several respects unique in the whole history of education. David Murray, who has more recently looked closely into the record of Millar's work, did not hesitate to rate him as 'the most celebrated and most successful teacher of his time'.†

Education must always remain a major concern of any people; and education in the Scotland of the later eighteenth century, and for that matter in the nineteenth as well, offers perhaps the best key to the leadership wielded throughout the Western world by that little nation in philosophy, science, law, medicine, theology and other areas of our cultural life. It is not an exaggeration to say that the Scottish universities, as educational institutions and as homes of scholarly and scientific research, were at that time rapidly coming to the forefront of universities anywhere in the West, Oxford and Cambridge not excepted.

* See below, p. 15 n.
† David Murray, *Memories of the Old College of Glasgow* (Glasgow, 1927), p. 221.

Only those of Holland continued, perhaps, to hold their own in this rivalry.

In the building up of one of these institutions of learning, Millar played no insignificant part. Along with men like Hutcheson, Simson, Adam Smith, Reid, Cullen and Black at Glasgow (the last two later at Edinburgh), and Maclaurin, Robison, Ferguson, Campbell, John and James Gregory, John and Alexander Monro and others elsewhere, he was helping to breathe new life into institutions of learning that had suffered a considerable decline under the religious and political strife of the preceding century or more.

His elevation of the law chair at Glasgow, for the period of his incumbency, to a position that easily outrivalled those at Edinburgh and in the other Scottish universities was admitted by all. His elevation of law teaching from mere instruction in the technicalities of the law in preparation for its professional practice, after the fashion of the Inns of Court, to the level of a genuinely liberal subject, deserving of a place in a university, was recognized both by his contemporaries and by the succeeding generation of lawyers and statesmen. His methods of instruction and the stimulation he gave to a whole generation of students in the study of jurisprudence and of civil history and politics generally were recognized as outstanding.

When the authentic biographer of Adam Smith, at whose feet Millar had sat and from whom he had received perhaps his chief inspiration, speaks, not of the master himself but of his pupil, as having been, in his opinion, 'the most effective and influential apostle of liberalism in Scotland in that day',* he points to a second area in which Millar's work takes on a significance reaching far beyond the simply personal and beyond a mere interest in his contribution to the study and teaching of law.

His mature years fell in a time of great political upheaval. Those were times that not only 'tried men's souls', but that touched also the deepest springs of men's thought and action. In the words of a friend of Millar's and a worthy antagonist but great admirer of Burke's who must have had both these men in mind:

Recent events have accumulated more terrible practical instruction on every subject of politics than could have been in other times acquired by the experience of ages. Men's wits, sharpened by their passions, have penetrated to the bottom of almost all political questions. The mind of that man must indeed be incurious and indocile who has either overlooked all these things, or reaped no instruction from the contemplation of them.†

* John Rae, *Life of Adam Smith* (London, 1895), pp. 53 f.

† Sir James Mackintosh, *A Discourse on the Study of the Law of Nature and Nations* (London, 1799), p. 30. Also the various editions of Mackintosh's works.

Millar participated actively, and I believe significantly, in this movement of thought and political agitation. In its Scottish manifestations he may not unfairly be called a key figure. His writings, along with those of Montesquieu, Hume, Smith and Ferguson, made up the principal diet of a rising generation of liberals, mostly young lawyers, who led the Scottish agitation for reform; and he was personally the inspiration of not a few of them. When the Reform of the British Parliament came to be effected some three decades after Millar's demise, we find not only among its supporters but among its leaders a number of his former students and others who had come under his influence.

A third element that stands out in his life and work is his contribution to social and political thought in its more theoretical aspects, to historical interpretation and to an understanding generally of the nature and development of social and political institutions. It was for this, in fact, related though it is to his more practical educational and political efforts, that this study was chiefly undertaken. And it is this that gives character and abiding worth to his writings.

An analysis of Millar's thought must, therefore, constitute the burden of the present study, however engaging the story of the life itself of this hitherto little-known figure may be. But Millar's thought, it must be remembered, was part of a larger thought-movement in Europe generally but particularly in eighteenth-century Scotland. This body of thought, which we shall discuss in some detail later, marked a sharp departure, on the historical side, from the speculations of Hooker, Hobbes, Locke and Berkeley on matters social and political, and stands in sharp contrast with many, though by no means all the tendencies of the French Enlightenment from Descartes to Voltaire, Rousseau and Condorcet. To see in the Enlightenment of the eighteenth century only a modified Cartesianism, a restatement of earlier ideas of 'natural law' in terms of 'natural rights' and of a physical naturalism, the apriorism of many of the *philosophes*, a blind faith in progress and in man's ability to make man, society and all political institutions over, unhistorically, on an abstract rational model—this would be to reveal, at least so far as Scottish thought is concerned, either a vast lacuna in one's knowledge of the facts, or an excessively romantic bias in their evaluation.*

This thought-movement was itself, in turn, only an element in a remarkable awakening, not only in the intellectual, but also in the moral and political, the literary and artistic, the cultural, and even, in a measure, the religious life of Scotland: an awakening that was in many ways unique in the whole history of Western thought and culture. Only

* See below p. 98 and note.

3

the Periclean Age in Greece, the Augustan Age in Rome, the Renaissance movement in Italy and beyond, the contemporary Encyclopedist movement in France and the advances in history, philosophy and science that we associate with the founding of the University of Berlin in the Germany of the early nineteenth century can fairly bear comparison. To call it the 'Augustan Age' of Scottish life and thought would hardly be an exaggeration. Comparable efforts in other times and places may have been more creative in pure science, or in art, or in religious life and thought. But viewed in its total range and vigour, in its influence, even in its own day, upon the thought of other countries, and in its foundation-laying role in the scientific labours of succeeding generations in philosophy, the natural sciences and in social and political thought, this awakening of the Scottish mind has few parallels indeed.

With all the limitations of his evolutionary naturalism, and with all the permeation of his historical analysis by his political biases and by his characteristically eighteenth-century devotion to the idea of progress, Millar's thought still stands in sharp contrast with the alleged and sometimes real 'rationalism' of the Enlightenment. Particularly in helping to give this eighteenth-century thought a distinctly sociological cast, in the broadest sense of that term, Millar played a very prominent part.

If a further reason were needed for wanting to make Millar's closer acquaintance, some students of intellectual history and of the history of liberalism in modern times will find this in the intimacy of his relations, both personal and intellectual, with his master, Adam Smith.

Millar was a student in the very first classes to which Smith lectured at Glasgow, if not indeed an attendant upon his lectures at Edinburgh before he came to Glasgow, and he gratefully acknowledged his indebtedness to Smith for many of his own ideas.

The reader who will take the pains to compare Millar's writings with Smith's long-lost and still much neglected *Lectures*, as made available to us from student-notes by Cannan, or with the more broadly historical and sociological portions of the *Wealth of Nations*, will find reflected in the former, not indeed as in a mirror, but in a kind of dynamic transformation and enlargement, important elements thrown out in the latter. So that, just as we owe much of our more intimate personal knowledge of the teacher, his manner in the classroom, the range, broad content and general character of his lectures, to the pen of his pupil (see below, App. I, pp. 401 ff.), so, too, a study of the life and thought of one of his most distinguished pupils should throw even further light on that of his great master.

4

PART I

CHIEFLY BIOGRAPHICAL

I

INTRODUCTION

The basic source for Millar's life and work must remain *An Account of [his] Life and Writings*,* by his nephew, John Craig, prefixed to the fourth edition (Edinburgh and London, 1806) of the *Origin of the Distinction of Ranks*. This account is uneven in many ways, and in some instances inaccurate. It leaves completely unanswered many questions that we should like very much to have answered. For all of its valuable analysis of his courses of lectures and of many of his basic ideas, and its excellent personal characterization of the man, it is still woefully limited in factual biographical detail, especially for the formative years of his life. It has the advantage of being written largely from personal knowledge and intimate association with its subject by a man with keen insight into human character; but perhaps also some disadvantages of friendly bias. At any rate, it is the only strictly biographical account we have of him except for an obituary statement published in the *Scots Magazine* for 1801 by the same author shortly after Millar's death.†

For the rest we are dependent on reviews of his works, items here and there in the memoirs of various contemporaries, the minutes of the Senate and of the Faculty of the University for the period of his professorship, a few items in the newspapers of the day, some notations in the official parish registers of births, deaths and marriages preserved in the Register House at Edinburgh, and casual items here and there. A few of Millar's letters have been preserved. Some inferences about his life and work can also be drawn from his published works and from surviving student-notes on his lectures.

A number of references to Millar, based chiefly on the sources already cited, will be found in the various histories of the University noted below and in the biographies of Adam Smith. To David Murray in particular we are indebted for a number of details on Millar's life that he gathered from various sources, and for his collection of student-notes on his lectures.

A source that would presumably have proved of great value to our study was unfortunately irretrievably lost only a few years ago. At any rate, we know that there were preserved at his one-time summer home until 1943 or 1944 several boxes of papers belonging to Millar, presum-

* Abbreviated in the notes below as *Life*.   † *Scots Magazine*, vol. LXIII (1801), pp. 527 f.

7

ably including lecture notes, unfinished manuscripts, letters, etc. In those war years, we are informed by a member of the family, the last occupant of Milheugh in the Millar family line, on vacating the premises, burned this material without further examining it.*

* Information from personal correspondence and other personal sources. (Cp. also W. R. Scott, *Adam Smith as Student and Professor* (Glasgow, 1937), p. 306 n. 3.)

II

BACKGROUND AND FORMATIVE YEARS

The life of Professor Millar of Milheugh falls in a period very remarkable indeed in the annals of intellectual achievement and has its setting amidst scenes of social, economic and political transformations scarcely less remarkable.

When the future professor, author, and champion of liberalism was born, in 1735, the first signs were just beginning to appear of that great awakening of the spirit in Scotland that was to give the world Hume, Adam Smith, Robertson, and many more of equal fame. When he died in 1801 that great movement in philosophy, letters, political speculation, historical interpretation and the liberalization of religious thought and feeling had, if not exactly ended, at least accomplished its main object and lost something of its original freshness and glory.

During that period Scotland had been transformed from a land and people not without elements of real greatness indeed, but almost primitive in their rusticity and general rural poverty, and thoroughly agrarian in outlook and orientation, into a land increasingly oriented toward a number of booming commercial and industrial centres. Its very soil in many places was undermined in the pursuit of coal and ore, and the face of its countryside marred by reeking 'bings' of mine tipple. Its people by the thousands were leaving behind them the scenes of 'the cottar's Saturday night', and the glens of the Highlands and the Islands, to find new outlets in Glasgow and the lower Clyde, in Edinburgh and Dundee, and generally along the Firths of the Clyde, the Forth and the Tay—or in Birmingham, London or the 'wilderness of America'.

Politically the Scottish people had finally, though somewhat slowly and at times reluctantly—particularly in the Highland regions—given up their Jacobite protests and accepted their new position in the United Kingdom as loyal subjects of the ruling House at Westminster. They had, along with the English but with not quite the same feelings in either case, gone through two wars, first with the France with whom they had long had many intimate associations, dynastically and otherwise, and then with the colonies with whom they had come to be even more closely united by ties of blood. Glasgow particularly, which had built up a tobacco trade with the colonies so thriving that it had become almost her very life-blood, suffered a severe shock when this trade was, for the time being, completely laid waste by the latter war. They had experienced also the tremendous impact of the French Revolution—those in authority, on the one hand, being driven to reactionary and repressive measures dangerous to the established British liberties; the lower, and to some extent the middle classes, on the other hand, being aroused to a political consciousness never before experienced in the same measure in Scotland.* Men had been stirred to the defence and to an attempted extension of those liberties in sharp criticism of their government, and there was a rising demand for parliamentary reform. Then came another war with France—a war that stirred up the deepest opposition, in fact evoked charges of almost criminal irresponsibility against the government by Fox and his followers, many of them Scottish, and that threatened, at times, the direst consequences to the nation. This war and the repressive anti-sedition measures that accompanied it in the mid-1790's, served at once to strengthen the spirit of faction among the people and to prepare them for a more effective voice in the councils of the nation.

To this whole movement of life and thought Millar was, as Rae said of Adam Smith, 'all antennae'. He was 'a part of all he met' in the double sense of making it intimately a part of his life and thought and of himself in his own measure contributing actively to its development.

But to begin in the beginning, Millar was born in the manse of the famous Kirk o' Shotts, about midway between Edinburgh and Glasgow, in Lanarkshire. A lone wall, once forming part of the old manse but now part of a garden wall to the rear of the present manse, and bearing the date 1700, marks the site of the house where he was born. The portion of the original parish records, preserved in the Register House at Edinburgh, that once no doubt contained his baptismal record is missing, but from other contemporary sources we know the date of his birth to be 22 June 1735.

His family was an old one of good standing in the parish of Blantyre near Glasgow, but it lacked the dignity of the neighbouring Hamiltons, the Maxwells of Calderwood, or of the Lords of Blantyre. The Millars had occupied the estate of Milheugh and operated its mill at least since Reformation times, if not since the days of Robert the Bruce—at least seven of the occupants, apparently without interruption, bearing the name of John Millar.†

His father, James Millar (1701–85), son of a John Millar of Milheugh in Blantyre, was a minister of the Church of Scotland, who served charges within the Synod of Glasgow and Ayr throughout a long

---

* See H. W. Meikle, *Scotland and the French Revolution* (Glasgow, 1912), especially ch. 1.

† See Appendix IV below.

ministry. He took his M.A. degree at Glasgow in 1720 and later a degree in divinity. Licensed to preach in 1726, he was two years later called to his first charge at the Kirk o' Shotts—where he found the doors barred, and the people rising in riotous protest, not against the new minister but against the manner of his appointment by the heritors, who felt themselves in no need of consulting the rank and file of the membership in the selection of a minister—and preached from a window in the inn instead. Whether or not we choose to see any symbolical significance in this for the future championship of liberty by his son, he was able to overcome the opposition and served this famous charge for ten years. In 1737 he transferred to the Second Church at Hamilton, about eleven miles from Glasgow, which he served until 1766, when he transferred to the First Church there, to serve it in turn until his death in 1785. He was considered 'a man of high respectability as a clergyman, equally distinguished by the strength of his understanding as by his talents in his profession'.*

In 1734 he married one Ann, daughter of Archibald Hamilton of Westburn and a first cousin to the distinguished Professor Cullen—a marriage of which her family disapproved, however, as being unworthy of their status, and which resulted in her isolation from them for the rest of her life. From this union John was born the next year as the oldest of four children.

For reasons we are not told but which might in some way have to do with his mother's estrangement from her brothers, or possibly with the law of entail, he spent most of his childhood up to the age of seven with his father's only and senior but unmarried brother John at Milheugh, which country seat he was later to inherit. Here he learned the rudiments of letters in preparation for entry into the grammar school at Hamilton, where he learned not only Latin but also Greek to prepare him for further study in his father's college. We may assume that he was at the same time well grounded by his parents in biblical lore and in the tenets of religion according to the faith of the Church of Scotland.

At the age of eleven, a tender age to become a student, but not an unusual one at that time, he entered the Old College or University of Glasgow where he spent at least the next six years in study. This study was directed first, as was that of perhaps a majority of the students in the University at that period, toward the service of the church; but the lad was soon aiming, as was also so frequently the case—witness Adam Smith, Adam Ferguson, James Mill, Thomas Thomson, and many others—at another vocation of his own choosing. He appears to

* Craig, *Life*, pp. 1 f.; John Hamilton Gray, *Autobiography of a Scottish Country Gentleman* (Edinburgh, 1868), pp. 17–30. Other sources below, p. 410.

have had, as his biographer suggests, 'some disinclination to fetter himself by established articles of belief', in a church that, as he saw it, 'holds out few inducements to the ambition of him who is conscious of superior talents'.*

Since Glasgow, a city of commerce and increasingly also of industry, though not entirely neglectful of the finer arts of life, was to be his place of abode and labour with few interruptions for the next fifty-five years, and as such was to exert a marked influence on his life and thought, it behoves us here to look briefly at it.

When Millar first came to live there, Glasgow was a sleepy college and cathedral town of some 18,000 souls, just waking from its medieval slumbers. 'Broom still grew on the Broomielaw' and the town-herd still made his morning round calling the cattle from their stables near the Trongate, the Saltmarket and the Gallowgate with his familiar horn, and driving them to pasture in the common meadows which are still known as the Cowcaddens, though now densely populated. St Enoch's Square was still a private garden;† the Clyde had not yet been deepened to the Broomielaw, and few ships larger than small fishing craft could come nearer than Greenock, Port Glasgow or Dumbarton. Life still centred chiefly around 'the Cross', on High Street, on the Trongate, and on the Gallowgate—the latter, true to its name, leading to the place that must have left shocking memories in the mind of many a child.

Still this city, which Defoe had even before this (1721) called 'one of the cleanliest, most beautiful and best built cities in Great Britain'‡ was coming rapidly to be the emporium of the West, and next to Edinburgh was easily the most important city in Scotland; and as such must often have fired Millar's youthful imagination. The lad could not but be moved by its throbbing life, its colourful scenes, its many tokens of the larger world beyond the Clyde and his native Lanarkshire, and, as he was later to realize and abundantly to reflect in his writings, of a transformation going on in the land of his fathers.

Glasgow lacked, indeed, the courtly life and more courtly manners of its rival in the east with the lively and colourful scenes of the Parliament Hall and the Court of Session. It lacked also largely the literary brilliance and other graces coming to be bestowed on its rival by the Muses. Yet the city of Kentigern or St Mungo of old, and the Glasgow of his own day, had its own appeals to the imagination. Ships were

---

* *Life*, p. v. Cf. also below, p. 41, Thomson's letter to his father; also Rae, *Adam Smith*, p. 57.

† Taken, in part verbatim, from Rae, *op. cit.* pp. 87 ff. See also Denholm, *History of Glasgow* (1798), pp. 112-49, and other histories.

‡ Defoe's *Tour*, quoted in *Chronicles of St Mungo* (Glasgow, 1843), p. 43.

beginning to bring at least near her gates the golden leaf and other precious cargoes from afar. The great tobacco merchants presented evidence in abundance of this in luxurious homes, splendid though noisy carriages, gay attire and festive boards. Highlanders and Lowlanders mingled freely on the city's streets and in the market place. 'Wild, shaggy, dwarfed cattle and ponies' could often be seen driven to market by men almost equally wild in appearance, who gazed in wonderment at the buildings and steeples, at shops filled with 'articles of luxury of which they knew not the use', at the men and women of fashion—in a word at the marvels of a growing, throbbing city.* Soon there were to be stage-coaches carrying men and wares and intelligence of the market and of the doings of Parliament post-haste from London, from Birmingham and Newcastle, to and from Edinburgh and Dundee. New faces were appearing in increasing numbers on its streets, in its shops and mills—men wearing strange garbs and speaking in strange dialects and worshipping in ways that were different.

If the mere boy of a student was still too much absorbed in his Greek and Latin, his logic and letters and his occasional student pranks to be thinking much on these things, his mind was still taking them in and in due time would be reflecting much upon them, upon the circumstances that brought about these changes, upon their impact upon the life of the nation and upon the ways of community living. Would the Campbells and the Macdonalds, the Stuarts and the Macgregors, remain the Highlanders they were, warlike, intensely clannish and generally poor, or would they mingle with the Bells, the Boyds, the Montgomerys and the Turnbulls, and be absorbed into the commercial and professional, the religious and political life of the community? Would the poet still be singing the simple piety of 'the Cottar's Saturday Night', or the shepherd idylls of 'Call [ing] the yowes to the knowes, call them where the heather grows' when men went down into the bowels of the earth to bring up the 'black stone' and were hearkening to the call of the marts of commerce or of the spindles and looms of the mills? And if the spirit of liberty might be advanced by these new interests and activities of men, did these not also contain the seeds, some of them at least, of the destruction of that liberty?†

The College itself, which the lad was now entering, was, like the other Scottish universities at this time, a school for boys in their middle and later teens almost more than a university proper. Yet it had the dignity of its nearly three hundred years; its halls and towers, the inner and outer squares, the 'professors' houses', the classrooms and the ancient and awesome 'Black Stone' or Blackstone '. . . that dreaded chair with

* Paraphrased from Scott's *Rob Roy*, ch. xix, near the end.　　† See Pt. IV, Selection vi.

bottom black, Ah, seat of terror to Collegiate pale!'* none of these was without a certain romantic appeal; and men of high scholarship taught there.

'Regenting', in which a given instructor carried a class upwards through all the Arts subjects, had given way shortly before this to professorial 'prelecting', each in his field of more limited and therefore more intensive scholarship, and Latin was rapidly giving way now to English as the language of instruction.

Like the other Scottish universities, the Old College of Glasgow was part of an educational system that aimed to reach all classes of the population and not merely the sons of the privileged. The English educational ideal of providing young gentlemen of leisure, and perhaps future statesmen, merely with a suitable environment and a cultural background in which they might develop freely in the company of their kind, was markedly absent at Glasgow. Rather the student was to be equipped with knowledge and provided with its tools, and to develop a frame of mind and habits of application, liberal indeed but useful also in the vocation of his early choice. The Puritan or 'Presbyterian' frame of mind and soul was, if anything, even stronger here than elsewhere in Scotland, and professors and students alike took themselves seriously in their work and in their conduct.†

Most of the students, coming from poor homes, lived frugally on simple, often even on very meagre rations, and even those who came from homes of greater abundance lived unostentatiously within the college walls or in near-by accommodation, sometimes in professors' homes. Piety was not infrequently a better passport into the college community than scholarship.

Of the professors some were excellent teachers, others were less skilled; but high scholarship was the rule. They lived modestly on very scanty salaries; only when classes were very large, as the Greek class frequently was, for example, did student fees bring up their income to a more comfortable level. Often they took in the sons of families of means as boarding students or 'resident pupils' to supplement their income. They lived, with few exceptions, in the 'professors' houses' within the college compound.

Of Millar's student days and early studies, and of the men who most entered into the shaping of his young mind, his biographer tells us

---

* No reference to the jurist; only to the awesome examination chair, so named after the black marble slab forming its seat. See Murray, *Old College*, pp. 79–92, for cuts and history.

† On the pragmatic, democratic character of Scottish as compared with English higher education at this time, see Gray, *op. cit.* pp. 69 f.; Murray, *op. cit.* pp. 464–67, 559–61; also *H.V.* vol. III, pp. 88 ff.

almost nothing. So little, indeed, that James Mill, in a review in his *Literary Journal,** takes him severely to task for this neglect; or rather, laments the tragic neglect generally, by biographers, of

the importance of the early part of life. When a man has risen to great intellectual and moral eminence [*sc.* as Millar had] the process by which his mind is formed is one of the most instructive circumstances which can be unveiled to mankind. [Of] the circumstances which kindled his ardour or those by which the flame was fed; [of] the studies in which [lads of promise like Millar] delighted, the books which they perused, the hours which they were accustomed to give to labour, and those which they resigned to relaxation, even the nature of the sports in which they indulged [biographers generally tell us but little].

And the man who gave so much to the education of his own son held this to be 'an egregious mistake' indeed.

No records have apparently been preserved of the classes he attended, but from a general knowledge of the Arts course requirements, and from the university records of the men then occupying the various chairs, we can draw some conclusions. A student in the Arts course would as a matter of course have taken Latin or 'Humanity', then taught by one Professor George Ross, and Greek under the much more distinguished Professor Moor, with whom Millar was later, as a young colleague, to fight many a battle royal. Moral philosophy he studied with Professor Craigie, immediate and not undistinguished successor to Professor Hutcheson, and logic with the less distinguished Professor Louden—to repeat, presumably both of them with Adam Smith during his first year, or more, at Glasgow. He very likely studied mathematics under the celebrated Robert Simson, re-discoverer and reviver of Euclid; and from his early family acquaintance with Professor Cullen, a kinsman by marriage of his mother's, and from his lively interest in chemistry in later life, it is probably safe to assume that he studied chemistry under this great scientist—as he may also have studied 'natural philosophy' with the elder Professor Dick.†

During his college years, and in private study in the years immediately following, he must have acquired a broad knowledge of history, jurisprudence, general philosophy and literature, including such a command of the Greek and Roman classics, we are told, as to enable him to cite and discuss freely passages from almost any author or work that might come under discussion. It would appear that association with his

* London, second series, vol. I, pp. 624–29; also Alexander Bain, *James Mill: A Biography* (London, 1882), pp. 56–8.

† For a complete list of professors, by chairs, by years, see Hay, *Inaugural Addresses*, pp. 175–8. For a convenient account of an arts student's general programme see Adam Smith's letter to Lord Shelburne, quoted by Scott, *Adam Smith as Student and Professor*, pp. 243–5.

uncle at Milheugh, during the long summer vacations and on other occasions, contributed not a little toward arousing his interest in problems of law and general jurisprudence and in the recent political and parliamentary history of Scotland and England.*

When Adam Smith came to Glasgow in 1751, the young student, just out of the Arts course, 'having come to the University for instruction, not merely to go through a common routine . . . eagerly seized the opportunity of hearing [his] Lectures' presumably chiefly on literary subjects from the logic chair, and on what Millar later himself called 'the history of civil society' from the moral philosophy chair. He was apparently so well prepared to enter into these subjects that his 'intelligence and ardour soon attracted Dr Smith's notice, and at this time was laid the foundation [as we have previously noticed] of that mutual esteem, which, during the few years they were afterwards professors in the same university, produced lasting intimacy and friendship'† and we may add, also intellectual co-operation.

Of Millar's activities, or even of his whereabouts, during the decade 1751–61, we have only very imperfect knowledge. During the first year, at least, he attended Smith's lectures at Glasgow. About two years before 'passing advocate' or being admitted to the bar, in Edinburgh, in mid-1760, he spent in the home of Lord Kames. According to Craig, this was soon after he 'had finished his studies at Glasgow'. From the parish records‡ we learn that on his permanent settlement at Glasgow he 'produced the lines' attesting his marriage in Edinburgh on 10 October, 1759, to a young woman whose acquaintance he had made in Glasgow. His brief practice at the bar in Edinburgh must also have fallen at about this time. From a letter cited by Murray we learn that he did attend the law lectures of Professor Lindesay—presumably some time after he had finished the Arts course. Watts tells us, in a letter about to be quoted, that he made Millar's acquaintance and associated with him frequently—Craig clearly implies, as a student, 'as a relaxation from study' on Millar's part—during his own early days in Glasgow; and we know Watts did not settle in Glasgow until 1754. We know, too, that, as a rule, if not even as a formal requirement, a prospective advocate or 'writer' had to spend at least five years as apprentice in a law office before 'passing advocate', and it would seem most likely that this also

---

* Craig tells us (*Life*, pp. ii, vi f.) that the uncle, John Millar, had studied law at Edinburgh, to become a Writer to the Signet, but soon gave up any law practice. The published volume of Writers to the Signet does not contain his name.

† *Life*, p. iv. Also *H.V.* vol. ii, p. 429. Tytler (*Memoirs*, vol. i, p. 190) lists Millar among those who attended Smith's lectures at Edinburgh before he came to Glasgow, but gives no source. This seems unlikely unless it was only for a short time.

‡ Register House, Edinburgh, under Glasgow marriages, 1761.

applied to Millar, who might have combined private study with such practice. The rest we must piece together as best we can. It would appear that he continued his studies at the University somewhat longer, and entered upon the tutorship somewhat earlier, than available records, on the surface, seem to indicate.

Watt's interesting letter, written in 1805, throws a welcome light on Millar's interests and accomplishments at this time:

I remember Mr. Millar was always looked up to as the oracle of the company; his attainments were greater than those of the others; he had more wit and much greater argumentative powers, of which he was not sparing, as those who engaged with him felt to their cost; at the same time he was perfectly good humoured, though he had an air of firmness which was apt to dismay his antagonist. In short, such as you knew him in age, he was in youth, allowing for his more matured judgement. Our conversations, beside the usual subjects with young men, turned principally upon literary subjects, religion, morality, belles-lettres, etc.; and to those conversations my mind owed its first bias to such subjects, in which they were all my superiors, I never having attended a college, and being then a mechanic.*

At about the age of twenty-two or twenty-three, then, he was, undoubtedly through the offices of their mutual friend, Adam Smith, invited by that distinguished, pioneering, always stimulating jurist and man of letters, Lord Kames, of the Court of Session, 'to reside in his family, and super-intend, in the quality of a preceptor, the education of his young son, Mr George Drummond-Home'. This was beyond question an event of major portent in his life, significant both for the development of his thought and for the shaping of his career. Kames had been chiefly responsible for Adam Smith's lecturing on rhetoric, jurisprudence, civil history, etc. at Edinburgh, which led to his professorship at Glasgow. Kames and Smith were Millar's chief supporters in his candidacy for the professorship of civil law there about two years later and, as we shall see, it was they who contributed more than anyone else toward shaping the basic lines of his interests and his thinking.

In his memoirs of Lord Kames Tytler, a young contemporary, says of this tutorship:

. . . Lord Kames found in young Millar a congenial ardour of intellect, a mind turned to philosophical speculation, a considerable fund of reading, and, what above all things he delighted in, a talent for supporting a metaphysical argument in conversation, with much ingenuity and vivacity. The tutor of the son became the pupil and companion of the father; and the two years before Mr Millar was called to the bar, were spent, with great improvement on his part, in acquiring those enlarged views of the union of law

---

* Quoted in J. Strang, *Glasgow and its Clubs* (London and Glasgow, 1857), pp. 156 f. Rae is in error in associating this letter (*op. cit.* pp. 98 f.) with a club of Adam Smith's.

with philosophy, which he afterward displayed with uncommon ability in his academical lectures on jurisprudence.*

His duties during these two years would have left him ample leisure for the pursuit of his private study both of law and of the history of civil and political institutions. Kames's private library would almost certainly have been at his disposal; and we are told by his former pupil that the two frequently spent many hours together discussing problems of law and finding solutions for problems that perplexed the young jurist. Millar's bar-examination *disputatio* is dedicated to Lord Kames and to Dr Thomas Millar, the Lord Advocate.

Kames was undoubtedly responsible for the unique privilege accorded the young advocate, scarcely twenty-five, of pleading cases not only in the 'Outer Room' of the highest court in the land, but in the 'Inner Room' itself, that is before the full assembled court of fifteen judges, a privilege usually accorded only to advocates of long experience.†

It was his residence in Kames's home, too, that provided opportunity for Millar's acquaintance with Hume, who came to regard the young jurist highly, counted him among his friends, followed his career with interest, and was later to send his own nephew to Glasgow for the explicit purpose of enjoying the advantage of study under this able and distinguished teacher, as was also Adam Smith to send his own cousin, David Douglas (see below, p. 39). Hume was the third in the trio of men who most strongly influenced Millar's thought. When later, in his *Elucidations*, Lord Kames took severely to task the teachers of law in the Scotland of his day as men who 'husband their reasoning faculty as if it would rust by exercise' and 'load the weak mind with a heap of interesting facts without giving any exercise to the judgement', he hastens to add in a footnote, 'I should merit censure equal to what I do liberally bestow on others, did I not except Mr John Millar, Professor of Roman law in the College of Glasgow.'‡

When in the early summer of 1761 the Chair of Civil Law at Glasgow was vacated by the death of Professor Hercules Lindesay, the young advocate not only enjoyed Kames's and Smith's support in his candidacy for this chair, but as their letters of support were dispatched to the Earl of Bute, who represented the interests of the crown in this crown-chair appointment, the very next day after Lindesay's death, and as Kames could hardly have been in the vicinity of Glasgow at this time, this move must have been prepared in detail before the vacancy occurred.

But this is getting ahead of our story.

---

* *Memoirs*, vol. 1, pp. 199 f. Also *Life*, p. vii.   † *Life*, p. ix.
‡ *Elucidations Respecting the Common and Statute Law of Scotland* (Edinburgh, 1777), Introduction, pp. vii f.

III

THE YEARS OF THE PROFESSORSHIP

In June 1761, at the almost daringly youthful age of only twenty-six, and but a year after his admission to the bar, Millar was elected to the Chair of Civil Law at Glasgow.

This chair had long been practically non-existent when it was newly founded less than fifty years before his accession (1712). Of his three predecessors, the first, William Forbes, and the last, Hercules Lindesay, had been men of ability and sound scholarship, and the latter a man of considerable vigour. William Crosse, on the other hand, held the chair for five years practically as a sinecure, seldom if ever lecturing at all, on the pretence that there were less than the required five students asking for the lectures; or he delegated the task to young Lindesay.* It was hardly a chair of distinction, and Millar's friends deemed his candidacy a move of doubtful wisdom, believing his prospects to be far better at the bar and later on the bench.

Whether or not we accept his biographer's view (*Life*, p. x) that he was moved in his choice chiefly by the needs of his newly established family—eminence at the bar or on the bench, with their corresponding emoluments, being but a distant prospect compared with the lesser but immediate rewards of this law chair—Millar himself seems to have had no doubts about the wisdom of his preference. The University considered the office an important one. In the minutes of the Senate meeting of 2 June 1761 we read that 'the supplying of this office being in the gift of the Crown . . . it is of the highest importance to the University to have it properly supplied'. Anxious 'that no time be lost in making application', the Senate immediately proposed Millar as a suitable candidate.†

Within three weeks a presentation was read in Mr Millar's favour, his customary inaugural discourse was heard and approved, the Confession of Faith duly signed before the Glasgow Presbytery, as was required of all professors in the University, and, we read in the minutes:

---

* The distinguished Viscount Stair (Sir James Dalrymple) is, however, also to be counted among Millar's predecessors at Glasgow, even though only as a 'regent'—there being, in reality, no law chair at Glasgow in the late seventeenth century.

† Murray, *Old College*, pp. 212–21; Coutts, *A History of the University of Glasgow* (Glasgow, 1909), pp. 234 f.; *Life*, pp. ix f.; *Univ. MSS.*, vol. 30, fos. 55, 61, 65.

The following oath was administered to him by the Clerk [of Senate]:

Ego, Ioannes Millar, Legis Professor in hac academia, a Rege nominatus, promitto sancteque polliceor, me, in muneris mihi demandati, ratione obeunda, studiose fideliterque pro mea tenuitate versaturum. [signed] Ioannes Millar.*

upon which he was solemnly admitted and received by all present and took his place as a member of the meeting.

How well he fulfilled that promise and what was his impact on the University and its successive student generations for the next forty years, will be best reflected, perhaps, in the immediately following chapters. Here only a few salient factual details can be noted and some general observations made.

First of all, his appointment was to lead to a phenomenal rise in the reputation and influence of his chair. It was soon without a rival in Scotland, and with the exception of Blackstone's Viner chair at Oxford, in any university in Great Britain—its reputation adding not a little to that of the University as a whole. It should be remembered, of course, in this connection, that universities were not at this time the principal instruments for the training of lawyers, that being a function more largely of the Inns of Court and similar agencies, or of apprenticeships in private law offices combined with private study.

In the words of his biographer, Craig:

From the absence of higher Courts of Justice, Glasgow lies under many obvious disadvantages as a school of law; and accordingly, the students of Law in that University previous to Mr Millar's appointment, seldom exceeded four or five and sometimes fell short even of that number. From the first moment of his appointment, there was a very general expectation that Millar would greatly improve, in this branch of education, the character of the University; but I believe his most sanguine friends never entertained the idea, that he could possibly raise it to that degree of celebrity, which it soon attained. The improvement, in a few years, became rapid: he had, frequently, about forty students of Civil Law; while those who attended his Lectures on Government, often amounted to a much greater number. To establish and maintain the reputation of his classes, became with him the principal object of his life; and never, perhaps, was an object followed out with more ardour and perseverance. (*Life*, pp. xi f.)

Another contemporary testifies: '. . . It is to hear his lectures . . . that students resort hither from all quarters of Britain' and he might

* In English equivalent, approximately: 'I, John Millar, Professor of Law in this University by appointment of the King, do promise and solemnly pledge myself studiously and faithfully to perform the duties of my office to the best of my strength and ability.'

have added, from foreign lands as well. 'Glasgow is, in short, famous as a school for Law, as Edinburgh is as a school for Medicine.'*

And to quote a somewhat later witness:

On his account the University of Glasgow was attended by all the most talented and distinguished of the high Whig aristocracy, among whom attendance upon the lectures of Professor Millar was regarded as a necessary portion of sound political education. He may be considered as having formed the minds of many of those who have been distinguished in the political world on the liberal side during the last fifty or sixty years.†

Such distinction and influence for his chair was not, however, to be achieved without the performance, first of all, of what might be called its routine functions.

The duties of the law chair were, officially, those of 'prelecting' on 'civil law', usually understood as the Roman law as contained in the Institutes and Pandects of Justinian, whenever five or more students presented themselves for instruction in that subject—and there were in his case always many more than that number—and generally to attend to the instruction, examination, etc. of students in this field. The chair was designated *iuris civilis* to distinguish it not so much from 'municipal law', or the law of a particular country or other political jurisdiction, which was hardly considered as meriting university status, or from 'criminal law', but rather from 'canon law', which in medieval universities was jealously guarded by the divinity interests.

These duties Millar promptly fulfilled by offering, first of all, a basic course in the Institutes of Justinian, with the aid of Heineccius as a text-book and soon also of a syllabus of his own, and with the reading of Grotius and other authorities recommended. This course, offered every year and running throughout the session, with lectures apparently five days a week, was broken into two parts. For about half the session he would run over the materials rather rapidly with the students, merely trying to make clear and fix in their minds the salient facts with regard to the various classes of rights and duties, to go over the same ground again, in the second half, with greater emphasis on underlying principles—including ethical and psychological foundations—interpretation, illustration, historical perspective and application to conditions of modern life. This latter half of the course was often spoken of as the course in jurisprudence. Beside the Institutes he also lectured on the Pandects. Available evidence would seem to indicate that these lectures on the Pandects constituted an independent course, given

* R. Heron, *Journey through Western Scotland in 1792* (2 vols, Perth, 1793), vol. II, p. 418.
† Gray, *Autobiography*, pp. 27–30.

annually and running like those on the Institutes, through the entire session. The evidence for this is not altogether clear, but at any rate he lectured on all three of them, the Institutes, the Pandects and general jurisprudence.*

In addition, Millar, from the beginning, or very nearly so, found time to offer each session a course in 'Public Law', or the 'Principles of Government', with lectures normally three days each week for the entire session; and every second year only, a course also in the Law of Scotland with lectures on the other two days.† The former had, obviously, a broad arts and citizenship appeal; the latter chiefly a vocational appeal. Toward the end of his career he also introduced a course on the Law of England, alternating with that on Scots Law. With the exception of the last-mentioned course, there was, if I am correctly informed, little if any change in the courses offered throughout the entire forty years of his professorship.‡

Lectures began usually about 10 November and ran to about the middle of May.§ Some three weeks before lectures began, notices of them usually appeared in the Glasgow papers, apparently as paid advertisements. The following may serve as examples:

John Millar, Professor of Law in the University of Glasgow, will begin his Prelections on Justinian's Institutes and Pandects on Monday, the First of Nov.; also on Monday the 8th of Nov. a Course of Lectures on Government and on Tue. the Ninth of Nov. a Course of Lectures on the Law of Scotland. (*Glasgow Journal*, 7–14 Oct. 1773.)

John Millar, Professor of Law in the University, begins his Prelections on Justinian's Institutes and Pandects, upon Monday the third day of November next. Also a Course of Lectures on Public Law, on Monday the tenth. And, A Course of Lectures on the Law of Scotland, on Tuesday the eleventh day of that month. (*Glasgow Mercury*, 23 Oct. 1783.)‖

---

* Murray (p. 223), from the various sources available to him, arrives at the following picture:

(1) The Institutes, 64 lectures. (2) The Pandects, 46 lectures. (3) Jurisprudence, 45 lectures. (4) Government, 46 lectures. (5) Scots Law, 50 lectures. (6) English Law, (?) lectures. Reid, writing in *c.* 1794, gives Millar's lecture programme as two hours daily, 'in his public department'. He does not yet mention the English Law course.

† On Saturdays there were few classes, most of the morning being given over to a general student-faculty convocation.

‡ It will be recalled there was only one law professorship at this time.

§ The Arts courses began in early October and continued to early June.

‖ Other such announcements will be found in, among other places, the *Glasgow Courier*: 20 October 1791, 15 September 1792, 24 October 1793; *Glasgow Mercury*: 14–21 October 1784, 27 October 1785; *Glasgow Chronicle*: 31 October 1776; *Glasgow Advertiser*: 12 September 1794, 21 September 1798; *Glasgow Journal*: 24 September 1793. These last September announcements are as a rule all-University announcements including law.

When lectures were about to begin, or at any rate before entering the class, students would present themselves to the professor individually, with their certificate of matriculation or other evidence of qualification, to pay him the required fee; after which they would attend classes, though it was often necessary for them to enter late and depart early from the College for reasons of expense and the need of earning to keep themselves in college.

Beside 'prelecting', Millar made it a practice to give examinations of some kind—daily as both Craig and Jardine inform us, with perhaps a more formal one on Monday mornings, as reported in the *Melbourne Papers*—with, of course, still more intensive examinations at the end for those taking degrees.* The lectures were given in English, following the example initiated, under great protest, by his predecessor, Hercules Lindesay. The examinations were, however, in part at least, given in Latin, because this would still be the language of the bar-examinations to 'pass advocate'.

Following all but universal practice, no doubt with examinations in mind, students would take more or less full notes on the professor's lectures—in most cases in long-hand, with the usual improvised short-hand, but in some cases quite clearly in a regular short-hand.† Often these notes would then be transcribed and written out more fully at the student's leisure—in some cases, it would appear, to be sold to other students.

Following a practice usual at the time (see above, p. 14), Millar more or less regularly took into his home—after the first few years when he was still too fully engaged in the preparation of his lectures—a number of 'resident pupils' or boarding students. Sometimes there were at least four of them. These were students of considerably more than average financial competence, and the additional income from such boarding fees was admittedly a principal reason for this practice, from the professors' standpoint. But in Millar's case, at least, there is clear evidence that these students were also selected on the basis of quality and promise of future achievement. In a number of instances, records have been preserved of the correspondence, during the summer, leading to their acceptance.‡ The private instruction of these students—supplementary, of course, to their work in the class—became an important part of Millar's instructional activity. In the words of his biographer:

* *Life*, pp. xiii f.; *Melbourne Papers*, p. 5; Jardine, see below, pp. 32 f.

† See below, Appendix III.

‡ Instances are those of Lauderdale, Hume, Melbourne, Mentieth. See below, pp. 36 ff. Also Scott, *Adam Smith*, pp. 292 f., 306 9.

To their instruction he devoted a considerable part of his time; he had much delight in conversing with them on their several studies, in leading them to inquire and to reflect, and, particularly, in encouraging such talents as promised future discoveries in science, or future eminence in the state. (*Life*, p. lxv.)

An important part of the duties of the chair was attendance at and participation in the meetings of the professors, as Faculty and as Senate, in the general administration of instruction, student discipline, the conferring of degrees, and the educational and business affairs of the College generally. This will be described in a later chapter; here it is necessary only to remark that this was a time-consuming function, sometimes and to some professors an irritating one, but to others of a more fighting temperament also offering the delights of battle.* To Millar these meetings clearly represented at once a considerable responsibility and an opportunity to promote the ends of the University's existence and of his own service to the community. His role here added not a little to his personal stature.

OUT-OF-COLLEGE ACTIVITIES

Next, it should be noted here that Millar's life and activities at Glasgow were by no means confined to the narrow limits of the college walls. Not only was the University in general integrated in a number of ways with the life of the larger community, at once reaching out into its civic, religious, educational, and to a lesser extent its political affairs, and being influenced in turn by its doings, subordinated to its religous controls, sharply scrutinized, often, in the conduct of her internal affairs by watchful, and not infrequently unfriendly eyes without. But Millar's own chair in particular was in various ways affected by the juridical life of the community, including the activities of the Faculty of Procurators, the 'lawyers' guild' so to speak, of Glasgow and its environs. Many of his students were apprentices or clerks in the law offices of the city, some of them preparing for their bar examinations. Citizens of Glasgow came to him frequently for consultation in legal matters or for his arbitration of cases under dispute, or engaged him as counsel in court trials.

* Reid remarks on these meetings in a letter written during the first year of his professorship there: 'There is no part of my time more disagreeably spent than in the College meetings, of which we have often five or six a week. And I should have been attending one this moment if a bad cold I have gotten had not furnished me with an excuse. These meetings are become more disagreeable by an evil spirit of party that seems to put us in a ferment, and, I am afraid, will produce bad consequences.' Letter to David Skene, 20 December 1765, in *Works*, p. 43.

This limited private law practice deserves a further word here both for its personal aspects and for its likely bearings upon the functions of his chair, tending as it would to offset to some extent the disadvantages of a law chair remote from a judicial centre like Edinburgh with its Court of Session, its Advocates Library, the Library of the Signet, etc.

We have already referred to the young advocate's brief practice in Edinburgh before entering upon his professorship at Glasgow. Of his continuing of it in the latter place his biographer gives us this valuable information.

Mr Millar, notwithstanding all [his other] occupations, still found time for a limited practice as a lawyer, a profession which he had not altogether abandoned, in undertaking the duties of a Public Teacher. He was very frequently consulted as Counsel, previously to the commencement of a law suit, or when any difficulty occurred in conveyancing; and the time he could spare from his other employments was occupied in determining causes referred to his arbitration. The delay and expense of law suits, partly unavoidable in a commercial country, but partly also owing to the constitution of the Court of Session, has rendered it extremely common for parties, when both are convinced of the justice of their claims, to refer their disputes to private arbitration. For the office of arbitrator, Mr Millar was singularly qualified. While, from the residence in a commercial town, he could easily be informed of the usages of merchants, he was led by his professional habits, to pay that attention to strict law, which is requisite to substantial justice in a country where all agreements are entered into with the knowledge that they may become the subjects of legal interpretation. His natural acuteness, too, led him to seize very readily the important circumstances of a case, and to detach them from such collateral topics as might have bewildered the judgement, and certainly must have protracted the investigation. His decisions were consequently prompt, but they never were inconsiderate. As the surest guard against error, he was in the habit, before pronouncing his awards, of submitting his opinion, with a short statement of the principles on which it rested, to the parties; and, not infrequently these statements were drawn up in a manner so clear and satisfactory, as to convince even the party against whose claim he intended to decide. (*Life*, pp. lxxxvii ff.)

For many years, Craig tells us, Millar was in the habit of appearing as counsel for unfortunates charged with crimes before the circuit courts when they were held in Glasgow.

...Thinking, with other philosophers, that the criminal laws of this country are, in many instances, unnecessarily and unjustly severe, he entered with warmth into the defence of those who, however profligate in their morals, were in danger of being subjected to punishments more than adequate to their offences. In the examination of witnesses, he showed uncommon skill and penetration; and his address to the Juries, besides containing a most acute and severe examination of such part of the evidence as seemed unfavourable to the prisoner, exhibited a clear view of whatever tended to establish his innocence, and, not infrequently, was terminated by a most powerful appeal to the feelings of his audience. (*Life*, pp. lxxxix f.)

His addresses to the jury were, by the testimony of those who frequently heard them, 'very brilliant and successful exertions of forensic eloquence'. Later in life, we are told, he declined to serve as counsel in these circuit court trials 'that he might not deprive younger lawyers of an opportunity for displaying their talents'.

Of Millar's political activities, particularly as they related to the anti-slave trade, parliamentary reform, the violent reaction to the Revolution in France, and the Pitt government policies in the war with France growing out of this reaction, we shall speak in another place; as also of his literary activities. Here it behoves us merely to add a few paragraphs on his family life and on what might be called the daily and yearly rounds of his life, neither of them entirely divorced, of course, from his professional career.

HOME AND FAMILY LIFE

About two years before entering upon his professorship, Millar married, as we have already seen, one Margaret Craig, a Glasgow woman of about his own age, apparently highly intelligent and possessed of many fine qualities of character. Over a period of eighteen years thirteen children were born to this union, five boys and eight girls, one boy and one girl, however, dying in infancy.

All four of his sons were enrolled in their father's university, two of them certainly, a third almost certainly, and fourth possibly, also attending his lectures. The oldest, John, a 'rising young lawyer', upon whose education his father had spent some of his finest education efforts and upon whose future he had pinned some of his fondest hopes, died in 'the back country' of Pennsylvania (see below, pp. 411 f.) before those hopes could be at all fully realized. The next, James, became Professor of Mathematics in the University, a post which he held until 1832, six years before his death in 1838. At one time he also lectured in English Law. The third, William, became a distinguished major in the artillery; and the youngest, Archibald, a Writer to the Signet in Edinburgh.

Of the seven daughters, one, Agnes, was married to Professor James Mylne, long occupant of the moral philosophy chair, following Reid after a brief interim occupancy by Professor Arthur, and a man of ability and of outspoken liberal political sympathies. Another, Margaret, was married to Dr John Thomson (his second marriage), distinguished Professor of Surgery at Edinburgh. Their son, Allen Thomson, was Professor of Anatomy in various Scottish universities, including Glasgow, and is said to have died with the reputation of being, in his time, the most learned physician in Scotland, and to have rated as a biologist second only to Huxley. His son in turn, and Professor Millar's great-grandson, therefore, was John Millar Thomson, LL.D., F.R.S., F.R.S.E., F.I.C., F.C.S., Professor and later Emeritus Professor of Chemistry at King's College, London, from 1887 to his death in 1933 (its Vice-Principal from 1905–14), thus bringing the line of Millar's distinguished descendants down to our own day.*

His second oldest daughter, Mary, died of consumption about ten years before the death of her father (1791); the oldest, and the three youngest, remained, so far as we know, unmarried and continued to live, after the father's departure and by a provision of his will, in his and their beloved Milheugh.

With this large family, sometimes still further enlarged by a number of student boarders, he lived, during the College session at least, in one or another of the 'professors' houses'† in the college compound—some of the children no doubt establishing residence elsewhere as the years went by and they reached adulthood. The long summer vacations, from late May to early November, were as a rule spent, in part at least, away from the College and the city, first in his father's manse at Hamilton; then on his Whitemoss farm at Kilbride, some eight or nine miles from Glasgow, given him by his uncle; and after 1784 at the old family estate of Milheugh, about the same distance from Glasgow, inherited, apparently under the law of entail, from the same uncle. Two at least of his colleagues, Professor Baillie, of divinity, and Jardine of the logic chair, were his neighbours in the country, their families being on the most intimate terms. The once famous Scottish poet, Joanna Baillie, daughter of the former, celebrated one of the Millar daughters in a curious bit of poetry.‡ So the Millar family was in more ways than one a part of the life of the College.

BEYOND GLASGOW

Millar held, as a rule, quite closely to his Glasgow and its environs. There were occasional visits to Edinburgh, to the Highlands and other parts of Scotland, and a few to the north of England. During the

* For sources see, beside *Life*, pp. cxxiv–vii, Murray, *op. cit.* p. 247, and Appendix IV. For J. M. Thomson, see *Who Was Who* (London, 1941), p. 1346.

† See, e.g., University Manuscripts, vol. 31, fo. 15, 8 March 1764.

‡ See Appendix IV.

summer months he often paid extended visits to the Earl of Lauderdale, one of his most distinguished former students, at Thirlestane Castle, Berwickshire. He made only two visits to London and none to foreign shores. In connection with his first visit to London, where he remained for two months, in 1774, he also paid visits to Oxford and Cambridge. On his second visit, in 1792, on which he was accompanied by his wife and oldest daughter, he was personally introduced to Fox, the Whig opposition leader of whom he had long been an ardent supporter and to whom his *Historical View*, and later his *Letters of Crito* were dedicated; attended important debates in Parliament; and visited with the Earl of Lauderdale, the Marquis of Lansdowne and other leaders of the Opposition, and with William Adam, a former student, apparently, who then stood high in the government. He also spent much time there with his life-long friend, Dr John Moore, formerly of Glasgow but then a distinguished physician in the metropolis and author of the novel *Zeluco*, a number of travel accounts widely acclaimed in his day, and an account of his sojourn in Paris during the days of the Revolution.

Dr Moore was one of the few men with whom he carried on a considerable correspondence, though we know he corresponded occasionally with such men as Adam Smith, David Hume, Edmund Burke, Dugald Stewart, the Earl of Lauderdale and a few others known, and no doubt others unknown to us.*

Outwardly Millar's forty years as professor in the University were uneventful enough, though his fame was very considerable. He went about his work quietly and without fanfare, but vigorously and with industry, always intent upon serving his students and his university well, both in the promotion of scholarship and in the defence of truth as he saw it, and in the advancement of liberal ideas and the cause of liberty. Inwardly his life was rich in the consciousness of the high regard and often deep affection in which a whole generation of students held him, and of the fruits of his labour in a new leadership that his former students were beginning to give to the life of the nation.

When he died at the age of sixty-five, still very much in the prime of his vigour, apparently,† (he died of an acute attack of pleurisy), his passing was outwardly marked by these simple notices: In the files of the *Glasgow Advertizer*—now the *Glasgow Herald*—for 5 June 1801 we find this unadorned notice:

* *Life*, pp. xcii f. including note.

† Professor Mackie (*University of Glasgow*, pp. 166 n., 187, 234) is led to believe, apparently chiefly on the basis of the low state of his chair under Davidson shortly after his demise, that there was a decline in Millar's effectiveness toward the end of his career. From the testimony of students in just these years this seems to the present author an unlikely interpretation, though we know his health did receive a shock some time before his last illness.

Died at Milheugh on the 30th ult. John Millar, Esq., Advocate and Professor of Law in the University of Glasgow.*

In the minutes of the University for the same date we read simply:

Mr John Millar, Professor of Law in this College, having died on the 30th May last and his office being in the gift of the Crown, the Faculty appoint a notification of his death to be made, and subscribed by the Principal and Clerk, and transmitted to His Majesty's Secretary of State for the Home Department.†

In the old churchyard at High Blantyre, but a brief walk from the still lovely Milheugh, the reader who will take the pains will find a so-called 'flat table-stone',‡ laid horizontally but elevated well above the sod, against a green background of myrtle and cedars, marking the resting place of Professor Millar and of his beloved wife. The inscription on the right half reads, simply:

To the memory of John Millar of Milheugh, Advocate, Esq., Professor of Law in the University of Glasgow. Born 22 June, 1735; died 30th May, 1801.

Inwardly his passing was perhaps better marked by the sentiments expressed in the following lines closing the obituary notice that appeared in the *Scots Magazine* shortly after his death:

By his death . . . his family lost a most affectionate father, his friends the life and soul of their society, the University her brightest ornament, and the country a firm and enlightened defender of her liberty.§

* Courtesy of the *Glasgow Herald*, from whose files of the *Advertizer* this note is taken.
† University Manuscripts, vol. 81, fo. 47.
‡ This designation will be found in an editor's note in Scott's *Old Mortality*. The author has, of course, visited the old churchyard.
§ *Scots Magazine*, vol. LXIII (1801), p. 528.

IV

THE PROFESSOR AND HIS STUDENTS

STUDENT IMPRESSIONS

Millar's impact upon his students was a very strong one. By his lectures from his chair, by his more informal after-lecture discussions with those who cared to remain, by his fireside 'Platonic exercises' with students admitted to this charmed circle in his home, by personal counsel and other forms of helpfulness to individual students, by his defence of students when he believed their rights infringed upon, he evoked considerable enthusiasm for his subject among students at the college and established a reputation that attracted students from far and wide. He not only left indelible memories with many of his students, but, more important, he aroused their intellectual curiosity, stimulated many of them to independent thinking, aided them in making vocational decisions and helped many of the abler ones to lay the foundations for careers of distinction in the years to come. They called him fondly 'cocky Millar', a 'jolly dog', and, in reminiscent retrospect, 'that second Gamaliel', the ideal teacher. The poet Campbell, author of 'The Pleasures of Hope' and 'Battle of the Baltic' rated him as in his time, the ablest of the distinguished professors at Glasgow, Young, of the Greek chair, ranking next to him.

In the following pages we shall, so far as possible, let students who knew him in and out of the class-room tell their own story of his impact upon them.

One of the keys to his influence upon his students was undoubtedly the force of his personality and the charm of his manner with young men. Campbell thus characterizes the professor who had so greatly inspired him in his student days:

. . . there was an air of the high-bred gentleman about Millar, that you saw nowhere else. Something that made you imagine such old Scottish patriots as Lord Belhaven, or Fletcher of Saltoun. He was a fine muscular man, somewhat above the middle size, with a square chest and shapely bust, a prominent chin, grey eyes that were unmatched in expression, and a head that would have become a Roman senator. He was said to be a capital fencer; and, to look at his light elastic step, when he was turned of sixty, disposed you to credit the report. But the glory was to see his intellectual gladiatorship, when he would slay or pink into convulsions some offensive

political antagonist. He spoke with no mincing affectation of English pronunciation; but his Scoto-English was as different from vulgar Scotch, as
that of St James's from St Giles's. Lastly he had a playfulness in his countenance and conversation that was graceful from its never going to excess.*

Equally important, however, was his intellectual temper, his ability
to make his subject become alive to his students, and his rare combination of moral seriousness with yet a spriteliness and good humour in his
'prelections' and in his conversations with them. To quote Campbell
again:

I heard him [Millar], when I was but sixteen, lecture on Roman law. A
dry subject enough it would have been in common hands; but in his hand
Heineccius was made a feast to the attention. His eyes, his voice, his figure,
were commanding; as if nature had made him for the purpose of giving
dignity and fascination to oral instruction. Such was the truth, cheerfulness
and courage that seemed to give erectness to his shapely bust, he might have
stood to the statuary [i.e., as sculptor's model] for a Roman orator; but he
was too much in earnest with his duty, and, too manly, to affect the orator;
but keeping close to his subject, he gave it a seriousness that was never tire-
some, and a gaiety that never seemed for a moment unillustrative or unnecessary. His cheerfulness appeared as indispensable as his gravity, and his
humour was as light as his seriousness was intensive. . . . His students were
always in the class before him, waiting for a treat. It was rumoured that he
was coming. There was a grave look of pleasure on every face when he began;
and I thought—it might be imagination—that there was a murmur of regret
when the time was at an end.†

On the manner of his exposition of his subject in his lectures the critic
and reviewer Francis Jeffrey, who too had been among his youthful
admirers, had this, among other things, to say:

. . . It is to little purpose, indeed, to make harangues to young men from
a velvet gown and an elbow chair. Their teacher must *talk* to them, after a
certain age, if he wishes to do them any good. He must put them on a level
with himself, and associate them in some measure in his inquiries. . . . He
must work with them, as well as for them; and, instead of appalling them
with the splendour of his attainments, he must encourage them, by shewing
how easily they may be made, and with what facility the notions which they
throw out in common conversation, may be improved into solid arguments,
and pursued to valuable conclusions. Mr Millar is the only public lecturer
we have known, who seems to have been fully aware of those facts; and, by
attending to them, he certainly delivered a series of most instructive lectures
in a more attractive and engaging manner than any other teacher we have

* William Beattie, *Life and Letters of Thomas Campbell* (3 vols. London, 1849), vol. 1,
pp. 158 f.

† Cyrus Redding, *Literary Reminiscences and Memoirs of Thomas Campbell* (2 vols. London,
1860), vol. 1, pp. 21 f.

heard of; commanding the attention of all descriptions of hearers, at the same time that he convinced their understandings; and not only putting them in possession of knowledge, but making it familiar and serviceable to them.*

In this manner, he continues farther on, he was able to give his lectures

an easy and attractive air, and imparted, to a profound and learned discussion, the charms of an animated and interesting conversation. No individual, indeed, ever did more to break down the old and unfortunate distinction between the wisdom of the academician and the wisdom of the man of the world: and as most of the topics that fell under his discussion, were of a kind that did not lose their interest beyond the walls of a college, so the views which he took of them, and the language in which they were conveyed, were completely adapted to the actual condition of society; and prepared those to whom they had been made familiar, to maintain and express them with precision, without running the risk of an imputation of pedantry or ignorance.

It will be admitted to have required no ordinary share of intrepidity, and confidence in the substantial merit of his instructions, to have enabled a professor thus to lay aside the shield of academic stateliness, and not only to expose his thoughts in the undress of extemporaneous expression, but to exhibit them, without any of the advantages of imposing or authoritative pretences, on the fair level of equal discussion, and with no other recommendations, but those of superior expediency or reason (p. 87).

On this his method and manner of teaching his biographer makes this further interesting comment.

Perhaps nothing contributed so much to the improvement of his pupils as the art with which he contrived to make them lay aside all timidity in his presence, and speak their sentiments without restraint. While he was thus enabled to judge of their abilities and attainments, he acquired, in addition to the respect due to his talents, that confidence and friendship which ensure the attention of young men, and renders the office of a teacher not undelightful.†

Some further light on this teaching method of Millar's comes from the pen of a former young colleague, Professor Jardine. He says:

It was in no small degree owing to his practice of examining, and of prescribing essays on subjects previously discussed in his lectures, that he acquired that high reputation as a professor of law which still [1825] attaches to his name. Every morning, before he began his address from the chair, he endeavoured to ascertain, by putting a number of questions to his pupils, whether they had been able to follow his reasoning on the preceding day, and

---

* Francis Jeffrey, in *Edinburgh Review*, vol. ix, pp. 86 f.   † *Life*, pp. lxvi f.

it was his custom, when the lecture was over, to remain some time in his lecture-room to converse with those students who were desirous of further information on the subject. By engaging with them in an easy dialogue, he contrived to remove obscurities, and to correct any errors into which they might have fallen. This meeting was called among the students, familiarly, 'the committee', from which they acknowledged that they reaped more benefit than from the lecture itself.*

On the matter of the related 'fireside' discussions Jeffrey, in his rectorial address, adds this significant comment, 'No young man admitted to his house ever forgot him, and the ablest used to say that the discussions into which he led them, domestically and convivially, were the most exciting and most instructive exercises in which they ever took part.'†

THE APPEAL OF HIS LECTURES

The general content of Millar's lectures will be briefly summarized elsewhere.‡ Here we can attempt only to characterize his manner of treatment of the subjects covered from the point of view of the liveliness of their appeal to his students.

Millar treated law not as a set of lifeless rules merely prescriptive in character, enforceable by the instruments of state but otherwise having little to do with the daily, vital concerns of life. Rather, he made the law a part of life itself. Who among his students would not have had glimpses of the problems of marriage or broken homes, of the limits of a husband's authority over his wife, or of a parent's over his or her children; or of problems of property and inheritance, as between husband and wife, between the oldest son and his younger brothers and sisters, or in a case of illegitimacy? Or again of problems of land-tenure, or of servitude, to the extent it still prevailed? Or of a man's right to compensation—to what extent and under what circumstances—if he was gored by his neighbour's bull, or if his sheep were killed by his neighbour's dog? What, to take an extreme example, were the rights of a student over against a professor who made improper use of his authority?

Or again, who among his students would not be interested in dif-

---

* George Jardine, *Outlines of Philosophy of Education* (Glasgow, 1818), pp. 465 f. A reviewer in the *Quarterly Review* (vol. XXXVI, p. 219) remarks to this passage that 'it clearly appears that the toil imposed upon a professor thus called upon to act in the double capacity of private and public teacher must be too irksome to find many imitators'. See, however, Murray, *op. cit.* p. 79, 'Teaching and examination have always been combined in the Scottish Universities.'

† Hay, *Inaugural Addresses*, pp. 6 f.   ‡ See below, pp. 57f.

Chiefly Biographical

ferences in customs and manners, and to some extent even in the law itself and its administration, between England and Scotland, between the Highlands and the Lowlands, between the countryside and the busy marts of Glasgow? How many of them had thought of the stories of Jacob and Laban, of the sabbath and the jubilee with its emancipation of servants or its relinquishment of debts, etc. as coming under principles of law rather than merely as something 'coming out of the Bible'? How many of them had thought of problems of prostitution, or of polygamy, as at all related to an unbalance in the sex-ratio, or to deferred marriages resulting from property, inheritance or class considerations?

Yet these and similar matters entered very much into Millar's lectures, and they were told with touches of wit or of cynicism here and there, or even with subtle references at times to persons and things he would not have spoken of openly in his lectures.

Of his lectures generally his biographer tells us that he was not merely desirous to convey to his students just views and accurate information; but he was anxious to convey them in a manner most likely to seize the attention, and to produce habits of original thought and philosophical investigation; thus rendering lectures, formerly considered as useful only to lawyers, the most important schools of general education. (*Life*, p. xii.)

On his lectures on government, in particular, Craig remarks:

To many of his students . . . who, without any intention of becoming practical lawyers had been sent to the University as to a seminary of liberal education, a course of Lectures on Public Law seemed more important than on almost any other science. In a free country every man may be said to be a politician; and the higher classes of society, those who chiefly resort to universities as general students, are frequently obliged, by their situation in life, to give opinions on various subjects of Government, which may have considerable influence on the welfare of their country. To them a knowledge of Public Law must be an object of the first importance, whether they look forward to the degree of estimation in which they would wish to be held in their respective counties, or listen to the voice of honourable ambition, which calls them to add lustre to their names, by defending the rights and augmenting the happiness of their fellow men. (*Life*, p. xlii.)

In these lectures

. . . The general student was delighted with the acuteness of the observations, the sagacity of the antiquarian researches, the number and elegance of the analogies, the comprehensiveness and consistency of the doctrines: the young Lawyer by tracing the progress and views of the Government, was instructed in the spirit and real intention of the laws: But to the future statesman, were opened up views of human society, of the nature and ends of Government, and of the influence of Public Institutions on the prosperity,

34

morals and happiness of states; views which could hardly fail to impress a veneration for liberty on his heart, and which, through his exertions, might essentially promote the welfare of his country. (*Life*, pp. lvi f.)

All of this, except for the last paragraphs quoted, still relates, however, more to the form and manner and style of his presentation than to any challenge presented by the vitality of his ideas themselves. Any abiding and life-transforming influence he may have exerted upon his students must be sought in the latter rather than in the former. This vitality of his ideas deserves a further word here.

It will be found, first of all, in their applicability, as above indicated, to the real-life problems of those who heard him, both as students and as prospective citizens and men in pursuit of their respective vocations. It will be found even more in their political implications, both explicitly and implicitly, in their liberalism, their forward look and their challenge to the *status quo*, as we shall see in a later chapter. Most of all, perhaps, it will be found in the challenge of what, for lack of a better expression, we shall call the secularizing tendencies of his thought in the broadest sense of that term. (See below, pp. 91 f.) By this we mean not only the fresh breezes of a humanistic, rational, historical outlook and the independence of the inquiring mind, in its implied attack upon dogmatism and the prevailing theological orthodoxy, but also a receptivity generally toward change, toward innovation, toward what might be called 'principial rationality', in every realm of experience. Above all, this meant, in Millar's case, viewing every subject, whether law, politics, history, morality, religion or art, in terms of what he called 'utility' as over against 'authority' and mere tradition. We should today perhaps call it a 'functional rationality', where every event, act, condition, institution or value is viewed and judged in its relation to the larger whole, to some end-goal of human striving and desire.

Herein would seem to lie the principal strength of Millar's appeal to his students.

HIS ABIDING INFLUENCE ON HIS STUDENTS

So much for the nature and basis of Millar's appeal to his students. More important, however, is the abiding influence he exerted upon those who sat at his feet, as reflected not in the enthusiasm of youth but in their achievements in the maturity of life and in any influence they in turn may have exerted on the public life of their time, either in the world of thought and scholarship or in the world of action.

Tytler, Professor of History at Edinburgh and somewhat critical of both Millar's political philosophy and of his method of historical construction, admits that 'the reputation of Millar's university as a school of jurisprudence rose from [his] acquisition' and that 'there were few who attended [his] lectures without . . . an increase of knowledge; or who perused his writings without deriving from them much information'.*

Ramsay of Ochtertyre, that indispensable witness to men of his time, was personally even more hostile to Millar's political philosophy. He held that 'there can be no doubt that a considerable number of the Faculty of Advocates were' as he viewed the matter, 'more or less tinged by Mr Millar's notions religious and political. . . .' But he admitted that 'Whatever may have been his demerits, . . . it is agreed that he made many excellent scholars. In fact, his general views of jurisprudence were masterly. . . .' He taught civil law 'with great ability and diligence. In a word, he is proof of what may be done by one single professor, acting steadily on a fixed plan for more than thirty years' (actually it was forty).†

Whether we take the following excerpt from a much later reviewer at its face value or deem it slightly overdrawn, it contains still, beyond question, much truth.

In vain did the exacting spirit of conformity to the tenets in vogue brood over Scotland, while session after session, to fresh relays of eager and delighted listeners, John Millar's eloquence fixed deeply in their minds the principles of free constitutional government. His class thus became a great training school for the lawyers and statesmen of the next generation; and many of them in after-life owned that Millar's prelections had first given the impulse which stimulated them throughout life . . . there can be no question that the bold lines of thought on which the 'Edinburgh Review' was afterwards constructed, were first laid down by his masterly hand.‡

Confirmation and illustration of such statements are abundantly provided by that remarkable array of men of achievement and great distinction in the late eighteenth and early nineteenth centuries who are counted among his former students. The list of them—incomplete, of course—which we give in a footnote below contains§ the names of a

---

* Alexander F. Tytler, *Memoirs of Lord Kames*, vol. I, p. 199.

† J. Ramsay, Ochtertyre Manuscripts, vol. III, p. 1860 (1855–60). Loaned to National Library, Edinburgh, by Mr Dundas, of Ochtertyre. Quoted with his permission.

‡ *Edinburgh Review*, vol. 135, no. 276 (1872), pp. 406 f. Article 'Charles Bell'.

§ David Murray has provided us with this impressive list of Millar's former students. We quote verbatim:

'. . . Amongst these were David Hume, professor of Scots Law in the University of Edinburgh and a judge of the Court of Exchequer; David Boyle of Shewalton, Lord Justice General of Scotland and Lord President of the Court of Session; Lord Gillies, Lord Reston [David Douglas, cousin of Adam Smith] and Lord Pitmilly, Judges of the Court of Session, and Sir Patrick Murray, one of the Barons of Exchequer; the Rt Hon. Sir David Rae of

Prime Minister and other members of the King's Council, of ambassadors of high rank, of attorneys of great distinction and of judges on the highest bench in the land, of prominent members of Parliament in both houses, and of authors, teachers and scholars of great distinction, as

St Catherines, Lord Advocate and M.P., the friend of Sir Walter Scott; Sir John Anstruther, Chief Justice of Bengal; James Kerr, Chief Justice of the Court of King's Bench at Quebec and Speaker of the Legislative Council of Quebec; Lord Cardross, afterwards Earl of Buchan; James Maitland, afterwards eighth Earl of Lauderdale, on whose recommendation the Hon. William Lamb, afterwards second Viscount Melbourne, and his brother Frederick Lamb, afterwards third Lord Melbourne, became students under Professor Millar; William Windham (1750–1810) the celebrated statesman, the friend of Dr Johnson; the Hon. Thomas Fitzmaurice, son of the Earl of Shelburne; Richard Wingfield, afterwards Lord Powerscourt; Thomas Douglas, fifth Earl of Selkirk, Commissioner to Canada for the settlement of the Colonies; Charles Stuart, afterwards Lord Rothesay, British Ambassador to many of the Courts of Europe; Charles Kinnaird, afterwards the eighth Lord Kinnaird; Sir Archibald Grant of Monymusk, afterwards Lord Saltoun; Robert Ferguson of Raith, M.P. for several Scottish constituencies; Sir James Grant Suttie, baronet of Prestongrange, a member both of the Scottish and of the English Bar. A large number of young men who intended to be called to the Scottish bar studied under Professor Millar, often eight in a session, many of whom rose to eminence and judicial positions. Graduates of Oxford and Cambridge, some of whom had already entered one of the Inns of Court, came to Glasgow to attend Professor Millar's lectures. James Reddie, afterwards the eminent Town Clerk of Glasgow, also studied under him, as did Thomas Campbell the poet and the unfortunate Thomas Muir of Huntershill, who attended his class for two sessions.' (*Old College*, pp. 221 f., quoted with permission of Jackson Son and Co., publishers to the University of Glasgow.)

To Murray's list we may add the following names of similar distinction: Thomas Thomson (see below); Sir James Moncreiff (Lord Wellwood), Dean of the Faculty of Advocates, active on the *Edinburgh Review*; Sir George Cranstoun, later Lord Corehouse, prominent Whig Lawyer, also an Edinburgh Reviewer; Lord William Craig of the Court of Session, eminent jurist of his time; William Adam, Lord Chief Commissioner of the Scottish Jury Court, member of the King's Council, Solicitor-General and later Attorney-General to the Prince of Wales; Sir William Rae, third Baronet of Esgrove and Lord Advocate; Simon Jefimovich Desnitzky, Professor of Roman Law and Russian Jurisprudence in the University of Moscow, said to be the first to lecture on civil law in any Russian university and 'one of the most influential professors of the Moscow University in the late eighteenth century', a member of the Russian Academy; also Ivan Andreevitch Tretiakov, Professor of Legislative science in the University of Moscow.

Among men of lesser renown are further to be named, Robert Davidson, successor to Millar's chair at Glasgow; Robert Reid, the 'Senex' of *Glasgow Past and Present*; John Craig, his nephew and biographer, author of several works on economics and political science; his sons John and James and almost certainly also Archibald; Charles Granville Stuart Mentieth, Baronet; Robert Colt, Robert Morehead and Alexander Campbell. Many others must remain nameless.

There is some doubt about Henry Petty-Fitzmaurice, Marquis of Lansdowne, though he speaks of Millar in a rectorial address as 'among his early memories'. He studied chiefly at Edinburgh and Oxford. Francis Jeffrey, Francis Horner, Lord Henry Brougham and George Bell, all prominent on the *Edinburgh Review*, have been named among his students, but probably by an erroneous interpretation of the phrase occurring somewhere that these 'had all received their first political instruction from Millar'.

It would be impossible to cite here the sources for this long list, but the evidence has in nearly all cases been carefully checked, or is taken on Murray's high authority. For individual students the *Matriculation Album of the University of Glasgow*, W. I. Addison ed., Glasgow, 1913, is most helpful. For the Russian students, see Scott, *op. cit.* Appendix VII.

well as of men of less pretension to high station in life. To only a few of these does space permit me to attend individually.

William Lamb, second Viscount Melbourne, was one of his ablest students and destined to a place of the highest distinction in the affairs of state as a leader in Parliament and an active supporter of parliamentary reform, as personal counsellor to the future queen and then to the young Queen Victoria herself, and as Prime Minister of the realm for eight years, first under William IV and then under Queen Victoria. After graduating from Cambridge he came to Glasgow with his younger brother Frederick, later third Viscount Melbourne, for the express purpose of studying under Millar, and he and his brother were 'resident pupils' in the professor's home in 1799 and 1800. As a young man of greater maturity and urbanity of outlook than most students at Glasgow, he was amused at the idolatry, almost, in which the, to him, somewhat provincial Scottish and Irish students held Millar. Yet he, too, developed the highest regard for the professor and was deeply influenced by him in his thought and outlook. They would take long walks together, discussing problems of law and politics, and presumably also of literature, philosophy and religion. He became so engrossed in Millar's philosophy that on his return to London, during vacations, his friends wondered at his departure from his traditions, and members of his family did not altogether approve of his politics. He was, however, too independent and pragmatically minded to become permanently engrossed in abstract theories of government and society, and his political position in later life came to reflect his family and class background more than his youthful enthusiasm for whiggish principles. Yet there can be little doubt about Millar's permanent influence upon him.*

James Maitland, eighth Earl of Lauderdale, also a resident student in his home and one of the few young men of noble rank among his students, early became a leader in Parliament, a strong advocate of parliamentary reform, leader of the opposition to the repressive sedition legislation in the hysterical early '90's and one of the principal members of Fox's Opposition to the Pitt government in the debates on the India Bill, the Anti-Slave Trade Bill and the early movement for parliamentary reform. He was supported in these activities by others of Millar's former students, such as the Earl of Buchan and William Adam. He also achieved distinction as an author on political and

* *Lord Melbourne's Papers*, Ll. C. Sanders, ed. (London, 1889), pp. 4–8, 14, 19 f. Also W. McC. Torrens, *Memoirs of the Rt Hon. William Lamb, Second Viscount Melbourne* (2 vols. London, 1878), vol. I, p. 39. Torrens quotes Lauderdale's letter of inquiry and of recommendation to Millar as 'resident pupil'. David Cecil, *The Young Melbourne* (London, 1939), pp. 65–67. There is a beautiful monument erected to the memory of the two brothers Lamb near the Duke of Wellington's burial-place in St Paul's, London.

economic subjects.* Millar's influence upon Lauderdale may be seen in the fact that he maintained intimate contact with him throughout life as he did with no other of his former students.†

Millar's most brilliant student, no doubt, was the younger David Hume, the future Professor of Scots Law in Edinburgh University, Principal Clerk of the Court of Session, and later Baron of the Exchequer, whom his uncle, the better-known historian and philosopher of the same name, sent to Glasgow to study under Millar after being assured that the professor could reserve a place for him in his home as 'resident student'‡—this in spite of the fact that the philosopher's political principles were on the surface considerably different from the professor's. Baron Hume's contributions to the science of law, particularly of the criminal law in Scotland, are of the very highest order.§ The importance of the connection between the two is strongly suggested by a reviewer of the 'State of the Universities' in the *Quarterly Review* (1827) when he observes that 'of late years there have been no professors of splendid reputation in any of the legal chairs [in the Scottish universities] except Mr Millar in civil law, at Glasgow, and Baron Hume in the municipal law of Scotland, at Edinburgh'.‖ This brilliant student was one of those who, if ever he had 'taken in the poison' of Millar's whiggery, that old Jupiter Carlyle speaks of (below, p. 69) was able to 'find antidote for this poison' and had 'strength of understanding to expel it'. He made no secret of his strong Tory sympathies. This is, however of minor importance compared with the fact that he received his first and major impulse toward creative work in the law at the feet of Professor Millar, both in his class and in his home. The two apparently kept up correspondence for some time (below, pp. 398 f.).

We have already noted the poet Campbell's personal impressions of the man at whose feet he had sat. His testimony to the impact of the teacher upon the life and thought of this highly imaginative and intelligent student, who never lost his great interest in liberal principles of politics, is even more significant. We quote from a letter of his.

... To say that Millar gave me *liberal* opinions, would be understating the obligation which I either owed, or imagined I owed, to him. He did more.

* *An Inquiry into the Nature and Origin of Public Wealth: and into the Cause of its Increase* (Edinburgh, 1804).

† C. Innes, *Memoirs of Andrew Dalzel* (Edinburgh, 1862), pp. 14, 22 f. Also Craig, *Life*, pp. xc f.

‡ See *Letters of David Hume*, J. T. T. Greig, ed. (2 vols. Clarendon Press, 1932), Letters nos. 507, 512. Also J. H. Burton, *Life and Correspondence of David Hume*.

§ See various publications by G. Campbell H. Paton of Baron Hume's lectures for the Stair Society, Edinburgh.

‖ *Quarterly Review* (London, 1828), vol. xxxvi, p. 228.

He made investigations into the principles of justice, and the rights and interests of society, so captivating to me, that I formed opinions for myself, and became an emancipated lover of truth.

I will not take upon me to say that Miller's tuition was profound; for his mind, with all its natural strength, had grown to maturity in an age, when, with the exception of Adam Smith and a few others, there appears to me to have been a dearth of deep-thinking men. . . . But John Millar had the magic secret of making you so curious in inquiry, and so much in love with truth, as to be independent of his specific tenets. Every lecture that he gave was a treat from beginning to end. . . .

The impulse which Miller's lectures had given to my mind, continued to act long after I had heard them. . . . Poetry itself, in my love of jurisprudence and history, was almost forgotten. . . . At that period [of his Highland tutorship] had I possessed but a few hundred pounds to have subsisted upon in studying law, I believe I should have bid adieu to the Muses, and gone to the bar; but I had no choice in the matter.*

All this is high tribute to any teacher. When the Reform movement was, some twenty-eight years after Millar's death, meeting with its first promise of final triumph, Campbell remarked to a friend, 'How he [Millar] would have rejoiced, had he been alive, at this triumph of free principles after the war he saw begun to put them down!'†

Even more personally illustrative is the experience of Thomas Thomson.‡ Like so many of the students of his day he, too, hailed from a manse—in the Burns country—and was intended by his fond and pious father for the service of the church. The correspondence of the father with his 'Tammie' is tenderly revealing, particularly when he asks whether he has been in receipt of a *valde bene*, an *optime* or only a *bene* in his examinations, and when he counsels him, 'But above all, dear Tammie, let no hurry, let nothing whatever make you neglect the duties of piety and devotion. If you are attentive and serious, which I pray God you may always be, these duties will be no task, no burden, but your most delightful employment.'

Tammie made a fine record at the University, and among other prizes earned a bursary at the age of eighteen to permit him to continue the study of divinity. But his preference for the society which he found in Professor Millar's house was beginning to bring about a change in the direction of his vocational thinking, as is shown by a letter dated 27 April 1789 from which we quote.

'My dear Father,' he begins (he is now aged about twenty-five),

* Beattie, *Life and Letters of Thomas Campbell*, vol. i, pp. 157–60.
† Redding, *op. cit.* vol. i, pp. 21 f.
‡ C. Innes, *Memoirs of Thomas Thomson* (Edinburgh, 1854), pp. 3–15.

For some time past my thoughts have been almost totally absorbed in reflecting on my present situation and future destination in life. In the many conversations we have had on this subject, perhaps we have both acted with too much reserve. . . . In adopting the clerical profession, I will own to you I should have doubts and scruples of a kind not easily to be lulled or conquered, and which my sincere veneration for the order would tend only to heighten and confirm.

Then, after some comments on the disadvantages of the ministry as a profession, its lack of 'alluring prospects', etc., he continues:

You will easily perceive that I speak here only as a man of *this world* and leave out of view those sublimer enjoyments which certainly must arise from reflection on a life well spent in the service of religion. On the other hand, the profession of the law, with some alarming disadvantages, exhibits many tempting inducements. The hazard of success is no doubt greater than in the church; but the object when attained, is also great in proportion. In the lottery of the law the blanks are more numerous than in that of the church, but the prizes are infinitely higher. At the same time, I can say upon good authority, that the hazard is now less formidable than it was formerly accounted. It is not the man of rank and independent fortune, who is reckoned to have the best chance of rising at the bar. Amidst the various dissipations which wealth and luxury hold out, the law is too dry and too laborious a study for him. It is the man of no fortune, who must solely depend on his own industry and exertions for subsistence, whose early habits of labour protect him from the temptations of idleness, and whose poverty obstructs the avenues to dissipation—it is a man of this description who is most likely to rise to eminence at the bar. Unless endowed by nature with an uncommon portion of stupidity, a lawyer in this situation may, in a few years, acquire a tolerable subsistence, and by resolution and steady perseverence may, in no very long time, attain a comfortable independency. This doctrine my friends Professors Millar and Jardine have frequently preached up to me, and with this have they encouraged me to try my fortune at the bar. After all this, you will be at no loss to discover how my inclinations at present lie. . . .*

I am, dear Father,
Your most dutiful son. T. T.

This letter speaks for itself. 'Tammie' did not go into the ministry, nor did he 'rise to eminence at the bar'; but he became Scotland's greatest scholar in the antiquities of her law, or in the words of Cockburn:

the most learned and judicious antiquary in Scotland. No one has done nearly so much to recover, to arrange, to explain, and to preserve our historical muniments. . . . His real merit, great as it may seem now, will seem

* *Ibid.* p. 4.

still greater five hundred years hence. . . . Had he not allowed his taste for antiquarian research to allure him from the common drudgery of his profession, he would have stood high in practice, as he always did in character, at the bar; and would now have been adorning the bench by his considerate wisdom and peculiar learning.*

Surely his father would have felt requited by this record for his son's loss to the ministry, and his former professor and counsellor found in Thomson a living monument to his faith in the potentialities of earnest young seekers after the truth.

Thus Millar the professor, the teacher of youth, figured large not only in the vocational preparation, but in the mental and moral development of literally hundreds of young men who came to Glasgow for their education over a period of forty years. That he played no small role also in the administrative affairs of the Old College as member of its Faculty and Senate, we shall attempt to show in the next chapter.

---

* H. Cockburn, *Life of Lord Jeffrey* (Edinburgh, 1872), vol. I, p. 135. The matriculation dates, or other known attendance dates, with matriculation number in ( ), are given here for students of Millar's we have singled out for special mention. The Earl of Buchan, 1762 (2198); William Adam, 1771–72 (no matr. recorded); Hume, 1775 (3576); Lauderdale, 1777 (3778); Thomson, 1782 (4234), also 1789; Douglas (Lord Reston), 1787 (4773); Campbell, 1798 (4994); Reddie, 1795 (5726); William and Frederick Lamb, 1799–1800 (no matr. recorded).

V

THE PROFESSOR AND HIS COLLEAGUES

Millar's relations with his colleagues and his role, both in the university community, outside his classroom, and in his larger community, are passed over very slightly by his biographer. As pieced together, however, from various sources,* they not only make an interesting story but take on considerable significance for the present study.

It should be remembered, first of all, that at this time the professors of the College did not constitute a large body. The general curriculum or ordinary Arts course consisted of only five 'classes', each having but one chair. These were Latin (generally called Humanity), Greek, Logic and Rhetoric, Moral Philosophy, and Natural Philosophy. In addition there was a separate professorship for Mathematics, subordinated more or less to the Chair of Natural Philosophy, and another for Practical Astronomy—making seven in all for the general Arts or Philosophy course.

To these are to be added, on the 'graduate' and professional level, the Principal, who had by law also to be Primarious Professor of Divinity, and three other chairs relating chiefly to the training of young men for the church: one for Divinity proper, one for Oriental Languages, and one for Ecclesiastical History. In the Law College there was only one chair. In Medicine there were by the constitution only two: one for the Theory and Practice of Medicine and one for Anatomy and Botany. To these two were, however, added at about this time, by the University itself and supported out of private University funds, three additional lectureships: one for Materia Medica, one for Chemistry and a third for Midwifery. These latter were not, however, accorded full status in Faculty and Senate.

Of these fourteen 'professorships' altogether, six were crown appointments: the Principalship and the chairs of Ecclesiastical History, Law, Medicine, Anatomy and Botany, and Astronomy. The others were 'nominated' by the governing body of the College itself.

In addition to these professors, a representative of the 'ministers of

---

* Grateful acknowledgement is made of the courtesy extended the author by Professor Fordyce, Clerk of Senate, and by his assistant, Mr Reid, of repeated access to these valuable, and for the purpose in hand indispensable manuscript tomes of minutes of the Senate and of the Faculty over a period of forty years.

Glasgow'—usually the minister of the 'High Church',* a Dean of Faculty and a Rector had a certain status in this governing body, chiefly in a visitorial capacity. The Dean of Faculty, usually and properly an outside person, though occasionally, then as even today, one of the professors, was more often than not a minister of the Glasgow Presbytery.† The Rector, whose position was partly honorific, but who in certain situations bore responsibilities far greater than those of the other visitors, was usually an alumnus of distinction or some benefactor of the College. He was elected annually by the professors and the students, jointly by vote according to the traditional 'four nations', though he was usually re-elected for a second term. The duties of the first two of these visitors were usually taken lightly, and those of the Rector were for ordinary purposes deputed to a Vice-Rector named from among the professors. The powers and duties of the Rector were in Millar's time, however, a matter of grave dispute both within the university community and in actions at law in the Court of Session.

These matters were of course regulated by law, either by the original charter, by the *Nova Erectio* of 1577, or by parliamentary action at various times, consequent upon 'royal visitations'.

This body, then, was the teaching and governing body of the College, operating, as just indicated, under a royal charter, and standing in certain definite relations to the church as well as to the civil government, but not responsible to any higher body except for the right of royal visitation, which occurred only at rare intervals, and for what might be called the 'monitory' powers of both the Glasgow Presbytery and the General Assembly of the Church of Scotland. There was also a certain benevolent interest in the affairs of the College or University by such spokesmen of the crown, or at least members of the nobility, as the neighbouring Duke of Hamilton and the Earl of Bute, who would certainly be consulted in the crown appointments and would expect also to have some voice in nominations to the other chairs.

The functional organization of this body need not engage us in any detail here. Broadly, as the 'Senate', also called the 'University', it looked after the strictly educational or academic functions; as the 'Faculty', also called the 'College', with the same membership so far as the professors were concerned, chiefly after the business, financial, 'bursary' and property-custodial functions. There was also for some purposes a University court, not to be confused with the University Court of a later day. In any case it was a remarkably autonomous

---

* The 'High Church' has no implications of 'prelacy', but is merely the designation at the time for the Church of Scotland Cathedral, on an elevation not far from the old university site.

† For the years 1782–4, 1786–8, 1790–2 and 1794–6, at least, the Dean of Faculty was Millar's brother-in-law, the Reverend Alexander Hutchison, minister at Hamilton.

body, even to the extent of the filling of vacancies when they occurred in any but the crown chairs—and there too its recommendations were usually followed—and voting its own salary scale, so far as salaries came out of university funds and not out of public or crown funds. The professors were, appearances sometimes to the contrary notwithstanding,* generally aware of their high responsibilities, and their position, in relation to the students, to the Glasgow community, and to the political and religious community generally, was one of considerable dignity.

Among Millar's colleagues in the early years of his professorship were the following: George Muirhead in Humanity, James Moor in Greek, Adam Smith in Moral Philosophy (followed after three years by Thomas Reid), James Williamson in Mathematics, James Clow in Logic and Rhetoric, John Anderson in Natural Philosophy, and Alexander Wilson, soon to be followed by his son Patrick Wilson, in Astronomy. The celebrated Robert Simson retired from the Mathematics chair just about the time Millar entered into his. In Anatomy and Chemistry there was the distinguished Joseph Black until 1766, when he moved to Edinburgh;† in Divinity Robert Trail and also Principal Leechman; in Oriental Languages Patrick Cumin and in Ecclesiastical History William Wight. Among replacements during Millar's time, besides Reid, were William Richardson in Humanity, John Young in Greek, George Jardine in Logic, James Baillie in Divinity, and also his own son James in Mathematics and his son-in-law, James Mylne, in Moral Philosophy, to name the more outstanding.

Of these the most renowned for scholarship, educational leadership, the advancement of science or publications of high merit were Adam Smith, Robert Simson, Joseph Black, Thomas Reid, James Moor and John Young in Greek, and perhaps William Leechman in Divinity. Those with whom Millar was most intimate in terms of either personal friendship, moral and intellectual rapport or effective collaboration, were Adam Smith, Joseph Black, George Jardine, James Baillie and William Wight. His strongest antagonist among them on purely philosophical grounds—though sympathetic on personal and political grounds—was Thomas Reid. A 'difficult' man because of a strange admixture of great ability, high scholastic merit and many fine traits of character with a multitude of personal foibles, was James Moor of the Greek class. But the most exasperating of his associates was John Anderson of the Experimental or Natural Philosophy (Physics) class. Anderson was a 'man of good parts' able, popular with his students,

* J. D. Mackie, *The University of Glasgow* (Glasgow, 1954), pp. 190 ff., 213.

† Professor Cullen (1710–90) transferred to Edinburgh in 1756; Professor Black (1728–99) in 1766.

who called him 'Jolly Jack Phosphorus', but 'impossible as a colleague', 'meddling and disputatious, obstinate and inconsiderate and involving the University in protracted, useless and costly litigation',* leading, at times, to serious disruption of morale and dangerous cleavages within the College, going so far as to raise the question of a royal visitation.†

An examination of the Senate and Faculty minutes for the forty years of Millar's occupancy of the Law Chair, where they bear on his role and activities, would seem to warrant the following generalizations.

First to be noted is that from the very beginning we find him serving on important committees, particularly on assignments involving legal matters, disputes over property, representation of the University in court, etc. In this his law training served the University in good stead. Later we find him also frequently elected chairman of the meeting, serving as Clerk of Senate or of Faculty, and at one time, at least, as Vice-Rector of the University.‡

Next, in the performance of these roles and in his participation in the solution of difficult problems of university administration or intra-mural conflict, he appears always to manifest a keen analytical mind and a constructive purpose. Holding strictly to the line, wasting no time on matters irrelevant or peripheral to the issue at hand, he quickly gets at the core of the problem, and, helping thus to clarify the issue, soon leads the meeting out of a badly tangled situation. Here again his legal training is clearly in evidence.

Further, in matters involving personal disputes and personal rancour and jealousies—and of these there were not a few—he is always seen to rise above personalities and to hold to principles, whether of law, of morality, of good administration, or of the honour and good name of the University in the community.

Again, he seems never to lack the courage to take an unpopular stand, or even to challenge those in authority, when a cause, as he sees it, bids him so to do. He is frequently in the minority and often on the losing side. Over and over again remarks like these occur in the minutes, 'Mr Millar wishes to have it marked that he dissents from the above resolu-

* Murray, *op. cit.* pp. 115 f. Also Coutts, *op. cit.* Index, and Millar's letters to Burke listed in Appendix I.

† As a parting bolt he hurled vengefully at his colleagues, whom, directly or by implication, he called 'drones', 'triflers', 'drunkards' and men 'negligent in their duty', testamentary plans for the foundation of a rival university (Anderson Institution), chiefly in applied fields—a plan that was in considerable measure carried out. For contemporary accounts see, e.g. Denholm, *History of Glasgow*, pp. 328–33, and *Glasgow Courier*, 6 October 1798.

‡ University Manuscripts, vol. 71, fo. 171 (1778): 'To execute the office and to have the full power given to the Rector by the *Nova Erectio* and such other powers' etc., the powers of visitation only excepted. For other offices see vol. 32, fo. 370; vol. 71, fos. 68, 370; vol. 75, fo. 81; vol. 78, fo. 16, *et al.*

tion for reasons to be given in a subsequent meeting'; 'Mr Millar, having been absent from the last meeting, desired to have it marked that he adhered to the dissent from the resolution,' etc. On one occasion where a committee had been appointed to attend to some improvements calling for a small expenditure of College funds, he charges the Principal with having proceeded in the matter without convoking the committee, and on another he even charges him with distortion if not falsification of the minutes of a meeting.*

Once more, he is frequently seen to head a committee or otherwise to be entrusted with the responsibility of looking to the improvement of the College in educational matters, such as working out a system for the arrangement and classification of the books in the library,† drawing up rules for the conferring of degrees and for admission to candidacy for such degrees, etc.‡

Significantly, he is frequently seen to come to the defence of students, whose status as students merely, should not, in his view, deprive them of basic rights to freedom of opinion, speech and action, or to a fair trial when accused of misconduct.

More frequently than others, it would appear, he is called upon to represent the University in her relations with the outside community, in legal matters, in receiving guests of honour, in official or semi-official correspondence; or in being sent on missions 'abroad'.

Finally, in such matters as 'political' appointments, nepotism, the selling, in effect, by a professor, of his chair to a successor of his own choice for a financial consideration, holding on to the salary, and if possible even to his house, after retirement, Millar is realistic enough to recognize that up to a point, in the absence of suitable retirement provisions, such practices had become a part of the university system. But he is zealous in opposing them when they lead to sinecures or threaten to burden the University and the profession with men of inferior ability, or otherwise lead to injustice of any kind.

Only a few of these observations and generalizations can be illustrated here from the records. The selections will, it is hoped, throw sidelights not only on the actor upon whom this study is focused, but also on the stage upon which he acted.

In a notorious trial within the University,§ in which a certain divinity student, David Woodburn, was charged with heresy, blasphemy and other conduct unbefitting a student—for example, remark-

---

* *Ibid.* vol. 38, fo. 161.　† *Ibid.* vol. 71, fo. 106.　‡ *Ibid.* vol. 71, fos. 112–15, 141.

§ University Manuscripts, vol. 31, fos. 273–373 *passim*; 32, 40–81 *passim*. Coutts, *History*, p. 333. Also Anon. (Mr Thom), *Trial of a Student of the College of Cluthra, in the Kingdom of Oceanea* (Glasgow, 1768), 76 pp.

ing, no doubt with a specific personal reference, that a student could learn more in the theatre than 'by attending the drowsy shops of Logic and Metaphysics'—Millar came strongly to the defence of the student. From the legal phraseology used it may be assumed that the very wording of the portion of the minutes which we give in a footnote below* is his.

After endless debate in this trial, that had apparently taken on a public character, with the populace of the city generally siding against the accusing professors, Millar and his friend Wight are still standing by their dissent on the ground that 'they see no reason to believe or suspect that [the accused] has been guilty of any impiety or wilful disrespect to religion; and with regard to the other articles, with which he has been charged, they apprehend them to be of too frivolous a nature to merit a formal prosecution.'

In another instance a colleague was charged with libel and assault against an unoffending and defenceless student. There is no need of baring here the unsavoury details of the case, but the wording of the charge, which is undoubtedly Millar's, is illuminating.

Whereas every professor in this college ought to exercise discipline over his students with prudence, temperance and moderation; and whereas violent passions and frantic behaviour in a professor when teaching his students must weaken his authority and hurt his usefulness; and whereas

* The following paragraphs lifted out of the very extensive minutes of the Senate covering the long-drawn-out trial most clearly reflect Millar's position on the affair, presumably largely in his own words:

'A very considerable number of the members of this meeting, having heard from many different persons that Mr Woodburn, a student in the university, is said to have spoken at sundry times in such a manner as to give great offence from an appearance of impiety, concerning our Blessed Saviour, concerning the Holy Ghost, concerning faith and grace, concerning the sacraments, and has also uttered several other things which are contrary to the duty of a student, which are said to be publicy known . . . [resolution follows. Then]

'Mr Millar desires leave . . . to have it marked that he dissents from the above resolution of the university meeting for the following reasons:

'1. Because he has never had occasion to hear the above-mentioned reports concerning the impiety of Mr Woodburn and therefore he thinks it would have been a proper step in the university meeting to have previously enquired in a private manner concerning the nature and circumstances of the above reports before resolving to make the matter public by taking a precognition of the case.

'2. Mr Millar is of the opinion that the articles mentioned in the above minutes, which are to be the ground of the precognition proposed, are conceived in too general and vague a manner; that they do not specify any particular instances of impiety in Mr Woodburn, concerning which the committee is appointed to enquire; that the minute mentions neither the places, the times, nor the persons, nor the expressions relative to the above-mentioned report. By the above minute therefore the committee is vested with a power of enquiring at large into the whole life and conversation, either public or private, of said Mr Woodburn and that not only with respect to the charge of impiety, but with respect to every breach of duty in Mr Woodburn as a student. This, Mr Millar apprehends to be an inquisitorial power which no court in Great Britain has a right to exercise.' (University Manuscripts, vol. 31, fos. 273 f.)

a professor by beating students while he is in a passion, with weapons capable of giving a deadly wound . . . ought to be censured and punished in such a manner as . . . may prevent the loss and dishonour that may arise to the college from such behaviour and discipline: Yet it is true that you, Dr—, professor of — in Glasgow college have been guilty of all or part of the enormities above mentioned insofar as in the room within the college called the — class, and between the hours of four and five afternoon upon the — day of —, . . . you [follows a very detailed description of his actions]. At least you, the said Dr —, in the place and at the time before mentioned did assault and beat said — and behave to him in a manner highly inconsistent with the proper discipline of the college, and highly unsuitable to the character and behaviour of a professor, which being proved before the Faculty of the Glasgow College together with the Rector and the Dean of the University of Glasgow or the majority thereof, you ought to be censured and punished according as such offence and such enormity deserve.*

In still another case an innocently offending student wounded the dignity of his professor by protesting that the punishment he had received for an unintentional mis-step was unwarranted, and that he, the student, also had certain rights in such a matter. When the professor thereupon severely insulted the student, called out the beadle and had him locked up in the gaol without hearing or bail, Millar and another professor bailed out the student and saw to it that he was given a fair trial.†

The matter of professors' houses in the college was an occasion of frequent wrangling in the meetings of the faculty. Professors coveted not only a house, but the right to a particular house, and desired at times to retain the occupancy of a given house even after their retirement or 'demission'. Mr Millar was once asked to serve on 'a committee to consider of proper regulations with regard to the removal of families from college houses in case of death, demission or deprivation of a professor'‡ and had often to do with the administering and up-keeping of these properties. At one time a professor had without authorization ordered major repairs made, charging them to the College. Mr Millar, with Mr Young

protested because the state of the repairs was not laid before the meeting by the committee which had been previously appointed for that purpose, and because they understood it to be a principle which had long been observed by the society that when a professor first occupied a college house and obtains repairs from the faculty, he is bound to keep the house afterwards in proper order unless so far as relates to the fabric. . . . Deviation from foregoing principle . . . will open the door to enormous demands which may occasion great abuses in the management of the college funds.§

* University Manuscripts, vol. 75, fos. 97 ff. '—' indicates deletion by present editor.
† *Ibid.* vol. 75, fo. 132.   ‡ *Ibid.* vol. 76, fo. 149.   § *Ibid.* vol. 78, fo. 250.

Millar was greatly and actively interested in the anti-slave trade movement of which Wilberforce was the great leader. When the University decided to honour this leader with its doctorate, this was undoubtedly done at his instigation. The recommendation of the committee, presumably drawn up by Millar, its chairman, reads in part:

A motion was made and seconded for conferring the honorary degree of Doctor of Laws on William Wilberforce, Esqr., member of Parliament for Yorkshire, as a mark of that esteem which this university entertain for his character and abilities, as well as of their high approbation of his exertions for the abolition of the African slave trade.

The Senate, having considered this proposal, think it highly becoming a society entrusted with the education of youth to take a public opportunity of expressing their unfeigned applause of a conduct so agreeable to the principles of humanity and virtue, and so consistent with the duty of a member of the legislature in a country enjoying the blessings of a free government.

The Senate of this university do therefore unanimously confer the degree of Doctor of Laws upon this said William Wilberforce, Esqr., and appoint Mr Millar [and others named] a committee to make out a diploma accordingly and to have the same conveyed to Mr Wilberforce by the first opportunity; and the Vice-Chancellor is hereby appointed to transmit an extract of this minute in a letter to Mr Wilberforce.

Signed etc.*

In a letter of grateful acknowledgement of this 'high honour bestowed upon him by so learned and respectable a body' Wilberforce wishes to look upon this as not merely a personal honour to himself: 'I rejoice in it also on other grounds, anticipating the credit it cannot fail to reflect on a cause in the success of which I am most deeply interested.'†

When a year later the University sent a petition to the House of Commons through Wilberforce in support of pending legislation to abolish the slave trade, this move was again presumably instigated by Millar who was also active in promoting public meetings and gathering signatures to a similar petition in the Glasgow community. The wording of this petition, too, in which he presumably had a hand, is interesting for the light it throws not only on its presumed author, but on the University itself, which did not often engage in activities of this kind. It reads in part:

. . . Both in our individual capacity, and as members of a public seminary, we think ourselves called upon, at this juncture, to express our disapprobation of the African Slave Trade, and humbly pray for its abolition as an

* *Ibid.* vol. 72, fos. 113 f. (27 April 1791).   † *Ibid.* vol. 72, fo. 117.

existing evil of infinite magnitude; as an evil which comprehends in it the most obvious violation of the feelings of nature, of the prescripts of morality, and of those doctrines and duties inculcated in the Gospel, which forms the basis of our most holy religion.

Deeply penetrated by the cries of justice and mercy, . . .

[Signed . . .]*

The year 1798 was a year of severe crisis and trial in Great Britain, owing to her involvement in the war with France, the outcome of which was most uncertain and the fiscal burdens heavy to the point of threatening ruin. A meeting of the faculty, 'recognizing the duty of communities as well as individuals . . . to contribute' to a 'voluntary pecuniary aid for the defence of the country,' under a so-called 'assessment tax act', 'voted £300 sterling to the defence of Great Britain in the present critical juncture'. This move Millar opposed vigorously as we see from his own words given in a footnote below.†

The occasions when Millar represented the University in her external relations are very many. When it was found necessary to consult some distinguished advocates at Edinburgh 'upon the legality of the sentence of the University meeting, by which, the Professorship of Ecclesiastical History was declared vacant' Mr Smith and Mr Millar were sent on that mission and were allowed 'to carry [thither] the University book in which the transactions relating to that affair are narrated'.‡ When Burke came to Glasgow for his inauguration to the rectorship, he, along with Adam Smith (then at Edinburgh), and

---

* *Ibid.* vol. 72, fo. 136 (1 February 1792).

† Against this resolution Mr. Millar protested for the following reasons:

'1mo. Because all the funds of the college are strictly appropriated to particular purposes; to the payment of the stipends of certain clergymen; to the maintenance of the Principal and professors and of a number of foundation scholars; to the support of college buildings; and to other pious uses immediately relative to the university. . . .

'2do. If the circumstances of public administration have at present suggested voluntary contributions for the service of the state, the contributors must be supposed to have the full and unlimited disposal of this money which they bestow in this manner. The effect of this contribution is merely to save or relieve others from taxes; and those who come forward with a free gift on this occasion are virtually making a present to those persons who may thus be exempted from taxation. . . .

'3^{tio}. It has been said that the contribution of this university is supported by the legislature, which expressly allows corporations to contribute as well as individuals. But surely the act of Parliament does not enter into the question, how far corporations are, in any case, entitled to alienate any part of their funds. It only authorizes them, where they have funds at their free disposal, to act as *legal persons* in subscribing toward this contribution.

'He therefore protests that the members of the faculty, who have voted for this application of the college money, shall be liable to repair the loss which is thereby brought upon the university, and hereupon takes instruments in the clerk's hands. To which protest Professor Cumin adhered.' (University Manuscripts, vol. 80, fos. 221–3.)

‡ *Ibid.* vol. 30, fos. 95–8. See also, for fuller account, Scott, *Adam Smith*, pp. 193–5.

Professors Dalzel and Dugald Stewart, who had come with him from Edinburgh, were entertained at dinner in Millar's home. And when under his rectorship serious difficulties confronted the University, growing out of the activities of Professor Anderson, already referred to, and correspondence was necessary in this and other matters, Millar is seen to carry on much of that correspondence though he was neither Vice-Rector nor Clerk of Senate or of Faculty at that time. Similarly when arrangements were in process for Adam Smith's inauguration to the same office, his former protégé is seen to carry on the correspondence.

When difficulties arose in the matter of the Balliol College, Oxford, Snell Exhibition, on which, incidentally, Adam Smith had studied there for six years, Millar was principally entrusted, along with Professor Jardine, with finding a solution for the problem. On receipt of his report, he was voted the special thanks of the meeting for his handling of a difficult situation.*

Again, in matters of land acquisition by the University—the University came in time to own a goodly amount of such property—or in difficulties with legal titles to properties, he is almost invariably seen to represent the University in the relevant courts.

One of the 'extra-curricular' interests and activities to which Millar was greatly attached took him, at least figuratively, beyond the college walls though not to any considerable extent away from his colleagues. This was his participation in the programme of the Glasgow Literary Society.

The Literary Society† was one of the many clubs for which Glasgow, like other Scottish centres of culture, was famous at this time, but one very closely associated with the life of the University by its membership, its place of meeting within her halls, and its concern with literary and scientific subjects. It was founded in 1752, shortly after Smith's coming to Glasgow, and apparently largely at his instigation, for the consideration of topics literary, philosophical, scientific, religious and political, and continued for at least some time after Millar's death.

Its membership was drawn first of all from among the professors at the College, but also from ministers in and about the city, and some physicians, advocates, merchants—in fact anyone who might be interested in its programme and willing to deliver a paper at least once a year, or pay a fine for failure to do so. Students in the College, perhaps only the more advanced ones, were also allowed to attend the meetings,

* *Ibid.* vol. 75, fos. 332 f.

† *Life*, pp. lviii–lxiv; *Notices and Documents Illustrative of the Literary History of Glasgow* (Maitland Club, Glasgow, 1831), pp. 15 f., 131, 132–5. Also James Cleland, *Annals of Glasgow* (2 vols. Glasgow, 1816), vol. II, pp. 447 f. and Denholm, *op. cit.* pp. 335 f.

though without the rights and duties of full membership. On its membership roster will be found the names of the most distinguished Glasgow figures of the time, such as Adam Smith, Robert Simson, the great mathematician, William Cullen, one of the fathers of modern chemistry, Thomas Reid, perhaps Scotland's greatest metaphysician, James Watt, the inventor, and the Foulis brothers, printers of fine books; also David Hume, Adam Ferguson and Edmund Burke—these latter perhaps as honorary members.*

The society met every Friday evening at half-past five from the first Friday of November to the second Friday of May. First a paper would be read, to be followed by more or less formal debate. Then all who cared to remain would retire to a favourite spot, usually a designated tavern, where more informal discussion of the same topic would be carried well into the night under 'convivial' circumstances. Surviving records give us a fair picture, though an incomplete one, of actual programmes, papers presented—some of them to be later published— topics discussed etc., but space does not permit our going into these, except to remark that the variety of these topics, the high literary and philosophical standing of many of the contributors, the seriousness of the discussions, are indicative of a keen and widespread interest in things of the mind, while at the same time the meetings gave outlet to social and convivial impulses that could not easily be met in other ways, and that made these occasions memorable in the lives of the participants.†

Of this society, then, Millar was an ardent devotee, allowing nothing to prevent his regular attendance, and always giving it his very best. He is known to have presented his share of papers before the society, but none of them, nor even a record of them, has been preserved. He was at his best in the debates, in which he sparred very freely, at times even with almost dangerous warmth—particularly with his strongest antagonist, Thomas Reid, against whom he ardently defended Hume's philosophy—on many religious and political issues of the day. The heat of these battles was, however, never allowed to rankle long, we are told, after the debates were concluded.‡ It was in these debates and in this

* Other names on the roster are those of Professors Leechman, Lindesay, Moor, Black, Millar, in fact most of the professors at the University; also James Oswald, William Dunlop, Lord Craig, of the Court of Session, and his father William Craig, distinguished Glasgow minister, Baron William Mure of Calderwood, Thomas Campbell, the poet, Thomas Muir, the renowned Scottish martyr, the Earl of Buchan, the Reverend John Lockhart, father of Scott's biographer, and others that might be mentioned.

† *Life*, pp. lviii–lxiv.

‡ Dugald Stewart says, on the relations of these two men, 'Nor was [Reid] less delighted with the good humoured opposition which his opinions never failed to encounter in the acuteness of Millar—then [1764 et seq.] in the vigour of his youthful genius, and warm from the lessons of a different school.' (*Works*, vol. x, p. 262.)

discussion of so wide a range of topics, that the breadth of Millar's scholarship and his unusually wide reading served him in especially good stead. In the words of his biographer:

In this [the more informal] part of the evening's amusement, Mr. Millar was as conspicuous, as in the previous discussions. His convivial talents, his unfailing vivacity and good humour, called out the powers of many, who would otherwise have remained silent and reserved; the liveliness of his fancy suggested infinite topics of conversation or of mirth; and his rich stores of information enabled him to supply endless sources of knowledge and amusement.*

Shortly after Millar's death Professor Jardine, of the logic chair and one of Millar's most intimate associates and friends, read before the Society an obituary paper that Craig drew heavily upon in preparing his biography. But this paper, like many others that would have interested us greatly, has been lost to posterity.

In some respects, this account of University activities is a record of stormy meetings and of internal dissention. More than could appear from our necessarily brief presentation, these conflicts within the University found their echoes outside in the larger community; as in turn, storms without, especially during the period of the French Revolution, the reactionary 'blackout', the war-strains of the nineties, had their impact on the life of the University. Professors were under attack for their 'whiggish' treason. One of the papers read by Professor Reid before the Literary Society dealt specifically with 'The Dangers of Political Innovation', reflecting, of course his reaction to the French Revolution.† Yet on the whole it is remarkable how calmly, how majestically almost, this body rode the waves of the storm. So calmly, in fact, that it might at first appear that these men lived in an ivory tower. Yet on closer view it becomes clear that they were not sheltered from the storm, but rather, in firm confidence in their business as a university, raised themselves above its turmoil and its violent partisanships. And this was not least the case in Millar's own conduct of his work and of his relations with his colleagues.

* *Life*, pp. lxi f.

† Reprinted from an account in *Glasgow Courier* (18 December 1794) in Archibald Arthur's *Discourses on Theological and Literary Subjects* (Glasgow, 1803), Appendix II, pp. 518–23. See also Alexander C. Fraser, *Thomas Reid* (London, 1898), pp. 115 f. Meikle (*Scotland and the French Revolution*, pp. 155 f.) is hardly warranted in calling this 'bowing to the storm'. Millar, with whom Reid had a remarkable affinity, *politically*, and who could never have been so accused, would have taken an almost identical stand.

VI

WRITINGS AND LECTURES

Millar was not a prolific writer. There are only three published works which can definitely be attributed to him. His first known publication, aside from an eight-page bar-examination *Disputatio*,* in Latin, which has been preserved, was a quarto volume of xv and 242 pages bearing the title of *Observations Concerning the Distinction of Ranks in Society*. It was published in 1771, ten years after he had entered upon the duties of his professorship at Glasgow. Eight years later this work appeared, twice revised† and considerably enlarged, under the new title of *The Origin of the Distinction of Ranks*, with the revealing descriptive sub-title 'or, An Inquiry into the Circumstances which Give Rise to Influence and Authority in the different Members of Society'.

In 1787, in the full maturity of his career, he published *An Historical View of the English Government from the Settlement of the Saxons in Britain to the Accession of the House of Stewart*. This quarto volume in two books, some 600 pages in all including an index, is dedicated 'To the Honourable Charles James Fox' and is, no doubt appropriately, spoken of in that dedication as an attempt 'to write a constitutional history of England'. There was a second, little-altered edition in 1790, and considerable progress was made on a second volume intended to bring the history down to his own time.

Millar did not live to carry out this plan fully, though he clearly intended to do so without great delay. His delay may well have been occasioned in considerable part, as his biographer suggests, by the distracting influence of the French Revolution and of its immediate aftermath—upsetting not only in an emotional way and by the devastating impact of years of war, but also by turning men's minds so strongly to vivid expectations for the immediate future as to make historical studies seem less important than political action for the realization of the promise of the Revolution.‡

Among his manuscripts his executors found, however, one apparently nearly ready for the press, carrying the history down to the Revolution of 1688, and other materials, some in finished and others in less finished form, clearly intended in part for a fourth Book to bring the

---

* See the Millar bibliography at the end of this book.   † *Ibid.*
‡ This is Craig's opinion, at least. *Life*, p. cxxx.

history down from the Revolution to his own time. The first of these was published as Volume III of a new edition of the *Historical View* (1803), Books I and II of the earlier editions now appearing as Volumes I and II. Other papers, not all of which were necessarily intended by their author for this purpose, they published as a fourth volume.*

From May to September 1796 Millar published in the *Scots Chronicle* of Edinburgh (see Appendix II) a series of fifteen letters under the pseudonym 'Crito', republished in pamphlet form the same year, still anonymously, as *Letters of Crito*, with a preface and a dedication to Mr Fox.† This sizeable pamphlet (some 26,500 words) is strictly political in character and consists chiefly of an attack on the war policies of the Pitt government.

There is a strong probability that a series of letters following closely upon the Crito letters in the *Scots Chronicle* under the signature 'Sidney', and within the same year published in pamphlet form as *Letters of Sidney on Inequality of Property*,‡ is also from Millar's pen (see Appendix II below). These letters, too, are strongly political though they have, perhaps, a stronger underpinning of theory than do the Crito letters.

Between 1788 and 1792 he contributed 'a number of articles'—if our identification of these review-articles is correct, a goodly number— to another new and strongly anti-Tory journalistic venture, the London *Analytical Review*. These are discussed below (p. 60) and in Appendix II.

Besides these materials published either during his lifetime or shortly thereafter, Millar is known to have left a number of manuscripts, papers read before the Literary Society, etc. that have been lost or destroyed. The most important of these was one on 'The Present State of the British Government', which is said to have been in a fairly finished form, but still not adjudged as fully warranting publication. Its loss has been much regretted.§

Like Adam Smith, Millar strongly disapproved of having any but finished productions exposed to public view. He held that John Home's reputation, for example, would have been much advanced with posterity, had he never published anything but his Douglas Tragedy.‖ He

---

* The whole now bore the sub-title 'From the Settlement of the Saxons in Britain to the Revolution in 1688: to which are sub-joined, some dissertations connected with the history of the Government from the Revolution to the present time'.

† The only files we have found of the *Scots Chronicle* which contain the original letters, both series, are in the Edinburgh Public Library. The pamphlet is dated Edinburgh and London, 1796. See Appendix II below.

‡ Edinburgh, 1796.   § *Life*, pp. cxxxii f.

‖ See letter, Millar to David Douglas, Appendix I.

was similarly reluctant to have personal letters, not originally intended for the public, later so exposed.

Of his letters written to various persons, in a correspondence that was never large, we have found copies thus far of only thirteen. Some of these will be found, in whole or part, in Appendix I to this volume.

Fortunately for the present study, there have been preserved a number of complete or partial sets of student-notes on his various courses of lectures. A brief characterization of these notes, some of which merit publication in part, will be found in Appendix III. On these various writings and lectures I offer here only such comment as has a biographical interest.

SCOPE AND CHARACTER OF THE LECTURES ON GOVERNMENT

The lectures on civil law and those on Scots and on English law need not detain us here. Of the lectures on government the first fifteen or sixteen, usually, were given to outlining the 'general principles of government', as he viewed them.* It is here that we have, in brief form, the most systematic presentation of his general view of society, government, the evolution of property and familial institutions, and of social and political institutions generally. Like all of the lectures in this course, these lectures reflect a broadly historical and historico-sociological more than a theoretical orientation. Millar does not always draw a clear line, in the execution of his design, between 'government' in its more formal aspects, on the one hand, and society, 'social control', stages of economic development, etc. on the other.

In the second part he applies these 'principles' to the development of political institutions in Athens and Sparta and among the Romans, and, in 'modern' or medieval and modern times, among the Germans, the French and the English,† with Scotland and Ireland included—the aim being admittedly more to illustrate his 'principles' than otherwise to write history. It is in these latter, in particular, that the basic materials are provided for his published *Historical View*.

The third part, consisting usually of another fifteen or sixteen lectures, offers a view of 'the present state of the Government of Great Britain', the constitution and powers of Parliament in its three divisions of King, Lords and Commons, and the different judicial establishments, civil and ecclesiastical, with the differences between the English and the Scottish

* See student lecture-notes, some with lecture-heads attached, Murray Collection, University of Glasgow Library. Also *Life*, pp. xliv–lvii.

† In the title of his *Historical View* and elsewhere he frequently uses the term 'English' for 'British' and 'England' for 'Great Britain' as was customary even in Scotland at the time.

duly noted—all with considerable attention also to their historical origin and development.

In all of these 'lectures on government' Millar treats of a wide range of topics beyond the merely 'governmental'. They include, for instance, sustenance and the general economic order; the institutions of property; the rank structure and the distribution of power generally in society; the forms of family life and of authority within the family; the origin and development of feudal institutions, including chivalry; religious institutions and ecclesiastical policy; the development of the arts and of science; the consequences of an excessive division of labour in modern industrial society; servitude, slavery and liberty. Many of these themes are, of course, more fully developed in his published works. There is little—one should probably say surprisingly little, for a man of his strong political convictions in a time of most intense political controversy when some of these lectures were given—that we should today consider polemical or controversial in character; unless we except his discussion of the royal prerogative, and of the character, tenets and policies of the Catholic Church.

THE GENERAL CHARACTER OF HIS WRITINGS

Millar's *Ranks* is intended, in the author's own words,* as an inquiry into 'the natural history of mankind in several important articles', and aimed in particular at showing the influence of basic technological and economic improvements, or 'the gradual progress of civilization and improvement' upon 'the manners, the laws and the government of a people'. The 'several articles' are, above all, property, the family and the positions and relation of the sexes, and the rank and power structure of society or its differentiation into classes seen in relation to 'the distribution of power'.

The book is clearly an outgrowth of his lectures on law, general jurisprudence and government, not in the sense that it in any way reflects their content and scope, but that it selects certain aspects of their subject-matter. The author draws heavily on ancient and medieval historical and legal sources and on travel literature and other modern historical and descriptive accounts of peoples outside the pale of modern European societies. The approach is thoroughly evolutionistic and represents, as will be shown later, a marked transition from a legal or juridical to a prevailingly sociological orientation.

In the *Historical View* the general plan is to review the successive periods of English, or more correctly 'British' constitutional history,

* Introduction to the *Ranks*, 3rd and 4th editions.

realizing that this government 'has not been formed at once, but has grown to maturity in a course of ages', that the foundations of our present constitution were laid in a very early period, and that 'by considering events in the order in which they happened . . . the causes of every single change will be more easily unfolded, and may be pointed out with greater simplicity'.

He hopes in this 'historical view' to answer questions like these:

. . . By what fortunate concurrence of events has a more extensive plan of civil freedom been established in this Island [than in other countries reviewed]? Was it by accident, or by design, or from the influence of peculiar situation, that our Saxon forefathers, originally distinguished as the most ferocious of all those barbarians who invaded the Roman provinces, have been enabled to embrace more comprehensive notions of liberty, and to sow the seeds of those political institutions which have been productive of such prosperity and happiness to a great and populous empire? (*H.V.* vol. I, pp. 7 f.) [His answer, as it applies here to the Saxon period in particular, but elsewhere to other periods and governments as well, is that it must not be supposed] that the whole has originated in much contrivance and foresight; and is the result of deep-laid schemes of policy [but that] the regulations established in [England as in other European] countries proceeded from no artificial or complicated plan of legislation; but were such as occurred successively to the people, for the supply of their immediate wants, and the removal of incidental inconveniences; in a word, that the feudal constitution was, everywhere, a kind of natural growth, produced by the peculiar situation and circumstances of the society. (*H.V.* vol. I, pp. 375 f.)

Both of Millar's major works were well received by the public and went through a goodly number of editions, particularly if we count also the pirated Dublin editions, and both were translated into the German, the *Ranks* also into the French and the Italian (?) languages. Excerpts from some of the reviews will be found in the footnote below.*

* A reviewer of Millar's *Ranks* in the *Critical Review* (vol. XXXI, pp. 432–42), on its first appearance in 1771, holds that the author has 'with great ability and with ingenuity given us a review of the manners and customs of men'; he emphasizes his careful use of historical sources and concludes by observing that 'few books have been published of later years that are more entitled to public favour and approbation'. The *Monthly Review* (vol. XLV, O.S., pp. 188–95) holds that Millar is pointing the way, on foundations laid by 'Hobbes, Mandeville, Temple, Bolingbroke, Hume, etc.' to a new and promising kind of historical investigation, and sees in the *Ranks* 'one of those works which only can be produced in an age superior to prejudice and guided by the spirit of a free and liberal philosophy'.

In reviewing his *English Government*, on its first appearance in 1787, the *Critical Review* (vol. LXIII, pp. 369–77, and vol. LXIV, pp. 49–57) dwells particularly on the author's philosophical-historical method, which he applies 'with clearness and ability', his observations being everywhere 'supported by reason and probability'. On the appearance of the 4-vol. edition, this same *Review* observes (third series, vol. II, pp. 410–15) that 'to found a philosophy of history requires a mind of no common powers and penetration'. The 'art of developing the secret spirit of the times . . . has been carried to a higher perfection by Professor Millar than

On the *Letters of Crito* and the *Letters of Sidney*, assuming them both to be his, it may be remarked here that they reveal aspects of Millar's mind and personality, and style of writing, little in evidence in his more formal writings. His stand is entirely in line with his theoretical and political position as elsewhere revealed, but he is less reserved, less cautious, clearly the politician fighting for causes he believes to be just and courageous in attacking parties and men in high places where he believes their policies wrong.

To the *Letters of Crito* we shall have occasion to return later. The *Letters of Sidney*—if they are Millar's—reveal his ability to adapt his principles to changing social and political situations without compromising them; to modify his earlier views regarding the constructive and stabilizing leadership-role of the better families, of the propertied classes, even of the upper 'middling ranks' without for a moment giving up his belief in the fundamental role of property in society; to broaden the application of the principles of liberty, and their corresponding responsibilities to the rank and file, without yet accepting universal suffrage.

His contributions to the *Analytical Review* present us with greater difficulties. The content of the numerous reviews signed 'M' is significant and most interesting. If we could be certain they are from Millar's pen we could state more categorically that they throw much new light on his literary tastes and scientific interests, on his educational philosophy and religious outlook, on his style of writing when under less critical restraint—as is evidenced also in the Crito and Sidney letters—and on the many-sidedness of his mind generally. But until we can be certain of his authorship of them, we must be content to state this only hypothetically.

Something remains to be said on Millar's writing habits and on the general qualities of his style as an author.

Of the former we know comparatively little. We have seen that he did not write out his lectures but 'prelected' freely from outline notes. How detailed these notes were we are not told, but there are some reasons to believe they were fairly extensive.*

by most of his Continental contemporaries'. The *Monthly Review*, reviewing this work in 1787 (vol. LXXVII, o.s., pp. 106–16), notes particularly Millar's unconventional but well-documented and in the main convincing interpretation of the origins of feudalism. The same periodical, reviewing the 1803 edition (vol. XLIX, n.s., pp. 16–26), stresses particularly the necessary corrective it offers, especially in vol. III, to Hume's account of the Stuart and Cromwellian period.

The high-church *British Critic*, reviewing this same work in 1806 (vol. XXXVII, 237–56, 592–611) is severe on Millar's devotion to 'his darling Democracy', but finds here proof of a man 'equally conversant with philosophy and with law' and with the then fashionable 'political economy', and holds that the work 'evinces that the author possessed a mind of large grasp'.

Reviews of his work by Jeffrey, James Mill and Herder are cited elsewhere.

* Craig (*Life*, pp. xx f.) informs us that he early prepared a syllabus of his law course for the convenience of his students.

We know that he read widely and in fields well beyond the confines of his professional interests, themselves none too narrow. Certainly he kept abreast of the latest publications in his own and related fields. For this purpose he had access, of course, to the resources of the College library, and no doubt also to the facilities of the Faculty of Procurators, and on occasion also to those of the libraries at Edinburgh. Once, at least, he spent some time in research in the libraries at Oxford on subjects not adequately covered in libraries nearer at hand. His own personal library must have been sizeable and well stocked.* This reading, it is clear, he assimilated and made so much his own as to enable him to draw freely upon it in his extemporary lectures, in debate and in informal discussion, and to incorporate its essence in his writings without, as it were, 'having the bones stick out'.

At the same time he must have taken extensive notes on his reading, for the actual composition of his works—and they were largely historical —was done chiefly away from libraries, in the long summer vacations spent, as we have already seen (above, pp. 27 f.) in more or less rural retirement, away from the distractions of lecturing, counselling and administrative duties.

In his revision for new editions of works already published, particularly of the *Ranks*, there is evidence not only of new materials added and of improvement effected in organization, but also of greater precision of statement, greater caution in generalization and a more systematic rounding out of his position.

The limitations of his style of writing have often been remarked, particularly in attempts to explain his early 'going out of sight'. But there were also positive values or elements of merit.

First, on what might be called the style of his thought more than of his language merely, Jeffrey has this to say:

The distinguishing feature of Millar's intellect was the great clearness and accuracy of his apprehension, and the singular sagacity with which he seized upon the true statement of a question, and disentangled the point in dispute from the mass of sophisticated argument in which it was frequently involved. His great delight was to simplify an intricate question, and to reduce a perplexed and elaborate system of argument to a few plain problems of common sense. . . .

To some of our readers, perhaps, it may afford a clearer conception of his intellectual character, to say, that it corresponded pretty nearly with the abstract idea that the learned of England entertain of a *Scotish* [sic] *philosopher*;

* Portions of his library were later given to the Library of the Faculty of Procurators; some remained at Milheugh until about 1943 or 1944, when they were apparently sold to Glasgow booksellers, and were in some cases still on their shelves, with the Milheugh bookplate, in 1950. See also Scott, *op. cit.* p. 306, n. 3.

a personage, that is, with little or no deference to the authority of great names, and not very apt to be startled at conclusions that seem to run counter to received opinions or existing institutions; acute, sagacious, and systematical; irreverent towards classical literature; rather indefatigable in argument, than patient in investigation; vigilant in the observation of facts, but not so strong in their number, as skilful in their application.*

On his style of writing, in particular, he further remarks, 'Everything is delivered with a studied perspicuity and a sort of elementary simplicity. The general truth of his theory is clearly and boldly asserted and details of the subject are sometimes passed over very slightly.' And again, 'He writes with great clearness and solidity; and is never for a moment trifling, loquacious or absurd; but he is not often captivating in his manner and makes you feel the weight of his matter rather too sensibly in his style. . . .'†

His language is, as one critic remarks,

'the expression rather than the ornament of his thoughts'. Clear, accurate, precise, it never fails to convey his ideas with a distinctness which precludes all misapprehension; but frequently [his language] conveys them in a manner neither the most striking nor the most alluring to the reader. . . . His object is to convey clear and accurate ideas; . . . it would [perhaps] be impossible to find a sentence in his book which can require a second perusal to be distinctly understood.‡

Yet though, in the words of Jeffrey again, 'the character of his genius is very clearly impressed' on both his oral and his written style, in his writings there 'is embodied . . . only a part of his singular sagacity, extensive learning, and liberal and penetrating judgement. But they reveal nothing of his magical vivacity, which made his conversation and his lectures still more full of delight than of instruction.'§ Or in the words of Campbell, again, his writings, as contrasted with his oral communication, 'always seem to me to be imperfect casts of his mind, like those casts of sculpture which want the diaphanous polish of the original marble'.||

It is clear that his passion for accuracy and precision, his fear of ornament and flourishes and of the possibility of superfluous illustration, and his caution generally, in writing for the more critical reading public, robbed his style of many of the qualities that fascinated in his more familiar oral communication. It was probably his dislike too, for any appearance of pedantry that led him, particularly in the *Historical*

* *Edinburgh Review*, vol. ix, pp. 155 f.   † *Ibid.*
‡ *Life*, pp. lxxxiv f.   § Hay, *Inaugural Addresses*, pp. 6 f.
|| Redding, *Literary Reminiscences and Memoirs of Thomas Campbell*, p. 20.

View, to be rather sparing in his footnote or other references to his authorities, though it is obvious that he made abundant use of those who had written before him on the subject he treats of. In the *Ranks* his sources are more fully cited.

Student-notes on his lectures could, of course, not possibly reflect much of the vividness of his style of lecturing, but even these do occasionally reflect bits of wit, humour, sarcasm or personal frankness that occur only rarely in his published works. Much the same holds for such of his letters as have been preserved.

The following classroom echo may perhaps not inappropriately bring this characterization of Millar's style to a close.

Once, when he was lecturing in his best style and spirit, an English student, though perfectly sober, and meaning no offence, was so carried away by interest in the subject, that, forgetting himself, he made a remark aloud to the Professor. It was as much against the etiquette as speaking to a parson in church. A look from John Millar was sufficient to bring any man to his recollection, and the face of the student who had offered the involuntary compliment, was instantly covered with blushes.*

* *Ibid.* p. 21.

VII

POLITICAL TENETS AND ACTIVITIES

A man's political tenets can never be completely divorced from his general philosophy of society and the state, nor his political endeavours from his educational or other activities by which he would be attempting to influence the behaviour of other men. This would be particularly true of a man of Millar's temper who always sought a theoretical, or at least a rational basis for any programme of action, and for whom the study of history, society and the 'principles of government' always had something of a moral challenge, and in that sense political, or at least pragmatic implications. For purposes of analysis, however, we must attempt to distinguish his political tenets, attitudes and activities from his other areas of thought and activity.

Millar was first and foremost an ardent believer in liberty and a zealous defender, in particular, of the liberties secured to the British people, through centuries of effort, by their constitution. His efforts to defend those liberties against encroachments by privileged groups or by an extension of the royal prerogative, and to advance them and to broaden their basis, was a dominant motive in all his activities, whether as teacher, as author or as citizen.

By liberty he did not, of course, mean freedom from the restraints of law, or from obligation to one's fellow-men, but freedom under law to live fully and without arbitrary restraints in the community of men. Far from being the enemy of liberty, law was for him on the contrary, its instrument and its chief support. And social obligation was for him as essential a part of citizenship in a free society as the right to protection against arbitrary and irresponsible uses of power. Unlike Godwin, whose *Political Justice* he must have known well, he accepted the customary and institutional controls of society, as making for order and stability and predictability, even though far, often, from conforming to ideal justice. Where these restrained liberty, he would be working for their correction; their uprooting he would advocate only when they became perverted from their essential social functions.

Most elementally, liberty meant for him freedom from enslavement, from serfdom, from subserviency to any power exerted by man over his fellow-men other than that sanctioned by the community in the interest of all men. More than this, it meant freedom from subserviency to arbitrary dominance however imposed—whether by an irresponsible monarch, by a landlord, a titled nobleman, a robed justice on the bench, a priest in the confessional, or a guardian of the orthodoxy of men's religious beliefs. It meant freedom from the very spirit of servility in every relationship of life.

But liberty meant for Millar also something more positive than that. It called for the promoting and perfecting and guarding of free institutions, such as just laws, humane judicial establishments, and forms of government responsive to the will of an enlightened public. By implication it meant also the protection of the public against the irresponsible rule of the ignorant, the unthinking, the easily excitable mob. To this latter end it also required educational establishments that would help set free the minds of men and destroy the power of ignorance and of superstition.

In short it meant the emancipation of men and the freeing of the human spirit not only *from* servitude of every kind, but *for* the enlargement of opportunity and for service to the community, above all to the national community. And though he did not, perhaps, use this language, it meant also freedom of every man to worship God in his own way and after the dictates of his own conscience.

As a student of history and as a 'historical sociologist' he was, of course, fully aware of the role, historically, of power, and of the attempt of the strong to dominate, often even to enslave, in the life of the community and of the state. But he could also point to the creation, by free men, of institutions to prevent the abuse of power and to subject it to the rule of law and of justice and equity. He exalted the Magna Charta and acclaimed the abolition of slavery and serfdom, the liberalizing of the rules of tenancy, the victory of reason over superstition and ecclesiastical domination. The Glorious Revolution of 1688 was for him the crowning event in English history because it curbed the attempted return of absolutism and of 'superstition' under the Stuarts.

Millar recognized that his own Scotland lived still, much more than England, under the rules, and in many ways under the spirit, of feudalism; and, too, under the thundering voice of Jehovah audible in Presbyterian doctrine and rule. A Highland clansman is far less independent in spirit than an English wagoner (*Ranks*, below, p. 295). But he also saw many signs of the breaking of these bands of feudalism and subserviency, partly through the advances of commerce, industry and urbanization, with resulting improvements in agriculture; partly through an intellectual awakening, the rise of a new philosophy and the liberalization of religious thought; perhaps most of all through the development and strengthening of an educational system, both on the grammar-school and the university levels, that, already clearly conceived by the Reformation fathers,* was now being implemented on a larger and more effective scale.

Any attempt to trace the working out of these tenets in Millar's thought and action will need to be guided by the following considerations.

First, while he believed with Hume that all governments rest on the principles both of utility and authority, that is on both the performance of necessary social functions, and on respect for superior power reinforced by symbols and by tradition, he also believed that 'the authority of every government is founded in *opinion*', and 'that the diffusion of knowledge'—we are tempted to add, especially of the kind of historical and sociological analysis he himself engaged in—'tends more and more to encourage and bring forward the principle of utility in all political discussion'. 'Blind respect and reverence paid to ancient institutions' gives way 'to a desire of examining their uses, of criticising their defects, and of appreciating their true merits'.† This would have tended to make him a Whig under any circumstances.

Next, Millar lived and worked, as we have already seen, in a time of rising political consciousness in Scotland, increasingly affecting, if not the masses, at least the middle class. A man of Millar's outlook, temper and convictions could not but be drawn into the affairs that were engaging the minds of men at this time.

Third, he had the socio-political insight to realize that any enlargement of governmental functions, particularly great increases in the national budget for military and other purposes, would tend to strengthen the executive as against the legislative arm of the government, and that under even a limited monarchy this would mean—unless Parliament in its more popular branch were thoroughly alerted to this danger—an increase in the royal prerogative. This Millar believed was a marked tendency of the British government since the Revolution of 1688, and in his own day a great danger to British liberties.‡

Add to these historical considerations two basic assumptions of Millar's and we have the key to much of his thinking and of his conduct in matters political. The first is a perhaps unconscious pervading assumption, the validity of which might well be questioned, that—in practice, whatever they might be in theory—the interests of the crown are naturally opposed to those of the people. The second is a firm conviction, the validity of which can hardly be questioned, 'that the

* See below, p. 77, and references given there.

† *H.V.* vol. III, p. 329; and below, Pt. IV, Selection II, esp. pp. 355–7.

‡ See below, pp. 74 f.

66

particular distribution of political privileges exerts its powerful influence on the civil rights enjoyed by the inhabitants, on their morals and on their general welfare'.

From this standpoint, then, we can understand at once why politics were so very important to Millar and why he adhered so strongly to the particular tenets he did espouse, and was so active in their defence and promotion.

Millar was, then, an ardent Whig and a follower of the party of Rockingham and of Fox, and 'did not perhaps bear any great antipathy', in the words of Jeffrey, 'to the name of "Republican" ';* but he was hardly a democrat, as we would understand that term today, in in either its egalitarian or in its 'government by the people' implications. Even less was he carried away by Utopian dreams of radical political reconstruction. As Jeffrey no doubt rightly says of him:

. . . there never was a mind, perhaps, less accessible to the illusions of that sentimental and ridiculous philanthropy which has led so many to the adoption of popular principles. He took a very cool and practical view of the condition of society; and neither wept over the imaginary miseries of the lower orders, nor shuddered at the imputed vices of the higher. He laughed at the dreams of perfectibility, and looked with profound contempt at those puerile schemes of equality that threatened to subvert the distinctions of property, or to degrade the natural aristocracy of virtues and of talents.†

He was opposed to all distinctions of privilege and power that were not accompanied by corresponding duties and services to the community. He opposed every measure of public policy that, as he saw it, tended to create inequalities not of virtue and merit but of unearned privilege, and that would limit the freedom of men. He did not, however, believe in the feasibility or wisdom of universal suffrage, but preferred, rather, to rest the franchise, so far as possible, on a 'union of talent and rank', that is on an aristocracy of merit, in the firm belief that such a political system was more likely, at least under existing conditions of education etc., than a more popular one, to achieve the good of all.

That he was nevertheless looked upon by many of his contemporaries as a 'radical', even as a 'dangerous man' must be understood partly from the conservative temper generally of the classes likely to take notice of his work at all, but more particularly from the alarm produced by the events in France in Millar's later years, or perhaps more accurately, fostered by the party in power on that occasion to preserve

---

* *Edinburgh Review*, vol. III, p. 158; and in general, *Life*, pp. xcix–cxx.
† *Edinburgh Review*, vol. III, p. 158.

the *status quo* and to keep themselves in power.* Let us look more closely at these charges and at the allegation that he abused the privileges of his chair to attempt to poison the minds of youth with doctrines hostile to the British Constitution, to the good order of society and even to the foundations of religion.

We know, of course, that in the immediate aftermath of the Revolution to be a 'republican' was already to border on treason; and Millar did not, like many fair-weather liberals, allow the excesses of the Revolution, provoked largely, as he viewed them, by interference from without, and which he deplored even more perhaps, than most, to dampen his faith in its fundamental principles. Of these principles, incidentally, 'Jacobinism' was, as Millar viewed the matter, a perversion, not their real expression. Because of its Jacobinical radicalism, 'he was never sanguine in his hopes for [the] final success' of the Revolution. He feared, rather, 'that the splendid attempt might end in the ruin of the friends of liberty and the aggravation of the public wrongs'—its excesses giving to the Tories in Britain an excuse for suppressing, or at least setting back for a long time, the movement for parliamentary reform that he deemed so essential to the preservation of liberty; and in fact 'injuring the cause of liberty everywhere in Europe' (*Life*, p. cxii). Yet he continued to believe in the justice of the cause of the French people and in the ultimate success of liberal principles. In fact we find him, on the second anniversary of the fall of the Bastille, acting as 'croupier' or co-chairman, with a Lieut.-Col. Dalrymple, of a dinner-meeting of the 'Friends of Liberty'—not to be confused, incidentally, with the 'Society of the Friends of the People'—at Glasgow, in celebration of that symbolically so significant event. Professors Jardine and Reid are also listed among the celebrants.†

Little wonder, then, that the father of the future founder and editor of the *Edinburgh Review* should have forbidden his son to attend the

---

* See on this point *Letters of Crito*; *Life*, p. cxviii; and W. T. Laprade, *England and the French Revolution* (Baltimore, Johns Hopkins University Studies, 1909), particularly pp. 118 ff., 129 ff.

† A meeting in commemoration of the fall of the Bastille, of which Millar was 'croupier' or co-chairman, was thus announced in the *Glasgow Mercury* of 5 July 1791:

'The 14. of July being the anniversary of the late glorious revolution in France, by which so many millions have been restored to their rights as men and citizens, the Friends of Liberty in Glasgow and neighbourhood are invited to celebrate the second anniversary of that revolution . . . in order to certify their joy at an event so important in itself and which is likely so essentially to promote the general liberty and happiness of the world.' J. Strang, *Glasgow and its Clubs* (1857), p. 167. Meikle, *Scotland and the French Revolution*, p. 71, cites an account of this meeting in the *Edinburgh Herald* for 18 July 1791. Professor Reid was also one of the conveners. The Lieut.-Col. Dalrymple who was chairman was one of the men, mentioned below, to be relieved of his commission, presumably because of his political activities.

professor's lectures and 'blamed himself for having allowed the mere vicinity of Millar's influence to corrupt and ruin' his son.* Or that old 'Jupiter' Carlyle should speak so disparagingly of the 'democratic principles and sceptical philosophy which young noblemen and gentlemen of legislative rank carried into the world with them from his law class', later displaying them 'to the no small danger of perversion to all those under their influence'. Carlyle notes that 'though some sound heads might find antidote to this poison before they went into the world, . . . yet, as it was connected with lax principles of religion, there might be not a few of such contexture of understanding as not to be cured'.†

Ramsay of Ochtertyre remarks that 'it was notorious that he was as desirous to make his pupils politicians and philosophers as lawyers', and considers more or less dubious the means he found 'to impress the minds of his young friends with a set of notions which were not likely to make them better subjects and better members of society'. He holds that 'he was, in truth, a most dangerous man in times when young men wished to be set free from every shackle which restrained their turbulent passions'.‡

The most vitriolic of such attacks was, however, that of a Glasgow critic who, in a series of letters to a local paper,§ signed himself 'Asmodeus'.‖ To quote from one of these letters:

> Were I a mortal father [which a demon could of course not be] I would certainly prefer finishing my son's education in a brothel to a school where his political principles were likely to become contaminated. . . . In some instances the teachers in the public seminaries of this kingdom profess themselves Republicans; . . . Men of that description should either relinquish their tenets or their places; for is there not gross inconsistency in their eating the King's bread and at the same time vilifying his government?
>
> The mildness of the British Constitution is strongly exemplified in the security in which these pests of society vomit forth their opinions. Were the like freedom taken with the executive government in their beloved land of *Liberty and Equality*, the lamp-iron or the scaffold would soon terminate their

---

* H. Cockburn, *Life of Lord Jeffrey* (2-vol. ed. Edinburgh, 1852), vol. 1, p. 12.

† Alexander Carlyle, *Autobiography* (London, 1910 ed.), pp. 516–18.

‡ John Ramsay, Ochtertyre Manuscripts, vol. 111, fos. 1855–60. In a footnote Ramsay relates this anecdote: Once when, in lecturing to his class, 'he asserted with great vehemence that all power was derived from the people, his favourite *dog* (one of the audience) fell to barking most outrageously. With difficulty he was silenced, but no sooner did his master resume his lecture than the poor cur renewed what the wags called his *protest*: He was turned out and no more admitted' (fo. 1857).

§ (Anon.) *Asmodeus; or, Strictures on the Glasgow Democrats* (Glasgow, 1793), first appearing as a series of letters in the *Glasgow Courier* (Autumn, 1793).

‖ 'Asmodeus' was the name of the legendary 'Prince of Seducing Demons' in Hebrew lore. See *Jewish Encyclopedia*, vol. 11, *s.v.* 'Asmodeus'; Tobit, iii. 8, vi. 14; also, *Testament of Solomon*.

career. But though the British Lion indeed pisseth upon these snarling curs, is it fitting that they should continue their practice with impunity?*

This letter is dated 29 August 1793. Millar is clearly the outstanding target. Just what these 'vomitings' were will be abundantly clear from materials presented elsewhere in this volume.

The general state of mind of which these accusations are a reflection can best be seen, perhaps, in the record of the trial of Thomas Muir and other members of the Society of the Friends of the People in Edinburgh in 1793. The charge made by Judge Braxfield, the able but notorious 'Hanging Judge', to the jury in this trial contained, among other things, the following:

. . . The British constitution is the best that ever was since the creation of the world and it is not possible to make it better. . . . There was a spirit of sedition in this country last winter which made every man uneasy. Yet Mr. Muir had at that time gone about amongst ignorant people making them forget their work and told them that a reform was absolutely necessary to preserve their liberty, which, if it had not been for him, they would never have thought was in danger. I do not doubt that this will appear to the jury, as it does to me, as sedition.

. . . what could he do in France [whither he had recently gone] at that period? Pretending to be an ambassador to a foreign country without lawful authority, that is rebellion! And what kind of folks were they ['those wretches, the leading men' in France]? I never liked the French all my days, and now I hate them. . . . Mr. Muir might have known that no attention can be paid to such a rabble [as the 'multitude of ignorant weavers' he had been haranguing]. What right had they to representation? . . . A government in every country should be just like a corporation, and in this country it is made up of the landed interest, which alone has the right to be represented. As for the rabble who have nothing but personal property, what hold has the nation on them? . . . they might pick up all their property on their backs and leave the country in the twinkling of an eye, but landed property cannot be removed.†

Thomas Muir, ardent advocate of parliamentary reform, and active in the 'Society of the Friends of the People', was convicted of sedition at Edinburgh in 1793 and sentenced to transportation (to Botany Bay) for fourteen years.

Or we may recall these reminiscences of Lord Cockburn from his childhood that fell in this period. 'How they raved! What sentiments! What principles!' exclaims this great liberal of a slightly later day of the conversations of his elders that filled his boyhood imagination with

---

* *Asmodeus*, pp. 2 f.

† Quoted, with slight variations, in various places. This from Peter Mackenzie's *Life of Thomas Muir*.

horrors, terrified his sleep with dreams of bloodshed till he 'hated liberty and the people as much as they did'. 'Everything rung and was connected with the Revolution in France; which for above twenty years was, or was made, the all in all. Everything, not this or that thing, but literally everything, was soaked in this one event.'*

Little wonder, too, that the elder Mill, who counts himself as in his youth also one of the victims of these Tory attacks, should be enraged at the very attempt of Millar's biographer to vindicate him in the face of these charges

To suppose that the worthless imputations of a persecuting and barbarous period, which is a disgrace in our history, should leave a stain on the memory of so sound a philosopher and so virtuous a man—for the hand of anyone now to wipe it off is to offer an insult to those of us who have survived these humiliating scenes.†

We, too, need not linger to answer these Tory charges except to remark that his real position was, from the evidence at hand, one of remarkable moderation. A contemporary account (1787) in a local paper‡ of a public meeting called to draw up an 'address to His Majesty' on a lively issue of the day and to gather signatures for the same, informs us that the meeting noted with satisfaction its pleasure at being honoured by the presence of men of such respectability as Professor Millar and another (unnamed) professor from the University. But when Millar rose to speak, 'with his usual animation and ability', he counselled caution and further deliberation on so important a step. His words provoked so noisy and protracted a protest 'that it was with the utmost difficulty that the chairman prevailed with them to hear him to the end'.

In a letter to Burke, then Rector of the University (15 August 1784), we find this most interesting note. In reply to Professor Anderson's charge against his colleagues of 'engaging with too much warmth in the politics of the times' he says:

. . . I am at a loss to discover what this refers to. . . . If we are charged with *lecturing* on politics, I am afraid the charge must fall principally upon myself, as lecturing upon public law. I certainly am guilty of endeavouring to

---

* Cockburn, *Memorials of his Time* (Edinburgh, 1856), pp. 45–7, 80.

† *Literary Journal* (see above, p. 15 n). The reference is to an apologetic note by his biographer (*Life*, p. cxix) to the effect that 'in the heat of debate' and 'at a time when political rancour rose to an unexampled height' Millar might at times have gone beyond the bounds of 'his cooler judgement'.

‡ *Caledonian Mercury*, 3 March 1784. Incidentally, the account notes that the address was voted by a majority of at least 20 to 1, and was signed, at the meeting and afterwards, of course, 'by upwards of 1100 individual citizens, possessed of at least four-fifths of the wealth of Glasgow'. See also Meikle, *op. cit.* p. 5.

explain the principles of our own government. I know that I have been accused of including Republican doctrines, but I am not conscious of having given any just ground for such an imputation. It has always been my endeavour to recommend that system of limited monarchy which was introduced at the Revolution [1688], an acquaintance with which I conceived to be as useful to young men of fortune as many other branches of science. I should think it petulance, if, in the capacity of a public lecturer, I were to meddle with the local and partial [i.e., partisan] politics of the day; and in order to avoid the suspicion of including anything of that nature, I have, on some late occasions, been careful to pass over in a more slight and general manner certain subjects which I used formerly to treat at more length. In short, if they were not too insignificant, I should have no objection that these lectures were subjected to any scrutiny whatever.*

As a private citizen he did, of course, engage openly in political activities. We have already noted his efforts, in and out of his official capacity, in behalf of the abolition of the slave trade. With his pen, and there is some reason to believe also in more direct ways, he attacked slavery wherever it existed and concerned himself with prison reform and the cause of improved education for the working classes.

His efforts on behalf of parliamentary reform have already been referred to.† They are understandable when we remember that even as late as thirty years after his death, Scotland, with a population of some 2,300,000, had only 3,000 electors, the burghs having in reality none at all since their representatives were sent up to Parliament by small self-perpetuating municipal councils whose members might be far more beholden to the crown than to the people over whom they had jurisdiction; and that the representation was extremely uneven. Glasgow, for example, still shared a single representative in Parliament with neighbouring Renfrew, Rutherglen and Dumbarton; while many a member represented but a small rural constituency, or in the case of the so-called 'parchment barons', in reality none at all.‡

But with the advent of the French Revolution, which 'from its first appearance riveted Millar's attention, and in its early progress excited his fondest hopes', his faith in the 'families of rank and talent' was considerably shaken. The Tory reaction at home to these events convinced him of the necessity of seeking a broader popular basis of representation than he had previously advocated. In fact he believed that:

the best and only solid refutation of [the more revolutionary popular doctrines] was such a reform of Parliament, as, in itself highly desirable, had

---

* Letter, Millar to Burke, 15 August 1784. With permission. See Appendix I.
† Above, p. 3.　　　　　‡ P. Hume Brown, *op. cit.* vol. III, pp. 333 f.

now become almost necessary, to rally the great body of the nation around the Constitution. Actuated by such motives, he became a zealous member of the Society of the Friends of the People, and, with those great characters whom he venerated, willingly exposed himself to obloquy in performing what he considered as an important duty to his country.*

This Society was one of a number of such organizations active in the early 'nineties, most of them new-formed at that time, in behalf of parliamentary reform. It was in the public mind obviously 'thrown into the same hopper' with the more radical societies, such as the various Corresponding Societies and Societies for Constitutional Information; though in reality it made every effort, if in fact it was not brought into being, to counteract the more revolutionary demands of other organizations and of other, often somewhat undisciplined, meetings in the larger industrial centres. This did not prevent spies being planted in the local meetings of the society and charges of sedition being brought against its members.

Just how active Millar himself was in this society, we do not know. Perhaps less so than Craig's statement would lead us to believe. Contemporary accounts of the meetings of the society in the local press† make no mention of his presence or participation, though other members of prominence are named.‡ Certainly he gave it his moral support, and at its top level in parliamentary circles he was looked upon as the inspiration of such of its 'misguided' leaders as Lauderdale, Lansdowne and others.§ On the local level, men like Thomas Muir and his own son John were clearly inspired by him.

The clearest expression, perhaps, of overt political activity on Millar's part will be found in his *Letters of Crito*, the purpose of which was, in his own words,

to point out the causes of this extraordinary phenomenon [that 'the mildest and most limited monarchy in the world has affected the greatest apprehension, lest the example of a political change, in a neighbouring country, should shake the foundations of her authority']; to explain the true motives by which our Ministry were induced to enter into a war with France; to ascertain the real object of that war, in contradistinction to those plausible pretences which they assumed in order to conceal their designs ... [etc.] (pp. viii f.).

* *Life*, pp. cxiv f. and generally pp. cxii ff.

† *Glasgow Courier*, various dates 8–29 December 1792 and 8–26 January 1793. Files in Mitchell Library, Glasgow.

‡ Two prominent leaders of the Glasgow society, Lieut.-Col. Dalrymple and Col. Macleod, soon after this 'received intimation from the Secretary of War that His Majesty has no further occasion for their services'. *Ibid*. 8 December 1792.

§ *Life and Letters of Sir Gilbert Elliot, first Earl of Minto*, ed. by the Countess of Minto (3 vols. London, 1874), vol. II, pp. 26 f.

He speaks much of 'this unfortunate contest', sees his country in a 'dangerous crisis', confronted by financial ruin, threatened mutiny in the navy, and 'impending calamities'.

We have here a very direct and bold attack upon the policies of the Pitt government—anonymous to be sure, but scarcely leaving doubt as to the authorship of the letters. He views the war as being as unprovoked as it was proving costly and ill-foreboding in its outcome, and threatening of the liberties of the English people—an unwarranted interference* in the internal affairs of a sister nation, on the false pretence of preventing the fire from spreading across the Channel, but in reality as a means of suppressing the demand for parliamentary reform at home. He lays the worst excesses of the revolutionists squarely at the doorstep of the European powers, and outstanding among them, of the Pitt government—the French being driven to them in sheer desperation for their liberty and for their survival as a nation. In his own words, these governments 'did not seem to look upon [the French] as fellow creatures, but as beasts of prey, to be hunted down and exterminated from the face of the globe' (*Crito*, p. 28). He advocates parliamentary reform to prevent, among other things, the possibility in the future of this kind of arbitrary and irresponsible foreign policy. He attempts to correct misrepresentations of the French and suggests ways out of present difficulties.

In its issue of 13–16 September 1793 the *Glasgow Advertizer* reports the presentation, through the Earl of Lauderdale, Millar's intimate friend, of 'a petition to His Majesty from the City of Glasgow, signed by upward of 40,000 praying His Majesty to end the present war'. It is inconceivable that Millar should not have been prominent among its promoters. He is alleged to have himself drawn up the petition.

Most of Millar's criticisms of the government, and his advocacy of reform, in the *Letters of Crito* and elsewhere, revolve about his convictions on the matter of the tendency toward an increase of the royal prerogative. Whether the king has merely a veto power in legislation—only rarely to be exercised with wisdom—or also, in practical effect, the initiative, was to Millar a most important matter. Where judges are appointed by the crown, or are in the pay of the crown, or where causes are to be tried that involve the personal interests of the crown, the rights of the people need always to be protected with peculiar care. While he believed that the advancement of commerce tended in general to broaden the spirit of liberty, he also held that great commercial and industrial interests could easily be influenced by the crown, and that therefore in times of economic progress the people needed to be guarded

* See above, p. 68 n.

against possible encroachments on their rights by the head of state. He advocated not only the abolition of the rotten borough system and of sinecures of all kinds, but the reduction of the national expenditure generally, fearing the tendency of the latter, by its very magnitude, to increase unduly the power of the crown.* Because of the danger of misappropriation of funds to uses inconsistent with the public interest, he advocated allotting such revenues as were necessary directly 'to the several heads of the public service', who would thus be strictly accountable for their expenditure rather than appropriating them to the crown, which could then easily shift them into channels of 'secret influence'. Offices should, so far as possible, be vested in freeholders of the several counties, or at least in persons altogether unconnected with the administration.†

On the matter of patronage and secret influence, the chief means of increasing the royal prerogative, Millar becomes particularly vocal.

To what a monstrous height has this abuse, which has continued for more than a century, been at length carried! How many officers, in church and state, obtain immense fortunes from the public for doing no work, or next to none! How many are often employed to perform the duty which might easily be performed by a single person!

And again:

... To what a height ... has this influence been raised in all the departments of government, and how extensively has it pervaded all ranks and descriptions of the inhabitants: in the army, in the church, at the bar, in the republic of letters, in finance, in mercantile and manufacturing corporations: not to mention pensioners and placemen; together with the various officers connected with the distribution of justice and the execution of the laws, the corps diplomatique, and the members of the king's confidential council. With what a powerful charm does it operate in regulating opinions, in healing grievances, in stifling clamours, in quieting the noisy patriot, in extinguishing the most furious opposition! It is the great opiate which inspires political courage, and lulls reflection; which animates the statesman to despise the resentment of the people; which drowns the memory of his former professions, and deadens, perhaps, the shame and remorse of pulling down the edifice which he had formerly reared.

... It is ... of infinite consequence to have a number of partisans scattered through the nation, at all times zealous to support the administration, and ready to extol their measures. In this way placemen, pensioners and expectants are of the most essential service to their employers. Like people stationed in different parts of a theatre to support a new play, they set up such an enthusiastic and noisy applause, as by giving an appearance of general

---

* *H.V.* vol. iv, pp. 83–99, more particularly pp. 95–7. Also *Crito*, Letter xv (below, Pt. IV, Selection ix).　　　　† *Life*, pp. cvi f.; student lecture-notes.

approbation, drowns all opposition, confounds the timid, and secures the concurrence of that immense class of persons who either want leisure or talents to judge for themselves. . . .*

Such a passage is, incidentally, notwithstanding its strong whiggish bias, remarkably revealing of its author's political insight.

A more subtle kind of 'politicking' will be found in the last chapter of the *Ranks*. After reviewing the history of master-servant relations, and the 'causes of the freedom acquired by the labouring people in the modern nations of Europe', he makes a more direct attack on modern survivals of slavery, both on economic and on moral and psychological grounds.

Referring to the survivals of slavery among colliers and salters in his own country, he remarks that, 'Considering the many advantages which a country derives from the freedom of the labouring people, it is to be regretted that any species of slavery should still remain in the dominions of Great Britain, in which liberty is generally so well understood, and so highly valued',† and he sees no great obstacles to its complete abolition. Where the same is not immediately feasible, as in the colonies where slavery is still a matter of much greater importance, he not only argues that self-interest demands 'that the negroes should be better treated, and even that they should be raised to a better condition', but insists that slavery is itself the cause of poor economic conditions there. Slavery he holds to be everywhere unfavourable to industry and to a desirable increase of the general population. It not only degrades and leads to the brutalizing of the slave, who is after all also a human being, but it must just as certainly lead to the degradation and brutalization of the master himself. But for this the reader will turn to the closing paragraphs of the *Ranks* itself.

The American reader, in particular, will appreciate both the psychological realism and the biting irony of the paragraph with which we may fittingly bring this discussion to a close.

It affords a curious spectacle to observe that the same people who talk in a high strain of political liberty [this in 1771] and who consider the privilege of imposing their own taxes as one of the inalienable rights of mankind, should make no scruple of reducing a great proportion of their fellow creatures into circumstances by which they are not only deprived of property, but almost of every species of right. Fortune perhaps has never produced a situation more calculated to ridicule a hypothesis, or to show how little the conduct of men is at the bottom directed by any philosophical principles.‡

* *H.V.* vol. IV, pp. 93, 95-7.
† *Ranks*, below, p. 319, and generally Chapter VI, Section iv.   ‡ *Ibid.* p. 321.

VIII

PHILOSOPHY OF EDUCATION, RELIGION AND LIFE

It behoves us now, in bringing this chiefly biographical portion of our study to a close, to bring the man Millar himself into a closer view: his traits of mind and character, his more intimate personal relationships, and that philosophy of education, religion and life that gave direction and character to his life and work.

Such a philosophy he did indeed clearly have, though it will be discovered more in the general conduct of his life than in any formal statement of it. Until we can accept with certainty his authorship of the 'M' articles in the *Analytical Review* (Appendix II), which focus so largely on just such matters, our characterization of it must be couched in rather general terms and with stronger reliance than were ideally desirable on a single source, and that one not completely above the suspicion of a family bias. Our best initial approach to its understanding will probably be a historical and institutional one.

Millar pays a great deal of attention to educational, and more particularly to religious and religious-educational establishments, in his writings and lectures. He is greatly interested in their historical development and their functional roles in society. The two are of course very closely tied together—more so in Scotland, perhaps, than almost anywhere else. The great reformers of the church were also reformers of education; or so at least their efforts were intended. Knox's *First Book of Discipline* made very specific provisions for an educational system that was unique in its scope, in its underlying assumptions and democratic implications, and in its envisaged functional interrelation of school, church and community, of education, religion and civic responsibility.* Slow as was the practical realization of this scheme in anything like its full original conception, its influence on Scottish life and thought, including the work of the universities, was profound. And Millar understood this very well.

---

* See *H.V.* vol. III, pp. 86–92; below, p. 382. Also Alexander Morgan, *The Rise and Progress of Scottish Education* (Edinburgh and London, 1927), pp. 49–53 *et passim*. P. Hume Brown calls this *First Book of Discipline* 'The most important document in Scottish history', its proposals, as a whole 'casting the mould in which the Scottish character and intellect have been formed for nearly four centuries'.

While focusing less on formal educational than on religious institutions, he is distinctly aware and appreciative of the educational functions of the church, which had in fact done much for education, even in the 'Dark Ages'. He also appreciates the educational establishments of feudalism and chivalry. He recognizes the limitations of Scotland's parish schools, but yet also their unique scope and their role in the development of the national character. He points out the effect of religious thought, even in its doctrinaire and disputatious aspects, on Scottish mentality, on the character of her scholarship, on the life of the universities. He recognizes clearly the unique character of the educational objectives of the Scottish universities, and is in sympathy with them.* Referring to the great intellectual ferment produced by the Reformation, with 'a disposition to inquire, and to embrace no tenets without examination', he says:

The same circumstances which tended in Scotland to multiply seminaries of education, contributed also to model those institutions according to utility and the conveniency of the inhabitants. While the principal schools and universities of England, from the remains of ancient prejudice, confined their attention, in a great measure, to the teaching of what are called the learned languages, those of Scotland extended their views in proportion to the changes which took place in the state of society, and comprehended, more or less, in their plan of instruction, the principles of those different sciences which came to be of use in the world. (*H.V.* vol. III, p. 89.)

Millar clearly recognized the role of education—not only in its formal, institutionalized aspects, but even more in its informal, 'incidental' aspects—in the shaping of the national character. But he also felt keenly that the new industrial order demanded a more effective educational programme to counteract and prevent the robotizing influence of an excessive division of labour. He advocated 'the institution of schools and seminaries to communicate, as far as possible, to the most useful but humble class of citizens [i.e., the working classes] that knowledge which their way of life has, in some degree, prevented them from acquiring'. The 'powerful tendency [of their mode of work] to render them ignorant and stupid', and to involve them 'in a thicker cloud of ignorance and prejudice' rendered this for him highly necessary both on humane and on political grounds.†

More important, he believed strongly in the educability of human nature, in the capacity of young minds for growth, and in the challenge to the teacher or professor to provide them with food for such growth,

---

* Same as note on p. 77; add Murray, *Old College*, pp. 462 ff. See also below, p. 382.
† *H.V.* vol. IV, pp. 144–61. See Pt. IV, Selection IV below.

not only in knowledge and the satisfaction of their intellectual curiosity —though he never neglected that—but in ideals to form the heart and character, and in such understanding of community life as would make for effective and responsible citizenship.

Most important of all, from our present standpoint, he carried out his precepts in his classroom and in his personal association with the more inquiring and promising of his students. While commanding the respect of his students with his talents and his scholarship, he was able also to win not only their confidence but even their friendship. He believed in his students, even in the meanest of them, and gave unstintingly of his time, his knowledge and his strength to the most deserving and promising of them. In doing so he was enabled to draw out the best that was in them. Moreover, he attempted always to remain just and fair. Rank and social position in his students—and there were future earls, viscounts and marquises among them, as well as sons of the humblest families—made little difference to him, except as such position was marked by better breeding, greater intellectual curiosity, greater ability or promise of future achievement.

His approach to religion, too, both in its doctrinal and ceremonial expression in belief and worship and in its institutional expression in the church and its various offices, is first of all a historical and comparative, and a functional one. Beliefs, conceptions of the Deity and modes of worship vary from place to place and from time to time, and change with advancing stages of civilization, with altering social, economic and political needs and situations. Millar views them largely as anthropomorphic reflections (*Ranks*, below, pp. 256 f., 310 ff.) of a given state of society, of given power structures in the state, of a given state of backwardness or enlightenment of men's conceptions of the world in which they live. He is, however, far from denying completely the truth and benevolent character of one religion and the falsity, the perversion, the superstitious character of another, or from refusing to evaluate the beliefs and practices of the church at different periods.

A religion or a doctrinal system based chiefly on fear and centring chiefly on 'penances and mortifications; from which nature is disposed to shrink; and which are submitted to for no other purpose but that of appeasing the wrath of an offended Diety' and to avert future punishment; while neglecting and disesteeming 'the real virtues of society whose intrinsic value recommends them to our observance'—this he considers a perversion. In particular, the glorification of extreme asceticism and of monastic celibacy, 'inveighing' against the married life of the secular clergy 'as inconsistent with the purity of a Christian pastor, and representing their wives in the light of concubines and prostitutes, and their children as bastards', these, like the attempt, generally, to keep the laity engrossed in ignorance and superstition, for no other reason, as he views the matter, than to enhance the power of the clergy, meet with his sharpest censure (*H.V.* vol. i, pp. 344–7; also pp. 144–6).

Yet underneath his historical relativism, and at times even cynicism, we see on occasion an entirely different Millar. He speaks then of the 'true religion' as over against mere 'superstition' and 'perverted' religion. For all his 'rationalism' he recognizes the element of mystery in life and in the universe, and man's weakness and his dependence on 'the Author of our being'. He recognizes it as the challenge of the spirit of the Christian religion, 'which considers all mankind as the children of the same Father, and as all equally the objects of his paternal care and affection', to 'inspire them with compassion for the miseries of each other, and [to] teach the opulent and the proud',* consideration and compassion for their less fortunate fellow-men. He recognizes the value of 'ceremony', but ceremonies devoid of spirit he despises. Ceremonies should be an aid to, and not a substitute for, 'impassioned morality'. Religion must teach men 'a true estimate of the real end of life'.†

Millar was shocked at attempts to justify a war-policy on grounds of religion, or to charge a whole people with irreligion because of a mere proposal for calendar reform or of the vain boastings of a few professed atheists among them. (See *Crito*, pp. 46–51.)

It would be a great weakness . . . to believe, that the Christian religion in general, or even in France, can be materially injured, either by this [attempted calendar-reform] or by the petulant and absurd opposition and derision which the vanity, or malice, of some individuals appears to have suggested. Christianity is founded upon a rock; and neither Thomas Paine, with his *Age of Reason*, nor Anarchasis Cloots with his *Representative of all Religions*, nor Fabre D'Eglantine, the abolisher of Sunday, with his *New Calendar*, nor even that profound philosopher who stood up in the French Assembly, and professed himself *An Atheist*, shall ever, as we are assured from the best authority, prevail against our holy religion. Christianity is an enlightened system, which introduced a purer morality than had formerly prevailed in the world, and more distinct views of a future state of rewards and punishments, by which the efforts of human laws for the suppression of crimes are better enforced and promoted. The more the light of truth is spread over the world, the more clearly are mankind enabled to see their

---

* Below, pp. 311–72; also pp. 136 f. and Pt. IV, Selection iv.

† The expression is from one of the 'M' articles in the *Analytical Review*, and so may or may not be his.

true interest; and the more will they be convinced of the futility of supporting a religion by which all the bands of human society are thus maintained and strengthened.

... For my own part, though I feel, from education, an attachment to the forms of religion established in this country, I am sensible that innovation, in matters of this kind, ought never to be attempted without very cogent reasons; yet, were I the inhabitant of a country, where, for good grounds, the old establishment had been abolished, I should, without hesitation, prefer [the] very liberal and apparently beneficial system [being introduced in America, and now apparently also in France]. (*Crito*, pp. 50 f.)

We see religious faith demonstrated in his own life. Formal observance of the rites of the church, in stated worship, in the baptism of his children and in the burial ceremony, is not, of course, proof of religious conviction or devotion; but facing manfully great trials in life—the sufferings and finally the loss, within five short years, of his eldest daughter, his beloved wife, and his eldest son, upon whom he had staked so many of his fondest hopes—enduring these 'with feeling but without weakness; like a man deprived of much happiness, but not abandoning himself to affliction'—*this is proof indeed of religion that is real and meaningful.† It was, however, in right and charitable and noble living, much more than in holy dying or in the contemplation of death, that he would have his own religious faith tested.

And this brings us to a brief review of his personal relations with his fellow-men and of the traits of mind and character he manifested in them.

It has already been indicated that Millar was very much a family man. A few further glimpses into his domestic life will prove revealing. Besides being a man of sanguine temperament, though self-restrained at times almost to a fault, he was a man of very fine sensibilities and always entered 'with the greatest warmth into the feelings of every person around him'. He attended personally with great care to the education, both moral and intellectual, of all of his children, and as they grew up, took them often into his confidence in his own intellectual pursuits. To quote his biographer:

He had long been in the habit of consulting Mrs Millar with regard to his literary works, and some of his children being [by the time his *Historical*

* *Life*, p. cxxv.

† The trial of his last hours, we are told, 'he nobly sustained. His last scene was altogether worthy of the part he had uniformly maintained on the stage of life. [He awaited the issue] with the most perfect composure. No symptom of impatience or of alarm ever escaped him: no thought gave him pain but the thought of being separated from his family, with whom he had long enjoyed the purest happiness, and to whose happiness his life was so important.' *Ibid.* cxxix.

View was in composition] competent judges of composition, he occasionally read over to his family the most amusing and interesting passages, and listened with much attention to their various criticisms. By these means, besides increasing the mutual confidence which ever subsisted between him and his family, he had the means of detecting any little errors which had escaped his own observation, and formed the taste while he improved the judgement of his children.*

Another echo of his family life, with four boarding students in residence, will be found in these notes from the *Melbourne Papers*. In a letter to his mother,† Lady Melbourne, Frederick, the younger of the Lamb brothers, writes—this was in the last year of Millar's life—'All the ladies [here] are contaminated with an itch for philosophy and learning, and such a set of fools it never was my lot to see. . . . They are all philosophers. . . .' That this matter of 'fools' is not to be taken too literally, and that such 'philosophy' did not rob this enlarged family life of all gaiety, is shown by the next observation. Besides remarking that one of the daughters was 'very pretty', and that his older brother William (the future Prime Minister) was reading poetry to these young ladies all the time, he gives an account of table manners and table scenes, observing among other things:

One exclusive custom I have remarked here is a devilish good one which ought to be adopted everywhere. After cheese they hand around the table a bottle of whisky and another of brandy, and the whole company, males and females, in general, indulge in a dram. It is very comfortable and exhilarating, and affords an opportunity for many jokes.‡

Of the economic basis of his family life we need only remark here that while a professor's salary was never large§—in most cases, till nearly the end of Millar's life, when salaries were being considerably enlarged, seldom over £50 per year, though in the case of Millar's crown chair £90 per year—this was, where classes were large, considerably added to by student fees. The commodious 'professors' houses' were rent-free except for casual maintenance costs, and both of his country homes, first Whitemoss and later Milheugh, would appear to have been largely a family inheritance. Beyond this Craig tells us merely that he was always ready to share what he could spare with those in need, and 'to contribute to every useful institution' to the extent that

his generosity sometimes exceeded what his limited fortune might altogether warrant. Nothing was so despicable in his mind as any sordid attention to

* *Life*, pp. lxxiii f.　　† *Melbourne Papers*, p. 5.　　‡ *Ibid.*
§ See in general, the histories of the University, below, p. 415.

money; and while he knew he could place his family in independent circumstances, he was less anxious about further accumulation.*

Both Millar's relations with his family and friends and colleagues and his personal leisure, were greatly enriched by a command of information that 'reached to almost every subject that was likely to occur in conversation'. To continue this quotation from Craig:

... He was completely master of whatever had been written on the sciences connected with the study of mind, and had added many opinions and combinations to the discoveries of others. The whole range of [known] history was familiar to him, and there was little in the manners or customs of any nation, which he could not state with accuracy, and account for with surprising quickness and ingenuity. Nor was he ignorant of the physical sciences, although his knowledge of them rather embraced the different theories by which the facts were explained, than showed a very intimate acquaintance with the facts themselves . . . , wherever there was an appearance of system his attention was roused so fully, that, for a time, it almost engrossed his mind. It was thus, that, after Lavoisier published his astonishing experiments, and no less astonishing system built on these experiments, Mr. Millar, for a whole winter, thought of nothing but chemistry; and so great was his veneration for that philosopher, that no circumstance in the French Revolution struck him with so much horror, as the murder of the man whom he considered as the brightest ornament of the age.†

'In literature and Belles Lettres,' Craig continues:

... Mr. Millar was completely conversant. In his youth he had read all the classics with such pleasure and discrimination, that, although his line of study was afterwards extremely different, he could always refer to the most impressive passages, and discuss, with much intelligence, their relative beauties and defects. His acquaintance with English poetry was also very general, though his taste might be considered as somewhat fastidious. Mediocrity, in everything, but particularly in verse, he was accustomed to treat with marked contempt. . . . Seldom have I known any person more alive to the higher kinds of poetry; to those striking and sublime allusions, that rich and varied imagery, that loftiness of thought, and dignity of expression, which delight the imagination and elevate the mind.‡

There is little doubt, however, that the 'rational principle' in his mind was stronger than the 'aesthetic' one. In his thinking, child of the Enlightenment that he was, everything, even the aesthetic and the religious itself, had in some way to be brought under the rule of reason.

* *Life*, p. cxxii. It may be of interest to note that in 1789, at least, he was among those who had a cash account in the Ship Bank of Glasgow. *Glasgow Past and Present*, vol. 1, p. 505.

† *Life*, pp. xciv f.   ‡ *Ibid.* pp. xcv f.

Abstract theories and abstruse speculations, whether in theology, philosophy or politics, interested him but little. Yet the universe about him, the experiences of men recorded in history and in accounts of travel, and the doings of men and women in the realities of the here and now, had for him somehow to be reduced to a rational order. To religion, as to art, poetry and music, he was sympathetic; but ignorance and superstition and prejudice he despised, and in irrational explanations of things he would have no part.

A wholesome diversion from his academic duties and scholarly and literary pursuits was offered Millar by his domestic life in rural surroundings during the long summer months. At Whitemoss, we are told, he engaged in many agricultural experiments, not all of which proved practical or profitable. Later at Milheugh he found great satisfaction in effecting various improvements in this country estate he loved so dearly, both on the practical side and in its beautification into what Craig calls 'one of the sweetest little retirements that could be desired'.

On the more personal side, there was in Millar a deep sense of reverence, more in evidence in a certain humility before the facts of life, in a deep regard for the great and the heroic, for courageous action, and in an almost fanatical regard for the sanctity of human personality in young and old, than in any act of formal worship. He entered easily into the mind and feelings, and even into the play of his students and of his children, but never to the extent of losing his sense of dignity and his respect for them as persons at once in being and still in the making. For sham, for make-believe and ostentation he had only contempt.

Those who knew him best remarked in him also a degree of personal pride. He was proud of his university, of his office, of his family. He is said at times also to have manifested a not undue pride in his own scholarly and academic achievements. He was quick to respond vigourously to everything that might reflect unfavourably on any of these, or might be considered insulting to his personal dignity. But we must distinguish sharply between pride and vanity. Of the former he had a great deal; of the latter he had no more, if we are correctly informed, than could easily be forgiven in any mortal of outstanding achievement.

Another characteristic of his personal make-up was a remarkable degree of both intellectual and moral integrity and an unswerving adherence to principle, in thought and action, and in all the relationships of life. Both intellectual shoddiness and pedantry he despised; hypocrisy in all forms he hated; venality, above all, he scorned in his deepest being, especially when men who pretended to science and learning, and who would be instructors of youth, 'sacrificed principle to interest'. He had, moreover, the courage to follow through his principles even when they brought him into conflict with prevailing beliefs, dogmas or political tenets, or called for great personal sacrifice. When 'the offer of a lucrative position which might have introduced him to high honours' came to him, he refused it because he felt that 'its acceptance might be construed into an engagement to support an administration whose measures he condemned'.*

In all his dealings there was an almost religious sense of fairness and disinterestedness, and a delicate sensibility to the feelings of others. He had, we are told,

an uncommon candour in judging of his own claims and those of others, . . . Never was his opinion warped by his private interest, never did he palliate or excuse that in himself, which he would have blamed in his friend. His conduct was uniformly guided by a most delicate attention to the rights, claims, and expectations of others, by the strictest sense of honour. Always aware of the tendency of a man's interest, and desires, to pervert his judgement, against such partiality and self-deception, he guarded with a most vigilant care, anxious not only to abstain from all injustice, but to avoid every suspicion, in his own mind, of his having done what any person informed of the circumstances, could possibly disapprove.†

Truth, justice, liberty, emancipation from servility, love of country— these were the great objects of his devotion, and this devotion was, in the deepest sense, his religion—the force that binds, that sustains, that gives meaning to life. Without these, all creeds, all ceremonial observances, were to him but an empty echo, meaningless, even a mockery. To remove from the eyes of young and old every veil that would obscure these moral values was to him the true 'enlightenment'. To help eliminate from the common life all things that constrained and enslaved instead of freely binding, and to encourage instead the spirit of freedom and true community of living—this was to him the meaning of liberty, and to this the best energies of his life were devoted.

This is not at all to attempt to make Millar out a saint or a model of moral perfection. All human virtues are contained in earthen vessels. If the record were more complete and were completely untouched by friendly bias, many foibles would no doubt come into view, and possibly even more serious flaws of character make their appearance. Our purpose here cannot be to glorify the man, but only to indicate the direction of his thinking and feeling, the strength of his convictions, the tenor of his private life and his personal relations with men—all of

* *Life*, p. xcviii. Mr Craig does not feel warranted to reveal details, but vouches for the authenticity of his statement.

† *Life*, pp. cxx f.

which were in all probability not a little related, also, to his work as teacher, 'politician' and author.

Had my sources been more abundant, I might have been able to draw a fuller picture, and perhaps, therefore, a truer one, of Millar's life and character. But even so, Millar stands before us as a man of strength and dignity. And, from his actions and his personality more, perhaps, than from anything he said and wrote, we can understand how he inspired a whole generation of young men to higher levels of thought and aspiration, and in many instances to really noble endeavour and devotion.

PART II

CHIEFLY THEORETICAL

IX

INTRODUCTION

In the five chapters that follow an attempt will be made to analyse Millar's social and political theory on the background of eighteenth-century Scottish thinking generally, and any contribution he may have made to such theory.

In this background emphasis will be placed particularly on the historical and sociological aspects of this remarkable movement of thought, because I believe that most of my readers will be less familiar with this aspect of the movement than with its philosophical and economic aspects.

After a brief consideration in Chapter XI of the development of Millar's thinking, his own theoretical position will be outlined in Chapters XII and XIII in sufficient detail to make clear the general lines of his thought, but yet with this advance reminder, that for a fuller documentation of the positions there ascribed to him, and for any adequate evaluation of his work, the reader will have to turn to Millar's writings themselves.* This will be made considerably easier by the reproduction in Part III of the full text of one of his major works, and in Part IV of pertinent selections from his other writings.

In a final chapter an attempt will be made to assess the impact of his work upon his contemporaries and upon later thinking on the problems to which he addressed himself.

In this approach to the question of Millar's contributions to social and political theory, which of course is the question that principally concerns us in this book, and in any attempt to fix his place in the history of ideas, the discriminating reader will avoid the mistake of looking here for a development of a given idea or theoretical position such as could reasonably be expected only after generations of co-operative effort by many scholars in history, anthropology and sociology, with more abundant materials and finer tools than could possibly have been available to a pioneer in the middle and later eighteenth century. To focus attention upon a field of interest and upon a set of problems that little engaged thinkers before him; to attempt a new *Fragestellung* and to raise questions that even far greater and more creative thinkers, such

---

* For editions and abbreviations of Millar's works cited in text and notes below, see above, p. xv.

as Bacon, Hobbes and Locke had scarcely raised in their approach to comparable problems, would seem in itself to be making a major contribution to thought. Millar did more, we believe, than merely to *raise* a number of such questions.

X

EIGHTEENTH-CENTURY SCOTTISH
THOUGHT

Indulge your passion for science, says [Nature], but let your science be
human, and such as may have a direct reference to action and society. . . .
Be a philosopher; but amidst all your philosophy, be still a man. (Hume,
'Of the Different Species of Philosophy'.)

Mention was made at the very beginning of this study of a remarkable
intellectual and cultural awakening in the Scotland of the second and
third quarters, roughly, of the eighteenth century, and in particular of a
movement of thought that we chose to call a historical, or more
accurately, a historico-sociological movement. It is necessary now to
develop, as briefly as possible, the implications of the position there
stated. The objective of this chapter is to provide the needed background
for an understanding and appreciation of Millar's thought in its more
theoretical aspects.*

This movement can be, perhaps, most broadly and most fundamentally
characterized in terms of its secularizing tendencies. By 'secular' we
mean, of course, not at all an indifference to, or negation of, the religious
idea, much less any tendency toward irreligion. We mean, first of all, a
focusing of attention upon the mundane, the humanistic, the concerns
—be they material or ideal—of the here and now, and an assertion of

---

* Neither the sources listed on p. 415 below nor the histories of philosophy or political
theory provide us with the needed background for the present chapter, except in the most
general way. The most useful single work is Gladys Bryson, *Man and Society: The Scottish Inquiry
of the Eighteenth Century* (Princeton, 1945). The author's *Adam Ferguson and the Beginnings of
Modern Sociology* (New York, 1930) provides some materials. C. R. Fay, *Adam Smith and the
Scotland of his Day* (Cambridge, 1956) will prove valuable. J. B. Black, *The Art of History* (New
York, 1926) is most useful for the historical approach, and H. W. Thompson, *A Scottish Man
of Feeling* [Henry Mackenzie] (London and New York, 1931), will prove a helpful supplement
at some points. See also Dugald Stewart's biographical sketches of Smith, Robertson and
Reid (*Collected Works*, vol. x).

The following articles deserve notice for limited aspects of the problem: Gordon Mackenzie, 'Lord Kames and the Mechanist Tradition', in *University of California Studies in English*,
vol. xiv (1943), pp. 93–121; A. L. Macfie, 'The Scottish Tradition in Economic Thought',
in *Scottish Journal of Political Economy*, vol. ii (1955), pp. 81–103; Duncan Forbes, 'Scientific
Whiggism; Adam Smith and John Millar' in *Cambridge Journal*, vol. vii (1954), pp. 643–70;
and R. L. Meek, 'The Scottish Contribution to Marxist Sociology', in *Democracy and the
Labour Movement*, ed. John Saville (London, 1954).

Chiefly Theoretical

the autonomy of the human personality, as contrasted with the other-worldly, the supernatural, the sacerdotal, a world of supra-mundane values and an excessive emphasis on man's dependency on a 'Supreme Being'. In this sense we observe here a marked tendency to conceive and explain our experience-world rationally, by 'natural' causes, rather than supernaturalistically or by appeal to miracles or to a special revelation. Divine right gives way to utilitarian theories of government and the state; faith in a special Providence to either broadly deistic conceptions or to something like Adam Smith's 'invisible hand'; concern with questions of theology is replaced by an equally lively concern with questions of economics and politics; and traditional accounts of things give way to inquiries into their 'nature and causes', if not also into their 'origin and development' in naturalistic terms. Such secularization was, in the case of Scotland, all the more remarkable for the traditional engrossment of the Scottish mind—or a considerable sector of it at least—in religious orthodoxy and theological speculation.*

But 'secularization', in sociological usage,† means more than this. It means also, in life itself, a change of values, from the customary, the traditional, the folk-oriented, the authoritative, the familial—and in that sense the 'sacred', to an adaptive, a functional, a utilitarian, an experimental, a contractual, an impersonal life-orientation, to the values usually associated with urbanization. Methodologically this means an empirical, historical, analytical approach; a lively sense of the real goings-on in the world in which we live and an attempt to explain them in terms compatible with everyday observations. Conduct comes to be judged by criteria of social motivation and functional utility, rather than by reference to divine sanctions. Detachment and scientific objectivity, rather than orthodoxy, come to be the ideal.

Above all secularization, as here conceived, implies an attitude toward change, an ability and a willingness to accept inevitable change and to adapt oneself to the requirements of ever-changing situations, or better still, in response to the demands of new values freely espoused. On the theoretical side this means a dynamic view of life and society, a developmental, evolutionary view of the world in which we live; and on the valuational side a faith in the 'idea of progress'.

* The thoughtful reader can hardly afford *not* to read Buckle (*History of Civilization in England*, vol. II, chs. v, vi) on the eighteenth-century Scottish mind. Intellectually undisciplined, with a fierce bias against the 'monkish rabble' and the theological mind, holding every Scot to be a 'deductive' thinker, every Frenchman an 'inductive' one, and every Englishman at least an empiricist, Buckle is yet informed, entertaining, provocative.

† See especially H. Becker, 'Current Sacred-Secular Theory and its Development' in Becker and Boskoff (eds.), *Modern Sociological Theory in Continuity and Change* (New York, 1957), pp. 133–85, and other of his works and articles there cited.

92

Now, these tendencies of thought, all clearly present in the Scotland of this time, were in themselves neither new in the eighteenth century nor characteristically Scottish. They had their roots, practically, in changing social and economic conditions by no means confined to Scotland; and philosophically, in the ideas of Descartes, Grotius, Hobbes, Locke, Newton and Shaftesbury. These seventeenth-century men were, like their disciples in the deistic movement, essentially secularists in spite of their inability in most cases to strip themselves completely, in one fell swoop as it were, of their sacred garments. Their ideas soon became the property of all Europe. Yet there was in the Scottish expression of these tendencies something at once new to the eighteenth century and peculiarly Scottish.

It is scarcely an accident that an essay, 'Of Liberty and Necessity', was written in Scotland where men had long and vigorously engaged in debate on 'free-will versus predestination'; or that its author should also have asked, 'How can politics be a science if laws and forms of government had not a uniform influence on society? What would be the foundation of morals if particular characters had no certain or determined power to produce particular sentiments, and if these sentiments had not constant operation on actions?'* Nor is it without significance that the man who asked these questions should not only be the author of what was perhaps the first 'natural history of religion' ever to be written, but that he should have written it without any sense of cynicism or irreligion; or that Adam Ferguson, an ordained minister, should have written one of the first 'natural histories of civil society',† as an outgrowth of a course in Moral Philosophy, that, like similar courses in all Scottish universities, treated of 'natural theology' and revealed religion as well as of history, morals, law and politics.

In fact it is most remarkable that the bearers of this new tradition not only remained, in spite of a mild anti-clericalism, friendly to the church and to the ideals of religion, but that so many of them were either ordained ministers, or had at least been trained originally for Christian ministry‡ and continued to take an active interest in the affairs of the church. Voltaire's 'écrasez l'infame' would be as un-

* Hume, *Works* (Boston, 1854), vol. IV, p. 102.

† Adam Ferguson, *History of Civil Society* (Edinburgh, 1767). Reid said of this work, while it was still in process, 'I hear [Ferguson] is about to publish, I don't know under what title, a natural history of man; exhibiting a view of him in the savage state, and in the several successive states of pasturage, agriculture and commerce.' Letter to David Skene, 20 December 1765. See *Works* (Hamilton, ed.), p. 42.

‡ Examples are Ferguson, Robertson, Reid, Hutcheson, Wallace; also Walker (Natural Philosophy, Edinburgh), John Home, Hugh Blair, Robert Henry, Gerard, and others. Among men headed at least at first toward the ministry are Adam Smith and Thomas Thomson.

thinkable here as an act of public worship of 'the Goddess of Reason'. Theological argumentation, philosophical penetration, reformation zeal and democratic educational ideals and practices were closely inter-related in this home of Presbyterianism.

A marked characteristic of this movement of thought was a combination of empiricism, realism and idealism that was peculiarly Scottish. 'Scottish realism' applied here in more senses than one. First, there was a marked tendency, even on high theoretical levels, to keep one's feet on the ground—a tendency to base theory always on the facts of everyday experience and to apply that same theory to the practical conduct of life. In matters religious the concerns of salvation and the soul within and the prescripts of biblical tradition were never far removed from the concerns of community life or from the conduct of men in the marketplace. Religion, education—whether in the parish schools, the grammar schools or the university—and the requirements of good citizenship were brought very close together, and they all seemed to reflect a wresting of a living from a niggardly soil and a struggle to tame both man and his environment 'stern and wild'. In economics, politics and law the hard facts of experience and observation were rarely left to stand unrelated to a larger theoretical or philosophical frame of reference; as on the other hand economic, political or legal principles without a concrete basis in experience and observation were to the Scots a thing quite unthinkable. The *Statistical Account* of Scotland,* prepared late in this period—incidentally with the aid chiefly of parish ministers throughout the country—was not highly 'statistical'† as we use that term today, but seldom has an account of the state of society of a whole nation been drawn up on a more solid descriptive basis, parish by parish, than was done in this remarkable early survey.

Of the recognition of social and economic and political change, both in the past and on the contemporary scene, we shall speak elsewhere. Here this further remark may be in place, that for all men's resort to a mechanistic terminology—Hume's mechanistic interpretation of 'the production and conduct of the passions' is an outstanding example—‡

---

* Sir John Sinclair, *Statistical Account of Scotland*, 21 vols. (Edinburgh, 1791–9).

† Sir John says of the title of this work he was editing from reports of ministers to whom this task was assigned, 'The idea I annex to the term "statistical" is an inquiry into the state of a country for the purpose of ascertaining the quantum of happiness enjoyed by its inhabitants and the means of its future improvements' (vol. xx, p. xiii). George Dempster is quoted (vol. i, p. viii) as saying of this work, 'that no publication of equal information and curiosity has appeared in Great Britain since Dooms-day Book'. See also vol. ii, pp. v–viii; vol. iii, pp. xi, xv f.; vol. xxi, p. vi.

‡ Hume, *Works*, vol. iv, p. 226. The passage reads, '. . . in the production and conduct of the passions, there is a certain regular mechanism, which is susceptible of as accurate a disquisition as the laws of motion, optics, hydrostatics or any part of natural philosophy.'

and for all their predilection for economic and other forms of 'environmental determinism', Scottish interpretations never really became materialistic, either in the physical sense, as with d'Holbach, with Hartley in his physiological psychology, and with Hobbes at least in his psychological terminology, nor in the moral sense that would deny or greatly minimize spiritual values. 'Moral philosophy' was still given priority over 'natural philosophy'; biologists and chemists like Gregory and Cullen remained still idealists at heart; geographical factors in social causation were subordinated to cultural and psychological ones; economic goods were still made to serve genuinely human ends, and property was treated in terms not primarily of 'things' possessed but of human rights.

Finally, these remarks should not be taken to imply that all thinking fell easily and readily into these patterns. The defence of more theological and more traditional ways of thinking still remained strong. Hume was to the very end counted a dangerous 'atheist', ostensibly because of his position on 'revealed' religion, miracles and the like, but no doubt also because of his whole 'sceptical' philosophy and consistent humanism and 'naturalism'; and Adam Smith greatly shocked the righteous by a public avowal of his conviction that this 'atheist' friend of his approached 'as nearly to the ideal of a perfectly wise and virtuous man as, perhaps, the nature of human frailty will permit'.* 'Moderatist' ministers in the pulpit who, while holding to biblical teaching had yet felt the invigorating breezes of Shaftesburyan Hellenism, were strongly suspected of preaching 'the husks of heathen morality instead of sound doctrine'. Some of the most enlightened and liberal minds of the time, like Reid, still occasionally spoke the more conventional theological language; and men who quite readily accepted the evolutionary hypothesis as applied to the history of civilization were reluctant to apply it to man himself in his physical being, although many discoveries and observation were already pointing strongly in that direction. Only Monboddo dared publicly to contemplate such a possibility. Kames, who did accept a natural history of the differentiation of the races of mankind, admits that if one were to apply the ordinary rules of logic to the known facts of comparative biology, anatomy and palæonology one would be led to similar conclusions as to the origin of man himself. But he continues to do lip-service, though it was perhaps only that, to biblical authority instead.† All of this need not, however,

---

* Smith informs us that his so innocent and heart-felt characterization of his late friend 'brought upon me ten times more abuse than the very violent attack I had made upon the whole commercial system of Great Britain'. Rae, *Life of Adam Smith*, p. 311; Scott, *Adam Smith as Student and Professor*, p. 383; Fay, *op. cit.* p. 27, n. 1.

† Kames, H. Home, *Sketches of the History of Mankind* (3 vols. Edinburgh, 1774), vol. 1, p. 39.

seriously qualify the above characterization. It is the leadership and the trend of thought that matter.

We proceed now to note and to sketch briefly four broad areas of interest and intellectual effort that do represent more distinctly Scottish contributions to thought at this time and that have a most immediate bearing on Millar's own thought. All of them can be seen to bear the marks, so far as they are not in fact a direct outgrowth of, practical problems of a judicial, political, economic and social character emerging in the life of the nation in the period between the Union of the Parliaments in 1707 and the coming of the French Revolution in 1789. And all of them partake of that unique combination of the pragmatic and the realistic, with that clear strain of idealism and that solid foundation in theory of which we spoke before.

The first of these areas we can dispose of very quickly: this is a rising interest in problems of law—of Scots law and Scottish justice, first of all, in a changed and changing political and economic situation, but an interest also broadening out into a comparison of legal and judicial systems and into problems of comparative and historical jurisprudence generally. Scots law, it should be remembered, remained closer to Roman law than did English common law, which did not recognize the authority of the Roman law at all, and its system of land ownership, tenure and inheritance were at this time still strongly under the influence of a feudalism that had largely disappeared in England. While the legal and judicial systems were not directly affected by the political Union except in minor details, inner conflicts between the Scottish and the English systems were bound to appear, and legal problems of adjustment to a changing agricultural, commercial and gradually also industrial situation were accordingly greater in Scotland than in England or elsewhere.

Little wonder, then, that even before the turn of the century such works were beginning to appear in Scotland as Sir George Mackenzie's *The Institutes of the Law of Scotland* (1684) and Sir James Dalrymple, Viscount Stair's *The Institutions of the Law of Scotland* (1681), to be followed after a few decades by the *Institutes* of the more scholarly Professor Forbes (1722, 1739) whose chair at Glasgow Millar was later to occupy, and by the *Principles* (1754) and the *Institutes* (1773) of John Erskine. Even before the middle of the century Kames was publishing his codifications and his *Remarkable Decisions* (1728), his *British Antiquities* (1747), and later his *Dictionary* and such comparative and historical studies as his *Historical Law Tracts*, (1758), *Equity* (1760) and *Elucidations* (1777). During the earlier part of the century, too, law chairs were being either new-founded or revived and strengthened, at least in the Universities of Glasgow and Edinburgh, and some law and general jurisprudence was soon being taught in all the universities. Shortly after the middle of the century the echoes of Blackstone's lectures at Oxford were also being heard in Scotland through his published *Commentaries* and in other ways. And later there were more intensive developments of the science of law by such able students as Baron Hume and George Bell (see above, p. 39).

A growing realization, in an age of increasing enlightenment of thought, feeling and sentiment, of the harshness, in many respects, of the law in Scotland—with a dismaying number even of minor offences still counting as capital crimes—no doubt gave rise to considerable reflection on problems of law and justice; as did also the presence of many judges of great ability and humane outlook on high Scottish benches at this time. A new spirit of philosophy, already mentioned, and of historical study, shortly to be discussed, were also having their effect.

A second area of interest and direction of effort will be found in a new concern, on a more empirical basis than had hitherto prevailed, with problems of government and public policy, including fiscal theory and 'political economy'.

In the broader 'political' field we need but cite here Hume's efforts to 'reduce politics to a science', his essays 'Of the First Principles of Government', 'Of the Origin of Government', 'Of the Original Contract', 'Of [Political] Parties', 'Of Civil Liberty', 'Of National Characters', 'Of the Rise and Progress of the Arts and Sciences', and the many essays on more purely economic subjects. With all their seeming casualness these essays are still highly original, strike bed-rock as had seldom been done before, and, taken together, lay the foundation to a surprising extent for future work in political science, economics and the social sciences generally.

In the more limited field of 'political economy' there appeared in Scotland a little later two fundamental treatises. Both represented landmarks in the discussion of this subject. To comment here on the *Wealth of Nations* in its general character or on its particular economic doctrines would be presumptuous. Three observations may, however, be permitted. First, the wording itself of its full title is significant: *An Inquiry into the Nature and Causes of the Wealth of Nations*. An 'inquiry', not a treatise or a pronouncement of principles *ex cathedra*; into 'the nature and causes' in typical eighteenth-century Scottish fashion; not of 'opulence' merely, but of 'wealth' with still some overtones of 'weal' or well-being, its increase, also implied; of 'nations', of national communities, not merely of entrepreneurs or of business enterprise, and of nations in their external trade relations clearly implied. Next, it is still a study, in considerable measure, in politics or public policy, not merely in the science of the production, distribution and consumption of wealth—thus reflecting its origin in a course of lectures in 'moral philosophy'. And third, it is, more than any of its predecessors and than most of its immediate successors, based on abundant and painstaking empirical observation and historical study, and partakes but little of the character of abstract speculation on principles and immutable laws, though the quest for principles, and in the broad sense for 'laws', is clearly in evidence in the treatment.

The other treatise referred to above is Sir James Steuart Denham's *Principles of Political Economy.** This today little-known work appeared a few years before the *Wealth of Nations*, and was well known to Smith, though he took little public cognizance of it. Though in itself a work of the highest merit, it cannot, in its influence, bear comparison with Smith's work. It is a more systematic and rounded treatise than the *Wealth of Nations*, is based on a scholarship scarcely less broad, and certainly not less sound; and reveals an insight into human nature, the psychology of living-standards and of consumption, and into economic processes, generally, scarcely less penetrating. It is profound in its insights into the political processes of social control by taxation and other means. In line with its title, it is a treatise on 'political economy' in the original Aristotelian meaning of both terms, rather than on the science of the production and distribution of wealth. Being still a mercantilist, though one of the last of them, Steuart has less faith in the benevolent operations of the 'invisible hand' in a *laissez faire* economy than does Smith.

The third aspect of this movement in Scottish thought to be reviewed here is what, for lack of a better term, we shall call its historical-mindedness.† We use this term with a threefold implication: first, there is the more obvious meaning of an interest in recorded history, historical research and historical interpretation; next is implied an interest in

---

* Sir James Steuart (Denham), *An Inquiry into the Principles of Political Economy* (2 vols. London, 1767).

† Space does not permit a discussion here of the controversy over the 'historical' or 'unhistorical' character of eighteenth-century thinking. We can only indicate our awareness of the attack upon these historians as offering little more than a rationalization of their own 'naturalistic', 'rationalistic', 'faith-in-progress' philosophy; to admit that we recognize some truth in their criticisms, but also a strong 'romantic' bias; and to cite a few authorities in the field. These are Fr. Meinecke, *Die Entstehung des Historismus* (2 vols., 2nd ed., Munich, 1946); R. G. Collingwood, *The Idea of History* (Oxford, 1946); James W. Thompson, *A History of History and Historical Writing* (2 vols. New York, 1942), especially vol. II—on the attack chiefly. More appreciative, E. Cassirer, *Die Philosophie der Aufklärung* (Tübingen, 1932), English translation available; and J. B. Black already cited. Also M. H. Mandelbaum, *The Problem of Historical Knowledge* (New York, 1938).

origins, in continuities through time in the development of social and political institutions, present of course also in the first meaning but viewed now on certain theoretical assumptions that can best be indicated by such terms as 'natural history', 'evolution', the 'idea of progress'; and finally, there is implied an empirical approach to socio-historical reality that attempts to see any subject under study—be it political, economic, literary, any particular custom, institution or what not—in the concreteness of a particular time and place in an organic relation to other phenomena, whether past or present, quite regardless of any time sequence.

All of these, it is contended here, were present in a marked degree in the Scottish thought of this time. The three of course overlapped and were considerably intertwined in practice, but they should be clearly distinguished in idea.

The historical turn of mind that embraced them all represents a distinct advance in the history of modern thought.

To take them up in reverse order, the last of these three manifestations can be disposed of by merely referring again to the empirical character of the best political writings of the time, to their frequent use of historical and of ethnographic materials, both on 'rude' and on more advanced societies, and to their frequent resort to institutional comparisons on a historical basis. Hume's *Essays*, the factual basis generally, the abundant historical illustrations and the many historical digressions in Smith's *Wealth of Nations*, and the *Historical Law Tracts* and other essays in like vein of Lord Kames, will serve as our best examples.

The second, the 'evolutionary' aspect, calls for somewhat more detailed treatment. By evolutionism—not to be confused with the 'idea of progress', though this confusion is often made—is here meant an attempt to reconstruct the 'natural history', to trace the origin and gradual development of social and political institutions and of civilization generally, in some kind of progressive order of stages, more or less uniform for all peoples or civilizations, and to explain them by the operation of forces or 'laws' inherent in the developmental processes themselves. Human nature is such a force in man's attempt to adapt to his environment and to improve his position. Any kind of 'Providential' order is excluded, and there is a playing down, at least, of the rational factor, of leadership roles and of any over-all political planning.

Generalizing, it may be stated that few ideas more deeply penetrated and more widely influenced the social, political and historical thought of the time than this evolutionary idea, in some of its aspects at least, and with few exceptions—Mandeville among them—it is new to this period. It pervades much of the thought of such major thinkers as

Hume, Smith and Ferguson. It is clearly present in such works as Gilbert Stuart's *View of Society in Europe in its Progress from Rudeness to Refinement* (1778), and in Robertson's *View of the Progress of Society in Europe* (1769) and in his *History of America* (1777),* though it does not dominate these more historical works. It becomes a dominant note in James Dunbar's *Essay on the History of Mankind in Rude and Cultivated Ages* (1780), in Monboddo's speculations on *The Origin and Progress of Language* (1773–92), and in Millar's *Origin of the Distinction of Ranks* and Ferguson's *History of Civil Society*.

From the last mentioned we quote a few key paragraphs without further comment.

The history of mankind is confined within a limited period, and from every quarter brings an intimation that human affairs have had a beginning. Nations distinguished by the possession of arts, and the felicity of their political establishments have been derived from a feeble original, and still preserve in their story the indications of a slow and gradual progress by which this distinction was gained.†

Mankind, when in their rude state, have a great uniformity of manners; but when civilized they are engaged in a variety of pursuits; they tread on a larger field and separate to a greater distance. If they are guided, however, by similar dispositions, and by like suggestions of nature, they will probably in the end as well as in the beginning of their progress, continue to agree in many particulars; and while communities admit, in their members, that diversity of ranks and professions which we have already described, as the consequence of the foundation of commerce, they will resemble each other in many effects of this distribution, and of other circumstances in which they nearly concur.‡

And again:

Mankind, in following the present sense of their minds, in striving to remove inconveniences, or to gain apparent and contiguous advantages, arrive at ends which even their imagination could not anticipate; and pass on, like other animals, in the tract of their nature, without perceiving its end. He who first said, 'I will appropriate this field; I will leave it to my heirs;' did not perceive, that he was laying the foundations of civil laws and political establishments. He who first ranged himself under a leader, did not perceive, that he was setting the example of a permanent subordination, under the pretence of which, the rapacious were to seize his possessions, and the arrogant to lay claim to his service.§

But it is history in the first of the three meanings indicated above that we wish here particularly to emphasize. What Black says of an interest

---

* See especially *Works* (Edinburgh, 1818), vol. IV, pp. 13–15, 246–54; and vol. IX, pp. 29–33.
† Ferguson, *An Essay on the History of Civil Society* (5th ed. London, 1782, used), p. 123.
‡ *Ibid.* p. 315.   § *Ibid.* p. 204.

in history in Europe generally at this time would seem to apply to Scotland in a peculiar measure; and it can hardly be an accident that two of the four authors he treats in detail in his *The Art of History* are products of the movement here under discussion and a third, Gibbon, at least closely associated with this tradition. We quote:

In all probability there has never been a period when history was so much in demand among the reading public in all European countries as in the latter part of the eighteenth century. It would be no exaggeration to say that the vogue of historical books between 1750 and the outbreak of the French Revolution was as great as the vogue of poetical literature in the age of Shakespeare and of the novel in the age of Scott.*

Such an interest in history might, of course, have remained a purely sentimental or romantic or patriotic one. That this was not the case, at least in Scotland, is evident from the reception given to its most solid historians. Hume, whom Adam Smith calls without reservations 'by far the most illustrious philosopher and historian of the present age',† and who was known in his time much more as a historian than as a philosopher, was, for all his failure adequately to pursue and utilize original sources, a historian of great skill, breadth and philosophical penetration. Robertson, hardly a mind of the same calibre and philosophical breadth and penetration, and sometimes appearing to give almost more attention to the style than to the substance of his writing, was, however, far more painstaking in the matter of primary sources, perhaps also more 'sociological' in his general orientation, and at any rate gave the world a number of histories of the very first order of importance. Gibbon, by later reputation outdistancing both of these men, was scarcely capable of conceiving a higher honour than to receive the accolade of both of these masters.‡ We shall confine ourselves, by way of illustration, to Hume and Robertson.§

---

* Black, *The Art of History*, p. 14. † *Wealth of Nations* (Cannan edition), vol. II, p. 275.

‡ '. . . the most ambitious wish I entertained was to deserve the approbation of Dr Robertson and Mr Hume. The candour of Robertson [in reviewing Gibbon's work] embraced his discipline; a letter from Hume over-paid the labour of ten years; but I have never presumed to accept a place in the triumvirate of British Historians.' *Autobiography* (ed. John Murray, London, 1896), pp. 311–13. Also letter, Gibbon to Robertson, 14 July 1777, quoted in part in Dugald Stewart, *Life and Writings of Robertson*, Section III.

§ Robert Henry's *History of Great Britain* (6 vols., 'written on a new plan', London, 1771–93), which Millar rated highly, especially for the author's assembling and utilizing of source materials on earliest British history, deserves mention here more for the scope of the 'new plan' than for the quality of its execution. Each of the ten books, covering a period marked at each end by some outstanding revolution, is divided into seven chapters, attempting to treat for each period the following topics: (1) Civil and military history; (2) Religious and Church affairs; (3) Constitution, government, laws and courts of justice; (4) Learning and seminaries of learning; (5) The arts, 'both useful and ornamental, necessary and pleasing';

For a general characterization and critical evaluation of both of them
we must refer the reader to Black's treatment of them in the work
already cited.* Here we can only remark, first of Hume, that it was
hardly an accident that the author of the *Treatise*, the *Inquiry* and the
Essays Moral, Political and Literary also wrote a great history, and that his
History reflects his views of human nature and politics perhaps as much
as his essays draw upon historical observation and experience. The
following passage, taken not from his *History* but from one of his essays,
is particularly pertinent here.

It is universally acknowledged, that there is a great uniformity among the
actions of men, in all nations and ages, and that human nature remains still
the same in its principles and operations. The same motives always produce
the same actions; the same events follow from the same causes. Ambition,
avarice, self-love, vanity, friendship, generosity, public spirit: these passions,
mixed in various degrees, and distributed throughout society, have been,
from the beginning of the world, and still are, the sources of all actions and
enterprises which have been observed among mankind. . . . Mankind are so
much the same, in all times and places, that history informs us of nothing new
or strange in this particular. . . . Nor are the earth, water, and other elements, examined by Aristotle and Hippocrates, more like to those which at
present lie under our observation, than the men described by Polybius and
Tacitus are to those who now govern the world.†

This is of course typically Humean, but it is only one side of the coin.
The other side is to be found in the same essay when the author cautions
the reader that no man in his right mind would press this position to the
point of excluding all historical individuality, uniqueness and variety
amidst such uniformity and regularity, or would fail to recognize 'the
great force of custom and education' in the moulding of the individual
mind and therefore also of the 'manners of men [differently] in different
ages and countries'.‡

Such statements, taken together with his essay, 'Of the Study of
History', should make it abundantly clear that Hume does not attempt to
construct history *a priori* out of his philosophical conceptions of human
nature and environmental forces.

Robertson deserves much more attention than space permits us to
give him here. For his sweeping view, on evolutionary principles, of

(6) Commerce, shipping, money, prices; and (7) The 'manners, virtues, vices, remarkable
customs, language, dress, diet and diversions of the people'.
The author admits unevenness, for lack of adequate sources for some periods, in carrying
through the plan. He fails to inform us, however, that Goguet, in the preface to his *Origin
of Laws, etc.* (see below, p. 116 n), which appeared thirteen years earlier, and a part of which
he had himself translated into English proposed to follow a very similar plan.

* Black, *op. cit.* chs. III and IV.　　† Hume, *Works*, vol. IV, pp. 94 f.　　‡ *Ibid.* p. 97.

the rise of modern European civilization, and for his attempt to view events in 'their mutual connection and dependence' and in their causal relations throughout, we must refer the reader above all to his remarkable *View of the Progress of Society in Europe* which serves as a full-volume introduction to his *History of Charles V,** and more particularly to its introductory chapter.

From his account of the impact of the Crusades on European culture we lift out this passage:

Although the attention of the historians of the Crusades was fixed on other objects than the state of society and manners among the nations which they invaded, although most of them had neither taste nor discernment enough to describe these, they relate, however, such signal acts of humanity and generosity in the conduct of Saladin, as well as some other leaders of the Mahometans, as give us a very high idea of their manners. It was not possible for the Crusaders to travel through so many countries, and to behold their various customs and institutions, without acquiring information and improvement. Their views enlarged; their prejudices wore off; new ideals crowded into their minds; and they must have been sensible, on many occasions, of the rusticity of their manners, when compared with those of a more polished people. These impressions were not so slight as to be effaced upon their return to their native countries. A close intercourse subsisted between the East and West during two centuries; new armies were continually marching from Europe to Asia, while former adventurers returned home and imported many of the customs to which they had been familiarized by a long residence abroad. Accordingly we discover, soon after the commencement of the Crusades, greater splendour in the courts of princes, greater pomp in public ceremonies, a more refined taste in pleasure and amusements, together with a more romantic spirit of enterprise, spreading gradually over Europe; and to these wild expeditions, the effect of superstition or folly, we owe the first gleam of light which tended to dispel barbarism and ignorance (pp. 31 f.).

Again, after discussing the impact of these events on the development of commerce and, the rise of cities, he makes these remarkable observations:

But in what way soever the representatives of cities first gained a place in the legislature, that event had great influence on the form and genius of government. It tempered the rigour of aristocratical oppression with a proper mixture of popular liberty; it secured to the great body of the people, who had formerly no representatives, active and powerful guardians of their rights and privileges; it established an intermediate power between the King and the nobles, to which each had recourse alternately, and which at some times opposed the usurpations of the former, on other occasions checked the

* Published Edinburgh, 1769. Quotations are from *Works* (Edinburgh, 1818), vol. IV.

encroachments of the latter. As soon as the representatives of communities gained any degree of credit and influence in the legislature, the spirit of laws [Montesquieu's phrase, of course] became different from what it had formerly been; it flowed from new principles; it was directed towards new objects; equality, order, the public good, and the redress of grievances, were phrases and ideas brought into use, and which grew to be familiar in the statutes and jurisprudence of the European nations. Almost all the efforts in favour of liberty in every country of Europe have been made by this new power in the legislature. In proportion as it rose to consideration and influence, the severity of the aristocratical spirit decreased; and the privileges of the people became gradually more extensive, as the ancient and exorbitant jurisdiction of the nobles was abridged (pp. 45 f.).

Here Clio has come fully into her own and her seat is one of genuine dignity and illumination. We have here a rare combination of carefully documented narrative history, a broad sociological orientation, and a due appreciation of ideal as well as economic and political factors in the shaping of history.

There remains the fourth aspect of this movement in Scottish thought —less explicit and less clearly marked, perhaps, than the others and therefore easily overlooked by the general student, but scarcely less fundamental and less characteristic of the movement—its sociological aspect, in the narrower sense of that term. We mean a peculiar awareness of the essentially societal nature of man's very existence, of his endeavours, activities, norms and institutions. Further, a search for the foundations of the state, of the economic order* and of the spiritual life itself in the relations of man to man, of the individual to the community is implied; and an attempt to explain change in all of them in 'scientific' rather than in moralistic or theological terms.

Again it is Hume who gives us our first and most searching leads here. In his own words:

Man, born in a family, is compelled to maintain society from necessity, from natural inclination and from habit. The same creature, in his further progress, is engaged to establish political society, in order to administer justice,

---

* On the broadly sociological orientation of Scottish thought, specifically in economics, see Macfie, *art. cit.* McCulloch may also be instanced (Introductory Discourse to *Wealth of Nations*, 1855 edition, p. xviii):

'The economist should study men in every different situation. He should resort to the history of society, arts, commerce and government; to the works of philosophers and travellers; to everything, in short, fitted to throw light on the progress of opulence and civilization. He should mark the successive changes which have taken place in the fortunes and conditions of the different ranks and orders of men in his own country and in others; ... above all he should analyze and compare the influence of different institutions and regulations, and carefully discriminate the various circumstances wherein advancing and declining societies differ from each other.'

without which there can be no peace among them, nor safety, nor mutual intercourse.*

The mutual dependence of men is so great in all societies, that scarcely any human action is entirely complete in itself, or is performed without some reference to the actions of others, which are requisite to make it answer fully to the intention of the agent.†

The human mind is of a very imitative nature; nor is it possible for any set of men to converse often together without acquiring a similitude of manners, and communicating to each other their vices as well as their virtues.‡

Again:

[In human society] it is necessary, in order to preserve stability in government, that the new brood should conform themselves to the established constitution, and nearly follow the path which their fathers, treading in the footsteps of theirs, have marked out to them.§

And finally:

. . . liberty is the perfection of civil society; but . . . authority must be acknowledged essential to its very existence: and in those contests which so often take place between one and the other, the latter may, on that account, challenge the preference.‖

Many similar passages could be cited, but here we have, in a few almost aphoristically pregnant sentences, in essence the foundations of a whole system of sociology as they had, perhaps, never been so clearly laid before. Most of the speculations in modern sociology up to about a generation ago have been little more than a commentary on such basic propositions.

Adam Smith's *Theory of Moral Sentiments*, too, is a treatise on social psychology almost more than on ethics. Here is the same recognition of human interdependence, of sympathy or 'empathy', imitativeness, the need for communication with one's fellows, of sensitivity to their approvals and disapprovals. A whole section is devoted to habit, custom, fashions, and the differences in manners and customs between different stages of civilization and advancement, between different nations, between different estates and professions. Conscience is recognized as essentially social in character; passions are either social or anti-social; ethics becomes, in effect, primarily social ethics. Much of this applies also to portions of the *Wealth of Nations*.

In the *Moral Sentiments*, the *Wealth of Nations*, and the *Lectures* there is an abundant recognition of the division of labour, not only in the

* *Works*, vol. III, p. 34.   † *Ibid*. vol. IV, p. 100.   ‡ *Ibid*. vol. III, p. 222.
§ *Ibid*. vol. III, p. 506.   ‖ *Ibid*. p. 38.

production of goods but in all human society, of the essentially social or societal character of most economic motivations, of conspicuous consumption, of standards of living and economic wants generally. Both the rivalry between the social classes and the willing subservience, often, of the lower classes to their superiors or betters, are clearly recognized; as are also varying social distances, at different times and in different societies, between the social classes. Differences in social attitudes and values, as well as in social structure, between rural and urban societies, are clearly recognized, as well as many other similar sociological and socio-psychological phenomena.*

Perhaps the most explicit and systematic treatment of this subject will, however, be found in Adam Ferguson's *History of Civil Society* and to a lesser extent also in his *Principles of Moral and Political Science*.

'Man is born in society, and in society he remains' he quotes from Montesquieu,† and he further assures us that:

Where there is a plurality of men, there is also a society; and in society there is a distribution of parts and cooperation of many to some common purpose or end.‡

From [man's union with his species] are derived not only the force but the very existence of his happiest emotions; not only the better part, but almost the whole of his rational character.§

The 'principle of opposition', of 'dissension', of 'rivalship', of conflict, is as deep-rooted in man's nature and as much a part of the life of society as the 'principle of union', and offers if anything the stronger driving force for the progress of society.

In human nature the associating principle is combined with a variety of considerations and circumstances, which lead mankind to vary their forms indefinitely, whether in respect to the number that compose their society, the direction under which a community is to act, or the object to which it is chiefly directed.‖

And finally, on a more specific matter:

Families may be considered as the elementary forms of society, or establishments the most indispensably necessary to the existence and preservation of the kind. As families may exist apart, and without any necessary communication of one group with another, so they still continue to be formed, in what-

---

* See particularly A. Small, *Adam Smith and Modern Sociology* (Chicago, 1907); and A. Salomon, 'Adam Smith as Sociologist', in *Social Research* (February 1945), pp. 22–44.

† *History of Civil Society*, p. 27.

‡ *Principles of Moral and Political Science* (2 vols. Edinburgh, 1792), vol. I, p. 21.

§ *History of Civil Society*, p. 30.

‖ *Principles of Moral and Political Science*, vol. I, p. 24.

ever numbers mankind may be leagued into larger communities: They are the nurseries of men; the basis of empires, as well as of nations and tribes; and the compartments of which the greatest fabrics of political establishment are composed. . . .*

From such passages it is clear that, however he may be inclined, occasionally, to moralize, or to fall into a flowery style, his writings represent beyond any question a considerable advance in sociological insight and interpretation, and move the problem of society as such into the very centre of historical and political thinking as had seldom if ever been done before.

In attempting now to draw these various threads together, we find that, except for a slight neglect of the more distinctly sociological factor, this has been much better done by a late contemporary than we could do it ourselves. We quote Dugald Stewart to the following effect:

That the capacities of the human mind have been in all ages the same, and that the diversity of phenomena exhibited by our species is the result merely of the different circumstances in which men are placed, has been long received as an incontrovertible logical maxim; or rather, such is the influence of early instruction that we are apt to regard it as one of the most obvious suggestions of common sense. And yet till about the time of Montesquieu, it was by no means so generally recognised by the learned as to have a sensible influence on the fashionable tone of thinking over Europe. The application of this fundamental and leading idea to the natural or *theoretical history* of society in all its various aspects;—to the history of languages, of the arts, of the sciences, of laws, of government, of manners, and of religion,—is the peculiar glory of the latter half of the eighteenth century, and forms a characteristic feature in its philosophy, which even the imagination of Bacon was unable to foresee.†

And expanding slightly on this in another place he says:

It is but lately only . . . that these important subjects [manners, customs, language, institutions, government, etc., treated by the methods of Theoretical or Conjectural History (Hume's *Natural History* or in French, *Histoire Raisonnée*)‡] have been considered in this point of view; the greater part of politicians before the time of Montesquieu having contented themselves with an historical statement of facts, and with a vague reference of laws to the wisdom of particular legislators, or to accidental circumstances, which it is now impossible to ascertain. Montesquieu, on the contrary, considered laws as originating chiefly from the circumstances of society, and attempted to account, from the changes in the condition of mankind, which take place in the different stages of their progress, for the corresponding alterations which

* *Ibid.* vol. I, p. 27.   † *Collected Works* (Hamilton ed.), vol. I, pp. 69 f.
‡ *Ibid.* vol. X, p. 34.

107

their institutions undergo. It is thus that in his occasional elucidations of the Roman jurisprudence, instead of bewildering himself among the erudition of scholiasts and of antiquaries, we frequently find him borrowing his lights from the most remote and unconnected quarters of the globe, and combining the casual observations of illiterate travellers and navigators, into a philosophical commentary on the history of law and manners.

The advances made in this line of inquiry since Montesquieu's time have been great. Lord Kames, in his *Historical Law Tracts*, has given us some excellent specimens of it, particularly in his *Essays on the History of Property and of Criminal Law*, and many ingenious speculations of the same kind occur in the works of Mr Millar.*

Stewart is here obviously groping for a concept like that of a comparative historical sociology. These quotations, therefore, with a direct reference to Millar himself, would seem the logical point from which to turn now to an account and analysis of Millar's own thought.

* *Ibid.* vol. x, pp. 35 f.

XI

THE DEVELOPMENT OF MILLAR'S THOUGHT

The background of Millar's thought on problems of politics and society has been presented in a measure of detail because without this there is danger that many readers would get a faulty impression of his contributions. They could not be expected to understand the larger implications of his position, at many points, and they would often be attributing to him a kind of originality to which he himself never pretended. Where his originality is to be found and what his real contributions were, should become clear in the chapters that follow.

But before proceeding to an analysis, in more or less systematic fashion, of his general theoretical position and of his application of it to various fields of interest, it seems desirable to inquire in this chapter into the dynamics of its development against the background given. Three questions will be asked and answered so far as the limitations of space and the availability of evidence permit. First, what was the general direction of the movement of his thought, as evinced in his lectures and in his published works? Second, what evidence do we find of an increasing maturity, of increasing breadth of outlook and depth of insight with his advance in years, or of more concrete application to the world of affairs? And finally, what, so far as we are able to determine them, were the dynamics, or more accurately, the 'kinetic' forces operating in the development and more final formulation of his ideas on various subjects?

The first question can be summarily answered by the observation that—discounting his engagement, early and late, with classical literature and with the history of civil society generally; or rather viewing these as themselves dynamic factors—his thought moved clearly from problems of law, in the narrower sense of civil law or of the Roman law, to a broader concern with problems of historical and comparative jurisprudence, to problems of government and public policy, toward an analysis of all of these in terms which we should today call essentially sociological.

In civil law itself, as distinguished from public law or government, he differentiates between rights and actions. Rights may proceed from the relation of husband and wife, parent and child, master and servant, guardian and guarded or minors. Rights may also be real or personal. Real rights may be in property, in servitude, in pledge or in personal privilege. Personal rights may arise from promise or contract, from crime or delinquency, or from equity or utility without the intervention of the two former. Actions involve the manner in which actions at law are commenced, procedure in determining causes, and the execution of sentences.*

Under 'jurisprudence' Millar treated, in the words of his biographer,

of such principles of law as pervade the codes of all nations, and have their origin in those sentiments of justice which are imprinted in the human heart.

He began by investigating the origin and foundation of each right in the natural principles of justice; and afterwards traced its progress through the different conditons of mankind; marking such deviations from the general rule as the known circumstances of particular nations might be expected to occasion, and accounting, in the most satisfactory manner, for those diversities in laws, which must otherwise have appeared irreconcilable with the idea that there is anything stable or precise in the moral sentiments of mankind.†

The general scope and character of his lectures on government has been indicated elsewhere (see above, pp. 33 f., 57 f.).

Without implying a clear-cut time sequence in this movement of Millar's thought, it is clear that he soon came to hold a broad view of 'the law', and considered the function of his chair in the University in a liberal or humanistic, rather than in a narrowly or technically legalistic manner. His general approach may well be described in terms of the following paragraphs lifted out of the report of the Royal Visiting Commission investigating the Scottish universities in the late 1820's:

The real interests of the community may be most materially sacrificed if the course of study of law shall be adapted wholly to the supposed convenience of a portion of the students. The country is deeply interested in the character, the independence and influence of the advocates to whom the defence of their property and liberties may be entrusted; and it will be in vain to hope that the independence and character of the bar can be maintained if the study of law is not conducted on an enlightened and philosophical plan.

The great extension of the subject only renders it more important to provide that the instruction of the students shall not be limited to the details of a technical art, and the philosophy and science of law sacrificed, in order to furnish materials for the manual of a practitioner. . . .

* James Reddie, *Inquiries in the Science of Law* (London, 1847), pp. 345 ff., 49 f., 160 f. (pages 1–216 of this edition are a reprint of the original 1840 edition, with a new preface. Pp. 217–459 are new). The paragraph is an indirect quotation from Reddie.
† *Life*, p. xxvi.

The Development of Millar's Thought

The manner in which the subject may be taught in the universities will necessarily determine, in a very great degree, the mode in which it will be generally studied.*

There is no explicit mention here of Millar, but when it is remembered that a number of the members of the Commission were former students of his† and that his former chair at Glasgow was shown by a rather severe grilling of its then incumbent to have deteriorated considerably, at least in this respect, since Millar's time,‡ it becomes extremely likely that these paragraphs had implicit reference to his exposition of the law.

Millar's general view of jurisprudence, of the historical development of legal and judicial establishments and of the science of law and government, are so clearly set forth in his essay on that subject (see below, Pt. IV, Selection II) that, except for the following key paragraph, we may here merely refer the reader to that source. The essay is no doubt in a manner 'autobiographical'.

The attempts to delineate systems of jurisprudence . . . opened at length a new source of speculation, by suggesting an inquiry into the circumstances which have occasioned various and opposite imperfections in the law of different countries, and which have prevented the practical systems, in any, from attaining that improvement which we find no difficulty in conceiving. In the prosecution of this inquiry, more especially by President Montesquieu, by Lord Kames, and by Dr. Smith, the attention of speculative lawyers has been directed to examine the first formation and subsequent advancement of civil society; the rise, the gradual development, and cultivation of arts and sciences; the acquisition and extension of property in all its different modifications, and the combined influence of these and other political causes, upon the manners and customs, the institutions and laws of any people. . . . (*H.V.*, below, p. 347.)

Here as elsewhere, Millar's thought may clearly be seen to move not only from the formal requirements of law, but from the realm of 'oughtness' generally, to the realm of the 'whatness' and the 'howness' of things in the collective life of men—asking no longer, chiefly, What ought men to do? or, What can they be compelled by public authority to do? or, Why should they render obedience to sovereign power? but

* *Report of the Royal Commission of Inquiry into the State of the Universities of Scotland* (London, 1831, etc.), vol. I (General Report), p. 54. See also pp. 321 ff., 337, 352, 376, 404, 557 ff. The Commission was appointed in 1826; the Glasgow hearings were in January 1828.

† Of the thirteen Commission members signing, David Boyle, William Rae and James Moncreiff, and possibly others, were former students; H. Home Drummond was the son of Millar's former pupil and grandson of Lord Kames. On the Glasgow sub-committee were two others, Lauderdale and Cranstoun (Corehouse).

‡ *Report of the Royal Commision of Inquiry*, vol. II, pp. 145–8.

III

rather, How do men actually behave, or tend to behave in their relations one with another in the life of the community? What manners, customs, institutions, etc. come to govern their behaviour? What transformations do they undergo? What uniformities and varieties do they manifest, and how can these best be explained on an empirical, rational basis?

This shift in basic orientation, which Millar of course shared with other of his contemporaries, and the fundamental importance of which in the history of thought must be apparent to every reader, is almost exactly what we mean by a turn toward sociological analysis.* That Millar's own thinking should have taken this turn will be the less surprising the more we keep in mind two considerations. The first is the general bias of the Scottish mind toward the sociological in the analysis of social, economic and political problems, as mentioned in the last chapter. (See above, p. 104.) The other is the marked similarity, after all, from the point of view of essential content, between the two

* By 'sociology' we mean, of course, not at all a study of 'welfare' problems merely, or 'social pathology', but a highly generalized social science. For present purposes 'sociology' should be conceived more nearly as a near-contemporary of Millar's conceived it than in terms of the present day. John Stuart Mill, who admitted borrowing the term from his contemporary Comte as a 'more compact' term than 'social science' and who thought very highly of Millar, gave us his conception of the subject in his 'Logic of the Social and Moral Sciences' (*System of Logic*, 1843), Book VI, Chapter IX, opening paragraphs. We quote with some abbreviation:

'There are two kinds of sociological inquiry. In the first the question proposed is, what effect will follow from a given cause, a certain general condition of social circumstances being presupposed.... But there is also a second inquiry, namely, what are the laws which determine those general circumstances. . . . what are the causes which produce, and the phenomena which characterize, states of society generally.

In order to conceive correctly the scope of the general science and distinguish it from the subordinate departments of sociological speculation, it is necessary to fix with precision the idea attached to the phrase 'a state of society'. What is called a state of society is the simultaneous state of all the general social facts or phenomena. Such are the degree of knowledge, and of intellectual and moral culture, existing in the community, and of every class of it; the state of industry; of wealth and its distribution; the habitual occupations of the community; their divisions into classes, and the relation of those classes to one another; the common beliefs which they entertain on all the subjects most important to mankind, and the degree of assurance with which those beliefs are held; their tastes and the character and degree of their aesthetic development; their form of government, and the more important of their laws and customs. . . .

When states of society, and the causes which produce them are spoken of as a subject of science, it is implied that there exists a natural correspondence among these different elements; that [only certain combinations] of these general social facts [are] possible; that, in short, there exist uniformities of coexistence between the states of the various social phenomena. . . .'

Today we may, of course, hold to a much more highly developed and specialized concept of the subject. For this we can here only refer the reader to works like the following:

George Gurvitch and W. Moore, *Twentieth Century Sociology* (New York, 1946).

H. E. Barnes and H. and Frances B. Becker, *Contemporary Social Theory* (New York, 1940.)

H. Becker and A. Boskoff (eds.), *Modern Sociological Theory in Continuity and Change* (New York 1957). R. K. Merton *et al.* (eds.) *Sociology Today: Problems and Prospects* (New York, 1959).

disciplines. For both law and sociology are basically concerned with inter-human relations, with the whole broad field of inter-human relations, be it in small groups or large, in the daily routines of life or in moments of great crisis or import, in the strictly personal ways or the more institutionalized aspects of community life.

The approach will be different, and so may the areas of concentration. There are no doubt aspects of almost every inter-human relationship that are little if at all amenable to the controls of law; there will be few, including the problems of law, and in particular those of equity, that do not involve questions of a sociological nature. The jurist will perhaps seek more exact definitions of situations, and will try to fix most rights and duties under prescription; the sociologist will be more prone to generalization, to searching the causes of events and actions, to studying the problems and processes of both institutionalization and of individuation. Both will find common ground in Millar's observation—at a time, of course, when there was no such discipline as 'sociology'—that 'Of all the sciences, law seems to be that which depends most upon experience, and in which mere speculative reasoning is of the least consequence' (*H.V.* vol. II, p. 339). He finds this particularly true of the Roman law as resting upon 'the accumulated experience and observation of ages and of the most extensive empire that ever existed in a civilized form'.

When in his 'searching for the causes' of different 'systems of law and government' he finds these in considerable measure in a variety of 'differences of situation' that 'must have a prodigious influence on the great body of a people', by 'giving direction to their inclinations and pursuits', 'productive of correspondent habits, dispositions and ways of thinking', Millar has clearly moved out of formal law into something we need no longer hesitate to call sociology.

So much for the general direction of the movement of his thought. If next we inquire into the development of Millar's mind from the point of view of scope of interests, breadth and maturity of outlook and pragmatic application, we may first of all refer the reader to the several places where this matter has already been touched upon. (See above, pp. 14 ff., 57 f., 83 f.)

It is clear that fresh breezes were in his youth beginning to blow in upon the situation in which he found himself, still somewhat stuffy with the traditionalism and barren orthodoxy of a period that had suffered much from defensive religious and political strife, and that the boy and youth sniffed the new atmosphere like the salty breezes from the sea. Hutcheson had not steeped his mind in vain in a Shaftesburyan Hellenism, and his spirit still hovered over Glasgow. History itself, including local Scottish and Glaswegian economic and civic history, were posing questions, as has been earlier indicated, that his alert mind could not allow to pass without some attempt, at least, at their answering.

Clearly his reading of the classics, and especially of the historians among them, was for him something more than a set of exercises in vocabulary and grammar. His early acquaintance with Scots law opened up, for him, questions that were not answered by Stair or Mackenzie or Erskine. His reading of the Old Testament—and, from his apt and frequent quotations from it later, he must have read it well —opened up more questions than who begat whom. It is obvious, above all, that Adam Smith's lectures on 'the history of civil society'* touched off a spark that burned for many a year and that his association with Lord Kames, and occasionally also with Hume, fed fuel to this flame.

Of his lectures during the earlier years of his professorship we know only the general areas covered, but little of the particular lines of his thinking; little, that is, except what can be inferred from the tremendous following he soon came to have among students from near and far—a following that, enthusiastic though it was, cannot be explained wholly by the appeal of his personality and the style of his lecturing—and from the ideas embodied in his *Ranks*, which, as already noted, appeared only ten years after he began to lecture, and which drew heavily upon those classroom lectures. New editions of this work, called for during the next ten years, reflect an enrichment of illustrative material, some improvement in organization and considerable improvement in style of writing, more attention, perhaps, to theoretical foundations and some broadening of historical outlook; but little change in basic ideas. These had clearly taken shape before he was thirty-five.

His *Historical View*, however, published in 1787, twenty-six years after he began to lecture, does give evidence not only of greater maturity of thought, but also of a much broader and more solid historical foundation for his political and sociological speculation. There is a greater concern with political questions and issues in both their historical and their contemporary aspects, and a sense of historical continuity and perspective in the treatment of the phenomena under review that is often distinctly lacking in the earlier work. If we may assume that the materials posthumously published as volumes III and IV of this work were written, or at least cast in their present form, during the last few years of his life—the essay on 'The Progress of Science Relative to Law and Government' certainly was, and most of the others presumably so—these throw considerable light on the

* For this designation, see below, p. 363 n.

development of his thought, particularly on the political, but also somewhat on the economic side, in this late period.

His later publications, above all his anonymous writings (see Appendix II), also evince a flexibility which enabled him to adapt his thinking to the requirements of a changing situation, particularly under the stresses and strains of the repercussions in Great Britain of the Revolution and the war in France.

Student-notes on his lectures—most of them from the late 'eighties, some a decade earlier, a few even later—offer us at once a more systematic view of the body of his thought than do either of his major published works—which address themselves chiefly to somewhat limited problems —and many glimpses, especially in the marginal notes and footnotes, into his reaction to current political and judicial events. They take us at times into the laboratory, as it were, of his thought in the making. But the limited period covered by the notes that have come down to us does not permit many conclusions on the quest before us.

His biographer does inform us that Millar's own lecture notes, which lay before him when he wrote his *Account*, contained much evidence of revisions, additions and other improvements up to 'a very short time before his death' (*Life*, p. xviii). But he gives us no leads as to any light these might throw on the development of his basic ideas.

For help on the nature of such development as of course did take place, dimly as we may be able to trace it in detail, we will do well to recall here some contemporary literary history. Montesquieu's *Spirit of Laws* was first published in 1748, and in English translation two years later when Millar was in his fourth year in the College. Rousseau's first prize-essay appeared while he was still a student (1750) and his *Origin of Inequality* (1754) before he was out of his teens. The *Social Contract* and *Émile* (both 1762) appeared shortly after he began to lecture. Hume's first writings appeared when Millar was but a boy; but his *Essays* appeared in their more final form (1752) when the young man was most likely to be interested in this kind of matter, and his *History* began to appear just a little later (1754) when he perhaps had more time to read. To Kames's ideas on law and history and comparative jurisprudence he was introduced in some measure even before they appeared in his publications. Adam Smith's ideas were familiar to him, as already noted, both from his lectures and from personal conversation, well before the appearance of the *Moral Sentiments* (1759) and of the *Wealth of Nations* (1776), the former twelve years before the appearance of his own *Ranks*, the latter eleven years before that of his *Historical View*. Robertson's *History of Scotland* appeared in 1759, and his theoretically more significant *View of the Progress of Society in Europe* (1769) when

Millar's *Ranks* must already have been well under way. Ferguson's *History of Civil Society* appeared in 1767, four years before Millar's comparable work. Goguet's *Origin of Laws*,* which McCulloch calls 'by far the best specimen ever given to the public of [the] species of history' Stewart called 'theoretical history',† and which Millar used extensively, appeared in 1758, and in English translation the year Millar began to lecture.

All of these works, and many other contemporary publications in the same or similar fields, Millar of course came to know; all but the very earliest of them presumably soon after their appearance. Some of them we know, and others we must assume, influenced him strongly though not always positively. Some, like the works of Paine and Godwin, and presumably also Condorcet, seem either to have left him cold or to have produced a negative reaction. He found them unrealistic, 'unhistorical', visionary.

How much he was influenced by Voltaire's *History* or *Essays on Manners*, or by his *Louis XIV*, is not clear. He makes no mention of them. Strangely enough, the same holds for Rousseau's *Social Contract*‡ and for Turgot's *Inaugural Discourses*, both of which should have interested him very considerably. Vico he probably did not come to know, but even had he known him, he would no doubt have been repelled by his theological dress more than attracted by the solid substance of his ideas.

The strong influence, both early and late, of Smith, Kames and Hume upon his intellectual bent and upon his thinking on particular subjects has already been indicated and can be easily traced in many passages in his writings. It was—certainly in the case of Smith and Hume—fundamental and far-reaching.

The influences that shaped Millar's mind were, however, far from being confined to these literary stimuli. Among non-literary influences may be mentioned, first of all, the judicial scene itself—court decisions, heresy and sedition trials, miscarriages of justice, conflicts between English and Scots law, and his own limited activity at the bar. All these must have raised many questions in his mind on the fundamental nature and the proper functions of the law and of legal and judicial establishments.

More important were his daily observations and his immediate experience of the dynamic economic scene about him, of the rapid economic transformation of his own Scotland, of his own Glasgow, in

---

* Antoine Y. Goguet, Prés. de, *The Origin of Laws, Arts and Science*, etc. (3 vols. Edinburgh, 1761. Translated by Robert Henry *et al*. French original, Paris, 1758).

† See his 'Sketch of the Life and Writings of Adam Smith' prefixed to his 1828 and later editions of the *Wealth of Nations* (1855 edition, p. xxi n.)   ‡ See, however, below, p. 383.

its many social, political and also legal manifestations and implications. To a man of his lively imagination this was undoubtedly of great importance in the shaping of his thought—always aided, of course, by his broad knowledge of history and of literary sources in the way of attempted interpretations of comparable phenomena.

Nor should we for a moment forget the dynamic impact of the current political situation upon his thought. The last of the Jacobite uprisings (Culloden Moor, 1745) was still one of his boyhood memories. Scotland's capital gave way only reluctantly to Westminster as the seat of government and general social and political influence; and Highland influences were strong in Glasgow. The Hanoverian house was not everywhere greeted with enthusiasm. The war with the colonies found many Scotsmen—partly for this reason, but perhaps even more because of many ties of blood, as already indicated—divided, not indeed in their loyalties but in their conflicting emotions and in their scepticism, often, concerning the policies of the Government. Millar was among these. The same applied, with unusual strength in Millar's case, to the experiences, already referred to, connected with the Revolution and the war with France. These raised fundamental questions of a political nature—both practical and theoretical—in Millar's mind.

Two factors that might appear of minor import should not be overlooked here. One is the peculiar character of Scottish education and of the Scottish universities to which attention has already been called (see above, pp. 1, 14); particularly the fact that these universities were not resorts of ease, luxury and polite intercourse for the sons of privilege, intended chiefly for future gentlemen of leisure. Students were prepared to be subjected to rigorous intellectual discipline to prepare them for positions of responsibility; and many of them at least, would in turn be critical of intellectual laxity on the part of their professors. Millar appears to have been peculiarly sensitive to such demands, and this probably had a marked influence upon his own intellectual discipline.

The other is the peculiar character of Scottish religious life. Only two of its many aspects can be briefly touched upon here. First, with all its seeming dogmatism religion in Scotland contained always a distinct moral challenge and had therefore both an individual and a community bearing. Its doctrinal tenets were never blindly accepted but were critically subjected to the tests at once of scripture, of reason and of daily life. And second, such was the strength of adherence to those tenets that anyone who was departing from them—and many did at this time—was under strong pressure to give an account of that departure that met the demands of the fundamental religious expectations of the community. Millar was inclined to be sceptical, or at least indifferent to religious dogma, and was clearly hostile to any form of clericalism; but there is evidence that he was very much alive to the moral demands of religion and could give a good account of his beliefs in keeping with the demands of an enlightened age.

The last factor to be discussed here is too important to be so summarily disposed of; namely, the influence on Millar's thinking, as on that of his contemporaries generally, of the new and widening horizons created by travel, by geographic and ethnographic exploration, particularly among 'primitive' and other distant peoples, and, of course, by the commercial expansion that accompanied them. This factor—not of course confined to this period, much less to Scotland alone—was nothing short of revolutionary in its impact upon men's thinking on problems of human nature, society, politics, the nature and origin and development of social and political institutions, and even on the nature of morals and religion themselves.

Travel and ethnographic accounts cannot, of course, themselves engage us here. They came in great abundance from missionaries, mercantile prospectors and explorers of various kinds. They came from Africa, India, China, Kamchatka and the isles of the Pacific, and of course from the Caribbean and from both Americas. Interest in them was great among the literate, including the philosophically minded as well as the general public. It matters little that many of them were uncritical, and some of them even quite fantastic—accounts of giants, and men with tails, for example. Most of them were genuinely informative and some of them remarkably objective, for all their distortion by European and 'Christian' lenses, in the pictures they gave of customs, manners, religious beliefs and ceremonies. They were often penetrating in their analysis of the social and political structures of strange, heretofore unknown and often extremely 'rude' peoples.* Whether men realized it or not, a new world was here being brought into their ken, a world very different from the experiences upon which they had built their notions of the propriety of things, their norms of conduct, their conceptions of the nature of human nature, of political establishments, and even of religion itself. The philosophically minded were set to thinking on these matters.

* This holds particularly for Lafitau. See notes to *Ranks*, below. The author may be permitted to remark here that despite Miss Lois Whitney's strictures (*Primitivism and the Idea of Progress in English Popular Literature of the Eighteenth Century* (Baltimore, 1934), p. 146 n.), made upon a similar statement by him in his *Adam Ferguson*, he still holds to this view. Lafitau's almost phantastically sweeping historical comparisons, and his biblical-historical literalism, do not detract seriously from his—for the time—remarkable ethnographic descriptions.

That some used these accounts as spring-boards for romantic dreams of a 'state of nature' free from the chains with which civilization had bound the children of nature, or even for luscious dreams of free-love under the palms of Otaheiti,* undisturbed by conscience, is not surprising. Much more important are the reflections they gave rise to among the thoughtful on comparative religion, government, family organization and property institutions, on the 'historical' origin and development of social and political institutions, on the validity of biblical literalism, and in a few brave minds here and there, even on the possibility of a simian origin of the sons of Adam themselves.

Men like Hume, Kames, Smith, Ferguson, Robertson, and outstandingly Millar himself, and others in lesser degree, realized that they were here being confronted not by fairy-tales, legends or theories, but by inescapable facts, by a whole body of factual knowledge, solid and not to be exorcised by argument, and inescapable in its implications. Before these hard facts dogmas of the divine origin of the state, of 'the law of nature' and many similar theories, were forced to give way, often slowly, and reluctantly, but inevitably; new conceptions of man and his universe had to take their place if men were to retain their intellectual integrity.

This new body of knowledge, mixed though it was with error and imperfectly understood, often, was soon related by these men, and again outstandingly by Millar, to the histories of Caesar, Tacitus, Polybius and Thucydides, to the poetry of Homer and to Macpherson's Ossian, to early and later accounts of the manners, customs, laws and religious beliefs of Picts, Scots, Britons and ancient Hebrews. Such comparisons from the living scene seem to have provoked reflection and speculation of a historico-sociological nature as a purely historical knowledge of the past had not previously done. The result was nothing short of revolutionary.

The importance of this factor it would be almost impossible to exaggerate. It was clearly realized by Millar and by some of his contemporaries.

A today little-known writer, W. J. Mickle, in an extended introduction to his translation of the Portuguese national epic, Camoens's *Lusiads*, exalted this on the commercial side into a veritable paean of praise to the civilizing influence of such broadened horizons. He emphasized the beneficent influence of commerce and saw this as most intimately related to 'the enlargement of mind', the improvement of 'every branch of philosophy and rational investigation'. 'The intercourse of mankind is the parent of both.' It is significant

* See especially C. B. Tinker, *Nature's Simple Plan* (Princeton, 1927).

that Millar's name is found among the subscribers to this remarkable volume.*

In the introduction to Cook's *Voyage to the Pacific*, it is suggested that in addition to all the other benefits conferred upon commerce, geography and science by these travels, men should 'not forget another very important object of study for which they have afforded to the speculative philosopher ample materials: I mean the study of human nature in various situations equally interesting as they are uncommon'. For all the instructiveness of Greek and Roman antiquities to the rational mind, the author suggests, one hour spent in 'surveying the numerous specimens of the ingenuity of our new discovered friends brought from the utmost recesses of the globe, to enlarge the British Museum' might teach men more than all the 'proofs of Roman magnificence' uncovered at Herculaneum. There follow speculations on the wide distribution and almost unbelievably distant overseas migrations of the Polynesians, with deductions from similarities and differences of customs, artifacts and language, of the utmost interest to the present-day anthropologist and ethnologist.†

Sir James Mackintosh, in his lecture on 'the law of nature and nations' already quoted (1798) states this even more clearly.

Many dark periods of history have since [Pufendorf's, Grotius's and Locke's time] been explored. Many hitherto unknown regions of the globe have been visited and described by travellers and navigators not less intelligent than intrepid. . . . We can [now] examine almost every variety of character, manners, opinions and feelings and prejudices of mankind into which they can be thrown, either by the rudeness of barbarism or by the capricious corruptions of refinement. . . . History . . . is now a museum, in which specimens of every variety of human nature may be studied. From these great accessions to knowledge, lawgivers and statesmen, but above all moralists and political philosophers, may reap the most important instruction. . . . What former age could have supplied the facts for such a work as that of Montesquieu?‡

Sir James was a great admirer and personal friend of Millar's.

No one of the factors here reviewed, nor all of them taken together, will account fully for the dynamics of the development of Millar's thought. The dialectics of the growth of thought and of the enlargement

---

* W. J. Mickle, Introduction to his translation of Camoens's *Lusiads* (Oxford, 1776). This remarkable piece, and the appearance of Millar's name among the subscribers, was brought to my attention by Mr. Shepperson of the Department of History, Edinburgh.

† Captain James Cook, *Voyage to the Pacific Ocean* (3 vols. London, 1784), vol. I, pp. lxvii ff.; vol. II, bk. iii, ch. xii, pp. 250 ff.

‡ Mackintosh, *Law of Nature and Nations*, pp. 25, 28. Also reprinted in various editions of his works.

of men's ideas are never as simple as that. But if we take all of them together, and remember that they were in interaction one with another
and reacted to by a keen and imaginative mind, we shall be able in
some measure, at least, to account for that development. They should
help us to understand the distance he travelled from the conventionalism
of thought that surrounded his youth to the historico-sociological interpretations and the political liberalism that marked his mature years.

XII

MILLAR'S THEORETICAL POSITION: GENERAL ASPECTS

If one were to attempt to characterize Millar's basic philosophy of history, society and politics by a single phrase, the most apt one would probably be 'evolutionary naturalism'; though we should quickly want to add that his evolutionary naturalism takes on so nearly mechanistic a character and is so much concerned with economic forces and basic sustenance techniques that 'economic determinism', not too sharply defined, comes a close second.

Phrases like 'the natural history of mankind', 'the natural progress of society from rudeness to civilized manners', the 'improvements which gradually arise in the state of society' and their influence upon 'the manners, the laws and the government of a people', 'the effects of commerce and manufactures—upon the morals of a people', seem to come as 'naturally' to his pen as does breathing to their author. Observations on 'property' as 'the foundation of all hereditary influence', the chief basis of 'the distinction of permanent ranks in society' and as 'the principal circumstance that contributes to reduce [men] under civil government' come with equal ease though on a slightly higher reflective level.

Francis Jeffrey, his sympathetic critic, attempts to summarize his position thus:

It was the leading principle . . . of all his speculations on law, morality, government, language, the arts, sciences and manners—that there is nothing produced by arbitrary or accidental causes; that no great change, institution, custom or ocurrence could be ascribed to the character or exertions of an individual, to the temperament or disposition of a nation, to occasional policy, or peculiar wisdom or folly: everything, on the contrary, he held arose spontaneously from the situation of the society, and was suggested or imposed irresistibly by the opportunities or necessities of their condition.*

And again:

It was the one great object of [men like Kames, Smith and Millar] to trace back the history of society to its most simple and universal elements—to resolve almost all that had been ascribed to positive institution into the spontaneous and irresistible development of certain obvious principles—and

* *Edinburgh Review*, vol. III (1803), p. 157.

to show with how little contrivance or political wisdom the most complicated and apparently artificial schemes of policy might have been erected. . . .*

Another contemporary, slightly less sympathetic to Millar's philosophy, charges Millar with following Montesquieu and of holding to a philosophy that

man is everywhere, and in all situations, the same animal; that his conduct is influenced by general laws, and that no considerable change in his condition happens through accidental circumstances, or individual actions, but that all arises necessarily by a uniform and natural progress which can be neither effectually resisted nor prematurely accelerated.†

Such phrases and characterizations come near enough to the heart of Millar's basic theoretical position; but they are too summary, too sweeping, too much in the abstract, to give an adequate, or even a fair picture of the real mind of the man. In general they are true; but in view of his application, in the concrete, of his 'principles' to the realities of both past history and present politics, they can still become almost a caricature.

After all he was only partially the 'mechanist', the 'naturalist', and only in a broad 'theoretical' way the economic determinist, though he was perhaps wholly the evolutionist. To say that he did not recognize 'accidental causes' in history, or the genuine leadership of great men as makers of history rather than merely its pawns, would be to fly in the face of his own words. To interpret his 'determinism' in such a way as to make him insensitive to the moral and political challenges of the great issues of his day would be no longer to describe the teacher of youth and the author of the *Ranks*, of the *Historical View* and particularly of the *Letters of Crito*, but to pursue to an unwarranted extent an abstraction.

If there remains in this an element of the paradox, or even an inner contradiction, it must be remembered that he was no more, in this sense, the philosopher than was his master Adam Smith. He was much more interested in a forceful idea than he was in metaphysical refinement or logical consistency, or in building a 'theory of history'. To the philosophical historian in him, looking backward and trying to explain a course of events, things might look quite different than to the moralist and the politician in him, facing the choices of the present and the challenge of the future.

Beyond this general characterization of Millar's thought, its tendencies can perhaps best be summarized in the statement that in him

---

* *Ibid.* vol. IX (1806), pp. 184 f.   † Tytler, *Memoirs of Kames*, vol. I, pp. 200 f.

the secularization, the rationalization, the naturalization and the socialization seen in a previous chapter to characterize the thought of his century, and that of the 'Augustan Age' of Scotland in particular, found so full and strong an expression as to make him more, perhaps, than any other of its representatives the harbinger of nineteenth-century thought in his field—so far, that is, as that century did not turn its back on the eighteenth-century Enlightenment altogether.

To proceed now to a closer view of his position in a number of fields, we may begin by the summary observation that Millar did not neglect such subjects as human nature, human learning, habit formation and custom, the moral sentiments and conduct norms, and motivational elements in human behaviour. His lecture courses on law and juris-prudence were always prefaced by an orientation in human nature, morals and ethical norms,* and he was possessed of no small measure of insight into these matters. But since he neither tried to build them into a theoretical system nor evinced any considerable originality in such formulations of them as he did attempt, these topics call for no further comment here, unless it be to point out such features as his attention to crowd-phenomena and mob-behaviour, and his understanding of the impact of urbanization, industrialization and modern means of com-munication on human attitudes, on the behaviour and mind and manners of men, and on the breaking down of custom, in cities, as contrasted with behaviour in rural isolation and in the agrarian way of life.†

On the historico-sociological level he does indeed offer us most interesting and illuminating accounts of variant moral codes, changing in adaptation to social and economic changes, 'the effects of commerce and manufactures, of opulence and civilization, upon the morals of a people'.

His political theory, that is his conception of the nature and functions of government and the state, cannot be disposed of so quickly. His treatment of this subject, too, is predominantly historical and sociologi-cal, and not to any marked extent philosophical, and in that sense theoretical. On such basic questions of political theory as the nature and basis of sovereignty, the grounds of obedience and of the consent of the governed, the just distribution of privilege and power, and so on, he has comparatively little to say, and even less that is new. And where he does introduce such topics, it is chiefly by way of historical description and sociological analysis. Only in his attack on vital political problems of the day, such as the extension of the royal prerogative, parliamentary

* *Life*, pp. xxi f., xli ff.; *H.V.*, below, pp. 340-3; also student-notes.
† *H.V.*, below, pp. 338 f., 382; also vol. IV, pp. 148 ff.

reform or the war with France, does he come nearer to a theoretical statement of the ends of government, the sociological basis of Whig and Tory tendencies in politics, etc.* On the origin and development of political institutions, on the economic and other factors underlying such institutions, on the historical transformations of the British constitution, etc., he has much indeed to say.

He does provide us, particularly in the first portion of his 'Lectures on Government'† and in the essay already mentioned (see Pt. IV, Selection II), with a more or less systematic approach to what he calls, at least, the 'principles of government'. The state is, for him, essentially an organ of power. Government, considered as authority organized under law, is intended ideally to serve the purposes of defence against external and internal enemies, and of the furthering of orderly relations among men, of justice, and of the general welfare. Obedience to its commands rests partly on habit and custom, partly on fear, partly on considerations of utility, but in no small measure also on men's worship of their superiors, on their love of ceremony and display, and on their love of the 'beauty of orderly relations'. Property is at once a basis of political power and prestige, and a determiner, to a large extent, of the political constitution. Its protection is a major function of government. Broad lines of policy are distinguished as fundamentally either Tory or Whig. The Tory policy rests chiefly on tradition, sentiment and symbolism, prestige factors and the desire of the privileged classes to maintain the *status quo* from the stand-point of interest. The Whig policy rests chiefly on considerations of utility and on the desire for human improvement. It looks to the future rather than chiefly to the past, and it results naturally from a scientific temper and a more analytical frame of mind.‡

---

* E.g., *H.V.*, below, pp. 350–7.; *Crito*, pp. 3, 9, 12, *et al.*

† We can cite only one example here:

'The first object of mankind is to procure subsistence, to obtain the necessaries, comforts and conveniences of life. Their next aim is to defend their persons and their acquisitions against the attacks of one another.

'It is evident, therefore, that the more inconsiderable the possessions of any people, their political regulation will be the more simple. And the more opulent a nation becomes, its government ought to be the more complicated.

'Property is at the same time the principal source of authority; so that the opulence of a people not only makes them in need of much regulation, but enables them to establish it.

'By tracing the progress of wealth we may thus expect to discover the progress of government.'

He then proceeds to establish four successive states of society: (1) Mere savages, 'people who live by hunting and fishing and by gathering the spontaneous fruits of the earth'; (2) Shepherds; (3) Husbandmen; and (4) Commercial peoples.

From James Millar's notes (in manuscript) on Lecture 3 of 'Lectures on Government'.

‡ See generally Pt. IV, Selection II below, esp. pp. 348–57.

Historically, Millar is quite aware that authority and power are often, if not as a rule, wielded in the interest of individual men, of a class or segment, merely, of the population—for the selfish purpose of the governing rather than for the welfare of the governed.* Again, inequalities, or more exactly inequities in the distribution of privilege and power between the different members or segments of the body politic, are clearly recognized. Institutions do not always serve the ends for which they are ideally intended; and laws themselves are sometimes used to oppress rather than to render justice. Yet fundamentally they liberate rather than enslave; and under liberty the very instruments of law provide the means for its own enlargement and for the advancement of the ideal ends of government.†

Inequalities of right, of power and of privileges enjoyed, moreover, are by no means always the result of oppression, exploitation or the irresponsible use of power. They will rest, often, on human-nature differentials, and on the desire of men to honour superiors. Justice, in a political rather than in a purely ethical sense, will be historically conditioned and relative to the social order, of necessity influenced by prevailing sentiments, habits, values and expectations in the various classes of society, and not based on any absolute conception, as with Godwin, for example. Policy aiming at a more just order of human relations needs to take cognizance of these socio-psychological elements in the situation.

We repeat, Millar's approach to the problems of justice, politics and government is chiefly historical and sociological. What is, in a concrete situation, engages him more than what ought to be; the factors and forces that produce given establishments, and the continuities in their historical development, concern him more than the measure in which perfection is reached. At the back of his historical analysis there is however, always a theoretical frame of reference; back of his educational and political efforts always a set of pragmatic as well as of ideal considerations. In his analysis, government and society are brought so close together, social and political institutions so closely interrelated, controls by custom, habit, example and social pressure so intimately intermingled with controls by law, that we are sometimes led to wonder whether he distinguished between the governmental and the non-governmental with sufficient clarity.

What puts Millar well in advance of his predecessors and contemporaries in the field of political discussion is, first of all, his attempt to delineate historically the development of the British constitution and to reduce it to its fundamental principles, or in his own words, 'to write a

* Below, p. 351.   † See also above, pp. 64 f.

constitutional history of England',* which would revolve about the central theme of the growth and 'diffusion of liberty through a multitude of people, spread over a wide extent of territory' (*H.V.* vol. I, p. 6).

The growth of the idea of liberty, and its implementation politically, he attempts to trace from its presence already in earliest Saxon times to its fullest realization in the Glorious Revolution of 1688—with, however, some set-back in the century that followed, owing to the increase of the royal prerogative, as we have seen elsewhere (above, p. 74). 'Without examining the principles upon which [our present constitution] is founded, we cannot form a just opinion concerning the nature of the superstructure' (*H.V.* vol. I, p. 6).

New is also his clear vision of the close interrelations of economic fact, social fact and political fact,† his clear grasp of the meaning of power relations in society generally, and the persistence of his effort to relate them all in a dynamic, evolutionary developmental pattern.

It is much the same with Millar's position on matters of economic theory. A reading particularly of his essay on 'The Advancement of Manufactures, Commerce and the Arts, etc.', to which the reader is referred (below, Pt. IV, Selection I), will make it clear that he is familiar with the literature of economics and has a firm grasp of its basic concepts; but he is hardly an economist, and his orientation is historical much more than it is theoretical, except in a broadly sociological sense. He accepts the anti-mercantilist principle of free-trade, but apparently with more reservations than were made by Smith. He is fearful of the consequences of monopoly. He is critical of those who would demand a favourable balance of trade at all costs, and of those who confuse bullion, or money in any form, with actual wealth. He understands clearly the nature of trade as a give-and-take for mutual advantage, and the role of supply and demand in fixing both the quantity and the price of commodities.

More than this, he is keenly aware of the significance not only of transportation, but of communication of any kind, and of the free intercourse of men, especially as provided in urban communities, in their economic as well as in their social and political implications. He sees the functional interrelationships and mutual interdependence between extractive industries, manufacturing and commerce, but especially the

---

* Professor Mackie remarks that Millar used this phrase 'forty years before it appeared, as we had supposed for the first time, in the title of Hallam's *Constitutional History of England*' (*History of the University of Glasgow*, p. 214 n.)

† He acknowledges his obligation in these matters to Adam Smith, Thomas Smith (*Commonwealth*) and Harrington (*Oceanea*). See among others, *H.V.* vol. II, pp. 482 ff.; vol. III, pp. 285 ff.; *Ranks*, below, pp. 196 n., 314 n.

dependence of agricultural advancement upon the market demand for farm surplus provided by the growing urban commercial and industrial centres. This, in turn, means for him a division of labour that reaches far beyond the mere production process into the complex structuring of the whole society in its rank make-up, its rural-urban division, etc. More, too, it would seem, than any of his predecessors, unless it be Adam Smith, he sensed the danger for the industrial worker, for the human spirit, for potential class conflict, of an excessive division of labour in the modern factory and its robotization of the industrial worker.*

If Millar made a distinctive contribution to economic theory, rather than merely to the historical and sociological interpretation of economic phenomena this will be found in large measure in his conception of, and strong emphasis upon, the role of capital in the production not merely of goods, but of profit. He distinguished clearly between the 'circulating' and the 'permanent' stock of the merchant and the manufacturer, between productive capital in the form of stocks of goods and machinery, on the one hand—which Smith had particularly emphasized—and, on the other hand, money or investment capital and credit institutions as used chiefly by a distinct group of finance capitalists—'the monied man who lives entirely upon his property, and is obliged to nobody for any part of his maintenance' (shades of Marx and Thorstein Veblen!).†

While Millar, to be sure, views this distinction in the passage referred to only from the point of view of its bearings on the spirit of subserviency and of independence, he no doubt understood it also in its wider bearings. The distinction is not only in itself significant, but Millar's statement of it is an almost prophetic one. Craig comments on the similarity between Millar's opinion on the nature of profit and that of Lauderdale in his *An Inquiry into the Nature and Origin of Public Wealth and into the Means and Causes of its Increase*, advancing as they both do upon the position of Adam Smith. From 'so much intimacy and friendship' and from the 'frequent and unreserved communications of sentiments' between Millar and his former pupil he concludes that the two had presumably worked together on the development of this doctrine. In his *Elements* he remarks: 'It is singular that Dr Smith should have omitted to explain in what manner the employment of capital produces profit otherwise than by the division of labour and the employment of machinery.'‡

* See Pt. IV Selection VI below.   † *H.V.* below, pp. 331 ff., esp. p. 334.

‡ John Craig, *Elements of Political Science* (3 vols. Edinburgh, 1814), vol. II, p. 71; also *Life*, p. xc.

Two elements in Millar's historico-sociological position—not unrelated to each other—deserve particular emphasis here because of their central place in his thinking, though their treatment can be the briefer because the materials are fully presented in his *Ranks*, to which the reader is referred for details. The first is his essentially evolutionistic treatment of the phenomena he seeks to interpret; the second is what may be loosely termed his 'techno-economic determinism'.

Millar everywhere goes on the assumption that 'there is . . . in man a disposition and capacity for improving his condition, by the assertion of which, he is carried on from one degree of advancement to another'; that this assertion revolves, particularly in the earlier stages, about subsistence and the satisfaction of man's material wants, such as food, clothing and shelter, though it increasingly involves also the cultivating of 'the feelings of humanity' and the establishing of 'property, the great source of distinction among individuals' and of government 'for distributing justice'; and that 'there is thus in human society, a natural progress from ignorance to knowledge, and from rude to civilized manners, the several stages of which are usually accompanied with peculiar laws and customs'.

In line with his strong emphasis upon the economic and technological basis of human existence, we note that his stages of this evolution are marked by a hunting and collecting economy, a shepherd or pastoral and nomadic economy, an agricultural economy—usually overlapping considerably with the preceding—and a commercial economy. The latter he divides, though not always explicitly, into commercial and industrial sub-stages—again with all three, industry, trade and agriculture always present, but in varying degrees.

As we saw in an earlier chapter, this evolutionary idea was anything but new, though on reading Millar one is often led to believe it original.

What is new is his application, and the manner of his application of the idea to certain broad areas of social and political content and the inclusion in it of his peculiar line of economic or techno-economic interpretation. These areas are outstandingly those of the relation of the sexes and of the sentiments attaching to sex and marriage, and the matter of 'rank' or status-differentials as these relate at once to the family and its role in the community and to the distribution of power or authority in its more political aspects. The 'intercourse of the sexes'—the term is broadly used—the role of mother-right and female headship or 'gynaikocracy' in very early society,* and later that of father-right or *patria potestas*, monogamy, polygamy and that 'unusual kind of

---

* See especially *Ranks*, below, pp. 198–202. Millar nowhere uses the term 'gynaikocracy' though the term was familiar to him from Lafitau and perhaps others.

polygamy'* today called polyandry, chivalry in feudal times—these are, some of them constantly, others at least frequently, among subjects discussed from this point of view. His clear recognition of the psycho-cultural, and therefore historically variant, rather than bio-psychic, and therefore innate, constant nature of sex-attitudes is, so far as we know, clearly anticipated only by Hume.† The transformations of familial institutions he views as tending, on the whole, to raise the various members of the family 'to a state of freedom and independence'.

Closely related to his conception of the evolution of the family is his view of the evolution and civilizing role of the institution of property. This can be most clearly seen in the quotations which follow.

The changes produced in the manners and customs of the Saxons, by their settlement in Britain, were such as might be expected, from their great change of situation which the people experienced, in passing from the state of shepherds to that of husbandmen. As in following the employment of the latter, they necessarily quitted the wandering life, and took up a fixed resi-dence, they were enabled to acquire *property in land*; with which it is probable they were formerly unacquainted. The introduction of landed property among mankind has uniformly proceeded from the advancement of agri-culture, by which they were led to cultivate the same ground for many years successively; and upon the principle that every man has a right to enjoy the fruit of his own labour, became entitled, first, to the immediate crops they had raised, and afterwards to the future possession of the ground itself, in order that they might obtain the benefit of the improvement which their long cultivation had produced. . . .

This alteration in their circumstances had necessarily a mighty influence upon the conduct of their military operations. As a great part of their property was now incapable of being transported, the inhabitants of each village were induced to fortify, in some degree, the place of their abode, for the preservation of their most valuable effects. . . .

The permanent residence of the people tended likewise to open a regular communication between different villages; the inhabitants of which, by re-maining constantly in the same neighbourhood, were led by degrees to con-tract a more intimate acquaintance. From the acquisition of landed posses-sions, which by their nature are less capable than moveables of being defended by the vigilance and personal prowess of the possessor, the necessity of public interposition, and of public regulations for the security of property, must have been more universally felt. . . .

The introduction of landed property contributed . . . to increase the influence and authority of individuals, by enabling them to maintain upon their estates a greater number of dependents than can be supported by persons whose possessions are merely moveable. The heads or leaders of particular families were thus raised to greater consideration; and, in the

* *Ranks*, below, p. 202.   † *Works*, especially vol. II, pp. 348 ff.; vol. III, pp. 199 ff.

130

respective communities of which they were members, obtained more completely the exclusive direction and management of public affairs. . . .
(*H.V.* vol. i, pp. 74–7.)

Viewing the same subject from a slightly different angle, he remarks
elsewhere, on the pastoral stage, that:

the invention of taming and pasturing cattle, which may be regarded as the
first remarkable improvement in the savage life, is productive of very important alterations in the state and manners of a people, . . . [that] the acquisition of property among shepherds had also a considerable effect upon
the commerce of the sexes, . . . [and] gives rise to a more remarkable and
permanent distinction of ranks. Some persons, by being more industrious or
more fortunate than others, are led in a short time to acquire more numerous
herds and flocks, and are thereby enabled to live in greater affluence, to
maintain a number of servants and retainers, and to increase, in proportion,
their power and dignity. As the superior fortune which is thus acquired by a
single person is apt to remain with his posterity, it creates a train of dependance in those who have been connected with the possessor; and the influence
which it occasions is gradually augmented, and transmitted from one
generation to another. (*Ranks*, below, pp. 203 f.)

Such passages speak clearly for themselves. If there is anything else
that is new in Millar's evolutionary approach, it is that he appears
already to be attempting to overcome the cruder speculative evolutionism of many of his contemporaries in favour of something more
genuinely historical, more clearly documented in historical fact;
though the ideas of 'natural development' and of 'progress' clearly
remain. It may also be noted here that most of his contemporaries, outstandingly Adam Ferguson, hold that that stage of civilization which is
marked by 'great opulence and luxury' tends to contain in itself the
seeds of its own destruction in 'national decadence and decline', after
the pattern of Rome. Millar rejects this idea, at least in part.

The above quotations have already introduced the second topic
which needs here to be illustrated and briefly discussed; namely,
Millar's so-called techno-economic determinism. His position on this
subject, to become so vital a theme of discussion and controversy in the
century that followed, is clearly marked, and, it would seem, an advanced one for his day. But again, let the author first speak for himself.

The distribution of property among any people is the principal circumstance that contributes to reduce them under civil government, and to
determine the form of their political constitution. The poor are naturally
dependent upon the rich, from whom they derive their subsistence; and,
according to the accidental differences of wealth possessed by individuals,
a subordination of ranks is gradually introduced, and different degrees of

power and authority are assumed without opposition, by particular persons, or bestowed upon them by the general voice of society. (*H.V.* vol. I, p. 127.)

. . . In every polished nation, the labour and application of the people is usually so divided, as to produce an endless variety of characters in those who follow different trades and professions. The soldier, the clergyman, the lawyer, the physician, the taylor, the farmer, the smith, the shopkeeper; all those who earn a livelihood by the exercise of separate employments, whether liberal or mechanical, are led, by the different objects in which they are conversant, to contract something peculiar in their behaviour and turn of thinking. . . . (*Ibid.* p. 45.)

And yet once more:

That the advancement of the arts, manufactures and commerce has a tendency to improve the virtue of justice in all its branches, appears indisputable. . . . By commerce and manufactures, the contracts and transactions of a country are multiplied almost without end; the possessions of individuals are extended and varied in proportion. . . . According as the intercourse of society is extended, it requires more and more mutual trust and confidence, which cannot be maintained without the uniform profession and rigid practice of honesty and fair dealing. (*H.V.*, below, p. 384.)

Putting all of these statements together now—and they would be hard to match for their force and clarity, their specific commitment and wealth of sociological suggestion, anywhere in the earlier literature of this subject—there can be no doubt that for Millar man's basic subsistence and sustenance activities, and the institutions aimed chiefly at their enhancement and control, were a primary factor in social causation, and that the ties between the evolution of property-institutions and that of political institutions generally, and of the social and political constitution, were very intimate ones. A few critical observations on his position, are however called for here.

First, it should be noted that Millar's techno-economic 'determinism', if it should be called that at all, is only a part of his more comprehensive conception of 'environmental determinism', his 'mechanistic' interpretation of social and political phenomena, previously discussed; and the strictures applied on it there, apply also here.

Next, we cannot but remark that his position clearly anticipates important elements of the so-called 'historical materialism' of the nineteenth century. It is not surprising that the distinguished German economist and historian of capitalism, Werner Sombart, should have called the *Ranks*, in which this doctrine is most clearly set forth, an 'astonishing' book, and should have ventured the judgement that nineteenth- and even twentieth-century theorists of the techno-economic interpretation of history were able to add nothing but details to what was already present, in embryo at least, in Millar's work. He held, no doubt with some exaggeration, that Millar so completely anticipated Engels's ideas in his mid-nineteenth-century study of the evolution of the family, that the latter contributed not a single idea not already present—again 'at least in embryo'—in the former. He paraphrases the title of the *Ranks* as 'a sociology of power-relations' (*eine Soziologie der Herrschaft*) and speaks of it as containing 'one of the most complete sociologies we have'.*

At the same time, upon closer examination, it is not difficult to point out limitations in Millar's development and use of this 'doctrine'. For example, he failed—at least in his exposition of the matter—to distinguish clearly such different things as basic sustenance activities, technological inventions, occupational roles, the production and distribution of wealth generally, and 'property', which is a moral and legal, almost more than it is a purely economic concept, as factors in social causation. Moreover, the purely economic aspects, the mode-of-work and plane-of-living aspects, the prestige aspects, and the power aspects of rank-distinctions, are in themselves very different things. To throw them all into a single hopper of 'the commercial and industrial arts' as causal factors, robs his argument of some of the convincing power it might otherwise have had.

Further he makes little attempt to develop his many observations into a rounded system, into a systematic theory of social causation, elaborated in theoretical detail and critically scrutinized. He drives the general idea home with a sledge-hammer, as it were; but fails to analyse it under a microscope. Perhaps it is unfair to impute to him any intention of doing so.

Nevertheless, what he does have to say on this subject, as we have attempted to illustrate and as the reader can further check with the sources themselves, remains an important part of Millar's thinking, and we believe registers a distinct advance in the history of social, political and historical interpretation. The possible influence of his ideas on the so-called 'historical materialism' of nineteenth-century thinkers will be briefly touched upon in our concluding chapter. (Below, pp. 157 ff.)

---

* Werner Sombart, 'Die Anfänge der Soziologie', in M. Palyi (ed.), *Hauptprobleme der Soziologie: Erinnerungsgabe an Max Weber* (2 vols. Munich-Leipzig, 1923), vol. I, pp. 11–14. With this evaluation we need not disagree seriously. It is unfortunate, however, that in his reference to Engels's study he fails to point out that this author fits Morgan's ethnographic data into an ideological frame of reference that was completely absent both in Morgan and in Millar.

XIII

MILLAR'S THEORETICAL POSITION: SOCIOLOGICAL ASPECTS

Turning now to aspects of Millar's thought that fall more clearly into sociological categories—the distinction is, of course, a somewhat arbitrary one; a number of topics discussed in the previous chapter could with almost equal propriety have been discussed under the present head—we begin by asking what was Millar's conception of society itself.

The term was, of course, then as now, variously used. It might mean merely fellowship, sociability, association of any kind with fellow human beings. Hume often so used the term. It might mean any more or less clearly marked-off group of people, large or small, permanent or ephemeral. It was often used—frequently by Millar himself—to designate 'civilization', or collective human living on a plane of civility or refinement and under a political order, as contrasted with the 'state of nature', or with 'rudeness' or savagery. It might also mean 'civil' society as distinguished from the political or ecclesiastical order of things.

For Millar it usually meant more than these, however. With or without explicit use of the particular term, Millar had a perfectly clear concept of a collective existence, a social order, a larger grouping of men with many sub-groupings, with a more or less clearly defined structure and with established rules for the performance of functions essential to the well-being of the whole group. It was something organic, functional, diversified with yet a unity in diversity—a product always, in some measure, of intelligence and human purpose. Never, or at least rarely, a product of pure rationality, and always a product in some measure of circumstantial adaptation, it was yet something very different from merely animal society or from a mere 'state of nature'.

Millar recognized clearly society's basis in tradition, the role of custom, the part played by language and by symbolic communication generally. He makes, in fact, much of communication and the enlargement of the means and opportunities for communication as conditions of civilizational advance—as, for example, in advancing urban as contrasted with primitive or simpler rural societies. 'The connections of society are [ever] being enlarged.' New conditions, themselves usually

134

arising out of man's innate 'disposition and capacity for improving his condition' are ever giving rise to new forms of control, legal, governmental and otherwise. 'The progress of commerce and manufactures has a tendency to change the manners and political state of the inhabitants' of a country. Under new conditions 'feudal institutions natural to a rude nation' tend to be abolished and forgotten; and 'upon the venerable stock of our ancient constitution' there are 'engrafted other customs and regulations more consistent with the genius and the circumstances of a civilized and opulent kingdom'.

'Society' is thus conceived in dynamic rather than in static terms, a living web of inter-human relationships, most of them governed by custom and by more or less formalized institutions, and yet ever in process of adaptation. Change, moreover, is never arbitrary or accidental; events are causally related, and change proceeds usually, as we have already seen, in some kind of progressive order of sequence. Under the operation of more or less uniform conditions, certain historical uniformities arise; but since these conditions are never exactly the same, there will also be, everywhere, historical diversity in human societies. The 'philosophical historian'—the term is his—will seek ever to trace 'the influence of early condition' and can establish an underlying national or group character in the various adaptive changes in a given society.

Society is thus for Millar ever involved in a kind of dialectic of growth and transformation, that looking backward it is the function of the historian to trace, looking inward the business of the 'philosophical historian' to attempt to explain and to understand, and looking forward the challenge of the educator and the statesman in some measure, at least, to direct toward desired goals. Millar's view of 'the general state of society'—he frequently uses the term—is undoubtedly very similar to that of Mill in the passage on 'sociological inquiry' referred to and in part quoted above (p. 112).

Any discussion of problems of society in its structural-functional aspects raises the question of the nature and function of social institutions and of the institutional structure of society. Millar does not address himself to an analysis of social institutions in the abstract. He was not trying to write a systematic sociology. But he has a great deal to say about institutions of various kinds in the concrete. Among the institutions most frequently discussed in his writings are governments in general and also particular forms of government, such as monarchical, absolute and limited, representative parliamentary government, etc.; legal and judicial establishments, such as the various kinds of courts, trial by jury, etc.; property in its various forms and the methods of its transmission by sale, primogeniture, entail, etc.; the family and marriage in their various forms; the church with its various forms of belief, worship, ceremonial and legal controls (canon law), and chivalry, as an aspect of feudalism in the Middle Ages.

All of these he views not as something given in nature but as historical productions, generally deeply rooted in custom, involving the co-operation of many individuals in differentiated roles and aiming more or less explicitly at the performance of essential functions in society. He views them as changing in their structure, in their methods of control and sometimes in their very functions themselves with the changing needs and educational levels, of society. These changes he views as, in the main, more or less unconscious adaptive changes; and yet he allows also for modification and improvement by responsible leadership, and for deterioration under irresponsible leadership.

Since some of these institutions have been briefly discussed in other connections, and most of them are treated more fully in his available writings, we can dispense with their further discussion here, where our interest lies chiefly in his conception merely, of these institutions and of their role in society. One exception may be made in a brief discussion of the church as a form of the institutionalization of religion in relation to other social functions.

We have elsewhere spoken of Millar's attitude toward religion and the church from the point of view of his personal philosophy. Here some further observations would seem to be called for on his view of institu-tionalized religion and its functions in society and the state, involving as this does his strongly anti-clerical view of Roman Catholic ecclesias-ticism.

He views religion much more in its social and political manifestations than in terms of personal faith and individual life adjustment. The church is for him an agency of social control much more than a body of believers. Both its doctrines and its ceremonies and often colourful ritual seem to him to serve ends of state and of power rather than truth and righteousness. Its organization, at least in medieval and early modern Europe, is closely integrated with that of the civil government. Canon law is viewed as more or less on a par with civil and municipal law; ecclesiastical courts are as much a part of the structure of govern-ment as are the various secular courts. The rank and power structure of the ecclesiastical hierarchy is very similar to that of the feudal and military hierarchy and rests on much the same foundations of landed and other property.*

In particular, the doctrinal system of the church, and the penances

* *H.V.* vol. I, chs. v, xiii, vol. ii, ch. iv.

resting thereon, he sees as deeply penetrating every corner of the human mind, taking a hold so firm, in fact, that 'the wisdom of after ages' has scarcely been able to break it, and as tending, if not always to enslave it by darkening and emotionally enthralling it, at least to limit the freedom of inquiry and the ready acceptance of new and more humane values. Particularly, 'the Roman Catholic religion may be regarded as a deeply laid system of superstition which took a firmer hold of the human mind than any other that has ever appeared in the world'. But the same tendencies are seldom completely absent even from the Protestant churches.* He does see it as a proper function of religion under any form to support 'the efforts of human laws for the suppression of crimes' as well as to inspire charity to the underprivileged, to inculcate a purer morality and to help maintain and strengthen 'all the bands of human society'.† He notes marked differences in the way in which the Roman Catholic, the Anglican, the Presbyterian and the Independent churches or religious parties in England and Scotland have related themselves to policies of state (see below, Pt. IV, Selection IV).

Millar is far from denying the benevolent, humanizing, stabilizing and even enlightening role of the church in the generally dark and harsh Middle Ages; but he appears always to return with great ease to 'ecclesiastical tyranny', 'ecclesiastical rapacity', to the church's exploitation of the people by appeal to ignorance and superstition and to its mixing even of its benevolent activities with selfish motives. The confessional is made to serve the ends of power; voluntary gifts are gradually transformed into compulsory tithes not only of the produce of the land, but 'of the annual industry as well, and even of the alms given to beggars, as well as of the hire earned by common prostitutes in the exercise of their profession' (*H.V.* vol. I, pp. 150 f.); the laws of marriage, inheritance and testamentary bequests are, for obvious reasons, made a part of canon rather than of civil law, to be administered by clergymen; and serfdom is opposed only where the church's own landed interests are not affected.‡

Two central themes stand out particularly in Millar's analysis of the structure and functions of society: its rank structure and its system of power-relations. The two are very closely related, as indicated in the very title of the first of his major works: *The Origin of the Distinction of Ranks: or, An Inquiry into the Circumstances which Give Rise to Influence and Authority in the Different Members of Society.* This may be due in part to the accident of the topic he chose to write on when he wanted to go before

---

* *H.V.*, below, p. 375.   † *Ranks*, below, p. 311; *Crito*, pp. 50 f.

‡ In general, *H.V.* vol. I, pp. 144, 149 ff., 157 ff.; vol. II, pp. 117, 135–38; vol. III, pp. 87 f.; vol IV, p. 157. *Ranks*, below, pp. 310–12.

the public, but there are reasons to believe that this was considerably more than an 'accident'.

By 'ranks' he means, of course, social classes or status differentials among the different members of the community, whether their lines are sharply or loosely drawn, whether they rest chiefly on an economic or occupational basis or on prestige values and family tradition, and therefore whether they are strictly hereditary or depend rather on individual achievement or merit and reveal, accordingly, a low or a high degree of vertical mobility.

The existence of such rank or status differentials in any but the very lowest orders of society is neither 'argued' nor disapproved of, even when the term 'inequality' is applied to them. As was the case with Adam Smith, the distinction of the lower or inferior, the 'middling' and the superior ranks of society, or variations of these, such as the 'labouring poor', the 'people of middling fortune' and the rich, are simply taken for granted. These enter so casually into their analysis of society as one of its 'natural' aspects, that there is only rarely an implied criticism. Or, if there is criticism, it is criticism of abuses, of 'artificiality', not of the rank structure itself. Differences in rank structure, in the sharpness, the rigidity of the lines that separate class from class, in the 'functional utility' of such stratification, at different times, in different societies—between agrarian and commercial-industrial societies, etc., are clearly recognized. In feudal societies the divisions will be sharply drawn; in commercial societies they will be loosely drawn and will fluctuate easily, and in both commercial and modern agrarian societies the ranks will often be so close together that, as in close-file marching, the toes of one rank will 'gall the kibes'* of the rank immediately before it. Ruling classes may perform vital leadership roles, or they may become parasitic. The lower classes may be reasonably intelligent and spirited in their own way, or they may become 'stupid' and wrapped in a 'thick cloud of ignorance and prejudice'. But a completely classless society is a vain imagination.

Rank distinctions and the power relations that go with them may arise, as Millar sees it, from various conditions and circumstances. They may have their origin in individual merit and achievement, such as military prowess, scholarship, religious leadership, success in the accumulation of land or flocks or other forms of wealth, or in distinctive services to the community. Often, as already indicated, they rest chiefly on family lineage and family position. Again they may rest on sheer domination and the use of force. They will, in many societies at least, also find marked support in the need of men to have someone to

* *H.V.*, below, p. 336

look up to as their superiors or betters. They are usually closely identified with occupational roles. But however they may arise and whatever form they may take on, they must at any rate be reckoned with in any attempt to view the social and political constitution realistically, as well as in any attempt to achieve a more equitable, a more just social order.*

Ranks and classes are, of course, even for Millar not completely interchangeable terms. They both clearly have status implications, but 'classes' and class distinctions begin to have, for Millar already, somewhat of an oppositional, and exploited-exploiting, an invidious character not always inherent in 'ranks' as such; though in the main, as already indicated, he looks upon the division of society into classes as arising 'from the natural course of things' in the evolution of society, when a given set of conditions prevail, and as tending historically toward a fourfold division, whether it be in Western Europe, in the Roman empire, in Egypt or in India. In early Anglo-Saxon society he distinguishes three classes: the military, the peasantry and the clergy (*H.V.* vol. I, pp. 134–40). In feudal society the whole English people came to be distinguished into four great classes; which from their differences in rank or employment, in characters and habits of living—elsewhere he adds, 'by their peculiar education, by their separate views of interest and by their professional character and manners'—were separated and kept at a distance from one another and acquired 'very different manners and ways of thinking'. These classes were: the military; the husbandman, whether peasant or husbandman of a higher order; the artisan, craftsman and the manufacturer, the tradesmen among them often becoming traders; and the clergy. Except for the latter, where celibacy prevails, children in these orders 'were commonly disposed to follow that way of life with which they had been early acquainted', being 'bred up in most cases for their father's employment before they could have any opportunity of comparing it with any other', their status thus tending to become hereditary. (*H.V.* vol. I, pp. 322–26.)

In modern industrial and commercial societies this order of ranks tends, in his thinking, toward a threefold division of society 'into landlords, capitalists and labourers', following the three different sources of wealth (*H.V.*, below, p. 331). With improvements in husbandry, however, farmers tend to approximate in circumstances to the manufacturers, and we tend to get two great classes instead of three: owners and wage-earners or labourers (pp. 334 f.). Millar also speaks frequently of the 'lower orders', or the 'labouring classes', the 'middling ranks', consisting chiefly of professional people and others with some

* E.g., *H.V.* vol. IV, pp. 155–61, also, below, pp. 381 f.

education, and the 'superior classes', made up more or less of the hereditary aristocracy. Or again in 'the dark ages', of 'two great classes, of which one is 'distinguished by knowledge and intelligence, the other by the opposite qualities'. The clergy chiefly formed the one; the laity, the military and the peasantry 'both equally sunk in ignorance and superstition, composed the other' (*H.V.* vol. IV, pp. 156 f.).

Next, inter-human relations, or at least those areas of the relations of man to man upon which he focuses his particular attention, are viewed by him as predominantly power-relations. Man is forever seeking power and authority over his fellow-men, whether it be chiefly in the way of prestige and special privilege and of a kind of homage effectively commanded; in the way of dominance, mastery and control; or in the way of exploitation of man by his fellow-men. Whether such dominion is exerted for purely personal satisfactions, or whether it becomes an instrument of the good order of the community, often freely submitted to by those dominated; whether it be exerted in the family, in the master-servant household relation, in the larger kinship group, in the more personal relations of community life, or in a whole nation—it remains still a power-relationship. As the abler, the more aggressive, the more favourably circumstanced succeed in imposing their will upon their opposites, superior-inferior relations, dominance and subordination, become a major aspect of the web of inter-human relations we call society, and, in particular, political society.

Furthermore, these power-relations, these social controls effectively exerted and often repeated, tend ever to become habitual, formalized, institutionalized, publicly recognized, and in the end publicly enforced through various kinds of establishment. Even ecclesiastical establishments may, by doctrinal tyrannies and by priestly bindings of the consciences of men no less than by canon law, wield controls no less powerful than those of the most absolute secular monarch. However wielded, and by whomsoever wielded, and for what purposes soever wielded, these controls remain still power-relations in human society.

Two important aspects of Millar's sociological thinking can be quickly disposed of here, the one because it has already, in effect, been discussed elsewhere, for example in the discussion of his so-called 'economic determinism'; the other because it is so very general in character and so completely pervades nearly all of his thinking as to make separate treatment of it here unnecessary if not in fact impossible. We refer to his conception of social causation and to his almost universal tendency toward empirical generalization in matters relating to society and culture.

Millar does not, of course, use the term 'social causation', or attempt to formulate a rounded theory of such causation, as we have already indicated elsewhere; but he is dealing with the concept all the time. It is involved in his very conception of natural law, in the empirical sense, in humanistic and social phenomena, and in his whole philosophy of the causal-relatedness, or of what Hume called 'necessity' in human actions and in the world of history. It pervades his outlook everywhere and is manifested in such phrases as the following: 'in searching for the causes of'; 'the effect of commerce, manufactures, etc. on the morals of a people'; 'the political consequences of the revolution'; 'the tendency of the advancement [of manufactures, etc.] to diffuse a spirit of liberty and independence'; 'the appetite of the sexes . . . is in the human species productive of sentiments and affections which are of great consequence to the general intercourse of society'.

Beyond such references, we need only call attention to the fact that Millar was well aware of the principle of multiple causation. In the very first paragraph of the introduction to the *Ranks*, for example, he lists a remarkable variety of factors producing varieties in laws, customs, and so on; and in the rest of that introduction he makes very clear that he rates human and cultural factors considerably higher than purely environmental or climatic factors, for example.

His marked tendency toward empirical generalization, too, so completely pervades his whole intellectual effort as to call for little special treatment here. Here are a few significant illustrations: 'In every human society there is a natural progress from ignorance to knowledge'; 'when men of inferior condition are enabled to live in affluence by their own industry . . . there we may expect that ideas of liberty will be universally diffused'; 'in every polished nation the labour and application of the people is usually so divided as to produce an endless variety of characters in those who follow the different trades and professions'; 'the diversions and amusements of any people are usually conformable to the progress they have made in the common arts of life'.

These examples will serve to illustrate at once Millar's flair for empirical generalization in matters of sociological interest, and something of the range of the problems that interested him. That some of his generalizations may not have stood the test of fuller knowledge, while others may strike us today as trite observations rather than discoveries, and that his attempted explanations may often over-simplify the problems before him, matters but little. It is the *Fragestellung*, the problems to which he addresses himself, the lines of his attack upon these problems, and the manner in which he brings them into a new focus of attention, that really matter.

Other areas of Millar's sociological interest could readily be singled out for illustration and discussion here, such as the relations of the sexes, the varieties of familial and property institutions and their evolutionary transformations; the impact of rural-agrarian and urban-industrial environments, respectively, on individual and collective behaviour; the influence of occupations generally, and of an excessive division of labour in particular, in industrial society, on behaviour patterns, on inter-human relations, on the spirit of liberty; the role of religious beliefs, practices and institutions in social control. But the matters discussed above will suffice to indicate his general sociological orientation.

Without developing any of them at this point, attention needs, however, still to be called here to at least those further aspects of his sociological analysis only incidentally if at all touched upon above.

First, Millar always distinguished clearly between nature and nurture, between the biological foundations and the cultural super-structure of the behaviour of men in society. Habit, custom, conscious and unconscious imitation, language, the communication of ideas, education, are for him of the very nature and making of human society. Society is a historical, and not in any large measure in the biological sense a 'natural' phenomenon.

Further, it needs to be re-emphasized here how very largely his political discussion, that is, his discussion of the nature and functions and policies of government—which are in a way his central theme—is everywhere given a sociological setting. Government rests on opinion, he is heard repeatedly to say (especially in *H.V.* vol. III, p. 329), and to be at all effective it must either be brought into accord with opinion or opinion must be brought into accord with the necessities of public policy. Government is the governing of men by men, not the rule over some kind of a vague 'public' by some kind of super-state. The criterion for the judging of any public policy, the justification for the very existence of a government, is service to the whole community, the long-range and far-sighted promotion of the general welfare, that is the good of a society of men. Political institutions are in their very nature social institutions, and the general state of society will be reflected in its government.*

Two elements essential to any rounded sociological scheme of things are, it must be admitted, considerably neglected, or at least under-emphasized in his thinking. One is the role of leadership in society, the extent to which men of insight, vision, ability and courage impress their stamp upon society. While not denying the fact, his over-all philosophy leads him, as we have already seen, to minimize it in his more theoretical analysis.

* *H.V.* vol. III, pp. 328 f.; below, pp. 351 ff.; *Crito*, p. 9.

The other is the role and importance of values to any understanding of human society. Again, he is far from denying the importance of values in a practical way. After all, economic well-being, the good of one's fellow-men, liberty, love of country, the sacredness of human personality—all of which he esteemed very highly—are such values of the highest order; but, as in the case of leadership, his theoretical scheme does not have much of a place for them.

Finally, it deserves to be remarked here, by way of reverting to an earlier observation on the movement of Millar's thought from law to sociological analysis, that in the final analysis he did not move as far from his original assignment as would on the surface appear. His selection of topics for discussion, his engrossment in power-relations in human society, and in social control, his concern with property and with authority in the family, and frequently even the manner of his treatment of non-juridical questions under discussion, clearly betray their origin in an early concern with problems of law and its function in the social order.

As a kind of postscript to the above, a few observations would seem to be called for here on Millar's historical method.

That his whole approach was essentially a historical one, has been emphasized throughout this analysis. That he drew heavily upon historical sources of various kinds can be easily demonstrated not only in the *Historical View* but in the *Ranks* as well. A reviewer in the *Critical Review* on the appearance of the latter remarks particularly its firm grounding in historical fact, without which 'speculations [and] conclusions with regard to the powers and dispositions of the human mind . . . will be vain and fruitless. . . . A careful perusal of many valuable historical monuments has furnished him with a variety of facts, and on these he founded his conclusions.'*

While his writings must in the end perhaps be considered political and sociological treatises more than histories—even the *Historical View* was just that, a sweeping over-all view of the trends of an institutional development, of the development of lines of public policy, rather than a detailed historical account of events and the actions of men, or an intensive historical analysis of a particular institution—they were never unhistorical. Less the antiquarian than the man of broad scholarship, much less the annalist than the analyst, not without his biases on such matters as the advance of the royal prerogative or the abuses of ecclesiastical power, their author yet drew his materials for analysis and generalization from a wide range of both primary and secondary historical sources and used those sources critically—being careful both

* *Critical Review*, vol. xxxi (1771), pp. 432f.

of his facts and of their interpretation, and of the conclusions he drew
from them.*

If his 'history' still looks toward what Professor Becker would call
'the heavenly city',† that is, toward the embodiment of social, moral and
political ideals and their gradual realization on earth, he was in that
only a child of his century, but not therefore less the historian for it.
He could not deny his belief in man's essential rationality, in the autonomy and dignity of human personality, in the progressive realization
of the ideal of liberty in the life of men and of nations.

Perhaps most important of all, Millar brings the experience of the
past and his observations upon the contemporary scene into the closest
possible relations one with the other: he makes history contribute toward an understanding of the present; he makes his experience of the
social, economic and political world in which he lived contribute toward
a deepening of his understanding of history and of the historical process.

Such, then, are the main lines of Millar's thinking on problems of
man and society, of government and economy, and of the historical
process generally and its interpretation. The summary observations of
these two chapters should provide a reasonably adequate introduction
to his writings themselves, some of which are being reproduced in this
volume.

---

* For Millar's own statement of sources and their use, see latter part of Introduction to
the *Ranks*. An illustration will be found in his treatment of the discovery of the *Institutes* and
Pandects of Justinian at Amalfi in 1137. Indirect criticism of Hume's evaluation of this
event (*History of England*, ch. XXIII, summation near end), he presents evidence of earlier
knowledge in the West of Justinian's work (*H.V.* vol. II, p. 321, and student-notes), and
attaches importance less to the rediscovery of Justinian than to the rise of a new interest in
problems of law at this time and the applicability men found of the Roman law to contemporary institutions. Other examples are his recognition of the meagreness of sources for
certain periods (*H.V.* vol. I, p. 179; vol. III, p. 15); the bigotry and narrowness of outlook of
the ecclesiastical annalists (*H.V.* vol. I, p. 179; vol. II, p. 215); and the observation that
changes sometimes take place so slowly and so gradually as to be easily overlooked by the
annalists (*H.V.* vol. I, p. 300).

† Carl L. Becker, *The Heavenly City of the Eighteenth Century Philosophers* (New Haven, 1932).

XIV

MILLAR'S IMPACT ON LATER THINKERS

We have treated our subject thus far as though a man's thought could be separated from his life's activities, and the thought of one man from the stream of thought that makes up the thinking of many, both at a given moment and down through the course of time. In reality, of course, neither of these is possible except as an expedient of analysis and of communication. In this concluding chapter Millar's life and thought will be viewed together again; and viewed in the larger perspective of a historical movement, as part of a web in the weaving, as it were, where neither the separate threads of the woof nor the warp that binds them in a time sequence can always be clearly distinguished. The question needs, however, still, to be asked here, What reception did his ideas meet with, what influence of an abiding character did his lectures and his publications wield on his contemporaries and on those who thought and wrote on similar subjects after him? The question is much easier to ask than to answer satisfactorily.

The first difficulty lies in the very nature of the problem before us. How can we hope to 'measure' or even otherwise to assess the impact of such an intangible as an 'idea', or of an idea-complex or mode of thinking, on another idea or idea-complex or on the mode of thinking of after-generations? The more so when we remember that there are a number of contributors, as there always will be, to a given idea-complex, and an even far greater number of respondents, each in his own way, to the stimulus it in turn provides? And what when that body of ideas becomes after a while a kind of unconscious assumption, something that is 'in the air'? Certainly the mere excellence of an idea or of a book, the originality or even the general validity of a theoretical position, are no guarantee of their being widely accepted or of their strongly influencing the thought of other men.

In Millar's case the problem is complicated by the fact that his published works went out of the public view rather earlier than one should have expected from the acclaim they had met during his lifetime. Did his ideas therefore cease to wield any influence at all? Certainly the allegation that his works were very soon completely forgotten— *gänzlich verschollen* in Werner Sombart's forceful phrase, 'died out to the last echo', as it were—need not be accepted without qualification, as we shall see below; but neither can it be lightly dismissed. Let us look at some of these allegations.

Some twenty-eight years after Millar's death the Scottish economist McCulloch speaks of his *Historical View* as 'a work over-rated when it first appeared, and now too much neglected'.*

Cosmo Innes, Professor of History at Edinburgh, writing in 1854, remarks that 'his historical work and writing on the philosophy of history are almost forgotten [despite a] merit that should have preserved them'; that a variety of circumstances, including 'a style without life' and a 'limited' philosophy 'condemned them to a premature oblivion'.†
McLennan, another Scotsman, tells us in his study of primitive marriage about two decades later, that he rediscovered Millar's *Ranks* just a hundred years after its publication, as a remarkable work that had 'gone out of sight'.‡

More recently the distinguished German sociologist and economic historian whose '*gänzlich verschollen*' we have just cited, remarks of the *Ranks* at least, that in spite of its astonishing anticipations of nine-teenth-century historical and sociological thought, and in spite of a number of translations and considerable commentary notice at the time, it soon disappeared completely from public view.§

Moreover, the reader who will take the pains to examine the histories of philosophy and of social and political theory by modern scholars, or the encyclopedias of the social sciences,‖ or who will but check the indexes of modern works of scholarship dealing with the subjects Millar dealt with, will seldom indeed find his name so much as men-tioned there. Even Flint, the Scottish historian of the philosophy of history, who knew the literature of his country well, fails to make any mention of him. There can be no doubting that the hopes and ex-pectations of his contemporaries that his works would 'go through many editions', that they 'would long continue to demand the respect and admiration of his readers', and that his influence both on political action and on political thought would be a far-reaching and lasting one, were destined to be disappointed. This situation calls for closer examina-tion.

To the extent that this 'going out of sight' was real rather than merely alleged, how can we most satisfactorily explain it?

In the first place, such 'historical slighting' is not at all unusual and

---

* *Op. cit.* p. iv (see above, p. 116 n).
† C. Innes, *Memoirs of Thomas Thomson*, pp. 10 f.
‡ J. F. McLennan, *Studies in Ancient History* (London, 1876), p. 420 n.
§ *Op. cit.* (see above, p. 133 n).
‖ Major exceptions are *Biographie Universelle: Ancienne et Moderne* (Michaud, Paris), and *Nouvelle Biographie Générale* (Paris, 1862 f.). Also the writings of Pitirim Sorokin.

should not surprise us overmuch. Mackintosh's *Vindiciae Gallicae*, which Reid once called 'one of the most ingenious essays in political philosophy he had ever met with',* was soon forgotten after the storm of the French Revolution had subsided—perhaps because its purpose had been accomplished—while Burke's *Reflections* on the same subject are still read after one and two-thirds centuries, for reasons quite other than those that attracted attention to them at the time. Ferguson's *History of Civil Society* which history in the long run rated much higher than his *Roman Republic*, was, except in Germany, where it appears to have had its strongest and most lasting influence, comparatively neglected, while the latter continued long to be read. Again, Adam Smith himself no doubt placed a far greater value on the socio-psychological, socio-historic and genuinely sociological elements in his writing than on his doctrines of 'the invisible hand', 'the impartial spectator', or his descriptions of the process of manufacturing a pin or a nail. Yet the former are largely forgotten, if they were ever much noticed at all, again except in Germany, while the latter are still frequently on the lips of men who have never read a page of his writing. And his insistence that 'consumption is the sole end and purpose of production; and [that] the interest of the producer ought to be attended to only so far as it may be necessary for promoting that of the consumer'† was silently passed over by those who made most of his theory of production and swore by his doctrine of laissez faire—often misinterpreted at that. So, too, Steuart's *Political Economy*, certainly a work of the highest merit in itself, but out of line with the growing popularity of *laissez faire* doctrines, went largely unnoticed, while the *Wealth of Nations* caught on tremendously.

Many circumstances and conditions, historical, psychological, political and otherwise, will determine the acceptance or non-acceptance of an idea or a book. Inherent merit is only one of them. Literary style may loom large with one generation of readers, but appear very secondary to another. Vital political ideas that have a strong appeal at one moment, may meet with an indifferent or even hostile reception with a turn of political fortunes.

Millar's so-called 'love of system', a fondness for broad generalization, 'philosophical' interpretations and more sweeping, panoramic views of history, may well have brought him into disfavour with a rising generation of scholars more interested in the intensive cultivation of narrower fields. Cosmo Innes's charge of a 'limited philosophy' may have

---

* Sir James Mackintosh, *Vindiciae Gallicae* (London, 1791). See also Frazer, *Thomas Reid* (above, p. 54 n.).

† *Wealth of Nations* (Cannan edition), vol. II, p. 159.

pointed to real limitations in Millar's naturalistic, evolutionary and environmental interpretations. But the same philosophy may also have had the merit, or demerit, of disturbing the complacency of men who enjoyed special privileges under the existing order.

We refer here not so much to any particular political tenets of Millar's, as to his substitution of the general 'principle of utility', or of a historical, functional, sociological analysis, for the principle of tradition, prescription, authority, for 'the right divine of kings to govern ill'.*

As the present author has elsewhere put it, 'even the most non-political elements in his work, his historical, analytical, functional approach to the problems of law, government and society, contained a threat to the established order of things that was clearly recognized by men of insight, and those responsible for the education of future leaders did their best to provide them with another diet'.† Men who predicted, however wrongly, that 'so jacobinical and scurrilous a work [as the first number of the *Edinburgh Review*] could not possibly reach a third number'‡ would hardly have considered Millar's writings proper material to be placed in the hands of youth.

Mention must also be made here of a not unrelated influence unfavourable to the acceptance of Millar's ideas—a rising tide of religious conservatism. By the end of the century 'moderatism' in religious thought was nearing low tide, and, in the words of a recent historian, 'the barren orthodoxy dear to a former generation soon resumed its sway . . . the light which had given so sustained a brilliance [in Scotland] to literature, and that other and newer light toward which the martyrs of her political freedom were struggling, had both gone out'.§

Not unrelated to this religious and political conservatism, though not always in itself illiberal, was another influence that may go farther than any other toward explaining the reaction of the early nineteenth century to the challenge of Millar's thought, and in fact to the whole movement of thought designated by Dugald Stewart as 'theoretical history'. We refer to the rise of Romanticism, and in particular to what

---

* *H.V.*, below, pp. 354 f.; and in general, Pt. IV, Selection II.

† Lehmann, 'John Millar: Historical Sociologist', in *British Journal of Sociology*, vol. II. no. 1 (March, 1952), pp. 30–46. See on this post-French-Revolutionary reaction also, J. Bonar, *Malthus and his Work* (London, 1885), p. 27: 'The close of the [18th] century saw the troubles of a European war added to the list [of politically retarding influences] and the tide of political reform ebbed for forty years (1792–1832). Because the French reform had gone too far, the English reform was not allowed to take its first steps.'

‡ See Innes, *op. cit.* p. 243.

§ Mathieson, *The Awakening of Scotland*, p. 241. This statement is preceded by, 'In the panic caused by the bloodshed and anarchy of the Revolution men saw in every liberal theologian a potential Jacobin: . . .'

might be called either 'historical romanticism' or 'romantic historicism' depending on the point of emphasis. To this we shall return later.

But are we not here, in some measure at least, fighting windmills? Did Millar really go as quickly and as completely 'out of sight' as has been alleged? Let us look at the record.

Millar's impact upon his contemporaries, and in particular upon his students, both personally and through his ideas, has been described earlier in this study, and what was said there needs not to be repeated here. The reader may, however, be reminded of these facts and considerations:

First, the more personal impact of the man can no more be sharply separated from the more impersonal impact of his thought than his moral outlook or philosophy of life and his political tenets can be from his historical, sociological and political analysis in its more theoretical aspects. Millar clearly taught his students to think and gave them food for thought as well as inspiring them to nobler aspirations and to liberal lines of action.

Next, many of his students, and others who had come under his influence, entered public life, as we have seen, as authors, as literary critics, as 'writers' and advocates of great distinction, a goodly number as occupants of benches in the highest courts of the land, as members of Parliament in both houses, and other high offices of state. In some cases there is clear evidence, in others at least a strong presumption, that they were to no small extent influenced by their former teacher in their writings, in their activities, in their conduct of office, and in their application of legal and political principles to the latter. His influence, along with that of his younger contemporary and in some ways rival, Dugald Stewart,* on Francis Jeffrey, George Bell, Moncreiff and other of the early Edinburgh Reviewers,† and the influence, in turn, of that most able and influential of all journals of literary and political opinion in Great Britain at that time‡ upon the movement that resulted in 1832 in the reform of Parliament, can hardly be questioned. His influence on such opponents of Tory repression in the 1790's and proponents of parliamentary reform as Lauderdale, both the elder and younger Lansdownes, Melbourne and others was publicly admitted.

Finally it should be noted that many of these men lived and worked, and carried both the memory of the man and the impact of his thought well toward the middle, and in a few cases even beyond the middle of the nineteenth century.

---

* See D. Stewart, *Collected Works*, vol. x, pp. l–lv (Memoir by J. Veitch).

† See esp. above, pp. 36 ff. and p. 21. Also, Rae, *Adam Smith*, pp. 53 f.

‡ G. N. Trevelyan, *Illustrated English Social History* (4 vols. London, 1942), vol. III, p. 157.

A Glasgow student speaks of Millar in a college publication some sixteen years after his death, not in an intended eulogy but in a paper on environmental and hereditary factors, respectively, in the determination of human achievement, as 'one of the greatest men Scotland ever produced'. If this is youthful exaggeration, it is nevertheless revealing.*

Before this, in 1808, Sir James Mackintosh, a man of truly Burkean stature and a personal friend of Millar's (Hay, *Inaugural Addresses*, p. 33) writes to a newly elected professor of history at Edinburgh, '. . . You come after Hume and Montesquieu; and let me strongly recommend to you the books of Professor Millar—his excellent treatise *On Ranks*, and even his tedious and unequal work on *The English Government*, which contains at least an excellent half volume of original matter' (*Memoirs* (Boston, 1853 ed.), vol. 1, p. 416).

The younger Marquis of Lansdowne, a distinguished Member of Parliament, and presumably though not quite certainly a former student, names Millar in fond recollection in a rectorial address in 1830, among 'those illustrious names' and 'beacons of light' who not only were 'ornaments' of their University, but who contributed 'to the progress of knowledge', to 'an enlargement of feeling and action' and toward 'bringing men and countries much closer to each other' until they 'are no longer the property merely of this city and this country, but have become the property of the world' and 'have created a fame which, far from being abated by the hand of time is now extending itself in countries almost totally unknown when the living presence of these eminent persons graced the scenes in which [he was then speaking]'.†

In 1837 Peter Mackenzie, author among other things of the life of martyr Muir, and perhaps too ardent a defender of liberty to be a completely unbiased witness, speaks still of Millar as 'one of the ablest jurists this country ever produced' and as one whose 'splendid writings are now admired by every lover of liberty throughout Europe'.‡

As late as 1849 the historian Macaulay in his rectorial address names Millar along with only such other names as Simson, Adam Smith, Black and Reid as among the most 'illustrious men who . . . taught and learned wisdom' at Glasgow in the eighteenth century.§

Even later, in 1860, the distinguished author and jurist, Henry Brougham, then elderly, still remembers the man who had strongly stimulated him in youth as the author who 'traced the history of the

---

* *The Student: a periodical paper* (Glasgow, 1817), pp. 39 f. (University of Glasgow Library).
† Hay, *Inaugural Addresses*, p. 96.
‡ Peter Mackenzie, *Life of Thomas Muir* (Glasgow, 1831), pp. vi f. Also above, p. 32.
§ Thomas B. Macaulay, 'Rectorial Address', 21 March 1849. Bound in with some editions of Hay, *Inaugural Addresses*.

constitution upon principles, freed from vulgar errors, empirical as well as absolutist'.* He had elsewhere spoken of his *Historical View* as an excellent work, though in many parts speculative and even fanciful',† and of Millar himself as, in his judgement, 'a man of strong understanding, well disciplined by study, and above all by legal study; . . . a mind of more vigour and manly cast [than President Montesquieu]'.‡

If we look now for concrete evidence of Millar's influence on the legal, social and political thought of those who wrote after him, rather than merely for echoes of his fame, we have already seen evidence of this in the work of such men as Baron Hume, the Earl of Lauderdale, Thomas Thomson and James Reddie,§ and we have heard Tytler testify that 'there were few who attended [his] lectures without an increase of knowledge; or who perused his writings without deriving from them much information' (above, p. 36); and Ramsay of Ochtertyre that 'it is agreed that he made many excellent scholars' (*ibid.*). Among 'disciples by indirection' we should certainly also include Brougham, Mackintosh, Francis Jeffrey and George Bell.

Nowhere in published works, though, is Millar's influence more clearly traceable than in Craig's *Elements of Political Science*.‖ This work, in three volumes (1814), reflects that influence at once in its general conception, in the particular legal, political and economic tenets adhered to, in the scope and organization of subjects treated, especially in the first volume, in the author's repeated references to his uncle's works and in specific acknowledgement of indebtedness to his lectures on jurisprudence. There is little evidence, however, that Craig's work was widely influential in his time or at any later time.

Three men of far greater influence on the political thought of a later day need, however, to be mentioned here. That Ricardo was greatly influenced in his thinking by Millar would be a hazardous claim indeed. It is interesting to note, however, that his friend James Mill strongly recommended the reading of Millar to him and that Ricardo later informed him that he had read Millar with great pleasure. Also his library is known to have contained a copy of Millar's *Ranks*.¶

James Mill himself, however, had come strongly under his influence, as we have already seen. He no doubt recommended his reading to

* Quoted in Murray, *op. cit.* p. 314.   § See above, pp. 36 ff.
† *The British Constitution* (London, 1861), p. 130 n.
‡ H. Brougham, *Political Philosophy* (3 vols. London, 1846), vol. III, pp. 15 f. Also, p. 41.
‖ John Craig, *Elements of Political Science* (3 vols. Edinburgh, 1814). See especially vol. I, pp. 198 ff. 214, 244; vol. II, pp. 70 f.

¶ David Ricardo, *Works and Correspondence* (Cambridge, 1952), vol. VII, pp. 195–97, 382 f. My attention was first called to these letters by Mr Meek of Glasgow.

other of his friends than Ricardo. In his history of India* he repeatedly pays tribute to Millar and conceives his broadly evolutionary and civilizational approach, particularly in Part II of that work, which Mill's biographer Bain calls a 'grand sociological display',† as done in the Millar tradition. In fact he views Millar there as a pioneer in the application of this fruitful and promising approach to problems of politics and history, and regrets that he has not yet found many imitators in it.

Millar's works were also among those included in the rather heavy diet imposed by his father on the young John Stuart Mill, as we learn from the *Autobiography*. Duncan Forbes calls the *Historical View* 'the text-book of English constitutional history used in the education of John Mill, who preferred Millar to Hallam'.‡ In fact in a—to be sure somewhat youthful—review, Mill speaks of Millar as 'perhaps the greatest of philosophical inquirers' into the history of past ages, quotes his *Ranks* at some length on the role of sex and of the sexes in savage, barbarian and civilized societies, and cites his *Historical View* as the only work in English known to the reviewer that deals at all adequately and truthfully, though far too sketchily, with the subject of chivalry and its setting in medieval feudal institutions. He sees in Millar 'almost the only writer we have [in English] who has made the Middle Ages a subject of philosophical investigation'. By comparison Hallam comes off very badly.§

Later, in a letter to Comte,‖ Mill counts himself with pride in the line of the Scottish thinkers, including Millar, and Comte in replying rejoices in this information and acknowledges his own obligation to these thinkers so near of kin, in many ways, to the French.

From his essay on Comte and from this personal correspondence, from a passage earlier quoted (above, p. 112 n), from his 'Logic of the Social Sciences', from his essays on 'Civilization' and 'A Few Observations on the French Revolution',¶ and other expressions of his thought

---

* James Mill, *History of British India* (9 vols. 4th edition, London, 1848), vol. II, p. 156; vol. I, pp. 182 f., 196, 445 f. See also Bain, *James Mill* and Mill's translation of Charles Villers, *The Spirit and Influence of the Reformation of Luther*, etc. (London, 1805), pp. 176 f., 232–7 where there are quotations from both the *Ranks* and the *Historical View*. Phrases like these occur: 'that sagacious contemplator of the progress of society'; 'the usual sagacity of that eminent author'; 'who has with so much knowledge and sagacity illustrated English history'.

† Bain, *James Mill*, p. 176 f.   ‡ D. Forbes, *op. cit.* (above, p. 91 n.), p. 669.

§ *Westminster Review*, vol. VI (1826), pp. 95 f., 102 f.

‖ *Lettres inédites de John Stuart Mill à Auguste Comte* (Paris, 1899), pp. 151, 162. Also pp. 356, 358, 366.

¶ J. S. Mill, *Dissertations and Discourses Political, Philosophical and Historical* (4 vols. London, 1859 and other editions).

that might be cited, it is clear that Mill was not only on the threshold of
nineteenth-century sociology, but had passed well over its threshold.
There are good reasons, therefore, to believe that Millar's influence on
the younger Mill, too, was a not inconsiderable one. One author* finds
similarities of the style of the two men that would point in the same
direction. Forbes, in the article already cited, no doubt rightly attributes
importance to Millar 'because in the development of the liberal "science
of history" he forms a link between Adam Smith and the Utilitarians'.†

Both of the Mills were thus undoubtedly among the more important
runners bearing on the torch of social and political thought that Millar
had helped to light.

McLennan, to whom reference has already been made, says of
Millar's *Ranks*:

> The reader will find an admirable review of the facts in connection with
> this matter [mother-right] and with ancient gynaikocracy in Professor
> Millar's *Origin of Ranks*, a work in which Bachofen has *almost* been antici-
> pated, and that by a treatment of the facts in every sense scientific. . . .;
> [a work] which every student of history should be acquainted with.‡

The following observations on Millar's influence abroad must be
considered purely exploratory. The matter calls for further research,
but it is known that his works early found their way into France,
Germany, Holland and America, and presumably also Italy and other
European countries—both in English, and in some cases in translation.§

In a course of lectures on law that have been called a 'landmark in
American jurisprudence' delivered by James Wilson in the new-
founded chair of law in the College of Philadelphia (later to become the
University of Pennsylvania) in 1790–91, Millar's *Historical View* (1787),
is cited not less than forty-five times as a source in English constitutional
history and constitutional law.‖ This law chair was the first but one to
be established in any college or university in the infant republic. Wilson,
its first incumbent, who was Scottish by birth and early training,
ranks alongside James Madison and Gouverneur Morris as a principal
'founding father' and framer of the American Constitution. He was by
common consent the ablest and most learned of the associate justices
on the Federal Supreme Court—much his own creation—in its first
constitution (1789–98), was a candidate for the Chief-Justiceship itself,

---

* J. H. Millar, *A Literary History of Scotland* (New York, 1903), p. 367. See also in general
his *Scottish Prose in the Seventeenth and Eighteenth Centuries* (Glasgow, 1912), pp. 246–264.

† D. Forbes, *op. cit.* p. 670. ‡ McLennan, *op. cit.* p. 420.

§ See Bibliography, p. 416 below.

‖ *Works of James Wilson*, Bird Wilson (ed.), (Philadelphia, 1804). New edition, J. de W.
Andrews, 2 vols. (Chicago, 1896). Millar references are chiefly in footnotes, but by Wilson
himself.

and has been considered by some the most important exponent of jurisprudence in early American legal history.*

In a rare-book collection in the Library of Congress will be found a copy of Millar's *Ranks* (third edition) bearing the personal autograph of James Madison, Jr., fourth President of the United States, presumably as its one-time owner. Madison, who had received his preparation for college at the hands of a Scottish born and bred schoolmaster and of a Princeton-educated minister, was one of the few Virginians to go to Princeton rather than to William and Mary. He there came under the influence of Princeton's Scottish born and bred President Witherspoon, who had, incidentally, brought a sizeable library with him from Scotland. Madison was a man of 'long and profound research in history, law and political economy'. He was 'the systematic philosopher' of the Constitutional Convention, and generally acknowledged 'the father of the Constitution' drawn up there. He has been called the most systematic exponent of the doctrine of 'economic determinism' after Harrington.†

A copy of the first edition of the *Ranks* found its way into the Harvard College library the very year after its publication (1772) and somewhat later a copy of the third edition bearing Millar's personal autograph.‡ Other libraries also early contained copies of his works.

These are but a few straws in the wind, but they are not without significance. Outside legal circles, and where Scottish influences were generally the strongest, in Princeton circles, a religious conservatism would have been unfriendly to many of Millar's ideas.

On his possible influence on German thought the evidence is meagre but in itself somewhat clearer. We know that up to about the turn of the century German scholars and men of letters were to a remarkable extent open to intellectual influences from 'the West', and especially through the medium of the Hanoverian University at Göttingen, from England and Scotland.

Herder, for example, was widely read and intimately familiar with the literature currently appearing abroad, and not least in England

---

* Charles P. Smith, *James Wilson: Founding Father (1742-98)*, (Chapel Hill, 1956). Especially chs. xx–xxii. Also Charles Warren, *A History of the American Bar* (Boston, 1911), pp. 340–9. The first college to have a law chair was William and Mary.

† For the facts and for sources, see Charles A. Beard, *An Economic Interpretation of the Constitution of the U.S.* (New York, 1948), pp. 14 ff., 152–75 *et passim*; also his *Economic Basis of Politics* (New York, 1922), pp. 29 ff. See also, Douglas Alastair, 'James Madison', in Willard Thorp (ed.), *The Lives of Eighteen from Princeton* (Princeton, 1946), especially pp. 137–43.

‡ Probably a gift of the author to his daughter-in-law, Robina Cullen Millar (see Appendix IV below), whose autograph it also bears.

and Scotland. Schiller, who was historian in his own right as well as poet and dramatist, was only slightly less so. Christian Garve, before Kant's rise to his full fame next to Mendelssohn the most renowned philosopher in Germany, translated Ferguson's *History of Civil Society* and Adam Smith's *Wealth of Nations* into German and promoted the circulation of such authors as Hutcheson, Kames, Steuart, and of English and French 'sociological' ideas generally.*

References to English and Scottish authors, and of course also to Rousseau and the Encyclopedists, occur over and over again in the personal correspondence and diaries of the leading authors of the day. In his correspondence and novels, Jacobi, friend of Goethe, repeatedly cites and even quotes at some length from Ferguson's *Civil Society*. In one passage he makes the leading character remark that the reading of this work marked a turning-point in his life. Ferguson had given him a new inspiration to read the ancients, had led him to new heights of speculation, had in fact produced such an awakening in him that he still considers this period as marking a transition to a more worthy existence.† This is a significant indication of the measure of the penetration of these writers and ideas even into the lay readership. Incidentally, Ferguson was, on a visit to Germany, voted into membership of the Berlin Academy of Science.

Goethe was not only acquainted with the Scottish philosophers but he assures us that they had long been held in high regard by German scholars and recommended them as being intelligible to ordinary understanding and as manifesting a desirable reconciliation of sensationalism (i.e. empiricism) with spiritualism, effecting a union of the real and the ideal, and thus creating a more satisfactory foundation for human thought and action than was to be found among German philosophers, whom he accuses of failing to 'lay hold on life'.‡

Kant, himself of Scottish descent on his father's side, was by his own admission aroused from his 'dogmatic slumbers' by Hume to have his 'investigations in the field of speculation [given] an entirely new direction'.§

---

* From first-hand examination of this literature, especially Garve, in German libraries. See also, *Allgemeine deutsche Biographie* (Leipzig, 1875 ff.).

† F. H. Jacobi, *Werke* (Leipzig, 1812), vol. VI, pp. 69–72, 166 f. (first published, 1792). Jacobi's interest in Ferguson was brought to my attention personally by Professor Pascal of Birmingham University.

‡ W. F. Goethe, *Sämtliche Werke* (Jubilaeumsausgabe, Stuttgart, etc., 1902 in 40 vols.) vol. XXXVIII, p. 217, with note, p. 322. P. H. Brown, in quoting this passage (*History of Scotland*, vol. III, pp. 297 f.; also *Surveys of Scottish History* (Glasgow, 1919), p. 135), does not inform us that Goethe's observations (1830) were occasioned by Carlyle's *Life of Schiller*.

§ I. Kant, *Prolegomena* (P. Carus's translation, Chicago, 1902), p. 7.

In all this we find only a few explicit references to Millar, but these few are significant. Herder, in a review* that does not otherwise interest us here, notes with surprise the failure of the author reviewed to make mention of Smith, Ferguson, Millar and others along with those he does mention, but then hastens to add that this was no doubt because the fame of these men was already such as to make their mention superfluous. Previously he had devoted an extended review to Millar's *Ranks*,† critical in many ways of the purely empirical and naturalistic approach of all the disciples of Montesquieu—the romantic already speaking!— but yet with due recognition of the merits of this production. The translator-editor of the *Historical View* in 1819 —it had apparently not been translated before—expressed the hope in his introduction that its liberalism might have a much needed quickening influence on German politics.‡ How widely these works were read in Germany we do not know. We only know that copies are found in all the older university libraries and *Staatsbibliotheken*.

We cannot but ask here whether this Scottish 'historical school', including Millar, may not have considerably influenced the Roman law studies of Savigny, the Roman historical studies of Niebuhr, the *Mutterrecht* studies of Bachofen, and finally the studies in 'historical materialism' of Marx and his followers. The evidence, so far as we have been able to trace it, is not altogether convincing.

Niebuhr, who knew the language well and was kindly disposed to the English, spent a year in study at Edinburgh in 1798–9, with some time also spent in London. He preferred the lectures of Playfair, Robinson and others in 'natural history' to those of Dugald Stewart and Tytler in political economy and history, though he read privately in these fields. In a letter to a friend he confesses to a 'mean opinion' of British scholarship in history and philosophy at this time, by comparison with the German, and believes Jacobi exaggerated in his praise of the former.§ Later, in his Roman history he comments most unfavourably on Ferguson and the speculative historians.|| Bachofen, who studied mother-right with characteristic German minuteness and intensity of scholarship, likewise dismissed the 'speculative historians', among whom

* J. G. Herder, *Sämtliche Werke* (Suphan edition in 33 vols., Berlin 1877 ff.), vol. xviii, p. 245.

† *Ibid.* vol. v, pp. 452–6. See also, vol. v, p. 550, and vol. vii, p. 103.

‡ John Millar, *Historische Entwicklung der englischen Staatsverfassung* (3 vols. Jena, 1819–21). Translated K[arl] E[rnst] S[chmid]. See translator's preface and postscript.

§ B. G. Niebuhr, *The Life and Letters of* (2nd ed. in 3 vols. London, 1852), vol. i, pp. 111, 113, 119, 129, 137 ff.

|| *Lectures on the History of Rome* (3 vols. 2nd ed. London, 1849), vol. iii, p. lxxxviii. *History of Rome* (3 vols. Cambridge, 1828), vol. i, pp. 65 f. See on this also, Duncan Forbes, *The Liberal Anglican Idea of History* (Cambridge, 1952), p. 71.

he may well have included Millar, with a single sentence or two, as offering nothing but utopian 'rational constructs'.* Adam Mueller, who lectured and wrote on 'the elements of statecraft' (1806 ff.)† early turned away from a youthful enthusiasm for Adam Smith to an almost slavish adoration of the 'romantic' Burke.

How much, if at all, Marx and the 'historical materialists' were directly or indirectly influenced by Millar, it would be difficult to determine. Certainly Marx and Engels were both widely,‡ and in some respects, at least, intimately§ acquainted with the Scottish economic and historico-sociological or 'classical sociological' literature of the eighteenth and early nineteenth centuries, particularly after Marx's 'settlement' in the British Museum in 1850—and not a little also with Scottish economic conditions and developments (e.g. *Capital*, pp. 807 ff.). They acknowledged their obligation to French and English writers‖—the latter perhaps more Scottish than English—for laying the foundations for their own work as the first to write histories of civil society and of trade and industry with a due recognition, though from a Marxian standpoint a still somewhat inadequate and one-sided treatment of the basic life-sustaining, economic and property functions in the civil society they were describing. If, for present purposes at least, we can divorce the political-polemical from the genuinely theoretical elements in their 'historical materialism', and if we remember, as we should, that a historical orientation, a historico-sociological empiricism, a thorough-going evolutionism, and a recognition of the social, even the sociological character of wealth and of the production process, was if anything an even more important element in that theory than merely the 'physical', the techno-economic basis of human society, this becomes a matter of first importance.

In the rough draft, *Grundrisse der Kritik der Politischen Oekonomie* (1857–8), where more than anywhere else, perhaps, we are admitted into the laboratory of the development of Marx's thought, we find citations of English and Scottish authors clearly dominating, in fact, Proudhon, Sismondi, Storch and Say apart, almost monopolizing the

* J. Bachofen, *Das Mutterrecht* (in *Werke*, Basel, 1949), vol. II, 1st half-vol., pp. 16 f. (first published 1861).

† Adam Mueller, *Die Elemente der Staatskunst* (3 vols. in 1, Berlin, 1809).

‡ See any standard edition of Marx, *Das Kapital* with a good index. Also *Poverty and Philosophy*; Marx-Engels, *Die deutsche Ideologie* especially (Berlin, 1953); and both Introduction and body of *Grundrisse der Kritik der Politischen Oekonomie* (rough draft, 1857–8, Moscow, 1939); *A History of Economic Theories* (Kautzky editor, McCarthy translator), New York, 1952.

§ E.g. his acquaintance with James Anderson's *The Bee* and the attacks made on Smith's orthodoxy. See *Capital*, p. 681. All references are to Eden & Cedar Paul one vol. edition.

‖ Marx-Engels, *Die deutsche Ideologie* (Berlin, *Grundrisse*, 1953), pp. 24 ff.

scene. Along with the English Ricardo, who provides the text, as it were, for this 764 large-page commentary, Adam Smith and Sir James Steuart make their appearance in the very first paragraph, soon to be followed by Lauderdale, James Mill and his only slightly less Scottish son John Stuart—all of whom appear again and again on this stage, in *Das Kapital* as also later. Hume, Ferguson, Adam Anderson (*History of Commerce*), James Anderson, David Buchanan, Andrew Ure (*Philosophy of Manufacture*, 1835, etc.) trail not very far behind. All of them are viewed critically, some of them, especially the parsons (*Pfaffen*) among them, at times cynically, but many of them, at least, still in terms of the highest appreciation. Ferguson, mistakenly viewed as the master of Adam Smith (the latter called his *élève*), is credited with being the first to develop the theory of the division of labour;* Steuart with being more 'historical' than the others; and Smith with being a 'genius', a daring innovator in the world of ideas and of basic conceptual formulation, and in a much profounder sense than either his French antecedents or than Ricardo, the founder of political economy.

Hodgskin, this time not a Scot but the Englishman who more nearly than anyone else, perhaps, anticipated specific elements in the Marxian doctrine, and who in one of his works repeatedly cites Millar's *Historical View* and quotes him at some length,† appears not less than ten times in the *Kritik* and a half-dozen times in *Das Kapital* (meaning volume I only) with quotations from *Property* as well as from *Popular Political Economy* and *Labour Defended*. The latter he calls 'an admirable work'.

If Marx never mentions Millar by name—and apparently he does not—this may conceivably be because he did not come to know him, but in the light of the above paragraph this seems very unlikely. It is more likely that he finds him to make no contributions to economic theory worth considering, and therefore simply includes him, nameless, among those 'bourgeois historians and economists' who, he admits, 'a long time before me expounded the historical development of the class

---

* *The Poverty of Philosophy* (New York, n.d.), p. 110. Also *Capital*, pp. 103, 373, 382, 383, 384.

† 'A Labourer' [Anonym for Thomas Hodgskin], *The Natural and Artificial Right of Property Contrasted* (in the form of letters addressed to Lord Brougham (London, 1832)), pp. 94, 119, 136 f. Rare; only copy located is in Kress Library, a Foxwell collection in the Baker Library of the Harvard University School of Business Administration. H. S. Foxwell, Cambridge scholar and authority on pre-Marxian socialism, observes, in support of the quality of this work, that Hodgskin 'quoted throughout from the best authorities on economics and philosophy, especially Locke, Adam Smith and Millar'. Introductory essay to Anton Menger, *Right to the Whole Produce of Labour* (London, 1899), pp. lv–lxv. See also his *Labour Defended against the Claims of Capital* (London, 1825); and *Popular Political Economy* (London, 1827). On Hodgskin, see studies by W. Stark, Carl Koepp, and M. B. Levin. The latter, *Thomas Hodgskin: A study in the Development of Ricardian Socialism* (Libr. Congr. Microfilm AC-1, No. 12, 313.)

struggle . . . and the economic analysis of classes', but who failed, according to him, to see the only aspect of this matter for which he himself claims any originality, namely, the peculiar and inevitable role of the class-struggle in the evolution of the classless society.*

Thus it would appear that Millar's influence, direct or indirect, on the 'economic determinists' cannot be entirely discounted.† Any direct influence on Marx's own teacher Hegel would seem highly unlikely.

On the whole we must conclude, at least tentatively, that three factors rendered unlikely any considerable influence of Millar on German thought generally: first, the rise of an intensive and critical historical scholarship that would be inclined to consider broadly generalizing and 'philosophically' oriented work like Millar's either superficial or otherwise of little value; second, a rising national consciousness that rendered men content with their own German achievements and scholarship; and third, the rise of a romanticism, in history and elsewhere, that was hostile often in the extreme to the Enlightenment and all its ways and works, including its 'rationalistic' and 'naturalistic' history.

So much for the more tangible evidence of the impact, limited though it may have been, of Millar's life and thought and writings on his contemporaries, on the thinking of those who came after him, at home and abroad, on matters social and political.

We might, of course, let the matter rest at this point; but it seems to us not only permissible but necessary, in bringing this study to its proper conclusion, to broaden our question to ask not only, What was the demonstrable impact of Millar's own writings on individual thinkers who came after him? but, What was the relation between the broader movement of thought in which Millar clearly figured and the trends and tendencies of thinking on questions of politics and society in the half-century or more that followed? In its broader bearings this involves, of course, the whole question of what Mill once called 'the reaction of the nineteenth to the eighteenth century'.‡ In any formulation it involves some doubt, already hinted at, of our ability, even under the most favourable conditions, to establish a causal nexus in matters of this kind.

---

* *Marx-Engels Correspondence 1846–95: a Selection* (1934), p. 57.

† See on this matter R. Pascal, 'The Scottish Historical School of the Eighteenth Century' in *Modern Quarterly*, vol. i, no. ii (March, 1938), pp. 167–79, and Meek's article cited above, p. 91. The author is not a little obligated to these two men for inducing him to make the closer acquaintance of such landmarks of human thought as *Die deutsche Ideologie* and the *Kritik*, even though in the end as in the beginning he still holds to an emphasis and a general point of view that remain his own.

‡ Preface to his *Dissertations and Discourses*.

Just as Millar's own thought fed of necessity on the thought of other men, even where we cannot clearly trace the lines of influence, so it is entirely reasonable to assume that when ideas which he had a share in formulating and promoting later became more or less the common property of thinking men, some of the credit for them must go to him, even where we cannot nail matters down by chapter and verse. As on the other hand, when a later generation turns its back on the prevailing philosophy of an earlier one, the 'going out of sight' of any one of its exponents need reflect but little on the merits of his work. Let us follow up for a moment the implications of these statements.

We referred above to the 'romantic' reaction, particularly in Germany, to the eighteenth-century Enlightenment. This needs to be slightly enlarged upon here in its broader bearings. To attempt to put the gist of the matter in a sentence or two: to the rationalism, the naturalism, the secularism, the 'scientism' if we will, including the 'theoretical history', that constituted this Enlightenment—with its appeal from tradition, from prescription, authority and a blind faith, often, in orthodoxy—to the rationality of things, to utilitarian values in society and the state, and to the dignity of the human individual in freedom, many thoughtful minds reacted in the early nineteenth century by attempting to recover more traditional values, to reappraise the irrational element in individual and community life. They appealed again to a religious faith, to a deeper, more 'historical' conception of history, to a more 'organic' view of man, society and the state. This was true particularly in Germany, somewhat less so in France, but also in England and Scotland. That in response particularly to the shock of events in France this romantic reaction took on, often, a 'reactionary' rather than merely a 'conservative' character, which was the very essence of the movement, is incidental and not of its essence, though it is important in the present connection.

How far, if at all, these two tendencies of thought and feeling, these expressions of liberalism and conservatism, respectively, can be reconciled, is a question of profound historical importance. Here we can only remark further that the matter has obviously a most immediate bearing on the subject before us.

Perhaps the best example, for present purposes, of this reaction will be found in the thundering voice of that other Scot, who, like James Mill, Sir James Mackintosh and many another 'went down to London' —that man of bold imagination, deep moral convictions and profound historical insights, Thomas Carlyle. His well-known essays, 'histories' and biographies represent, of course, not only his reaction against the Benthamite 'felicific calculus' and his attempt to introduce German romanticism into English thought, but more generally the attempt of a man with an aroused social conscience to recover a sense of the irrational, of the more deeply moral elements in life, and to probe more deeply into the nature of human nature than the eighteenth-century rationalists, whether philosophers, poets or historians, had done. We might also cite Coleridge's philosophical and theological speculations, or the 'liberal Anglican historians'* recently brought to our closer attention by Duncan Forbes in his book by that title.

On the other side of the picture, many early and mid-nineteenth-century thinkers, perhaps a majority of them continued in the eighteenth-century tradition and built with fewer reservations on its foundations.

This is of course most obvious in the physical and biological sciences, including evolutionary geology and biological evolution. It is also true to a considerable extent of economic speculation and of the development of economics as a science. It is clearly true, though perhaps often without due acknowledgement, of the theoretical elements in so-called 'historical materialism'; much less so, if at all, of its revolutionary elements, which conflicted as strongly with middle-class liberalism as with upper-class conservatism.

Of perhaps most immediate pertinence to our present concern, it is nowhere more true than in the continued interest in 'scientific history', in the study of social origins, the comparative study of early legal, political, social and religious institutions on a broader basis of historical, ethnographic and geographic knowledge than was available to eighteenth-century students. Whether its students proceeded chiefly along evolutionary lines, using the 'comparative method' and the theory of 'contemporary ancestry', as in the case of Tylor, Spencer, McLennan,† L. H. Morgan and their followers, or along more critically historical lines, as in the case of Sir Henry Maine, it is difficult to imagine that their efforts could have been the same without the foundations laid by the men we have passed in review and other eighteenth-century students of jurisprudence, social and political institutions, etc. The fact that their roots were seldom clearly exposed to the surface—most of these men were not history-minded—does not mean that they lacked historical roots. And many of the roots, which they of course did have, clearly reached down into eighteenth-century Scottish soil.

In illustration of an attempted reconciliation of the two centuries, we cite again the younger Mill, in certain aspects, at least, of his many-

* D. Forbes, *op. cit.*

† McLennan would seem to be quite aware of this in his introductory chapter, 'Legal Symbolism and Primitive Life', to the work above cited.

faceted thought. Strongly influenced by Bentham, and as we have seen, not a little also by Millar himself, he was also able to appreciate a Coleridge, as he has himself reminded us,* and to befriend, and work with, up to a point, a Carlyle. He remained a liberal and in some ways even a radical in his sympathies. He took little interest in the mere 'child's play'† of a purely narrative history, but was profoundly interested in 'scientific history', in 'social science', and was therefore able to give to utilitarian thought a more sociological cast than either Bentham or James Mill had done. Because he held to the values of eighteenth-century liberalism without being blind to its weaknesses, and recognized values in early nineteenth-century conservatism without becoming engrossed therein, he was able to mediate between the two and thus to enrich the thought of his time—and of his century.

It is on this background that any further attempt to trace the influence of Millar's thought and to evaluate his place in the history of social and political thought, and in particular of sociological thinking, must finally be thrown.

That inquiry will not, however, be further pursued here. For the present we can only remind the reader in conclusion that Millar, too, stood in more ways than one between the eighteenth-century rationalist revolt against unreason, dogma and tradition and the late eighteenth- and early nineteenth-century romantic revolt, or at least conservative reaction against an often unhistorical eighteenth-century rationalism. Distinctly a liberal, if not from a Tory standpoint even a radical, he was yet a conservative from the standpoint of a Godwin, the Ricardian socialists and the more revolutionary movements of the second and third quarters of the nineteenth century. A strong believer in the idea of progress and in man's essential rationality, he was yet too historically minded to contemplate any sudden or revolutionary, and in that sense radical transformation of the social and political order. An ardent defender of liberty and of essential human rights for all, and in that sense an 'apostle of liberalism', he yet believed too strongly in property and an aristocracy of merit to contemplate a levelling of all distinctions of rank.

In this battle of ideas, both on the pragmatic-political and on the historico-sociological levels, Millar was beyond question a fighter on the liberal side. To lift the conflict above partisanship, however, and to mediate between those who allowed their worship of the past and of the *status quo* to blind them to the many defects of the present social and political structure, and those who allowed their worship of the future

* J. S. Mill, *Dissertations and Discussions*, Preface, and essays on Bentham and on Coleridge.
† The three phrases in quotation marks are Mill's own.

and their impatience with the slow processes of history and of realistic political action to lead them to destroy the very house they would be repairing by an untimely pulling out of its under-pinnings, was the central goal of his educational and literary as of his political efforts. To point out the manner of his working toward this goal and the extent to which he realized it, and thus to fix his place in history, has been the purpose of the present study.

PART III

THE
ORIGIN OF THE
DISTINCTION OF RANKS

BY

JOHN MILLAR

BEING A
REPRINT OF THE THIRD EDITION
PRINTED FOR JOHN MURRAY
IN 1779

EDITOR'S INTRODUCTION

The following inquiry is intended to illustrate the natural history of mankind in several important articles. This is attempted by pointing out the more obvious and common improvements which gradually arise in the state of society, and by showing the influence of these upon the manners, the laws, and the government of a people.

(From Millar's Introduction.)

Reproduced herewith is the full text of Millar's *Origin of the Distinction of Ranks*. The text used is that of the third edition (1779; reprinted also in 1781), which is the last edition prepared by Millar himself.

The original title (1771 edition; unmodified in 2nd edition, 1773), *Observations Concerning the Distinction of Ranks in Society*, and the revised title with a significant descriptive sub-title added, were undoubtedly both suggested by a chapter-subdivision head in Adam Smith's *Moral Sentiments* that reads, 'Of the Origin of Ambition and of the Distinction of Ranks'.

The revisions and additions in the second edition are, with two or three exceptions indicated in footnotes to the present text, of minor significance, consisting chiefly of stylistic improvements, the occasional re-structuring of a paragraph, and the breaking down of the chapters into sections. Changes in the third edition are somewhat more far-reaching, consisting, beside further improvements in style and exposition, of a considerable enlargement of the 'preface', now designated 'introduction', the breaking down of Chapter IV, now considerably enlarged, into two chapters, IV and V, the old Chapter V, also somewhat enlarged, now becoming Chapter VI. There are other revisions and additions of paragraphs here and there, and the occasional lifting of a footnote into the text proper, foreign-language quotations sometimes in English translation. All substantial changes in the third edition from the first, and most of those already occurring in the second, are indicated by a set of symbols and other footnotes explained below. Minor and mere stylistic changes are not indicated beyond this reference to them here. The text of the fourth edition, issued by his nephew Craig in 1806, differs in no way from that of the third, except for a difference in pagination and the correction of a few typographical errors—and of course the prefixing of the biographical sketch.

For the convenience of those readers who may wish to compare different editions, the pagination of the third edition is retained in brackets in the contents list of the present one, and a note at the end of this Introduction provides a table to facilitate comparison with other editions, at least by chapter and section-head pages.

In the footnotes, Latin and French quotations are usually given in English translation, our own or, where available, some standard translation. In the text proper the original is retained. With this modification, all footnotes that give the source of quotations, or provide illustration or further exposition of a topic, are, with a few exceptions indicated in the notes, retained. Source-citations that merely give the authority or authorities for a general statement, or suggest further reading, are omitted without notice as serving little purpose today. Instead there is presented at the end of this introduction a note indicating in roughly classified form the more important authorities cited, whether omitted or retained here, with some indication of the frequency of their citation.

The origin of this work in the author's lectures on law, general jurisprudence and government, its objectives, and general reception by the public, have been briefly indicated elsewhere. Its content, its theoretical substructure and general approach to the problem of society and the organization of power, and the quality of the argument, the reader can best examine for himself—with or without the leads provided in the analytical portion of the present volume. Here there is need further to point to only a few matters that might easily escape the reader on his first approach to this work.

The first is Millar's wide draft upon travel, ethnographic and historical literature that took his readers outside the conventional sphere of European history and society and the critical use he makes of sources with a 'philosophical' orientation quite different from his own, or with a purpose in their recording quite different from the present one. (See above, 118 ff., 143.)

Next, only a careful reading, and some reflection, will reveal how many of the basic quests and categories of law and jurisprudence are still reflected in this work that appears on the surface so far removed from the 'dry bones of the law'. Witness the status of the father or of the mother, the relation of the sexes, the rights and duties of the sovereign, or of servants, the prominent role of status and of property in the discussion—all very much matters of law, for all the other bearings they may also take on. (See above, pp. 33 f., 58, 109 f.)

Finally, that this remarkable work is thoroughly evolutionist in basic orientation, and deeply permeated, if not in fact dominated by a 'deterministic' philosophy, particularly as related to the basic technology of man's maintenance activities, to property and the family, is so obvious 'that he may run that reads it'. But two things need pointing out in this connection, though both of them have been discussed earlier in this volume:

First, such evolutionism is not nearly as original as might appear on the surface. Millar no doubt gave it a more concrete form and a wider application; but the idea itself, in its application to society and politics, had already come very much to dominate, first the thoughtful mind, but increasingly even the popular mind, if not of Europe generally, certainly of the Scotland of the middle and later eighteenth century. It was part of an almost revolutionary historical movement.

In the second place, his evolutionism, far from leading him into a revolutionist camp, confirmed him rather in an essentially middle-class outlook. For all his sympathies with 'men in the lower stations in life', he yet opposes everything that might be called 'levelling'. He emphasizes strongly the techno-economic factors in the evolution of society and the role of property in the social and political order, and makes much of the tendency of economic advance to broaden the basis of liberty. He pleads the claims of the 'labouring poor' upon the elemental humanity and decency of those in more privileged positions, and is almost passionate in his demand for the abolition of the last survivals of slavery and serfdom; but he is also a firm believer in an aristocracy of merit, in the 'union of talent and rank'. His evolutionism made him an out-and-out liberal Whig, with high hopes at first for the success of the Revolution across the Channel, but of the 'revolutionary' we find but few traces in the author of *The Origin of the Distinction of Ranks*.

Notes

NOTES
Explanation of Footnotes

A raised '*r*' in front of a paragraph, or occasionally elsewhere in a paragraph, indicates that this paragraph, or the remainder of the paragraph, represents a considerable revision of the text of the original edition. An '*a*' similarly placed indicates that that paragraph (or remainder of paragraph) is 'added', that is entirely new. Where the revision or addition requires comment, a note symbol rather than a raised letter will precede the paragraph. Where more than two paragraphs are involved, the number of paragraphs, including the one bearing the note, is indicated in a footnote. 'N. om.' indicates that a footnote of possible significance is omitted in this reprint.

Notes by this editor are always in square brackets. All notes in square brackets are this editor's except for a few inserts by a previous editor in quoted passages.

Principal Authors and Works Cited in the 'Ranks'

In view of the fact that source-citations not involving direct quotations were as a rule omitted in this reprinting of the *Ranks*, we give the following roughly classified lists of the more frequently cited or more important authors, indicating in brackets the frequency of citation if they are mentioned three or more times:

Classical authors, historical and literary: Caesar, *de bell. Gall.* (10); Tacitus, *de mor. Germ.* (8); Herodotus, *History* (6); Homer, *Iliad* and *Odyssey* (7); Dionysius Halicarnassus, *Rom. Antiq.* (4); Thucydides (3); Plutarch (3); Cicero (3). Also, Aristotle, Athenaeus, Diodorus Siculus, Pliny, Polybius, Strabo, Herodian, Plautus, Horace's *Satires*, Potter's *Greek Antiquities*, and some seventeen other citations.

Bible: Old Testament (17); New Testament (8).

Law, private and public, ancient and modern: Justinian, *Inst.* and *Pandects* (10); Heineccius (8); Potgiesserus, *Servitude* (8); Boulainvilliers, *Lettres sur le Parlement de France* (6); Bouquet, *Le droit publique de France*. Also Thomas Smith, *Commonwealth*; Wright, *Tenancy*; Grotius; Signon, *Roman and Athenian Antiquities*; Ulpian, *Fragments*; Spellman, *Glossary*; and some thirty other citations.

Travel and non-European history: Histoire générale des voyages (28); Charlevoix, *Journal historique* (6); Kolben, *Good Hope* (6); Lafitau, *Moeurs* (6); *Travels of the Jesuits* (4); D'Arvieux, *Arabia* (3); Le Compte, *China* (3); Le Poivre, *Voyages d'une philosophe* (3). Also, *Present State of Russia* (1722); *History of Kamtschatka*; Gmelin, *Siberia*; Le Brun, *Russia*; Recault, *Ottoman Empire*;

Notes

Recueil des voyages des Indes; Herrera, *Voyage of Columbus*; Bank's *Voyages*; Shaw's *Travels*; John Byron's *Narrative*; John Cook's *Travels*; *Recherche philosophique sur les Américains*; Chardin, *Travels*; Dampier, *Travels*; and some fifteen other citations.

Modern history: Modern *Universal History* (11); Abbé de Velly, *Histoire de France* (3); Abbé de Mably, *Histoire de France* (2); Goguet, *History of Laws*, etc. (2). Also, Robertson, *Charles V*; Adam Anderson, *History of Commerce*; and some seven or eight others.

Modern literary and philosophic works and authors: 'Ossian' (4); Montesquieu (3); Hume (2). Also Kames, Adam Smith, Gilbert Stuart, Robert Wallace, Montaigne, Johnson's *Volpone*, Spenser, and several others.

Pagination Key for Different Editions of the 'Ranks'
(By chapter and section heads as of 3rd edition)

Ch.: Sec.		This ed.	3rd ed.	1st ed.	2nd ed.	4th ed.
Intro.		175	1	i	i	1
I:	I	183	17	1	1	14
	II	198	57	29	37	47
	III	203	69	37	48	57
	IV	208	81	45	59	67
	V	218	106	63	82	87
	VI	224	120	74	95	99
II:	I	229	133	79	103	109
	II	238	157	101	129	128
III:	I	244	171	115	145	140
	II	254	197	137	171	161
IV:	I	262	215	153	191	176
	II	271	238	168*	204*	195
V:	I	284	269	178	228	220
	II	289	282	184	239	230
	III	292	289	188	244	236
VI:	I	296	297	193	251	243
	II	299	305	200	260	250
	III	305	319	211	273	261
	IV	315	344	232	298	282

* Approximate only; revision and difference of chapter division.

CONTENTS

*Figures in square brackets show the page
numbers in the third edition*

Contents

INTRODUCTION*

Those who have examined the manners and customs of nations have had chiefly two objects in view. By observing the systems of law established in different parts of the world, and by remarking the consequences with which they are attended, men have endeavoured to reap advantage from the experience of others, and to make a selection of such institutions and modes of government as appear most worthy of being adopted.

To investigate the causes of different usages has been likewise esteemed an useful as well as an entertaining speculation. When we contemplate the amazing diversity to be found in the laws of different countries, and even of the same country at different periods, our curiosity is naturally excited to enquire in what manner mankind have been led to embrace such different rules of conduct; and at the same time it is evident, that, unless we are acquainted with the circumstances which have recommended any set of regulations, we cannot form a just notion of their utility, or even determine, in any case, how far they are practicable.

In searching for the causes of those peculiar systems of law and government which have appeared in the world, we must undoubtedly resort, first of all, to the differences of situation, which have suggested different views and motives of action to the inhabitants of particular countries. Of this kind, are the fertility or barrenness of the soil, the nature of its productions, the species of labour requisite for procuring subsistence, the number of individuals collected together in one community, their proficiency in arts, the advantages which they enjoy for entering into mutual transactions, and for maintaining an intimate correspondence. The variety that frequently occurs in these, and such other particulars, must have a prodigious influence upon the great body of a people; as, by giving a peculiar direction to their inclinations and pursuits, it must be productive of correspondent habits, dispositions, and ways of thinking.

When we survey the present state of the globe, we find that, in many parts of it, the inhabitants are so destitute of culture, as to appear little above the condition of brute animals; and even when we peruse the remote history of polished nations, we have seldom any difficulty in

* [Except for the first and last and one other paragraph, this introduction represents a complete rewriting and considerable enlargement of the 'Preface' to the original edition, which consists largely of a prospectus of contents.]

175

tracing them to a state of the same rudeness and barbarism. There is, however, in man a disposition and capacity for improving his condition, by the exertion of which, he is carried on from one degree of advancement to another; and the similarity of his wants, as well as of the faculties by which those wants are supplied, has every where produced a remarkable uniformity in the several steps of his progression. A nation of savages, who feel the want of almost every thing requisite for the support of life, must have their attention directed to a small number of objects, to the acquisition of food and clothing, or the procuring shelter from the inclemencies of the weather; and their ideas and feelings, in conformity to their situation, must, of course, be narrow and contracted. Their first efforts are naturally calculated to increase the means of subsistence, by catching or ensnaring wild animals, or by gathering the spontaneous fruits of the earth; and the experience, acquired in the exercise of these employments, is apt, successively, to point out the methods of taming and rearing cattle, and of cultivating the ground. According as men have been successful in these great improvements, and find less difficulty in the attainment of bare necessaries, their prospects are gradually enlarged, their appetites and desires are more and more awakened and called forth in pursuit of the several conveniencies of life; and the various branches of manufacture, together with commerce, its inseparable attendant, and with science and literature, the natural offspring of ease and affluence, are introduced, and brought to maturity. By such gradual advances in rendering their situation more comfortable, the most important alterations are produced in the state and condition of a people: their numbers are increased; the connections of society are extended; and men, being less oppressed with their own wants, are more at liberty to cultivate the feelings of humanity: property, the great source of distinction among individuals, is established; and the various rights of mankind, arising from their multiplied connections, are recognised and protected: the laws of a country are thereby rendered numerous; and a more complex form of government becomes necessary, for distributing justice, and for preventing the disorders which proceed from the jarring interests and passions of a large and opulent community. It is evident, at the same time, that these, and such other effects of improvement, which have so great a tendency to vary the state of mankind, and their manner of life, will be productive of suitable variations in their taste and sentiments, and in their general system of behaviour.

There is thus, in human society, a natural progress from ignorance to knowledge, and from rude, to civilized manners, the several stages of which are usually accompanied with peculiar laws and customs. Various accidental causes, indeed, have contributed to accelerate, or to retard this advancement in different countries. It has even happened that nations, being placed in such unfavourable circumstances as to render them long stationary at a particular period, have been so habituated to the peculiar manners of that age, as to retain a strong tincture of those peculiarities, through every subsequent revolution. This appears to have occasioned some of the chief varieties which take place in the maxims and customs of nations equally civilized.

The character and genius of a nation may, perhaps, be considered as nearly the same with that of every other in similar circumstances; but the case is very different with respect to individuals, among whom there is often a great diversity, proceeding from no fixed causes that are capable of being ascertained. Thus, in a multitude of dice thrown together at random, the result, at different times, will be nearly equal; but in one or two throws of a single die, very different numbers may often be produced. It is to be expected, therefore, that, though the greater part of the political system of any country be derived from the combined influence of the whole people, a variety of peculiar institutions will sometimes take their origin from the casual interposition of particular persons, who happen to be placed at the head of a community, and to be possessed of singular abilities, and views of policy. This has been regarded, by many writers, as the great source of those differences which are to be found in the laws, and government of different nations. It is thus that Brama is supposed to have introduced the peculiar customs of Indostan; that Lycurgus is believed to have formed the singular character of the Lacedemonians; and that Solon is looked upon as the author of that very different style of manners which prevailed at Athens. It is thus, also, that the English constitution is understood to have arisen from the uncommon genius, and patriotic spirit of King Alfred. In short, there is scarcely any people, ancient or modern, who do not boast of some early monarch, or statesman, to whom it is pretended they owe whatever is remarkable in their form of government.

But, notwithstanding the concurring testimony of historians, concerning the great political changes introduced by the lawgivers of a remote age, there may be reason to doubt, whether the effect of their interpositions has ever been so extensive as is generally supposed. Before an individual can be invested with so much authority, and possessed of such reflection and foresight as would induce him to act in the capacity of a legislator, he must, probably, have been educated and brought up in the knowledge of those natural manners and customs, .which, for ages perhaps, have prevailed among his countrymen. Under the influence of all the prejudices derived from ancient usage, he will commonly be disposed to prefer the system already established to any other, of which the effects have not been ascertained by experience; or if in any case he should venture to entertain a different opinion, he must be sensible that, from the general prepossession in favour of the ancient establishment, an attempt to overturn it, or to vary it in any considerable degree, would be a dangerous measure, extremely unpopular in itself, and likely to be attended with troublesome consequences.

As the greater part of those heroes and sages that are reputed to have been the founders and modellers of states, are only recorded by uncertain tradition, or by fabulous history, we may be allowed to suspect that, from the obscurity in which they are placed, or from the admiration of distant posterity, their labours have been exaggerated, and misrepresented. It is even extremely probable, that those patriotic statesmen, whose existence is well ascertained, and whose laws have been justly celebrated, were at great pains to accommodate their regulations to the situation of the people for whom they were intended; and that, instead of being actuated by a projecting spirit, or attempting from visionary speculations of remote utility, to produce any violent reformation, they confined themselves to such moderate improvements as, by deviating little from the former usage, were in some measure supported by experience, and coincided with the prevailing opinions of the country. All the ancient systems of legislation that have been handed down to us with any degree of authenticity, show evident marks of their having been framed with such reasonable views; and in none of them is this more remarkable than in the regulations of the Spartan Lawgiver, which appear, in every respect, agreeable to the primitive manners of that simple and barbarous people, for whose benefit they were promulgated.

Among the several circumstances which may affect the gradual improvements of society, the difference of climate is one of the most remarkable. In warm countries, the earth is often extremely fertile, and with little culture is capable of producing whatever is necessary for substance. To labour under the extreme heat of the sun is, at the same time, exceedingly troublesome and oppressive. The inhabitants, therefore, of such countries, while they enjoy a degree of affluence, and, while by the mildness of the climate they are exempted from many inconveniencies and wants, are seldom disposed to any laborious exertion, and thus, acquiring habits of indolence, become addicted to sensual pleasure, and liable to all those infirmities which are nourished by idleness and sloth. The people who live in a cold country find, on the contrary, that little or nothing is to be obtained without labour; and being subjected to numberless hardships, while they are forced to contend with the ruggedness of the soil, and the severity of the seasons, in earning their scanty provision, they become active and industrious, and acquire those dispositions and talents which proceed from the constant and vigorous exercise both of the mind and body.

Some philosophers* are of opinion, that the difference of heat and cold, of moisture and dryness, or other qualities of the climate, have a more immediate influence upon the character and conduct of nations, by operating insensibly upon the human body, and by effecting correspondent alterations in the temper. It is pretended that great heat, by relaxing the fibres, and by extending the surface of the skin, where the action of the nerves is chiefly performed, occasions great sensibility to all external impressions; which is accompanied with proportionable vivacity of ideas and feelings. The inhabitants of a hot country are, upon this account, supposed to be naturally deficient in courage, and in that steadiness of attention which is necessary for the higher exertions of judgment; while they are no less distinguished by their extreme delicacy of taste, and liveliness of imagination. The weakness, too, of their bodily organs prevents them from consuming a great quantity of food, though their excessive perspiration, the effect of the climate, requires continual supplies of such thin liquors as are proper to repair the waste of their fluids. In this situation, therefore, temperance in eating and drinking becomes a constitutional virtue.

The inhabitants of a cold region, are said, on the other hand, to acquire an opposite complexion. As cold tends to brace the fibres, and to contract the operation of the nerves, it is held to produce a vigorous constitution of body, with little sensibility or vivacity; from which we may expect activity, courage, and resolution, together with such calm and steady views of objects, as are usually connected with a clear understanding. The vigorous constitutions of men, in a cold climate, are also supposed to demand great supplies of strong food, and to create a particular inclination for intoxicating liquors.

In some such manner as this, it is imagined that the character of different nations arises, in a great measure, from the air which they breathe, and from the soil upon which they are maintained. How far these conjectures have any real foundation, it seems difficult to determine. We are too little acquainted with the structure of the human body, to discover how it is affected by such physical circumstances, or to discern the alterations in the state of the mind, which may possibly proceed from a different conformation of bodily organs; and in the history of the world, we see no regular marks of that secret influence which has

* [Reference no doubt chiefly to Montesquieu, but see also below, p. 184]

been ascribed to the air and climate, but, on the contrary, may commonly explain the great differences in the manners and customs of mankind from other causes, the existence of which is capable of being more clearly ascertained.*

How many nations are to be found, whose situation in point of climate is apparently similar, and, yet, whose character and political institutions are entirely opposite? Compare, in this respect, the mildness and moderation of the Chinese, with the rough manners and intolerant principles of their neighbours in Japan. What a contrast is exhibited by people at no greater distance than were the ancient Athenians and Lacedemonians? Can it be conceived that the difference between the climate of France and that of Spain, or between that of Greece and of the neighbouring provinces of the Turkish empire, will account for the different usages and manners of the present inhabitants? How is it possible to explain those national peculiarities that have been remarked in the English, the Irish, and the Scotch, from the different temperature of the weather under which they have lived?

The different manners of people in the same country, at different periods, are no less remarkable, and afford evidence yet more satisfactory, that national character depends very little upon the immediate operation of climate. The inhabitants of Sparta are, at present, under the influence of the same physical circumstances as in the days of Leonidas. The modern Italians live in the country of the ancient Romans.

† The following Inquiry is intended to illustrate the natural history of mankind in several important articles. This is attempted, by pointing out the more obvious and common improvements which gradually arise in the state of society, and by showing the influence of these upon the manners, the laws, and the government of a people.

With regard to the facts made use of in the following discourse, the reader, who is conversant in history, will readily perceive the difficulty of obtaining proper materials for speculations of this nature. Historians of reputation have commonly overlooked the transactions of early ages, as not deserving to be remembered; and even in the history of later and more cultivated periods, they have been more solicitous to give an exact account of battles, and public negotiations, than of the interior police and government of a country. Our information, therefore, with regard to the state of mankind in the rude parts of the world, is chiefly derived from the relations of travellers, whose character and situation

* [Millar no doubt had Hume's essay 'Of National Characters' clearly in mind here.]

† [This and the concluding paragraph are retained without alteration (except for three words changed) from preface to first edition.]

in life, neither set them above the suspicion of being easily deceived, nor of endeavouring to misrepresent the facts which they have related. From the number, however, and the variety of those relations, they acquire, in many cases, a degree of authority, upon which we may depend with security, and to which the narration of any single person, how respectable soever, can have no pretension. When illiterate men, ignorant of the writings of each other, and who, unless upon religious subjects, had no speculative systems to warp their opinions, have, in distant ages and countries, described the manners of people in similar circumstances, the reader has an opportunity of comparing their several descriptions, and from their agreement or disagreement is enabled to ascertain the credit that is due to them. According to this method of judging, which throws the veracity of the relater very much out of the question, we may be convinced of the truth of extraordinary facts, as well as of those that are more agreeable to our own experience. It may even be remarked, that in proportion to the singularity of any event, it is the more improbable that different persons, who design to impose upon the world, but who have no concert with each other, should agree in relating it. When to all this, we are able to add the reasons of those particular customs which have been uniformly reported, the evidence becomes as complete as the nature of the thing will admit. We cannot refuse our assent to such evidence, without falling into a degree of scepticism by which the credibility of all historical testimony would be in a great measure destroyed. This observation, it is hoped, will serve as an apology for the multiplicity of facts that are sometimes stated in confirmation of the following remarks. At the same time, from an apprehension of being tedious, the author has, on other occasions, selected only a few, from a greater number to the same purpose, that might easily have been procured.

CHAPTER I

Of the rank and condition of women in different ages

SECTION I

The effects of poverty and barbarism, with respect to the condition of women

Of all our passions, it should seem that those which unite the sexes are most easily affected by the peculiar circumstances in which we are placed, and most liable to be influenced by the power of habit and education. Upon this account they exhibit the most wonderful variety of appearances, and, in different ages and countries, have produced the greatest diversity of manners and customs.

The state of mankind in the rudest period of society, is extremely unfavourable to the improvement of these passions. A savage who earns his food by hunting and fishing, or by gathering the spontaneous fruits of the earth, is incapable of attaining any considerable refinement in his pleasures. He finds so much difficulty, and is exposed to so many hardships in procuring mere necessaries, that he has no leisure or encouragement to aim at the luxuries and conveniencies of life. His wants are few, in proportion to the narrowness of his circumstances. With him, the great object is to be able to satisfy his hunger, and, after the utmost exertions of labour and activity, to enjoy the relief of idleness and repose. He has no time for cultivating a correspondence with the other sex, nor for attending to those enjoyments which result from it; and his desires being neither cherished by affluence, nor inflamed by indulgence, are allowed to remain in that moderate state which renders them barely sufficient for the continuation of the species.

The facility with which he may commonly gratify these appetites, is another circumstance by which his situation is peculiarly distinguished. In the most rude and barbarous ages, little or no property can be acquired by particular persons; and, consequently, there are no differences of rank to interrupt the free intercourse of the sexes. The pride of family as well as the insolence of wealth, is unknown; and there are no distinctions among individuals, but those which arise from their age and experience, from their strength, courage, and other personal qualities. The members of different families, being all nearly upon a level, maintain the most familiar intercourse with one another, and, when impelled by natural instinct, give way to their mutual desires without hesitation or reluctance. They are unacquainted with those refinements which create a strong preference of particular objects, and with those artificial rules of decency and decorum which might lay a restraint upon their conduct.

It cannot be supposed, therefore, that the passions of sex will rise to any considerable height in the breast of a savage. He must have little regard for pleasures which he can purchase at so easy a rate. He meets with no difficulties nor disappointments to enhance the value of his enjoyment, or to rouse and animate him in the pursuit of it. He arrives at the end of his wishes, before they have sufficiently occupied his thoughts, or engaged him in those delightful anticipations of happiness which the imagination is apt to display in the most flattering colours. He is a stranger to that long continued solicitude, those alternate hopes and fears, which agitate and torment the lover, and which, by awakening the sensibility, while they relax the vigour of his mind, render his prevailing inclinations more irresistible.

ʳThe phlegmatic disposition of savages, in this particular, has accordingly been often remarked as a distinguishing part of their character. There is good reason to believe that, in the state of simplicity which precedes all cultivation and improvement, the intercourse of the sexes is chiefly regulated by the primary intention of nature; that it is of consequence totally interrupted by the periods of pregnancy; and that the same laws, with respect to the difference of seasons, which govern the constitution of inferior animals, have also an influence upon the desires of the human species.*

It is true, that, even in early ages, some sort of marriage, or per-

---

* A late ingenious author imagines that this coldness of constitution is peculiar to the natives of America; and he accounts for it, in a most whimsical manner, from the moisture of the climate, by which the inhabitants of that country are, in his opinion, rendered inferior, both in mind and body, to those of the old world. (Recherches philosophiques sur les Americains.) But though it must, perhaps, be admitted that particular climates have some influence upon the passions of sex, yet, in most parts of the world, the character of savages, in this respect, exhibits a remarkable uniformity. (See an account of the Samoiedes, histoire generale des voyages, tome 18 pp. 509, 510.—Of the inhabitants of Kamtschatka, ibid. tome 19, liv. 2, chap. 4.)

Even among people somewhat advanced beyond the mere savage life, we frequently meet with traces of a similar temperament. 'The virginity of youth,' says Tacitus of the Germans, 'is late treasured, and puberty therefore inexhaustible; nor for the girls is there any hothouse forcing.

'So their life is one of fenced-in chastity. There is no arena with its seductions, no dinnertables with their provocations to corrupt them.' Tacitus, de mor. Germ. § 20, 19.

The same circumstance is mentioned by Caesar concerning the character of the ancient Gauls. 'Those who retain their chastity longest are held in highest honour by their fellow men; for continence, so they believe, makes a man taller, hardier, more muscular.' Caesar, de bell. Gall. lib. 6, § 21.

manent union between persons of different sexes, has been almost universally established. But when we examine the nature of this primitive alliance, it appears to have been derived from motives very little connected with those passions which we are at present considering. When a child has been produced by the accidental correspondence of his parents, it is to be expected that, from the influence of natural affection, they will be excited to assist one another in making some provision for his maintenance. For this purpose, they are led to take up their residence together, that they may act in concert with each other, and unite their efforts in the preservation and care of their offspring.

ªAmong inferior animals, we may discern the influence of the same principle in forming an association between individuals of different sexes. The connexion indeed, in this case, is commonly of short duration; because the young animal is soon in a condition to provide for its own subsistence. In some of the species of birds, however, the young which are hatched at one time, are frequently incapable of procuring their own food before the mother begins to lay eggs a-new; and the male and female are, therefore, apt to contract a more permanent attachment. To this circumstance we may ascribe the imagined fidelity of the turtle, as well as the poetical honours that have been paid to the gentleness of the dove; an animal which, notwithstanding the character it has so universally acquired, appears remarkable for its peevish and quarrelsome temper. Among common poultry, on the contrary, whose offspring is reared without much assistance even from the dam, the disposition to unite in pairs is scarcely observable.

But the long culture which is necessary in rearing the human species, will generally afford to the parents a second pledge of their commerce, before their assistance can be withdrawn from the former. Their attention, therefore, is extended from one object to another, as long as the mother is capable of child-bearing; and their union is thus continued by the same causes which first gave rise to it. Even after this period, they will naturally be disposed to remain in a society to which they have been so long accustomed: more especially, as by living at the head of a numerous family, they enjoy a degree of ease, respect, and security, of which they would otherwise be deprived, and have reason, in their old age, to expect the assistance and protection of their posterity, under all those diseases and infirmities by which they are rendered incapable of providing for themselves.*

* It seems unnecessary to observe, that what is here said with regard to marriage, together with many other Remarks which follow concerning the manners of early nations, can only be applied to those who had lost all knowledge of the original institutions, which, as the sacred scriptures inform us, were communicated to mankind by an extraordinary revelation from heaven.

These were in all probability the first inducements to marriage among the rude and barbarous inhabitants of the earth. As it appears to have taken its origin from the accidental and unforeseen exertions of parental affection, we may suppose that it would be commenced without any previous contract between the parties, concerning the terms or duration of their correspondence. Thus, among the Romans, it should seem that the most ancient marriage was formed merely *by use*; that is, by the parties, living constantly together for the space of a year; a period which, in the ordinary course of things, was sufficient to involve them in the care of a family.* [a]It is believed that the early Greeks were accustomed to marry in the same simple manner.† The Kalmuck Tartars have, at present, a similar practice. Among them, it is usual for a young pair to retire, and live together as man and wife for one year; and if, during this time, the woman has produced a child, their marriage is understood to be completed; but if not, they either separate at pleasure or agree to make another year's trial. Traces of this primitive custom may still be discovered in the law of Scotland; according to which, a marriage dissolved within a *year and day*, and without a child, has no legal consequences, but restores the property of either party to the same situation as if no such alliance had ever existed.

Time and experience gradually improved this connexion, and discovered the many advantages of which it is productive. The consideration of those advantages, together with the influence of fashion and example, contributed to promote its universal establishment. The anxiety of parties, or of their relations, to avoid those disputes and inconveniences with which it was frequently attended, made them endeavour, by an express stipulation, to settle the conditions of their union, and produced a solemn and formal celebration of marriage. The utility of this contract, as it makes a regular provision for multiplying the inhabitants of a country, gave rise to a variety of public regulations for promoting the institution in general, for directing its particular forms, and for discouraging the vague and irregular commerce of the sexes.

The marriages, however, of rude people, according to all accounts, are usually contracted without any previous attachment between the parties, and with little regard to the gratification of their mutual passions. A savage is seldom or never determined to marry from the particular inclinations of sex, but commonly enters into that connexion

* Cicero, pro Flacco, Heineccius, antiq. Roman.

† See Brisson, de vet. rit. nuptiar.

[Footnote references like these will hereafter be omitted, without indicating such omissions, unless there are special reasons for retaining them.]

when he arrives at an age, and finds himself in circumstances, which render the acquisition of a family expedient or necessary to his comfortable subsistence. He discovers no preference of any particular woman, but leaves it to his parents, or other relations, to make choice of a person whom it is thought proper that he should marry: He is not even at the trouble of paying her a visit, but allows them to begin and finish the bargain, without concerning himself at all in the matter: If his proposals are rejected, he hears it without the least disturbance; or if he meets with a favourable reception, he is equally unmoved; and the marriage is completed, on both sides, with the most perfect indifference.*

From the extreme insensibility, observable in the character of all savage nations, it is no wonder they should entertain very gross ideas concerning those female virtues which, in a polished nation, are supposed to constitute the honour and dignity of the sex.

The Indians of America think it no stain upon a woman's character, that she has violated the laws of chastity before marriage: nay, if we can give credit to travellers who have visited that country, a trespass of this kind is a circumstance by which a woman is recommended to a husband; who is apt to value her the more, from the consideration that she has been valued by others, and, on the other hand, thinks that he has sufficient ground for putting her away, when he has reason to suspect that she has been overlooked.

Young women, among the Lydians, were not accustomed to marry, until they had earned their doweries by prostitution.

The Babylonians had a public regulation, founded upon their religion, and probably handed down from very remote antiquity, that every woman, of whatever rank should, once in her life submit to a public prostitution in the temple of Venus. A religious ceremony of a like

* Father Lafitau takes notice of a particular custom among the savages of America, which shows the indifference with which their marriages are usually contracted, and marks, at the same time, the inattention of that people to the gratification of their passions. 'There is an ancient custom, among most of the savage nations, of passing the first year after the contraction of a marriage without consummating it. To propose otherwise before such time has expired would be to offer an insult to the bride, who would take this to mean that one sought this alliance more for sensual gratification than out of esteem for her person. And although the young couple spend their nights together, this is done without prejudice to this ancient usage. The relatives of the bride keep close watch on their part and are careful to maintain a large fire before their sleeping-mat, which continually lights up their doings and which serves to guarantee that nothing occurs contrary to the prescribed order.'

Joseph Lafitau, moeurs des sauvages Ameriquains [Paris, 2 vols. 1724, 4to.] tom. i, p. 564. [Paris, 1724, 4 vol. ed., vol. ii, pp. 263 f.]

In some parts of Great Britain, the common people hold it a point of decorum, that, after the ceremony of marriage, the married persons should sleep together one night without consummation.

nature is said to have been observed in some parts of the Island of Cyprus.

The infidelity of a married woman is naturally viewed in a different light, and, upon account of the inconveniences with which it is attended, is often regarded as an offence that deserves to be severely punished. To introduce a spurious offspring into the family; to form a connexion with a stranger, by which the wife is diverted from her proper employments and duties, and by which she may be influenced to embezzle the goods committed to her charge; these are circumstances, that even in a rude period, are apt to awaken the jealousy of the husband, and to excite his indignation and resentment. There are nations, however, who have disregarded even these considerations, and who have looked upon the strict preservation of conjugal fidelity as a matter of no consequence.

Among the ancient Massagetae, it was usual for persons who resided in the same part of the country to possess their wives in common. The same custom is said, by Diodorus Siculus, to have taken place among the ancient Troglodites, and the Icthyophagi, inhabiting the coast of the Red Sea.

Caesar observes that, in Britain, ten or a dozen persons, chiefly near relations, were accustomed to maintain a community of wives; but that the offspring of such promiscuous intercourse was reputed to belong to that man who had been first connected with the mother.

a Some authors, from a laudable desire of vindicating our forefathers, have called this fact in question, and have been willing to believe, that, in this particular, Caesar was imposed upon by the simple accommodation of those persons who lodged in the same cottage. But it is difficult to conceive that the judicious and well informed conqueror of Gaul, who had been long acquainted with the manners of rude people, and was of a disposition to look upon this as a matter of curiosity, would have made so slight an inquiry, or satisfied himself with so superficial an examination, as might expose him to such a gross deception.*

The custom of lending a wife to a friend, that he might have children by her, appears to have been universal among the ancient Greeks and Romans, and even when these nations had become wealthy and civilized, was openly countenanced by persons of the highest rank and character. It is said to have been recommended, in

---

* 'Ten, and even twelve [men] have wives in common, and especially brothers, or parents and their children amongst themselves; but if there be any issue by these wives, they are reputed to be the children of those by whom, respectively, each was first espoused when a virgin.' Caesar, de bell. Gall. lib. 5, § 14.

a particular manner, to the Spartans, by the celebrated institutions of Lycurgus.*

In the country of Kamtschatka, there are several tribes of savages, who esteem it an ordinary mark of politeness, when they entertain a friend, to offer him the enjoyment of their wife or their daughter; and whoever refuses a civility of this kind, to his guest, is supposed to have intended an affront; and his behaviour is resented accordingly. In Louisiana, upon the coast of Guinea, in several parts of the East Indies, in Pegu, Siam, Cochinchina, and Cambodia, the inhabitants are, in like manner, accustomed, for a small present, to make an offer of their women to all strangers who have occasion to visit the country.

† Among all men who have made any considerable advances towards refinement, sentiments of modesty are connected with the intercourse of the sexes. These sentiments are derived from the very different manner in which individuals are affected, when under the immediate influence of desire, and upon other occasions. After the violence of passion has subsided, and when the mind returns to its usual state of tranquillity, its former emotions appear, in some measure, extravagant, and disproportioned to the object which excited them. But if, with all our partiality, the recollection of our own appetites, in the case here alluded to, be seldom agreeable even to ourselves, we have good reason to conclude that an open display of them will be extremely offensive to

---

* Plutarch, *in vita Lycurg.* [Also]

> Soon as the sun dispelled the chilly night,
> The sounding doors flew wide, and from the tomb
> Of dead Hortensius grieving Marcia came.
> First joined in wedlock to a greater man
> Three children did she bear to grace his home:
> Then Cato to Hortensius gave the dame
> To be a fruitful mother of his sons
> And join their houses in a closer tie.
> And now the last sad offices were done
> She came with hair dishevelled, beaten breast,
> And ashes on her brow, and features worn
> With grief; thus only pleasing to the man.
> 'When youth was in me and maternal power
> I did thy bidding, Cato, and revived
> A second husband: now in years grown old
> Ne'er to be parted I return to thee.
> Renew our former pledges undefiled:
> Give back the name of wife: . . . .
> Although the times were warlike and the fates
> Called to the fray, etc.'

Lucan, Pharsal. lib. [11. 326–43, 350, translated by Sir E. Ridley.]

[Five paragraphs largely new.]

others. Those who are not actuated by the same desires must behold our enjoyment with disgust: those who are, must look upon it with jealousy and rivalship. It is to be expected, therefore, that, according as men become sensible of this, they will endeavour to remove such disagreeable appearances. They will be disposed to throw a veil over those pleasures, and to cover from the public eye those thoughts and inclinations, which, they know by experience, would expose them to contempt and aversion. The dictates of nature, in this respect, are inculcated by the force of education; our own feelings are continually gathering strength by a comparison with those of the people around us; and we blush at every deviation from that concealment and reserve which we have been taught to maintain, and which long practice has rendered habitual. Certain rules of decency and decorum with relation to dress, the modes of expression, and general deportment, are thus introduced; and as these contribute, in a high degree to improve and embellish the commerce of society, they are regarded as peculiarly indispensable to that sex, in which, for obvious reasons, the greatest delicacy and propriety is required.

But mere savages are little acquainted with such refinements. Their situation and manner of life prevent them, either from considering the intercourse of the sexes as an object of importance, or from attending to those circumstances which might suggest the propriety of concealing it. Conscious of nothing blameable in that instinct which nature has bestowed upon them, they are not ashamed of its ordinary gratifications; and they affect no disguise, as to this particular, either in their words or in their actions.

From the account given by Herodotus of the Massagetae, it appears that those barbarians were strangers to reserve or modesty in the commerce of the sexes. The same circumstance is mentioned by Caesar, in describing the ancient Germans; a people who had made some improvements in their manner of life.* The form of courtship among the Hottentots, by which the lover is permitted to overcome the reluctance of his mistress, may be considered as a plain indication of similar manners, and exhibits a striking picture of primitive rudeness and simplicity.

When Mr. Banks was in the Island of Otaheite, in 1769, he received a visit from some ladies, who made him a present of cloth, attended with very uncommon ceremonies, of which the following account is published by Dr. Hawkesworth.

---

* 'In the matter of sex there is no prudery, men and women bathing together in the rivers, and wearing skins or short cloaks of reindeer-hide which leaves most of the body naked.' Caesar, de bell. Gall. lib. 6, § 21.

There were nine pieces; and having laid three pieces one upon another, the foremost of the women, who seemed to be the principal, and who was called Oorattooa, stepped upon them, and taking up her garments all round her to the waist, turned about, and with great composure and deliberation, and with an air of perfect innocence and simplicity, three times: when this was done, she dropped the veil, and stepping off the cloth, three more pieces were laid on, and she repeated the ceremony: then stepping off as before, the last three were laid on, and the ceremony was repeated in the same manner the third time.*

Though the inhabitants of that country are, almost without labour, supplied with great plenty of food, and may therefore be supposed more addicted to pleasure than is usual among savages in a colder climate, yet they appear to have no such differences of wealth as might restrain the free indulgence of their appetites, and by that means produce a degree of refinement in their passions.

Upon the discovery of the new world by Columbus, the natives appeared to have no idea of clothing as a matter of decency: for, though the men made use of a garment, the women, it is said, had not the least covering. The nakedness, however, of these Indians, when authorised by custom, had probably no more tendency to promote debauchery than similar circumstances can be supposed to have upon inferior animals. Rude nations are usually distinguished by greater freedom and plainness of behaviour, according as they are farther removed from luxury and intemperance.

In the Odyssey, when Telemachus arrives at Pylos, he is stripped naked, bathed, and annointed by the king's daughter.

> While these officious tend the rites divine,
> The last fair branch of the Nestorian line,
> Sweet Polycaste, took the pleasing toil
> To bathe the prince, and pour the fragrant oil.
> O'er his fair limbs a flowery vest he threw,
> And issued, like a god, to mortal view.†

A remarkable instance of this plainness and simplicity occurs in the behaviour of Ruth to Boaz her kinsman.

* Voyages for making discoveries in the Southern Hemisphere, vol. 2, chap. 12.
In the same publication, an account of a still more remarkable exhibition, made in that Island, is given as follows: 'A young man, near six feet high, performed the rites of Venus with a little girl about eleven or twelve years of age, before several of our people, and a great number of the natives, without the least sense of its being indecent or improper, but, as appeared, in perfect conformity to the custom of the place. Among the spectators were several women of superior rank, particularly Oberea, who may properly be said to have assisted at the ceremony; for they gave instructions to the girl how to perform her part, which, young as she was, she did not seem to stand in need of.' Ibid.
† Pope's translation of the Odyssey, bk. 4, l. 58.

And when Boaz had eaten and drunk and his heart was merry, he went to lie down at the end of the heap of corn: and she came softly, and uncovered his feet and laid her down.

And it came to pass at midnight, that the man was afraid, and turned himself: and behold a woman lay at his feet.

And he said, Who art thou? And she answered, I am Ruth, thine handmaid: spread therefore thy skirt over thine handmaid, for thou art a near kinsman.*

The influence of such manners must be extremely unfavourable to the rank and dignity of the women; who are deprived of that consideration and respect which, in a polished nation, they are accustomed to derive from the passion between the sexes. It is, at the same time, impossible, in a rude age, that they should procure esteem by such employments as they have any occasion to exercise.

† Among those who are almost continually employed in war, or in hunting, and who, by their manner of life, are exposed to numberless hardships and dangers, activity, strength, courage, and military skill, are the chief accomplishments that are held in high estimation. These accomplishments, which in all ages excite a degree of admiration, are, in a barbarous country, the principal sources of rank and dignity; as they are most immediately useful to the people in procuring food, and in providing for their personal safety, the two great objects which they have constantly in view. When the members of a rude tribe return from an expedition, every man is respected in proportion to the actions which he has performed; and that person is distinguished at the feast who has been so fortunate as to signalize himself in the field. The various incidents of the battle, or of the chase, occupy their thoughts, and become an interesting subject of conversation. Those who are old take pleasure in relating the deeds of former times, by which their own reputation has been established, and in communicating to the young those observations which they have treasured up, or those rules of conduct which appear most worthy of attention. The son, when he goes out to battle, is armed with the sword of his fathers, and, when he calls to mind the renown which they have acquired, is excited to a noble emulation of their achievements.

The inferiority of the women, in this respect, may be easily imagined. From their situation, indeed, they naturally acquire a degree of firmness and intrepidity which appears surprising to persons only acquainted with the manners of polished nations. It is usual for them to accompany the men in their expeditions either for hunting or for war; and it sometimes happens that individuals are excited, by the

* Ruth, chap. iii, ver. 7, 8, 9.   † [Enlarged.]

general spirit of the times, to engage in battle, so as even to gain a reputation by their exploits. But whatever may have happened in some extraordinary cases, we may venture to conclude, that the female character is by no means suited to martial employments; and that, in barbarous, as well as in refined periods, the women are, for the most part, incapable of rivalling the other sex in point of strength and courage. Their attention, therefore, is generally limited to an humbler province. It falls upon them to manage all the inferior concerns of the household, and to perform such domestic offices as the particular circumstances of the people have introduced: offices which, however useful, yet requiring little dexterity or skill, and being attended with no exertion of splendid talents, are naturally regarded as mean and servile, and unworthy to engage the attention of persons who command respect by their military accomplishments.

From these observations we may form an idea of the state and condition of the women in the ages most remote from improvement. Having little attention paid them, either upon account of those pleasures to which they are subservient, or of those occupations which they are qualified to exercise, they are degraded below the other sex, and reduced under that authority which the strong acquire over the weak: an authority, which, in early periods, is subject to no limitation from the government, and is therefore exerted with a degree of harshness and severity suited to the dispositions of the people.

We accordingly find that, in those periods, the women of a family are usually treated as the servants or slaves of the men. Nothing can exceed the dependance and subjection in which they are kept, or the toil and drudgery which they are obliged to undergo. They are forced to labour without intermission in digging roots, in drawing water, in carrying wood, in milking the cattle, in dressing the victuals, in rearing the children, and in those other kinds of work which their situation has taught them to perform. The husband, when he is not engaged in some warlike exercise, indulges himself in idleness, and devolves upon his wife the whole burden of his domestic affairs. He disdains to assist her in these employments: she sleeps in a different bed, and is seldom permitted to have any conversation or correspondence with him.

Among the negroes upon the slave-coast, the wife is never allowed to appear before the husband, or to receive any thing from his hands, without putting herself into a kneeling posture.

In the empire of Congo, and in the greater part of those nations which inhabit the southern coast of Africa, the women of a family are seldom allowed to eat with the men. The husband sits alone at table, and the wife commonly stands at his back, to guard him from the flies, to serve him with his victuals, or to furnish him with his pipe and his tobacco. After he has finished his meal, she is allowed to eat what remains; but without sitting down, which it seems would be inconsistent with the inferiority and submission that is thought suitable to her sex. When a Hottentot and his wife have come into the service of a European, and are entertained in the same house, the master is under the necessity of allotting to each of them a distinct portion of victuals; which, out of regard to the general usage of their country, they always devour at a distance from one another.

In the account lately given by Commodore Byron of the Indians of South America, we are told, that:

the men exercise a most despotic authority over their wives, whom they consider in the same view they do any other part of their property; and dispose of them accordingly: even their common treatment of them is cruel; for though the toil and hazard of procuring food lies entirely upon the women, yet they are not suffered to touch any part of it till the husband is satisfied; and then he assigns them their portion, which is generally very scanty, and such as he has not a stomach for himself.

The same author informs us, that he observed a like arbitrary behaviour in many other nations of savages with whom he has since become acquainted.*

From the servile condition of the women in barbarous countries, they are rendered in a great measure incapable of property, and are supposed to have no share in the estate of that particular family to which they belong. Whatever has been acquired by their labour is under the sole administration and disposal of those male relations and friends, by whom they are protected, and from whom they receive a precarious subsistence. Upon the death of a proprietor, his estate is continued in the possession of his sons, or transmitted to his other male relations; and his daughters are so far from being entitled to a share of the succession, that they are even considered as a part of the inheritance, which the heir has the power of managing at pleasure.

At the Cape of Good Hope, in the kingdom of Benin, and in general upon the whole southern and western coast of Africa, no female is ever admitted to the succession of any estate, either real or personal.

The same custom is said to be observed among the Tartars; and there is some reason to believe that it has been anciently established among all the inhabitants of Chaldea and Arabia.

From the famous decision of this point related by Moses, it appears that, in his time, the succession of females had been without a precedent;

---

* Byron's Narrative.

and, by his appointment, they were only permitted to inherit upon a failure of males of the same degree.

Then came the daughters of Zelophehad—and they stood before Moses, and before Eleazar the priest, and before the princes, and all the congregation, by the door of the tabernacle of the congregation, saying:

Our father died in the wilderness, and he was not in the company of them that gathered themselves together against the Lord in the company of Korah; but died in his own sin, and had no sons.

Why should the name of our father be done away from among his family, because he hath no son? Give unto us therefore a possession among the brethren of our father.

And Moses brought their cause before the Lord.

And the Lord spake unto Moses, saying:

The daughters of Zelophehad speak right; thou shalt surely give them a possession of an inheritance among their father's brethren, and thou shalt cause the inheritance of their father to pass unto them.

And thou shalt speak unto the children of Israel, saying, If a man die, and have no son, then ye shall cause his inheritance to pass unto his daughter.*

In all those German nations which over-ran and subdued the different provinces of the Roman empire, the same notions were entertained concerning the inferiority of the women; and the same rules of succession were naturally introduced. It is probable that, according to the original customs which prevailed in all these nations, daughters, and all other female relations, were entirely excluded from the right of inheritance; but that afterwards, when the increase of opulence and luxury had raised them to higher consideration, they were admitted to succeed after the males of the same degree.

In a country where the women are universally regarded as the slaves of the other sex, it is natural to expect that they should be bought and sold, like any other species of property. To marry a wife must there be the same thing as to purchase a female servant, who is to be entrusted, under the husband's direction, with a great part of the domestic economy.

Thus, in all savage nations, whether in Asia, Africa, or America, the wife is commonly bought by the husband from the father, or those other relations who have an authority over her; and the conclusion of a bargain of this nature, together with the payment of the price, has therefore become the most usual form of solemnity in the celebration of their marriages.†

* Numbers, chap. xxvii, ver. 1–8.

† [Many references om.]

'The present law still fortunately holds that when a woman having a husband departs this life childless, the husband of the deceased wife may not demand her dowery, which was given for her.' Leges Burgundior. tit. 14, 3.

This appears to be the real foundation of what is related by historians; that in some parts of the world it is usual for the husband to give a dowery to the wife or her relations, instead of the wife bringing along with her a dowery to the husband.

'Dotem non uxor marito, sed uxori maritus offert,' is the expression used by Tacitus in speaking of this practice among the ancient German nations.*

When Shechem wanted to marry the daughter of Jacob—'He said unto her father, and unto her brethren, Let me find grace in your eyes, and what ye shall say unto me I will give.

'Ask me never so much dowery and gift, And I will give according as ye shall say unto me: but give me the damsel to wife.'†

When David married the daughter of king Saul, he was obliged to pay a dowery of a very singular nature.‡

§ This ancient custom, that the husband should buy his wife from her relations, remains at present among the Chinese; who, notwithstanding their opulence, and their improvement in arts, are still so wonderfully tenacious of the usages introduced in a barbarous period.

Sir Thomas Smith takes notice, that, according to the old law of England, 'the woman, at the church-door, was given of her father, or some other man of the next of her kin, into the hands of the husband; and he laid down *gold* and *silver* for her upon the book, as *though he did buy her.*'‖ In the early history of France we meet with a similar practice; of which there are traces remaining in the present marriage ceremony of that country.

Upon the same principle, the husband is generally understood to have the power of selling his wife, or of putting her away at pleasure.¶

It may however be remarked, that this is a privilege, which, from the manners of a rude people, he seldom has reason to exercise. The wife, who is the mother of his children, is generally the most proper person to be employed in the office of rearing and maintaining them. As she advances in years, she is likely to advance in prudence and discretion; a circumstance of too much importance to be counterbalanced by any considerations relating to the appetite between the sexes. Nothing but some extraordinary crime that she has committed, will move the husband to put away so useful a servant, with whom he has long been acquainted, and whose labour, attention, and fidelity, are commonly of more value than all the money she will bring in a market. Divorces are therefore rarely to be met with in the history of early nations.

---

* Tacitus, de mor. Germ. † Genesis, chap. xxiv, ver. 11, 12.
‡ 1 Samuel, chap. xviii, ver. 25. § [Three paragraphs largely new.]
‖ The Commonwealth of England, bk. 3, chap. 8. ¶ [Many references om.]

But though the wife is not apt to incur the settled displeasure of her husband, which might lead him to banish her from the family, she may often experience the sudden and fatal effects of his anger and resentment. When unlimited power is committed to the hands of a savage, it cannot fail, upon many occasions, to be grossly abused. He looks upon her in the same light with his other domestic servants, and expects from her the same implicit obedience to his will. The least opposition kindles his resentment; and from the natural ferocity of his temper, he is frequently excited to behave with a degree of brutality which, in some cases, may prove the unhappy occasion of her death.

Among the ancient inhabitants of Gaul, the husband exercised the power of life and death over his wives, and treated them with all the severity of an absolute and tyrannical master. In that country, whenever a person of distinction was thought to have died a violent death, his wives lay under the same suspicion of guilt with his other domestic servants; and in order to discover who had committed the crime, they were all subjected to the torture.*

But of all the different branches of power with which in a rude age the husband is usually invested, we meet with the fullest and most complete illustration in the ancient law of the Romans. By that law, a wife was originally considered as, in every respect, the slave of her husband.† She might be sold by him, or she might be put to death by an arbitrary exertion of his authority. From the ceremonies which were used in the more solemn and regular celebration of marriage, it seems probable that, in early times, the wife was purchased with a real price from her relations.‡ She was held incapable of having any estate of her own, and whatever she possessed at the time of her marriage became the absolute property of her husband.

ᵃ It will be thought, perhaps, a mortifying picture that is here presented to us, when we contemplate the barbarous treatment of the female sex in early times, and the rude state of those passions which may be considered as the origin of society. But this rudeness and barbarism, so universally discovered in the early inhabitants of the world, is not unsuitable to the mean condition in which they are placed, and to the numberless hardships and difficulties which they are obliged to encounter. When men are in danger of perishing for hunger; when they

* Husbands have the same power of life and death over their wives as over their children. When the head of a noble family dies his relatives meet, and if there is suspicion of foul play the widow is examined under torture, just as we examine slaves.' Caesar, de bell. Gall. lib. 6, § 18.

† She was said 'convenire in manum mariti,' and was precisely in the same condition with a 'filia-familias.'

‡ The ceremonies of 'coemptio.'

are exerting their utmost efforts to procure the bare necessaries of life; when they are unable to shelter themselves from beasts of prey, or from enemies of their own kind, no less ferocious; their constitution would surely be ill adapted to their circumstances, were they endowed with a refined taste of pleasure, and capable of feeling the delicate distresses and enjoyments of love, accompanied with all those elegant sentiments, which, in a civilized and enlightened age, are naturally derived from that passion. Dispositions of this nature would be altogether misplaced in the breast of a savage: They would even be exceedingly hurtful, by turning his attention from real wants, to the pursuit of imaginary, and what, in his situation, must be accounted fantastical gratifications. Neither will it escape observation, that this refinement would be totally inconsistent with the other parts of his character. Nations who have so little regard to property as to live in the continual exercise of theft and rapine; who are so destitute of humanity, as, in cold blood, to put their captives to death with the most excruciating tortures; who have the shocking barbarity to feed upon their fellow-creatures, a practice rarely to be found among the fiercest and most rapacious of the brute animals; such nations, it is evident, would entirely depart from their ordinary habits and principles of action, were they to display much tenderness or benevolence, in consequence of that blind appetite which unites the sexes. It ought, at the same time to be remembered, that, how poor and wretched soever the aspect of human nature in this early state, it contains the seeds of improvement, which, by long care and culture, are capable of being brought to maturity; so that the lower its primitive condition, it requires the greater exertions of labour and activity, and calls for a more extensive operation of those wonderful powers and faculties, which, in a gradual progression from such rude beginnings, have led to the noblest discoveries in art or science, and to the most exalted refinement of taste and manners.

SECTION II

The influence acquired by the mother of a family, before marriage is completely established

Such are the natural effects of poverty and barbarism, with respect to the passions of sex, and with respect to the rank in society which the women are permitted to enjoy. There is one circumstance, however, in the manners of a rude age, that merits particular attention; as it appears, in some countries, to have produced a remarkable exception to the foregoing observations.

Although marriage, for the reasons formerly mentioned, is undoubtedly a very early institution, yet some little time and experience are necessary before it can be fully established in a barbarous community; and we read of several nations, among whom it is either unknown, or takes place in a very imperfect and limited manner.

To a people who are little acquainted with that institution it will appear, that children have much more connexion with their mother than with their father. If a woman has no notion of attachment or fidelity to any particular person, if notwithstanding her occasional intercourse with different individuals she continues to live by herself, or with her own relations, the child which she has borne, and which she maintains under her own inspection, must be regarded as a member of her own family; and the father, who lives at a distance, can have no opportunity of establishing an authority over it. We may in general conclude, that the same ideas which obtain in a polished nation, with regard to bastards, will, in those primitive times, be extended to all, or the greater part of the children produced in the country.

Thus, among the Lycians, children were accustomed to take their names from their mother, and not from their father; so that if any person was desired to give an account of the family to which he belonged, he was naturally led to recount his maternal genealogy in the female line. The same custom took place among the ancient inhabitants of Attica; as it does at present among several tribes of the natives of North America, and of the Indians upon the coast of Malabar.*

In this situation, the mother of a numerous family, who lives at a distance from her other relations, will often be raised to a degree of rank and dignity to which, from her sex, she would not otherwise be entitled. Her children being, in their early years, maintained and protected by her care and tenderness, and having been accustomed to submit to her authority, will be apt, even after they are grown up, and have arrived at their full strength and vigour, to behave to her with some degree of reverence and filial affection. Although they have no admiration of her military talents, they may respect her upon account of her experience and wisdom; and although they should not themselves be always very scrupulous in paying her an implicit obedience, they

* Herodot. hist. lib. 1.—See Goguet's Origin of Laws, etc. vol. 2, book 1.—Charlevoix, Journal historique d'un voyage de l'Amer. Nouveaux voyages aux Indes Orientales, tom. 2, p. 20.—Mod. Univ. Hist. vol. 6, p. 561.
 Vestiges of the same practice are also to be found in the writings of the Roman Lawyers. Extensive quotation om.]

will probably be disposed to espouse her quarrel, or to support her interest against every other person.

ᵃ We are informed, indeed, that when a young Hottentot is of age to be received into the society of *men*, it is usual for him to beat and abuse his mother, by way of triumph at being freed from her tuition. Such behaviour may happen in a rude country, where, after marriage is established, the superior strength of the husband has raised him to the head of his family, and where his authority has of course annihilated that of the wife, or at least greatly reduced her consideration and importance. But in a country where children have no acquaintance with their father, and are not indebted to him for subsistence and protection, they can hardly fail, during a considerable part of their life, to regard their mother as the principal person in the family.

This is in all probability the source of that influence which appears to have been possessed by the women in several rude and barbarous parts of the world.

In the island of Formosa, it is said, that in forming that slight and transient union between the sexes, to which our travellers, in conformity to the customs of Europe, have given the name of marriage, the husband quits his own family, and passes into that of his wife, where he continues to reside as long as his connexion with her remains.ᵃ The same custom is said to be established among the people called Moxos, in Peru.

In the Ladrone islands the wife is absolute mistress of the house, and the husband is not at liberty to dispose of any thing without her permission. She chastises him, or puts him away, at pleasure; and whenever a separation happens, she not only retains all her moveables, but also her children, who consider the next husband she takes as their father.

The North American tribes are accustomed to admit their women into their public councils, and even to allow them the privilege of being first called to give their opinion upon every subject of deliberation. Females, indeed, are held incapable of enjoying the office of chief, but through them the succession to that dignity is continued; and therefore, upon the death of a chief, he is succeeded, not by his own son, but by that of his sister; and in default of the sister's son, by his nearest relation in the female line. When his whole family happens to be extinct, the right of naming a successor is claimed by the noblest matron of the village.

It is observed, however, by an author who has given us the fullest account of all these particulars, that the women of North America do not arrive at this influence and dignity till after a certain age, and after their children are in a condition to procure them respect; that before this period they are commonly treated as the slaves of the men; and that there is no country in the world where the female sex is in general more neglected and despised.

Among the ancient inhabitants of Attica, the women had, in like manner, a share in public deliberations. This custom continued till the reign of Cecrops, when a revolution was produced, of which the following fabulous relation has been given by historians. It is said, that after the building of Athens, Minerva and Nepture became competitors for the honour of giving a name to the city, and that Cecrops called a public assembly of the men and women in order to determine the difference. The women were interested upon the part of Minerva; the men upon that of Neptune; and the former carried the point by the majority of one vote. Soon after, there happened an inundation of the sea, which occasioned much damage, and greatly terrified the inhabitants, who believed that this calamity proceeded from the vengeance of Neptune for the affront he had suffered. To appease him, they resolved to punish the female sex, by whom the offence was committed, and determined that no woman should for the future be admitted into the public assemblies, nor any child be allowed to bear the name of its mother.

It may explain this piece of ancient mythology to observe, that in the reign of Cecrops marriage was first established among the Athenians. In consequence of this establishment the children were no longer accustomed to bear the name of their mother, but that of their father, who, from his superior strength and military talents, became the head and governor of the family; and as the influence of the women was thereby greatly diminished, it was to be expected that they should, in a little time, be entirely excluded from those great assemblies which deliberated upon public affairs.

Among the ancient Britons we find, in like manner, that the women were accustomed to vote in the public assemblies. The rude and imperfect institution of marriage, and the community of wives, that anciently took place in Britain, must have prevented the children from acquiring any considerable connexion with their father, and have disposed them to follow the condition of their mother, as well as to support her interest and dignity.

When a woman, by being at the head of a large family, is thus advanced to influence and authority, and becomes a sort of female chief, she naturally maintains a number of servants, and endeavours to live with suitable splendour and magnificence. In proportion to her affluence, she has the greater temptation to indulge her sensual appetites and, in a period when the sexes are but little accustomed to control or disguise their inclinations, she may, in some cases, be led into a correspondence with different male retainers, who happen to reside in her family, and over whom she exercises an authority resembling that of a master.

* The above remark may account for what is related by historians; that, in some provinces of the ancient Median empire, it was customary for women to entertain a number of husbands, as in others, it was usual for men to entertain a number of wives or concubines. The dominion of the ancient Medes comprehended many extensive territories; in some of which, the inhabitants were extremely barbarous; in others, no less opulent and luxurious.

This unusual kind of polygamy, if I may be allowed to use that expression, is established at present upon the coast of Malabar,† as well as in some cantons of the Iroquois in North America; and though there is no practice more inconsistent with the views and manners of a civilized nation, it has in all probability been adopted by many individuals, in every country where the inhabitants were unacquainted with the regular institution of marriage.‡

§ It is highly probable, that the celebrated traditions of the *Amazons*, inhabiting the most barbarous regions of Scythia, and the relations of a similar people in some parts of America, have arisen from the state of manners now under consideration. Though these accounts are evidently mixed with fable, and appear to contain much exaggeration, we can hardly suppose that they would have been propagated by so many authors, and have created such universal attention, had they been entirely destitute of real foundation. In a country where marriage is unknown, females are commonly exalted to be the heads of families, or chiefs, and thus acquire an authority, which, notwithstanding their inferiority in strength, may extend to the direction of war, as well as of other transactions. So extraordinary a spectacle as that of a military

---

* [Enlarged.]

† Modern Universal History, vol. 16.—Capt. Hamilton says, that upon the coast of Malabar a woman is not allowed to have more than twelve husbands.

‡ Father Tachard, superior of the French Missionary Jesuits in the East Indies, gives the following account of the inhabitants in the neighbourhood of Calicut. 'In this country,' says he, called Malleami, 'there are *castes*, as in the rest of India. Most of them observe the same customs; and, in particular, they all entertain a like contempt for the religion and manners of the Europeans. But a circumstance, that perhaps is not found elsewhere, and which I myself could scarce believe, is that among these barbarians, and *especially the noble castes*, a woman is allowed, by the laws, to have several husbands. Some of these have had ten husbands together, all of whom they look upon as so many slaves that their charms have subjected.' Lettres edifiantes et curieuses, translated by Mr Lockman, vol. 1, p. 168.

§ [Largely new.]

enterprise conducted by women, and where the men acted in a subordinate capacity, must have filled the enemy with wonder and astonishment, and might easily give rise to those fictions of a *female republic*, and of other circumstances equally marvellous, which we meet with in ancient writers.

> Ducit Amazonidum lunatis agmina peltis
> Pentheslea furens, mediisque in milibus ardet,
> Aurea subnectens exsertae cingula mammae,
> Bellatrix, audetque viris concurrere virgo.

SECTION III

The refinement of the passions of sex, in the pastoral ages

*When we examine the circumstances which occasion the depression of the women, and the low estimation in which they are held, in a simple and barbarous age, we may easily imagine in what manner their condition is varied and improved in the subsequent periods of society. Their condition is naturally improved by every circumstance which tends to create more attention to the pleasures of sex, and to increase the value of those occupations that are suited to the female character; by the cultivation of the arts of life; by the advancement of opulence; and by the gradual refinement of taste and manners. From a view of the progress of society, in these respects, we may, in a great measure, account for the diversity that occurs among different nations, in relation to the rank of the sexes, their dispositions and sentiments towards each other, and the regulations which they have established in the several branches of their domestic economy.

The invention of taming and pasturing cattle, which may be regarded as the first remarkable improvement in the savage life, is productive of very important alterations in the state and manners of a people.

A shepherd is more regularly supplied with food, and is commonly subjected to fewer hardships and calamities than those who live by hunting and fishing. In proportion to the size of his family, the number of his flocks may in some measure be increased; while the labour which is requisite for their management can never be very oppressive. Being thus provided with necessaries, he is led to the pursuit of those objects which may render his situation more easy and comfortable; and among

* [Revised, enlarged.]

these the enjoyments derived from the intercourse of the sexes claim a principal share, and become an object of attention.

The leisure, tranquillity, and retirement of a pastoral life, seem calculated in a peculiar manner to favour the indulgence of those indolent gratifications. From higher notions of refinement a nicer distinction is made with regard to the objects of desire; and the mere animal pleasure is more frequently accompanied with a correspondence of inclination and sentiment. As this must occasion a great diversity in the taste of individuals, it proves, on many occasions, an obstruction to their happiness, and prevents the lover from meeting with a proper return to his passion. But the delays and the uneasiness to which he is thereby subjected, far from repressing the ardour of his wishes, serve only to increase it; and, amid the idleness and freedom from other cares which his situation affords, he is often wholly occupied by the same tender ideas, which are apt to inflame his imagination, and to become the principal subject of such artless expressive songs as he is capable of composing for his ordinary pastime and amusement.

^a In consequence of these improvements the virtue of chastity begins to be recognized; for when love becomes a passion, instead of being a mere sensual appetite, it is natural to think that those affections which are not dissipated by variety of enjoyment, will be the purest and the strongest.

The acquisition of property among shepherds has also a considerable effect upon the commerce of the sexes.

Those who have no other fund for their subsistence but the natural fruits of the earth, or the game which the country affords, are acquainted with no other distinctions in the rank of individuals, but such as arise from their personal accomplishments; distinctions which are never continued for any length of time in the same family, and which therefore can never be productive of any lasting influence and authority. But the invention of taming and pasturing cattle gives rise to a more remarkable and permanent distinction of ranks. Some persons, by being more industrious or more fortunate than others, are led in a short time to acquire more numerous herds and flocks, and are thereby enabled to live in greater affluence, to maintain a number of servants and retainers, and to increase, in proportion, their power and dignity. As the superior fortune which is thus acquired by a single person is apt to remain with his posterity, it creates a train of dependence in those who have been connected with the possessor; and the influence which it occasions is gradually augmented, and transmitted from one generation to another.

^a The degree of wealth acquired by single families of shepherds is

greater than may at first be imagined. In the eastern parts of Tartary, where the inhabitants are chiefly maintained upon the flesh of reindeer, many of the rich possess ten or twenty thousand of those animals; and one of the chiefs of that country, according to an account lately published, was proprietor of no less than an hundred thousand.

ʳThe introduction of wealth, and the distinction of ranks with which it is attended, must interrupt the communication of the sexes, and, in many cases, render it difficult for them to gratify their wishes. As particular persons become opulent, they are led to entertain suitable notions of their own dignity; and, while they aim at superior elegance and refinement in their pleasures, they disdain to contract an alliance with their own dependents, or with people of inferior condition. If great families, upon an equal footing, happen to reside in the same neighbourhood, they are frequently engaged in mutual depredations, and are obliged to have a watchful eye upon the conduct of each other, in order to defend their persons and their property. The animosities and quarrels which arise from their ambition or desire of plunder, and which are fomented by reciprocal injuries, dispose them, in all cases, to behave to one another with distance and reserve, and sometimes prove an insuperable bar to their correspondence.

* Among persons living upon such terms, the passions of sex cannot be gratified with the same facility as among hunters and fishers. The forms of behaviour, naturally introduced among individuals jealous of each other, have a tendency to check all familiarity between them, and to render their approaches towards an intimacy proportionably slow and gradual. The rivalship subsisting between different families, and the mutual prejudices which they have long indulged, must often induce them to oppose the union of their respective relations: And thus the inclinations of individuals having in vain been smothered by opposition, will break forth with greater vigour, and rise at length to a higher pitch, in proportion to the difficulties which they have surmounted.

Upon the eastern coast of Tartary, it is said that such tribes as are accustomed to the pasturing of cattle discover some sort of jealousy with regard to the chastity of their women; a circumstance regarded as of no importance by those inhabitants of the same country who procure their subsistence merely by fishing.

From what is related of the patriarch Jacob, it would seem, that whole families or tribes of shepherds which were anciently scattered over the country of Arabia, had attained some degree of improvement in their manners.

* [Revised already in 2nd edition.]

And Jacob loved Rachel; and said, I will serve thee seven years for Rachel thy younger daughter.

And Laban said, It is better that I give her to thee than that I should give her to another man: abide with me.

And Jacob served seven years for Rachel: and they seemed unto him but a few days, for the love he had to her.*

In the compositions of Ossian, which describe the manners of a people acquainted with pasturage, there is often a degree of tenderness and delicacy of sentiment which can hardly be equalled in the most refined productions of a civilized age. Some allowance no doubt must be made for the heightening of a poet possessed of uncommon genius and sensibility; but, at the same time, it is probable, that the real history of his countrymen was the groundwork of those events which he has related, and of those tragical effects which he frequently ascribes to the passion between the sexes.†

Lorma sat in Aldo's hall, at the light of a flaming oak: the night came, but he did not return, and the soul of Lorma is sad.—What detains thee, Hunter of Cona? for thou didst promise to return.—Has the deer been distant far, and do the dark winds sigh round thee on the heath? I am in the land of strangers, where is my friend, but Aldo? Come from thy echoing hills, O my best beloved!

Her eyes are turned towards the gate, and she listens to the rustling blast. She thinks it is Aldo's tread, and joy rises in her face:—but sorrow returns again, like a thin cloud on the moon.—And thou wilt not return, my love? Let me behold the face of the hill. The moon is in the east. Calm and bright is the breast of the lake! When shall I behold his dogs returning from the chase? When shall I hear his voice loud and distant on the wind? Come from thy echoing hills, Hunter of Woody Cona!

---

* Genesis, chap. xxix, ver. 18, 19, 20.

† *a*As this poet was chiefly employed in describing grand and sublime objects, he has seldom had occasion to introduce any images taken from the pastoral life. From the following passages, however, there can be no doubt that, in his time, the people in the West-Highlands of Scotland, as well as upon the neighbouring coast of Ireland, were acquainted with pasturage. 'The deer descend from the hill. No hunter at a distance is seen. No whistling *cow-herd* is nigh' Carric-thura.

'Let Cuchullin,' said Cairbar, 'divide the *herd* on the hill. His breast is the seat of justice. Depart, thou light of beauty. I went and *divided the herd*. One bull of snow remained. I gave that bull to Cairbar. The wrath of Deugala rose.' Fingal, B. II.

I am informed that, in the Erse language, the word used to denote a man who has nothing, signifies properly one who has no *head of cattle*; which affords a presumption that, in the countries where this language was spoken, pastorage was nearly coeval with property. It is, at the same time difficult to imagine, that people should possess the art of managing a chariot drawn by horses, without having previously learnt something of the management of herds and flocks: Not to mention, that, in those parts of Britain which were known to the Romans, the pasturing of cattle was understood for ages before the time when Ossian is supposed to have lived.

His thin ghost appeared on a rock, like the watery beams of the moon, when it rushes from between two clouds, and the midnight shower is on the field.—She followed the empty form over the heath, for she knew that her hero fell.—I heard her approaching cries on the wind, like the mournful voice of the breeze, when it sighs on the grass of the cave.

She came, she found her hero: her voice was heard no more: silent she rolled her sad eyes; she was pale as a watery cloud, that rises from the lake to the beam of the moon.

Few were her days on Cona: she sunk into the tomb: Fingal commanded his bards, and they sung over the death of Lorma. The daughters of Morven mourned her for one day in the year, when the dark winds of autumn returned.*

a In the agreeable pictures of the *golden age*, handed down from remote antiquity, we may discover the opinion that was generally entertained of the situation and manners of shepherds. Hence that particular species of poetry, which is now appropriated by fashion, to describe the pleasures of rural retirement, accompanied with innocence and simplicity, and with the indulgence of all the tender passions. There is good reason to believe, that these representations of the pastoral life were not inconsistent with the real condition of shepherds, and that the poets, who were the first historians, have only embellished the traditions of early times. In Arcadia, in Sicily, and in some parts of Italy, where the climate was favourable to the rearing of cattle, or where the inhabitants were but little exposed to the depredations of their neighbours, it is probable that the refinement natural to the pastoral state was carried to a great height. This refinement was the more likely to become the subject of exaggeration and poetical embellishment; as, from a view of the progressive improvements in society, it was contrasted, on the one hand, with the barbarous manners of mere savages; and, on the other, with the opposite style of behaviour in polished nations, who, being constantly engaged in the pursuit of gain, and immersed in the cares of business, have contracted habits of industry, avarice, and selfishness.

> *a* Nondum caesa suis, peregrinum ut viseret orbem,
> Montibus, in liquidas pinus descenderat undas:
> Nullaque mortales, praeter sua, littora norant.
> Nondum praecipites cingebant oppida fossae:
> Non tuba directi, non aeris cornua flexi,
> Non galeae, non ensis erant. Sine militis usu
> Mollia securae peragebant otia mentes.
> Ipsa quoque immunis, rastroque intacta, nec ullis
> Saucia vomeribus, per se dabat omnia tellus;

* The battle of Lora.

Contentique cibis, nullo cogente, creatis,
Arbuteos foetus, montanaque fraga legebant;
Cornaque, et in duris haerentia mora rubetis;
Et quae deciderant patula Jovis arbore glandes:
Ver erat eternum, placidique tepentibus auris
Mulcebant zephyri, natos sine semine flores.

SECTION IV

The consequences of the introduction of agriculture, with respect to the intercourse of the sexes

The passions which relate to the commerce of the sexes may be still raised to a greater height, when men are acquainted with the cultivation of the ground, and have made some progress in the different branches of husbandry.

᾽ The improvement of agriculture, which in most parts of the world has been posterior to the art of taming and rearing cattle, is productive of very important alterations in the state of society; more especially with respect to the subject of our present inquiry. Although this employment requires greater industry and labour than is necessary among men who have only the care of herds and flocks; yet by producing plenty of vegetable as well as of animal food, it multiplies the comforts and conveniences of life, and therefore excites in mankind a stronger desire of obtaining those pleasures to which they are prompted by their natural appetites. It also obliges men to fix their residence in the neighbourhood of that spot where their labour is chiefly to be employed, and thereby gives rise to property in land, the most valuable and permanent species of wealth; by the unequal distribution of which a greater disproportion is made in the fortune and rank of individuals, and the causes of their dissension and jealousy are, of course, extended.

In the heroic times of Greece, we may, in some measure, discern the effect of these circumstances upon the character and manners of the people.

The inhabitants of that country were then divided into clans or tribes, who, having for the most part begun the practice of agriculture, had quitted the wandering life of shepherds, and established a number of separate independent villages. As those little societies maintained a constant rivalship with each other, and were frequently engaged in actual hostilities, they were far from being in circumstances to encourage a familiar correspondence; and when in particular cases a formal visit

208

had produced an interview between them, it was often attended with such consequences as might be expected from the restraints to which they were usually subjected. A man of wealth and distinction, having conceived a violent passion for the wife or the daughter of a neighbouring prince, was disposed to encounter every danger in order to gratify his desires; and, after seducing the lady, or carrying her away by force, he was generally involved in a war with her relations, and with such as chose to assist them in vindicating the honour of their family. Disorders of this kind were for a considerable time the source of the chief animosities among the different states of Greece, as well as between them and the inhabitants of Asia Minor; and the rape of Io, of Europa, of Medea, and of Helen, are mentioned as the ground of successive quarrels, which in the end were productive of the most distinguished military enterprise that is recorded in the history of those periods.

But notwithstanding these events, from which it appears that the passions of sex had often a considerable influence upon the conduct of the people, there is no reason to imagine that the Greeks, in those times, had entirely shaken off their ancient barbarous manners, or in their ideas with respect to the women, had attained any high degree of delicacy.

In the Iliad, the wife of Menelaus is considered as of little more value than the treasure which had been stolen along with her. The restitution of the lady and of that treasure is always mentioned in the same breath, and seems to be regarded as a full reparation of the injury which Menelaus had sustained: and though it was known that Helen had made a voluntary elopement with Paris, yet her husband neither discovers any resentment upon that account, nor seems unwilling to receive her again into favour.

Even the wife of Ulysses, whose virtue in refusing the suitors is highly celebrated in the Odyssey, is supposed to derive her principal merit from preserving to her husband's family the dowery which she had brought along with her, and which, it seems, upon her second marriage, must have been restored to her father Icarius.

And though Telemachus is always represented as a pious and dutiful son, we find him reproving his mother in a manner which shows he had no very high notion of her dignity, or of the respect which belonged to her sex.

> Your widowed hours, apart, with female toil,
> And various labours of the loom, beguile;
> There rule, from palace cares remote and free;
> That care to man belongs, and most to me.*

* Pope's Odyssey, book 1, l. 453.

Penelope, so far from being offended at this language, appears to consider it as a mark of uncommon prudence and judgment in so young a person.

> Mature beyond his years, the queen admires
> His sage reply, and with her train retires.

* In all parts of the world, where the advancement of agriculture has introduced the appropriation of landed estates, it will be found that the manners of the inhabitants are such, as indicate considerable improvements in the commerce of the sexes.

But the acquisition of property in land, the jealousy arising from the distinction of ranks, and the animosities which are apt to be produced by the neighbourhood of great independent families, appear to have been attended with the most remarkable consequences in those barbarous nations, who, about the fifth century, invaded the Roman empire, and afterwards settled in the different provinces which they had conquered.

† As those nations were small, and as they acquired an extensive territory, the different tribes or families of which they were composed spread themselves over the country, and were permitted to occupy very large estates. Particular chieftains or heads of families became great and powerful in proportion to their wealth, which enabled them to support a numerous train of retainers and followers. A great number of these were united under a sovereign; for the different parts of a Roman province, having a dependence upon one another, fell naturally into the hands of the same military leader, and were erected into one kingdom. But, in a rude age, unaccustomed to subordination, the monarch could have little authority over such wide dominions. The opulent proprietors of land, disdaining submission to regular government, lived in the constant exercise of predatory incursions upon their neighbours; and every separate family, being in a great measure left without protection from the public, was under the necessity of providing for its own defence. The disorders arising from private wars between different families of the same kingdom, were not effectually repressed for many centuries; during which time the same causes continued to operate in forming the character and manners of the people, and gave rise to a set of customs and institutions of which we have no example in any other age or country.

The high notions of military honour, and the romantic love and gallantry, by which the modern nations of Europe have been so much distinguished, were equally derived from those particular circumstances.

* [Paragraph already added in 2nd edition.]   † [Four paragraphs revised.]

As war was the principal employment of those nations, so it was carried on in a manner somewhat peculiar to themselves. Their military enterprises were less frequently undertaken against a foreign enemy than against the inhabitants of a neighbouring district; and on these latter occasions, the chief warriors of either party, were, from the smallness of their numbers, known to each other, and distinguished by the respective degrees of strength or valour which they possessed. The members of different families, who had long been at variance, were therefore animated with a strong personal animosity; and as, in the time of an engagement, they were disposed to single out one another, a battle was frequently nothing more than a number of separate duels between combatants inspired with mutual jealousy, and contending for superiority in military prowess. As the individuals of different parties were inflamed by opposition, those of the same party, conscious of acting under the particular observation of all their companions, were excited to vie with each other in the performance of such exploits as might procure admiration and applause. In this situation they not only contracted habits which rendered them cool and intrepid in danger, but at the same time acquired a remarkable generosity of sentiment in the exercise of their mutual hostilities. Persons, who aspired to superior rank and influence, fought merely to obtain a reputation in arms, and affected to look upon every other consideration as mean and ignoble. Having this object in view, they thought it disgraceful to assault an enemy when unprepared for his defence, or without putting him upon his guard by a previous challenge; and they disdained to practise unfair means in order to gain a victory, or to use it with insolence and barbarity. These notions of honour were productive of certain rules and maxims, by which the gentry were directed in their whole manner of fighting, and from which they never deviated without bringing an indelible stain upon their character.

The ideas of personal dignity, which were thus raised to so high a pitch among neighbouring families, were incompatible with any regular distribution of justice. Men of wealth and distinction were unwilling to apply to a magistrate in order to procure redress for the injuries or affronts which they sustained; because this would have amounted to a confession that they were unable to assert their character and rank, by taking vengeance upon the offender. If a law-suit had arisen in matters of property, it commonly happened in the progress of the dispute, that one of the parties gave such offence to the other, as occasioned their deciding the difference by the sword. The judge, who found himself incapable of preventing this determination, endeavoured to render it less hurtful to society, by discouraging the friends of either party from interfering in the quarrel. With this view, he assumed the privilege of regulating the forms, and even became a spectator of the combat; which in that age, no less prone to superstition than intoxicated with the love of military glory, was considered as an immediate appeal to the judgment of heaven. These judicial combats, though they did not introduce the custom of duelling, had certainly a tendency to render it more universal, and to settle a variety of observances with which it came to be attended.

The diversions of a people have always a relation to their general character and manners. It was therefore to be expected that such war-like nations would be extremely addicted to martial exercises, and that the members of different tribes or families, when not engaged in actual hostilities, would be accustomed to challenge one another to a trial of their strength, activity, or military skill. Hence the origin of jousts and tournaments; those images of war, which were frequently exhibited by men of rank and which tended still farther to improve those nice punc-tilios of behaviour that were commonly practised by the military people in every serious contest.

From this prevailing spirit of the times, the art of war became the study of everyone who was desirous of maintaining the character of a gentleman. The youth were early initiated in the profession of arms, and served a sort of apprenticeship under persons of distinguished eminence. The young squire became in reality the servant of that leader to whom he had attached himself, and whose virtues were set before him as a model for imitation. He was taught to perform with ease and dexterity those exercises which were either ornamental or useful; and, at the same time, he endeavoured to acquire those talents and accomplish-ments which were thought suitable to his profession. He was taught to look upon it as his duty to check the insolent, to restrain the oppressor, to protect the weak and defenceless; to behave with frankness and humanity even to an enemy, with modesty and politeness to all. According to the proficiency which he had made, he was honoured with new titles and marks of distinction, till at length he arrived at the dignity of knighthood; a dignity which even the greatest potentates were ambitious of acquiring, as it was supposed to ascertain the most complete military education, and the attainment of such qualifications as were then universally admired and respected.

ª The same ambition, in persons of an exalted military rank, which gave rise to the institution of chivalry, was afterwards productive of the different *orders of knighthood*, by which, from a variety of similar establish-ments in the several kingdoms of Europe, a subdivision was made in the degrees of honour conferred upon individuals.

The situation of mankind in those periods had also a manifest tendency to heighten and improve the passion between the sexes. It was not to be expected that those opulent chiefs, who maintained a constant opposition to each other, would allow any sort of familiarity to take place between the members of their respective families. Retired in their own castles, and surrounded with their numerous vassals, they looked upon their neighbours either as inferior to them in rank, or as enemies. They behaved to each other with that ceremonious civility which the laws of chivalry required; but, at the same time, with that reserve and caution which a regard to their own safety made it necessary for them to observe. The young knight, as he marched to the tournament, saw at a distance the daughter of the chieftain by whom the show was exhibited; and it was even with difficulty that he could obtain access to her, in order to declare the sentiments with which she had inspired him. He was entertained by her relations with that cold respect which demonstrated that their dignity was alarmed by his aspiring to contract an alliance with them. The lady herself was taught to assume the pride of her family, and to think that no person was worthy of her affection who did not possess an exalted rank and character. To have given way to a sudden inclination would have disgraced her for ever in the opinion of all her kindred; and it was only by a long course of attention, and of the most respectful service, that the lover could hope for any favour from his mistress.*

The barbarous state of the country at that time, and the injuries to which the inhabitants, especially those of the weaker sex, were frequently exposed, gave ample scope for the display of military talents; and the knight, who had nothing to do at home, was encouraged to wander from place to place, and from one court to another, in quest of adventures; in which he endeavoured to advance his reputation in arms, and to recommend himself to the fair of whom he was enamoured, by fighting with every person who was so inconsiderate as to dispute her unrivalled beauty, virtue, or personal accomplishments. Thus, while his thoughts were constantly fixed upon the same object, and while his imagination, inflamed by absence and repeated disappointments, was employed in heightening all those charms by which his desires were continually excited, his passion was at length wrought up to the highest pitch, and uniting with the love of same, became the ruling principle,

---

* Among the Franks, so early as the compilation of the Salique law, it appears that a high degree of reserve was practised between the sexes. M. L'Abbé Velly quotes, from that ancient code, the following article, 'Any man who has shaken hands with a free woman shall be made to pay a penalty, of fifteen gold sous.' And he adds, 'If our century is admittedly more polished than that of our ancient legislators, it is at least neither so respectful nor so reserved.' Histoire de France. tom. i, p. 134. [This note added in 2nd edition.]

which gave a particular turn and direction to all his sentiments and opinions.

As there were many persons in the same situation, they were naturally inspired with similar sentiments. Rivals to one another in military glory, they were often competitors, as it is expressed by Milton, 'to win her grace whom all commend'; and the same emulation which disposed them to aim at pre-eminence in the one respect, excited them with no less eagerness to dispute the preference in the other. Their dispositions and manner of thinking became fashionable, and were gradually diffused by the force of education and example. To be in love was looked upon as one of the necessary qualifications of a knight; and he was no less ambitious of showing his constancy and fidelity to his mistress, than of displaying his military virtues. He assumed the title of her slave, or servant. By this he distinguished himself in every combat; and his success was supposed to redound to her honour, no less than to his own. If she had bestowed upon him a present to be worn in the field of battle in token of her regard, it was considered as a pledge of victory, and as laying upon him the strongest obligation to render himself worthy of the favour.

The sincere and faithful passion, which commonly occupied the heart of every warrior, and which he professed upon all occasions, was naturally productive of the utmost purity of manners, and of great respect and veneration for the female sex. The delicacy of sentiment which prevailed, had a tendency to divert the attention from sensual pleasure, and created a general abhorrence of debauchery. Persons who felt a strong propensity to magnify and exalt the object of their own wishes, were easily led to make allowance for the same disposition in their neighbours; and such individuals as made a point of defending the reputation and dignity of that particular lady to whom they were devoted, became extremely cautious, lest by any insinuation or impropriety of behaviour, they should hurt the character of another, and be exposed to the just resentment of those by whom she was protected. A woman who deviated so far from the established maxims of the age as to violate the laws of chastity, was indeed deserted by every body, and was universally condemned and insulted.* But those who adhered to

* M. de la Curne de Sainte Palaye has collected some extraordinary instances of that zeal with which those who enjoyed the honour of knighthood endeavoured to expose any lady who had lost her reputation.—'Et vous diray encore plus,' says an old author, 'comme j'ay ouy racompter à plusieurs Chevaliers qui virent celluy Messire Geoffroy, qui disoit que quand il chevauchoit par les champs, et il veoit le chasteau ou manoir de quelque Dame, il demandoit tousjours à qui il estoit; et quand on lui disoit, *il est a celle*, se le Dame estoit *blasmee de son honneur*, il se fust plustost detournè d'une demi lieue qu'il ne fust venu jusques devant la porte; et là prenoit ung petit de croye qu'il portoit, et notoit cetter porte, et y faisoit ung signet, et s'en venoit.'

the strict rules of virtue, and maintained an unblemished reputation, were treated like beings of a superior order. The love of God and of the ladies was one of the first lessons inculcated upon every young person who was initiated into the military profession. He was instructed with care in all those forms of behaviour which, according to the received notions of gallantry and politeness, were settled with the most frivolous exactness. He was frequently put under the tuition of some matron of rank and distinction, who in this particular directed his education, and to whom he was under a necessity of revealing all his sentiments, thoughts, and actions. An oath was imposed upon him, by which he became bound to vindicate the honour of the ladies, as well as to defend them from every species of injustice; and the uncourteous knight who behaved to them with rudeness, or who ventured to injure and insult them, became the object of general indignation and vengeance, and was treated as the common enemy of all those who were actuated by the true and genuine principles of chivalry.*

The sentiments of military honour, and the love and gallantry so universally diffused among those nations, which were displayed in all the amusements and diversions of the people, had necessarily a remarkable influence upon the genius and taste of their literary compositions. Men were pleased with a recital of what they admired in real life; and the first poetical historians endeavoured to embellish those events which had struck their imagination, and appeared the most worthy of being preserved.

Such was the employment of the bards, who about the eleventh century are said, along with their minstrels, to have attended the festivals and entertainments of princes, and to have sung, with the accompaniment of musical instruments, a variety of small poetical pieces of their own composition, describing the heroic sentiments, as well as the love and gallantry of the times.

They were succeeded by the writers of romance, who related a longer and more connected series of adventures, in which were exhibited the most extravagant instances of valour and generosity, of patience and fortitude, of respect to the ladies, of disinterested love, and inviolable fidelity; subjects the most capable of warming the imagination, and of producing the most sublime and refined descriptions; but which were often disgraced by the unskilfulness of the author, and by that excessive propensity to exaggeration, and turn for the marvellous, which prevailed in those ages of darkness and superstition. These performances, however, with all their faults, may be regarded as striking monuments of the Gothic taste and genius, to which there is

* [See further, *H.V.*, vol. I, pp. 113-26.]

nothing similar in the writings of antiquity, and at the same time as useful records, that contain some of the outlines of the history, together with a faithful picture of the manners and customs of those remarkable periods.

This observation is in some measure applicable to the Epic poetry which followed, and which, with little more correctness, but with the graces of versification, described the same heroic and tender sentiments, though tinctured by the peculiar genius and character of different writers.

a The romance of Charlemain and his twelve peers, ascribed to archibishop Turpin, a cotemporary of that monarch, but which is supposed to be a work of the eleventh century, furnished materials for the *Morgante*, the *Orlando Innamorato*, and the *Orlando Furioso*. The last of these poems, which entirely eclipsed the reputation of the two former, whatever may be its merit to an Italian, in easiness and harmony of expression, is a bundle of incoherent adventures, discovering neither unity of design, nor any selection of such objects as are fitted to excite admiration. The *Gierusalemme Liberata*, to the system of enchantment, and romantic exploits which modern times had introduced, has united the regularity of the ancient Greek and Roman poets; and though the author's talents for the pathetic seem inferior to his powers of description, the whole structure of his admirable poem is sufficient to show the advantages, in point of sublimity, derived from the manners and institutions of chivalry. The fabulous legends of Prince Arthur, and his knights of the round table, suggested the groundwork of Spenser's *Fairy Queen*; but the writer, instead of improving upon the Gothic model, has thought proper to cover it with a veil of allegory; which is too dark to have much beauty of its own; and which, notwithstanding the strength of imagery frequently displayed, destroys the appearance of reality, necessary, in works of imagination, to interest the affections.

* When the improvement of public shows had given rise to dramatic performances, the same sort of manners was adopted in those entertainments; and the first tragedies, unless when founded upon religious subjects, represented love as the grand spring and mover of every action, the source of all those hopes and fears with which the principal persons were successively agitated, and of that distress and misery in which they were finally involved. This is the more remarkable, because, from the rigid morals of that age, women were not permitted to act in those representations; and therefore the parts allotted to them, which were performed by men, were usually so conducted by the poet as to bear a very small proportion to the rest of the piece.

* [Enlarged.]

The first deviation from this general taste of composition in works of entertainment may be discovered in Italy, where the revival of letters was early attended with some relaxation of the Gothic institutions and manners.

The advancement of the Italian states in commerce and manufactures so early as the thirteenth century, had produced a degree of opulence and luxury, and was followed, soon after, by the cultivation of the fine arts, and the improvement of taste and science. The principal towns of Italy came thus to be filled with tradesmen and merchants, whose unwarlike dispositions, conformable to their manner of life, were readily communicated to those who had intercourse with them. To this we may add the influence of the clergy, who resorted in great numbers to Rome, as the fountain of ecclesiastical preferment, and who, embracing different views and principles from those of the military profession, were enabled to propagate their opinions and sentiments among the greater part of the inhabitants.

The decay of the military spirit among the Italians was manifest from their disuse of duelling, the most refined method of executing private revenge, and from their substituting in place of it the more artful but cowardly practice of poisoning. Their taste of writing was in like manner varied according to this alteration of their circumstances; and the people began to relish those ludicrous descriptions of low life and of licentious manners which we meet with in the tales of Boccace, and many other writers, entirely repugnant to the gravity and decorum of former times, and which appear to have taken their origin from the monks, in consequence of such dispositions and habits as their constrained and unnatural situation had a tendency to produce. This kind of composition, however, appears to have been the peculiar growth of Italy; and those authors who attempted to introduce it into other countries, as was done by Chaucer in England, are only servile imitators, or rather mere translators of the Italians.

In the other countries of Europe, the manners introduced by chivalry were more firmly rooted, and acquiring stability from custom, may still be observed to have a good deal of influence upon the taste and sentiments even of the present age. When a change of circumstances, more than the inimitable ridicule of Cervantes, had contributed to explode the ancient romances, they were succeeded by those serious novels which, in France and England, are still the favourite entertainment, and which represent, in a more moderate degree, the sentiments of military honour, as well as the love and gallantry which prevailed in the writings of a former period. The fashion of those times has also remained with us in our theatrical compositions; and scarce any author, till very lately, seems to have thought that a tragedy without a love-plot could be attended with success.

a The great respect and veneration for the ladies, which prevailed in a former period, has still a considerable influence upon our behaviour towards them, and has occasioned their being treated with a degree of politeness, delicacy, and attention, that was unknown to the Greeks and Romans, and perhaps to all the nations of antiquity. This has given an air of refinement to the intercourse of the sexes, which contributes to heighten the elegant pleasures of society, and may therefore be considered as a valuable improvement, arising from the extravagance of Gothic institutions and manners.

SECTION V

Changes in the condition of women, arising from the improvement of useful arts and manufactures

*One of the most remarkable differences between man and other animals consists in that wonderful capacity for the improvement of his faculties with which he is endowed. Never satisfied with any particular attainment, he is continually impelled by his desires from the pursuit of one object to that of another; and his activity is called forth in the prosecution of the several arts which render his situation more easy and agreeable. This progress however is slow and gradual; at the same time that, from the uniformity of the human constitution, it is accompanied with similar appearances in different parts of the world. When agriculture has created abundance of provisions, people extend their views to other circumstances of smaller importance. They endeavour to be clothed and lodged, as well as maintained, in a more comfortable manner; and they engage in such occupations as are calculated for these useful purposes. By the application of their labour to a variety of objects, commodities of different kinds are produced. These are exchanged for one another, according to the demand of different individuals; and thus manufactures, together with commerce, are at length introduced into a country.

These improvements are the source of very important changes in the state of society, and particularly in relation to the women. The advancement of people in manufactures and commerce has a natural tendency to remove those circumstances which prevented the free intercourse of

* [Paragraph already added in 2nd edition.]

the sexes, and contributed to heighten and inflame their passions. From the cultivation of the arts of peace, the different members of society are more and more united, and have occasion to enter into a greater variety of transactions for their mutual benefit. As they become more civilized, they perceive the advantages of establishing a regular government; and different tribes who lived in a state of independence, are restrained from injuring one another, and reduced under subjection to the laws. Their former animosities, the cause of so much disturbance, are no longer cherished by fresh provocation, and at length are buried in oblivion. Being no longer withheld by mutual fear and jealousy, they are led by degrees to contract an acquaintance, and to carry on a more intimate correspondence. The men and women of different families are permitted to converse with more ease and freedom, and meet with less opposition to the indulgence of their inclinations.

But while the fair sex become less frequently the objects of those romantic and extravagant passions, which in some measure arise from the disorders of society, they are more universally regarded upon account of their useful or agreeable talents.

When men begin to disuse their ancient barbarous practices, when their attention is not wholly engrossed by the pursuit of military reputation, when they have made some progress in arts, and have attained to a proportional degree of refinement, they are necessarily led to set a value upon those female accomplishments and virtues which have so much influence upon every species of improvement, and which contribute in so many different ways to multiply the comforts of life. In this situation, the women become, neither the slaves, nor the idols of the other sex, but the friends and companions. The wife obtains that rank and station which appears most agreeable to reason, being suited to her character and talents. Loaded by nature with the first and most immediate concern in rearing and maintaining the children, she is endowed with such dispositions as fit her for the discharge of this important duty, and is at the same time particularly qualified for all such employments as require skill and dexterity more than strength, which are so necessary in the interior management of the family. *ª* Possessed of peculiar delicacy, and sensibility, whether derived from original constitution, or from her way of life, she is capable of securing the esteem and affection of her husband, by dividing his cares, by sharing his joys, and by soothing his misfortunes.

The regard, which is thus shown to the useful talents and accomplishments of the women, cannot fail to operate in directing their education, and in forming their manners. They learn to suit their behaviour to the circumstances in which they are placed, and to that particular standard of propriety and excellence which is set before them. Being respected upon account of their diligence and proficiency in the various branches of domestic economy, they naturally endeavour to improve and extend those valuable qualifications. They are taught to apply with assiduity to those occupations which fall under their province, and to look upon idleness as the greatest blemish in the female character. They are instructed betimes in whatever will qualify them for the duties of their station, and is thought conducive to the ornament of private life. Engaged in these solid pursuits, they are less apt to be distinguished by such brilliant accomplishments as make a figure in the circle of gaiety and amusement. Accustomed to live in retirement, and to keep company with their nearest relations and friends, they are inspired with all that modesty and diffidence which is natural to persons unacquainted with promiscuous conversation; and their affections are neither dissipated by pleasure, nor corrupted by the vicious customs of the world. As their attention is principally bestowed upon the members of their own family, they are led in a particular manner to improve those feelings of the heart which are excited by these tender connections, and they are trained up in the practice of all domestic virtues.

The celebrated character, drawn by Solomon, of the virtuous woman, is highly expressive of those ideas and sentiments, which are commonly entertained by a people advancing in commerce and in the arts of life.

She seeketh wool and flax, and worketh willingly with her hands.

She is like the merchant ships, she bringeth her food from afar.

She riseth also while it is yet night, and giveth meat to her household, and a portion to her maidens.

She considereth a field and buyeth it: with the fruit of her hands she planteth a vineyard.

She perceiveth that her merchandise is good: her candle goeth not out by night.

She layeth her hands to the spindle, and her hands hold the distaff.

She stretcheth out her hand to the poor; yea, she reacheth forth her hands to the needy.

She is not afraid of the snow for her household: for all her household are cloathed with scarlet.

She maketh herself coverings of tapestry, her cloathing is silk and purple.

Her husband is known in the gates, when he sitteth among the elders of the land.

She maketh fine linen, and selleth it, and delivereth girdles unto the merchant.

Strength and honour are her cloathing, and she shall rejoice in time to come.

She openeth her mouth with wisdom, and in her tongue is the law of kindness.

She looketh well to the ways of her household, and eateth not the bread of idleness.*

In many of the Greek states, during their most flourishing periods, it appears, that the women were viewed nearly in the same light, and that their education was chiefly calculated to improve their industry and talents, so as to render them useful members of society. Their attention seems to have been engrossed by the care of their own families, and by those smaller branches of manufacture which they were qualified to exercise. They were usually lodged in a remote apartment of the house, and were seldom visited by any person except their near relations. Their modesty and reserve, and their notions of a behaviour suited to the female character, were such as might be expected from their retired manner of life. They never appeared abroad without being covered with a veil, and were not allowed to be present at any public entertainment. 'As for you, women,' says Pericles, in one of the orations in Thucydides, 'it ought to be the constant aim of your sex to avoid being talked of by the public; and it is your highest commendation that you should never be the objects either of applause or censure.'†

Lysias, in one of his orations, has introduced a widow, the mother of several children, who considers her appearing in public as one of the most desperate measures to which she could be driven by her misfortunes. She prays and entreats her son-in-law to call together her relations and friends, that she might inform them of her situation. 'I have,' says she, 'never before been accustomed to speak in the presence of men; but I am compelled by my sufferings to complain of the injuries I have met with.'‡

§ In another oration, composed by the same author, a citizen, accused of murdering his wife's gallant, gives the following simple narrative of his domestic economy.

When I first entered into the married state, Athenians! I endeavoured to observe a medium between the harsh severity of some husbands, and the easy fondness of others. My wife, though treated with kindness, was watched with attention. As a husband, I rendered her situation agreeable; but as a woman, she was left neither the entire mistress of my fortune, nor of her own actions. When she became a mother, this new endearment softened and overcame the prudent caution of my former conduct, and engaged me to repose

* Proverbs, chap xxxi, ver. 13, etc.   † Thucydides, lib. 2.
‡ Lysias, Orat. cont. Diogit.   § [Three paragraphs added.]

in her an unlimited confidence. During a short time, Athenians! I had no occasion to repent of this alteration: she proved a most excellent wife; and, highly circumspect in her private behaviour, she managed my affairs with the utmost diligence and frugality. But since the death of my mother, she has been the cause of all my calamities. *Then she first got abroad to attend the funeral,* and being observed by Eratosthenes, was soon after seduced by him. This he affected by means of our female slave, whom he watched going to market, and whom, by fair promises and flattery, he drew over to his designs.

It is necessary you should be informed, Athenians! that my house consists of two floors; the floor above is laid out in a similar manner to that below; *this lodges the men, that above is destined for the women.* Upon the birth of our son, my wife suckled him herself; and to relieve her from the fatigue of going below stairs as often as it was necessary to bathe him, I yielded up the ground floor to the women, and kept above stairs myself. She still continued, however, to sleep with me during the night; and when the child was peevish, and fell a-crying, she frequently went below stairs, and offered it the breast. This practice was long continued without any suspicion on my part, who, simple man that I was! regarded my spouse as a prodigy of virtue.*

Solon is said to have made regulations for preventing the women from violating those decorums which were esteemed essential to their character. He appointed that no matron should go from home with more than three garments, nor a larger quantity of provisions than could be purchased for an obolus. He also provided, that when any matron went abroad, she should always have an attendant, and a lighted torch carried before her.

ᵃAt Athens, a man was not permitted to approach the apartment of his step-mother, or her children, though living in the same house; which is given, by Mr. Hume, as the reason why, by the Athenian laws, one might marry his half-sister by the father; for as these relations had no more intercourse than the men and women of different families, there was no greater danger of any criminal correspondence between them.

It is probable, that the recluse situation of the Grecian women, which was adapted to the circumstances of the people upon their first advancement in arts, was afterwards maintained from an inviolable respect to their ancient institutions.† The democratical form of government, which came to be established in most parts of Greece, had, at the same time, a tendency to occupy the people in the management of public affairs, and to engage them in those pursuits of ambition, from which the women were naturally excluded. It must however be admitted that, while such a state of manners might be conducive to the more solid enjoyments of life, it undoubtedly prevented the two sexes from im-

* See the oration of Lysias, in defence of Euphiletus, translated by Dr Gillies.
† [This sentence added.]

proving the arts of conversation, and from giving a polish to the expression of their thoughts and sentiments. Hence it is, that the Greeks, notwithstanding their learning and good sense, were remarkably deficient in delicacy and politeness, and were so little judges of propriety in wit and humour, as to relish the low ribaldry of an Aristophanes, at a period when they were entertained with the sublime eloquence of a Demosthenes, and with the pathetic compositions of a Euripides and a Sophocles.

The military character in ancient Greece, considered with respect to politeness, and compared with the same character in modern times, seems to afford a good illustration of what has been observed. Soldiers, as they are men of the world, have usually such manners as are formed by company and conversation. But in ancient Greece they were no less remarkable for rusticity and ill-manners, than in the modern nations of Europe they are distinguished by politeness and good-breeding; for Menander, the comic poet, says, that he can hardly conceive such a character as that of a polite soldier to be formed even by the power of the Deity.

* When the Romans, towards the middle of the Commonwealth, had become in some degree civilized, it is probable that the condition of their women was nearly the same with that of the Greeks in the period abovementioned. But it appears that, at Rome, the circumstances of the people underwent very rapid changes in this particular. By the conquest of many opulent nations, great wealth was suddenly imported into the capital of the empire; which corrupted the ancient manners of the inhabitants, and produced a great revolution in their taste and sentiments.

In the modern nations of Europe, we may also observe that the introduction of arts, and of regular government, had an immediate influence upon the relative condition and behaviour of the sexes. When the disorders incident to the Gothic system had subsided, the women began to be valued upon account of their useful talents and accomplishments; and their consideration and rank, making allowance for some remains of that romantic spirit which had prevailed in a former period, came to be chiefly determined by the importance of those departments which they occupied, in carrying on the business, and maintaining the intercourse of society. The manners introduced by such views of the female character are still in some measure preserved, in those European countries which have been least affected by the late rapid advances of luxury and refinement.

* [Two new paragraphs substituted for old.]

SECTION VI

The effects of great opulence, and the culture of the elegant arts, upon the relative condition of the sexes

The progressive improvements of a country are still attended with farther variations in the sentiments and manners of the inhabitants.

The first attention of a people is directed to the acquisition of the mere necessaries of life, and to the exercise of those occupations which are most immediately requisite for subsistence. According as they are successful in these pursuits, they feel a gradual increase of their wants, and are excited with fresh vigour and activity to search for the means of supplying them. The advancement of the more useful arts is followed by the cultivation of those which are subservient to pleasure and entertainment. Mankind, in proportion to the progress they have made in multiplying the conveniences of their situation, become more refined in their taste, and luxurious in their manner of living. Exempted from labour, and placed in great affluence, they endeavour to improve their enjoyments, and become addicted to all those amusements and diversions which give an exercise to their minds, and relieve them from languor and weariness, the effects of idleness and dissipation. In such a state, the pleasures which nature has grafted upon the love between the sexes, become the source of an elegant correspondence, and are likely to have a general influence upon the commerce of society. Women of condition come to be more universally admired and courted upon account of the agreeable qualities which they possess, and upon account of the amusement which their conversation affords. They are encouraged to quit that retirement which was formerly esteemed so suitable to their character, to enlarge the sphere of their acquaintance, and to appear in mixed company, and in public meetings of pleasure. They lay aside the spindle and the distaff, and engage in other employments more agreeable to the fashion. As they are introduced more into public life, they are led to cultivate those talents which are adapted to the intercourse of the world, and to distinguish themselves by polite accomplishments that tend to heighten their personal attractions, and to excite those peculiar sentiments and passions of which they are the natural objects.

These improvements, in the state and accomplishments of the women, might be illustrated from a view of the manners in the different nations of Europe. They have been carried to the greatest height in France, and in some parts of Italy, where the fine arts have received the highest cultivation, and where a taste for refined and elegant amusement has been generally diffused. The same improvements have made their way into England and Germany; though the attention of the people to the more necessary and useful arts, and their slow advancement in those which are subservient to entertainment, has, in these countries, prevented the intercourse of the sexes from being equally extended. Even in Spain, where, from the defects of administration, or from whatever causes, the arts have for a long time been almost entirely neglected, the same effects of refinement are at length beginning to appear, by the admission of the women to that freedom which they have in the other countries of Europe.

Thus we may observe, that in refined and polished nations there is the same free communication between the sexes as in the ages of rudeness and barbarism. In the latter, women enjoy the most unbounded liberty, because it is thought of no consequence what use they shall make of it. In the former, they are entitled to the same freedom, upon account of those agreeable qualities which they possess, and the rank and dignity which they hold as members of society.

^{r} It should seem, however, that there are certain limits beyond which it is impossible to push the real improvements arising from wealth and opulence. In a simple age, the free intercourse of the sexes is attended with no bad consequences; but in opulent and luxurious nations, it gives rise to licentious and dissolute manners, inconsistent with good order, and with the general interest of society. The love of pleasure, when carried to excess, is apt to weaken and destroy those passions which it endeavours to gratify, and to pervert those appetites which nature has bestowed upon mankind for the most beneficial purposes. The natural tendency, therefore, of great luxury and dissipation is to diminish the rank and dignity of the women, by preventing all refinement in their connection with the other sex, and rendering them only subservient to the purposes of animal enjoyment.

> * Prima peregrinos obscena pecunia mores
> Intulit; et turpi fregerunt secula luxû
> Divitiae molles. Quid enim Venus ebria curat?

The voluptuousness of the Eastern nations, arising from a degree of advancement in the arts joined, perhaps, to the effect of their climate, and the facility with which they are able to procure subsistence, has introduced the practice of polygamy; by which the women are reduced into a state of slavery and confinement, and a great proportion of

---

* [Added already in 2nd edition.]

the inhabitants are employed in such offices as render them incapable of contributing, either to the population, or to the useful improvements of the country.*

† The excessive opulence of Rome, about the end of the common-wealth, and after the establishment of the despotism, gave rise to a degree of debauchery of which we have no example in any other European nation. This did not introduce polygamy, which was re-pugnant to the regular and well established police of a former period; though Julius Caesar is said to have prepared a law by which the *emperor* should be allowed to have as many wives as he thought fit. But the luxury of the people, being restrained in this way, came to be the more indulged in every other; and the common prostitution of the women was carried to a height that must have been extremely un-favourable to the multiplication of the species; while the liberty of divorce was so much extended and abused, that, among persons of condition, marriage became a very slight and transient connection.‡

The frequency of divorce, among the Romans, was attended with bad consequences, which were felt in every part of their domestic economy. As the husband and wife had a separation constantly in view, they could repose little confidence in each other, but were continually occupied by separate considerations of interest. In such a situation, they were not likely to form a strong attachment, or to bestow much atten-tion to the joint concerns of their family. So far otherwise, the practice of stealing from each other, in expectation of a divorce, became so

---

* What is here said with respect to polygamy is only applicable to that institution as it takes place among opulent and luxurious nations; for in barbarous countries, where it is introduced in a great measure from motives of conveniency, and where it is accompanied with little or no jealousy, it cannot have the same consequences.

† [Remainder of chapter added.]

‡ By the Roman law, about this period, divorces were granted upon any pretence whatever, and might be procured at the desire of either party. At the same time, the manners, which produced this law, disposed the people very frequently to lay hold of the privilege which it gave them; in so much that we read of few Romans of rank who had not been once divorced, if not oftener. To mention only persons of the gravest and most respectable character: M. Brutus repudiated his wife Claudia, though there was no stain upon her reputation. Cicero put away his wife Terentia, after she had lived with him thirty years, and also his second wife Publilia, whom he had married in his old age. His daughter Tullia was repudiated by Dola-bella. Terentia, after she was divorced from Cicero, is said to have had three successive husbands, the first of whom was Cicero's enemy, Sallust the historian. It was formerly mentioned that M. Cato, after his wife Marcia had brought him three children, gave her away to his friend Hortensius. Many of those trifling causes which gave rise to divorce are taken notice of by Valerius Maximus. Seneca declares that some women of illustrious rank were accustomed to reckon their years, not by the number of consuls, but of husbands. [De beneficiis.] As a further proof of the profligacy of that age, it is observed that men were sometimes induced to marry from the prospect merely of enriching themselves by the for-feiture of the wife's dower, when she committed adultery. Valerius Maximus, lib. 6, c. 3.

general that it was not branded with the name of theft, but, like other fashionable vices, received a softening appellation.*

The bad agreement between married persons, together with the common infidelity of the wife, had a natural tendency to alienate the affections of a father from his children, and led him, in many cases, not only to neglect their education, but even to deprive them of their paternal inheritance. This appears to have been one great cause of that propensity, discovered by the people, to convey their estates by *will*; which, from the many statutes that were made, and the equitable decisions of judges that were given, in order to rectify the abuse, has rendered that branch of the Roman law, relating to testaments, more extensive and complicated than any other. The frequency of such deeds, to the prejudice of the heirs at law, created swarms of those legacy-hunters,† whose trade, as we learn from Horace, afforded the most infallible means of growing rich; and the same circumstance gave also great encouragement to the forgery or falsification of *wills*, a species of fraud which is much taken notice of by the writers of those times, and which has been improperly regarded as one of the general effects of opulence and luxury.‡

In those voluptuous ages of Rome, it should seem that the inhabitants were too much dissipated by pleasure to feel any violent passion for an individual, and the correspondence of the sexes was too undistinguishing to be attended with much delicacy of sentiment. It may accordingly be remarked, that the writers of the Augustan age, who have afforded so many models of composition in other branches, have left no work of imagination, describing the manners of their own countrymen, in which love is supposed to be productive of any tragical, or very serious effects. Neither that part of the Eneid which relates to the death of Dido, nor the love-epistles of Ovid, both of which are founded upon events in a remote age, and in distant countries, can properly be considered as exceptions to what is here alleged. It also merits attention that when the Roman poets have occasion to represent their own senti-

---

* The action for the recovery of such stolen goods was not called *conditio furtiva*, but *actio rerum amotarum*.

† *Heredipetae*.

‡ 'Do thou, O prophet, tell me forthwith how I may amass riches, and heaps of money. In troth I have told you and tell you again. Use your craft to lie at catch for the last wills of old men: and do not, if one or two cunning chaps escape by biting the bait off the hook, either lay aside hope, or quit the art, though disappointed in your aim.'
[See the whole of the 5th Satire, B. 2 of Horace.]
[Bracket note in original. Selection, 1, 21–6. Literal prose translation C. Smart, ed.]
The Volpone, of Johnson, is entirely founded upon this part of ancient manners; but the ridicule of that performance is in a great measure lost, as the original from which it is drawn, and of which it is a faithful copy, has no place in any modern country.

ments in this particular, the subject of their description, not to mention more irregular appetites, is either the love of a concubine, or an intrigue with a married woman. This is not less apparent from the grave and tender elegies of Tibullus and Propertius, than from the gay and more licentious writings of Horace, of Ovid, and of Catullus. The style of those compositions, and the manners from which it was derived, while they degraded the women of virtue, contributed, no doubt, to exalt the character of a kept-mistress. The different situation of modern nations, in this respect, is perhaps the reason why they have no term corresponding to that of *amica* in Latin.

The acquisition of great wealth, and the improvement of the elegant arts, together with the free intercourse of the sexes, have, in some of the modern European nations, had similar consequences to what they produced in ancient Rome, by introducing a strong disposition to pleasure. This is most especially remarkable in France and Italy, the countries in which opulence was first acquired, and in which the improvements of society are supposed to have made the greatest advances. But in these countries, the authority obtained by the clergy after the establishment of the Christian religion, and the notions which they endeavoured to inculcate with regard to abstinence from every sensual gratification, have concurred with the influence of the former usage and laws, not only to exclude polygamy, but in a great measure to prevent the dissolution of marriage by voluntary divorce. Many disorders, therefore, which were felt in the luxurious ages of Rome, have thus been avoided; and in modern Europe, the chief effect of debauchery, beside the encouragement given to common prostitution, has been to turn the attention, from the pursuits of business or ambition, to the amusements of gallantry; or rather to convert these last into a serious occupation.

* It is not intended, however, in this discourse, to consider those variations, in the state of women, which arise from the civil or religious government of a people, or from such other causes as are peculiar to the inhabitants of different countries. The revolutions that I have mentioned, in the condition and manners of the sexes, are chiefly derived from the progress of mankind in the common arts of life, and therefore make a part in the general history of society.

---

* [Already added in different form in 2nd edition.]

CHAPTER II

Of the jurisdiction and authority of a father over his children

SECTION I

The power of a father in early ages

The jurisdiction and authority which, in early times, a father exercised over his children, was of the same nature with that of a husband over his wife. Before the institution of regular government, the strong are permitted to oppress the weak; and in a rude nation, every one is apt to abuse that power which he happens to possess.

* After marriage is completely established in a community, the husband, as has been formerly observed, becomes the head of his family, and assumes the direction and government of all its members. It is to be expected, indeed, that in the exercise of this authority, he should have an inclination to promote the welfare and prosperity of his children. The helpless and miserable state in which they are produced, can hardly fail to excite his pity, and to solicit in a peculiar manner the protection of that person from whom they have derived their existence. Being thereby induced to undertake the burden of rearing and maintaining them, he is more warmly engaged in their behalf in proportion to the efforts which he has made for their benefit, and his affection for them is increased by every new mark of his kindness. While they grow up under his culture and tuition, and begin to lisp the endearing names of a parent, he has the satisfaction of observing their progress towards maturity, and of discovering the seeds of those dispositions and talents, from the future display of which he draws the most flattering expectations. By retaining them afterwards in his family, which is the foundation of a constant intercourse, by procuring their assistance in the labour to which he is subjected, by connecting them with all his plans and views of interest, his attachment is usually continued and strengthened from the same habits and principles which, in other cases, give rise to friendship or acquaintance. As these sentiments are felt in common by the father and mother, it is natural to suppose that their affection for each other will be, in some measure, reflected upon their offspring, and will become an additional motive of attention to the objects of their united care and tenderness.

* [Two paragraphs revised and enlarged.]

Such is, probably, the origin of that parental fondness, which has been found so extensive and universal that it is commonly regarded as the effect of an immediate propensity. But how strongly soever a father may be disposed to promote the happiness of his children, this disposition, in the breast of a savage, is often counteracted by a regard to his own preservation, and smothered by the misery with which he is loaded. In many cases he is forced to abandon them entirely, and suffer them to perish by hunger, or be devoured by wild beasts. From his necessitous circumstances, he is sometimes laid under the temptation of selling his children for slaves. Even those whom the father finds it not inconvenient to support, are subjected to a variety of hardships from the natural ferocity of his temper; and if on some occasions they are treated with the utmost indulgence, they are, on others, no less exposed to the sudden and dreadful effects of his anger. As the resentment of a savage is easily kindled, and raised to an excessive pitch; as he behaves like a sovereign in his own family, where he has never been accustomed to bear opposition or control, we need not wonder that, when provoked by unusual disrespect or contradiction, he should be roused and hurried on to commit the most barbarous of all actions, the murder of his own child.

The children, in their early years, are under the necessity of submitting to the severe and arbitrary will of their father. From their inferiority in strength, they are in no condition to dispute his commands; and being incapable of maintaining themselves, they depend entirely upon him for subsistence. To him they must apply for assistance, whenever they are exposed to danger, or threatened with injustice; and looking upon him as the source of all their enjoyments, they have every motive to court his favour and to avoid his displeasure.

The respect and reverence which is paid to the father, upon account of his wisdom and experience, is another circumstance that contributes to support his power and authority.

Among savages, who are strangers to the art of writing, and who have scarcely any method of recording facts, the experience and observation of each individual are almost the only means of procuring knowledge; and the only persons who can attain a superior degree of wisdom and sagacity are those who have lived to a considerable age.

It also merits attention that, in rude and ignorant nations, the least superiority in knowledge and wisdom is the source of great honour and distinction. The man who understands any operation of nature, unknown to the vulgar, is beheld with superstitious awe and veneration. As they cannot penetrate into the ways by which he has procured his information, they are disposed to magnify his extraordinary endowments; and they feel an unbounded admiration of that skill and learning which they are unable to comprehend. They suppose that nothing is beyond the compass of his abilities, and apply to him for counsel and direction in every new and difficult emergency. They are apt to imagine that he holds commerce with invisible beings, and to believe that he is capable of seeing into futurity, as well as of altering the course of human events by the wonderful power of his art. Thus, in the dark ages, a slight acquaintance with the heavenly bodies gave rise to the absurd pretensions of judicial astrology; and a little knowledge of chemistry, or medicine, was supposed to reveal the invaluable secret of rendering ourselves immortal.

As in all barbarous countries old men are distinguished by their great experience and wisdom, they are upon this account universally respected, and commonly attain superior influence and authority.

Among the Greeks, at the siege of Troy, the man who had lived three ages was treated with uncommon deference, and was their principal adviser and director in all important deliberations.

'Dost thou not see, O Gual,' says Morni in one of the poems of Ossian, 'how the steps of my age are honoured? Morni moves forth, and the young meet him with reverence, and turn their eyes, with silent joy, on his course.'*

The Jewish lawgiver, whose system of laws was in many respects accommodated to the circumstances of an early people, has thought proper to enforce the respect due to old age, by making it the subject of a particular precept. 'See that thou rise up before the hoary head, and honour the face of the old man.'†

'I am young,' says the son of Barachel, 'and ye are very old, wherefore I was afraid, and durst not show you mine opinion. I said days should speak, and multitude of years teach wisdom.'‡

When any of the Tartar nations have occasion to elect a khan or leader, they regard experience and wisdom more than any other circumstance; and for that reason they commonly prefer the oldest person of the royal family.§ It is the same circumstance that, in the infancy of government, has given rise to a senate or council of the elders, which is commonly invested with the chief direction and management of all public affairs.

So inseparably connected are age and authority in early periods, that in the language of rude nations the same word which signifies an old man is generally employed to denote a ruler or magistrate.

Among the Chinese, who, from their little intercourse with strangers,

---

* Lathmon.   † Leviticus, chap. xix, ver. 32.
‡ Job, chap. xxxii.   § Histoire generale des voyages.

are remarkably attached to their ancient usages, the art of writing, notwithstanding their improvement in manufactures, is still beyond the reach of the vulgar. This people have accordingly preserved that high admiration of the advantages arising from long experience and observation, which we commonly met with in times of ignorance and simplicity. Among them, neither birth, nor riches nor honours, nor dignities, can make a man forget that reverence which is due to grey hairs; and the sovereign himself never fails to respect old age, even in persons of the lowest condition.

The difference in this particular, between the manners of a rude and polished nation may be illustrated from the following anecdote concerning two Grecian states, which, in point of what is commonly called refinement, were remarkably distinguished from each other.

It happened, at Athens, during a public representation of some play, exhibited in honour of the commonwealth, that an old gentleman came too late for a place suitable to his age and quality. Many of the young gentlemen, who observed the difficulty and confusion he was in, made signs to him that they would accommodate him, if he came where they sat. The good man bustled through the crowd accordingly; but when he came to the seats to which he was invited, the jest was to sit close, and, as he stood out of countenance, expose him to the whole audience. The frolic went round all the Athenian benches. But on those occasions there were also particular places assigned for foreigners: when the good man skulked towards the boxes appointed for the Lacedemonians, that honest people, more virtuous than polite, rose up all to a man, and with the greatest respect received him among them. The Athenians, being suddenly touched with a sense of the Spartan virtue and their own degeneracy, gave a thunder of applause; and the old man cried out, The Athenians understand what is good, but the Lacedemonians practise it.*

We may easily imagine that this admiration and reverence, which is excited by wisdom and knowledge, must in a particular manner affect the conduct of children with respect to their father. The experience of the father must always appear greatly superior to that of his children, and becomes the more remarkable, according as he advances in years, and decays in bodily strength. He is placed in a situation where that experience is constantly displayed to them, and where, being exerted for their preservation and welfare, it is regarded in the most favourable light. From him they learn those contrivances which they make use

---

* Notwithstanding that old men are commonly so much respected among savages, they are sometimes put to death when so far advanced in years as to have lost the use of their faculties. This shows, that the estimation in which they are held does not proceed from a principle of humanity, but from a regard to the useful knowledge they are supposed to possess.

of in procuring their food, and the various stratagems which they put
in practice against their enemies. By him they are instructed in the
different branches of their domestic economy, and are directed what
measures to pursue in all those difficulties and distresses in which they
may be involved. They hear with wonder the exploits he has performed,
the precautions he has taken to avoid the evils with which he was
surrounded, or the address and dexterity he has employed to extricate
himself from those misfortunes which had befallen him; and, from his
observation of the past, they treasure up lessons of prudence, by which
they may regulate their future behaviour. If ever they depart from his
counsel, and follow their own headstrong inclination, they are commonly
taught by the event to repent of their folly and rashness, and are struck
with new admiration of his uncommon penetration and foresight. They
regard him in the light of a superior being, and imagine that the gifts
of fortune are at his disposal. They dread his curse, as the cause of every
misfortune; and they esteem his blessing of more value than the richest
inheritance.

When Phenix, in the Iliad, bewails his misfortune in having no
children, he imputes it to the curse of his father, which he had incurred
in his youth.

> My sire with curses loads my hated head,
> And cries, Ye furies! barren be his bed!
> Infernal Jove, the vengeful Fiends below,
> And ruthless Proserpine confirm'd his vow.*

'And Esau said unto his father, Hast thou but one blessing, my
father? Bless me, even me also, O my father! And Esau lift up his voice
and wept.'†

To these observations it may be added, that the authority of the
father is confirmed and rendered more universal, by the force and
influence of custom.

We naturally retain, after we are old, those habits of respect and
submission which we received in our youth; and we find it difficult
to put ourselves upon a level with those persons whom we have long
regarded as greatly our superiors. The slave, who has been bred up in a
low situation, does not immediately, upon obtaining his freedom, lay
aside those sentiments which he has been accustomed to feel. He retains
for some time the idea of his former dependence, and notwithstanding
the change of his circumstances, is disposed to continue that respect
and reverence which he owed to his master. We find that the legislature,
in some countries, has even regarded and enforced these natural senti-

---

* Pope's translation of the Iliad, book 9, l. 582.   † Genesis, chap. xxvii, ver. 38.

ments. By the Roman law a freed man was, through the whole of his life, obliged to pay to his patron certain attendance on public occasions, and to show him particular marks of honour and distinction. If ever he failed in the observance of these duties, he was thought unworthy of his liberty, and was again reduced to be the slave of that person to whom he had behaved in so unbecoming a manner.

A son who, in a barbarous age, has been accustomed from his infancy to serve and to obey his father, is in the same manner disposed for the future to continue that service and obedience. Even after he is grown up, and has arrived at his full strength of body, and maturity of judgment, he retains the early impressions of his youth, and remains in a great measure under the yoke of that authority to which he has hitherto submitted. He shrinks at the angry countenance of his father, and trembles at the power of that arm whose severe discipline he has so often experienced, and of whose valour and dexterity he has so often been a witness. He thinks it the highest presumption to dispute the wisdom and propriety of those commands to which he has always listened, as to an oracle, and which he has been taught to regard as the infallible rule of his conduct. He is naturally led to acquiesce in that jurisdiction which he has seen exerted on so many different occasions, and which he finds to be uniformly acknowledged by all the members of the family. In proportion to the rigour with which he is treated, his temper will be more thoroughly subdued, and his habits of implicit submission and obedience will be the stronger. He looks upon his father as invested by heaven with an unlimited power and authority over all his children, and imagines that, whatever hardships they may suffer, their rebelling against him, or resistance to his will, would be the same species of impiety, as to call in question the authority of the Deity, and arraign the severe dispensations with which, in the government of the world, he is sometimes pleased to visit his creatures.

From these dispositions, which commonly prevail among the members of his family, the father can have no difficulty to enforce his orders, wherever compulsion may be necessary. In order to correct the depravity, or to conquer the rebellious disposition of any single child, he can make use of that influence which he possesses over the rest, who will regard the disobedience of their brother with horror and detestation, and be ready to contribute their assistance in punishing his transgression.

In the history of early nations, we meet with a great variety of facts, to illustrate the nature and extent of that jurisdiction and authority which originally belonged to the father, as the head and governor of his family.

Of the Authority of a Father over his Children

We are informed by Caesar, that among the Gauls the father had the power of life and death over his children; and there is reason to believe, that, in the ancient German nations, his jurisdiction was no less extensive.

By the early laws and customs of Arabia, every head of a family seems, in like manner, to have enjoyed an absolute power over his descendants. When the sons of Jacob proposed to carry their brother Benjamin along with them into Egypt, and their father discovered an unwillingness to part with him, 'Rueben spake unto his father, saying, Slay my two sons, if I bring him not to thee: deliver him into my hand, and I will bring him to thee again.'* Moses appears to have intended that the father should not, in ordinary cases, be at liberty to take away the life of his children in private; as may be concluded from this particular institution, that a stubborn and rebellious son should be stoned to death before the elders of the city.† It was further enacted by this legislator, that a man might sell his daughter for a slave or concubine to those of his own nation, though he was not permitted to dispose of her to a stranger.

If a man sell his daughter to be a maidservant, she shall not go out as the menservants do.

If she please not her master, who hath betrothed her to himself, then shall he let her be redeemed: to sell her to a strange nation he shall have no power, seeing he hath dealt deceitfully with her.‡

In the empire of Russia, the paternal jurisdiction was formerly understood to be altogether supreme and unlimited. Peter the Great appear to have been so little aware that the customs of his own country might differ from those of other nations, that in his public declaration to his clergy, and to the states civil and military, relative to the trial of his son, he appeals to all the world, and affirms, that, according to all laws human and divine, and, above all, according to those of Russia, a father, even among private persons, has a full and absolute right to judge his children, without appeal, and without taking the advice of any person.

Among the Tartars, nothing can exceed the respect and reverence which the children usually pay to their father. They look upon him as the sovereign lord and master of his family, and consider it as their duty to serve him upon all occasions. In those parts of Tartary which have any intercourse with the great nations of Asia, it is also common for the father to sell his children of both sexes; and from thence the women and

* Genesis, chap. xlii, ver. 37.   † Deuteronomy, chap. xxi, ver. 18.
‡ Exodus, chap. xxi, ver. 7.

eunuchs, in the harams and seraglios, belonging to men of wealth and distinction in those countries, are said to be frequently procured.

Upon the coast of Africa, the power of the father is carried to the most excessive pitch, and exercised with the utmost severity. It is too well known to be denied, that, in order to supply the European market, he often disposes of his own children for slaves; and that the chief part of a man's wealth is supposed to consist of the number of his descendants. Upon the slave-coast, the children are accustomed to throw themselves upon their knees, as often as they come into the presence of their father.

The following account, given by Commodore Byron, may serve in some measure to show the spirit with which the savages of South America are apt to govern the members of their family.

Here [says he] I must relate a little anecdote of our Christian Cacique. He and his wife had gone off, at some distance from the shore, in their canoe, when she dived for sea-eggs; but not meeting with great success, they returned a good deal out of humour. A little boy of theirs, about three years old, whom they appeared to be doatingly fond of, watching for his father and mother's return, ran into the surf to meet them: the father handed a basket of sea-eggs to the child, which being too heavy for him to carry, he let it fall; upon which the father jumped out of the canoe, and catching the boy up in his arms, dashed him with the utmost violence against the stones. The poor little creature lay motionless and bleeding, and in that condition was taken up by the mother, but died soon after. She appeared inconsolable for some time; but the brute his father shewed little concern about it.*

The exposition of infants, so common in a great part of the nations of antiquity, is a proof that the different heads of families were under no restraint or control in the management of their domestic concerns. This barbarous practice was probably introduced in those rude ages when the father was often incapable of maintaining his children, and from the influence of old usage, was permitted to remain in later times, when the plea of necessity could no longer be urged in its vindication. How shocking soever it may appear to us, the custom of exposing infant-children was universal among the ancient inhabitants of Greece, and was never abolished even by such of the Greek states as were most distinguished for their learning and politeness.†

According to the laws and customs of the Romans, the father had

* Narrative of the honourable John Byron.

† Ælian mentions the Thebans alone as having made a law forbidding the exposition of infants under a capital punishment, and ordaining, that if the parents were indigent, their children, upon application to the magistrate, should be maintained and brought up as slaves. Ælian, var. hist. lib. 2, cap. 7.

anciently an unlimited power of putting his children to death, and of selling them for slaves. While they remained in his family, they were incapable of having any estate of their own, and whatever they acquired, either by their own industry, or by the donations of others, became immediately the property of their father. Though with respect to every other person they were regarded as free, yet with respect to their father they were considered as in a state of absolute slavery and subjection; and they could neither marry, nor enter into any other contract, without his approbation and consent.*

In one respect, the power of a father over his sons appears, in ancient Rome, to have extended even farther than that of a master over his slaves. If upon any occasion a son had been sold by his father, and had afterwards obtained his freedom from the purchaser, he did not thereby become independent, but was again reduced under the paternal dominion. The same consequence followed, if he had been sold and manumitted a second time; and it was only after a third purchase, that the power of his father was altogether dissolved, and that he was permitted to enjoy any real and permanent advantage from the bounty of his master.

This peculiarity is said to have been derived from a statute of Romulus, adopted into the laws of the twelve tables, and affords a sufficient proof that the Romans had anciently no idea of a child living in the family, without being considered as the slave of his father.

In those early ages, when this practice was first introduced, the Roman state was composed of a few clans, or families of barbarians, the members of which had usually a strong attachment to one another, and were at variance with most of their neighbours. When a son therefore had been banished from his family by the avarice of his father, we may suppose that, as soon as he was at liberty, he would not think of remaining in a foreign tribe, or of submitting to the hardships of procuring his food in a state of solitude, but that he would rather choose to return to his own kindred, and again submit to that jurisdiction, which was more useful from the protection it afforded, than painful from the service and obedience which it required.

It is probable, however, that if in this manner a child had been

---

* Dionysius of Halicarnassus, lib. 11, l. 11. Dig. de lib. et postum. § 3. Inst. per quas person. ciuq. [cuiq.] adquir. l. ult. Cod. de impub. et al. subst. l. 4. Dig. de judic. § 6. Inst. de inut. stip.

Upon the same principle a father might claim his son from any person, by the ordinary action upon property, lib. 1. § 2. Dig. de rei vind. If a son had been stolen from his father, the 'actio furti' was given against the thief, l. 38. Dig. de furt. When children were sold by their father, the form of conveyance was the same which was used in the transference of that valuable property which was called 'res mancipi', Cai. Inst. l. 6, 3.

frequently separated from the company of his relations, he would at length grow weary of returning to a society in which he was the object of so little affection, and in which he was treated with so much contempt. How long he would be disposed to maintain his former connexions, and how often he would be willing to restore that property which his father had abandoned, seems, from the nature of the thing, impossible to ascertain. ʳBut whatever might be the conduct of the son, it seems to have been intended by the statute of Romulus, that, after a third sale, the property of the father should be finally extinguished, and that he should never afterwards recover a power which he had exercised with such immoderate severity.

SECTION II

The influence of the improvement of arts upon the jurisdiction of the father

Such was the power, in early times, possessed by the head of a family. But the gradual advancement of a people in civilized manners, and their subjection to regular government, have a natural tendency to limit and restrain this primitive jurisdiction. When different families are united in a larger society, the several members of which have an intimate correspondence with each other, it may be expected that the exercise of domestic authority will begin to excite the attention of the public. The near relations of a family, who have a concern for the welfare of the children, and who have an opportunity of observing the manner in which they are treated, will naturally interpose by their good offices, and endeavour to screen them from injustice and oppression. The abuses which, on some occasions, are known and represented with all their aggravating circumstances, will excite indignation and resentment, and will at length give rise to such regulations as are necessary for preventing the like disorders for the future.

Those improvements in the state of society, which are the common effects of opulence and refinement, will at the same time dispose the father to use his power with greater moderation. By living in affluence and security, he is more at leisure to exert the social affections, and to cultivate those arts which tend to soften and humanize the temper. Being often engaged in the business and conversation of the world, and finding, in many cases, the necessity of conforming to the humours of those with whom he converses, he becomes less impatient of contradiction, and less apt to give way to the irregular sallies of passion. His parental affection, though not perhaps more violent, becomes at least more steady and uniform; and while it prompts him to undergo the labour that may be requisite in providing for his family, it is not incompatible with that discretion which leads him to bear with the frowardness, the folly and imprudence of his children, and in his behaviour towards them, to avoid equally the excess of severity and of indulgence.

On the other hand, the progress of arts and manufactures will contribute to undermine and weaken his power, and even to raise the members of his family to a state of freedom and independence.

In those rude and simple periods when men are chiefly employed in hunting and fishing, in pasturing cattle, or in cultivating the ground, the children are commonly brought up in the house of their father; and continuing in his family as long as he lives, they have no occasion to acquire any separate property, but depend entirely for subsistence upon that hereditary estate, of which he is the sole disposer and manager. Their situation, however, in this, as well as in many other respects, is greatly altered by the introduction of commerce and manufactures. In a commercial country, a great part of the inhabitants are employed in such a manner as tends to disperse the members of a family, and often requires that they should live at a distance from one another.

The children, at an early period of life, are obliged to leave their home, in order to be instructed in those trades and professions by which it is proposed they should earn a livelihood, and afterwards to settle in those parts of the country which they find convenient for prosecuting their several employments. By this alteration of circumstances they are emancipated from their father's authority. They are put in a condition to procure a maintainance without having recourse to his bounty, and by their own labour and industry are frequently possessed of opulent fortunes. As they live in separate families of their own, of which they have the entire direction, and are placed at such a distance from their father, that he has no longer an opportunity of observing and controlling their behaviour, it is natural to suppose that their former habits will be gradually laid aside and forgotten.

When we examine the laws and customs of polished nations, they appear to coincide with the foregoing remarks, and leave no room to doubt that, in most countries, the paternal jurisdiction has been reduced within narrower bounds, in proportion to the ordinary improvements of society.

The Romans, who for several centuries were constantly employed in war, and for that reason gave little attention to the arts of peace, discovered more attachment to their barbarous usages than perhaps any other nation that arose to wealth and splendour; and their ancient practice, with respect to the power of the father, was therefore permitted to remain in the most flourishing periods of their government. The alterations in this particular, which were at length found expedient, having, for the most part, occurred in times of light and knowledge, are recorded with some degree of accuracy, and as they mark the progress of a great people in an important branch of policy, may deserve to be particularly considered.

*a*We know nothing with certainty concerning the attempts which, in a very remote period, are supposed to have been made for restraining the exposition of infants. By a law of Romulus, parents are said to have been obliged to maintain their male children, and the eldest female, unless where a child was, by two of the neighbours called for the purpose, declared to be a monster. A regulation of the same nature is mentioned among the laws of the twelve tables; but there is ground to believe that little regard was paid to it; and even under the emperors, the exposing of new-born children, of either sex, appears to have been exceedingly common.

The first effectual regulations in favour of children were those which bestowed upon them a privilege of acquiring property independent of their father. During the free government of Rome, as war was the chief employment in which a Roman citizen thought proper to engage, and by which he had any opportunity of gaining a fortune, it appeared highly reasonable, that when he hazarded his person in the service of his country, he should be allowed to reap the fruit of his labour, and be entitled to the full enjoyment of whatever he had acquired. With this view, it was enacted by Julius and by Augustus Caesar, that whatever was gained by a son, in the military profession, should be considered as his own estate, and that he should be at liberty to dispose of it at pleasure.*

Some time after, when the practice of the law had also become a lucrative profession, it was further established, that whatever a son acquired in the exercise of this employment, should in like manner become his own property, and should in no respect belong to the father.†

In a later age, when no employment was considered as too mean for the subjects of the Roman empire, the son became proprietor of what he could procure by the practice of the mechanical arts, and of whatever he obtained by donations, or by succession to his mother or

---

* It was called 'peculium castrense.'   † Peculium quasi castrense.

maternal relations; though the *usufruct* of those acquisitions was, in ordinary cases, bestowed upon the father.*

It is uncertain at what time the Romans first began to limit the father in the power of selling his children for slaves. It appears, that before the reign of the emperor Dioclesian this privilege was entirely abolished, except in a singular case, in which it remained to the latest periods of the empire. To remove the temptation of abandoning new-born children, a permission was given to sell them, but with provision that they might, at any time after, be redeemed from the purchaser, by restoring the price which he had paid.

Exclusive of infants, the power over the life of children was first subjected to any limitation in the reign of Trajan, and of Hadrian his successor, who interposed, in some particular cases, to punish the wanton exercise of paternal authority. In the time of the emperor Severus, the father was not allowed to put his children to death in private, but when they committed a crime of an atrocious nature, was directed to accuse them before a magistrate, to whom he was impowered, in that case, to prescribe the particular punishment which he chose to have inflicted. At length this part of his jurisdiction was finally abolished by the emperor Constantine, who ordained that if a father took away the life of his child he should be deemed guilty of parricide.

These were the principal steps by which the Romans endeavoured to correct this remarkable part of their ancient law. It was natural to begin with the reformation of those particulars in which the greatest abuses were committed, and thence to proceed to others, which, however absurd in appearance, were less severely felt, and less productive of disorder and oppression. It seldom happened that a father, though permitted by law, was so hardened to the feelings of humanity and natural affection, as to be capable of imbruing his hands in the blood of a child whom he had brought up in his family; and accordingly no more than three or four instances of that nature are mentioned in the whole Roman history. He might oftener be tempted to neglect his children immediately after their birth, or be reconciled to the measure of reaping a certain profit at the expense of their freedom. But the part of his prerogative which he would probably exert in the most arbitrary manner, was that which related to the maintenance of his family, and the management of that property which had been procured by their industry and labour. Thus we find that, beside the early and ineffectual attempts to prevent the neglect of infants, the interpositions of the

* The subject so acquired was called *peculium adventitium*. Constantine made the first regulations concerning it, which were extended by his successors, especially by the emperor Justinian. Vid. Tit. Cod. de bon. matern.—Tit. de bon. quae lib.

Roman legislature were directed first to secure the property, afterwards the liberty, and last of all the life and personal safety of the children.*

ʳ Upon comparing the manners of different countries, with regard to the subject of our present inquiry, it will be found that whereever polygamy is established, the authority enjoyed by the head of every family is usually carried to a greater height, and is more apt to remain in its full force, notwithstanding the improvements which, in other respects, the people may have attained. By the institution of polygamy, the children belonging to a person of opulent fortune, are commonly rendered so numerous as greatly to diminish the influence of paternal affection: not to mention that the confinement of his wives, and the jealousy, hatred, and dissension, which prevail among them, are productive of such intrigues to supplant or destroy one another, and to promote the interest of their respective children, that the husband, in order to repress these disorders, finds it necessary to preserve a strict discipline in his family, and to hold all its members in extreme subjection. This will suggest a reason for what is observed by Aristotle, that among the Persians, in his time, the power of a father over his children was no less absolute as that of a master over his slaves.

In the empire of China, the same circumstance, together with that aversion which the people discover to every sort of innovation, has also enabled the father to maintain a great part of his original jurisdiction.† The father is said to have there the privilege of selling his children whenever he thinks proper; but if he intends to put them to death, it is necessary that he should bring them before a magistrate, and publicly accuse them. At the same time, whatever be the crime of which they are accused, they are held to be guilty, without any other proof but the bare assertion of the father.‡

The custom of exposing infants was not restrained in China till very lately. Father Noel, in a relation presented to the general of the Jesuits in 1703, takes notice, that at Pekin a number of children were usually dropped or exposed every morning in the streets.

As Pekin is excessively populous [continues that pious and Catholic father] and those who have more children than they can maintain do not scruple to drop them in places of public resort, where they either die miserably, or are devoured by beasts; one of our first cares is to send, every morning,

---

* Aristot. Ethic: lib. 6. cap. 10.

† Though in China a man is not allowed to have more wives than one, yet he may have any number of concubines; which, in the point under consideration, must have nearly the same effect. Le Compte's memoirs of China.

‡ Ibid.

catechists into the different parts of that great city, in order to baptize such of those children as are not dead. About twenty or thirty thousand children are exposed yearly, and of these our catechists baptize about three thousand; and had we twenty or thirty catechists, few of the children in question would die unbaptized.*

In those European nations which have made the greatest improvements in commerce and manufactures, great liberty is usually enjoyed by the members of every family; and the children are no farther subjected to the father than seems necessary for their own advantage. When they come to be of age, they have the full enjoyment and disposal of any separate property which they happen to acquire; and even during their father's life, they are in some cases entitled to a fixed provision out of the family estate.

It can hardly be doubted that these regulations, which tend to moderate the excessive and arbitrary power assumed by the head of a family, are supported by every consideration of justice and utility. The opinion of Sir Robert Filmer, who founds the doctrine of passive obedience to a monarch, upon the unlimited submission which children owe to their father, seems, at this day, unworthy of the serious refutation which it has met with, and could only have gained reputation when men were just beginning to reflect upon the first principles of government. To say that a king ought to enjoy absolute power because a father has enjoyed it, is to defend one system of oppression by the example of another.

The interest of those who are governed is the chief circumstance which ought to regulate the powers committed to a father, as well as those committed to a civil magistrate; and whenever the prerogative of either is further extended than is requisite for this great end, it immediately degenerates into usurpation, and is to be regarded as a violation of the natural rights of mankind.

The tendency, however, of a commercial age is rather towards the opposite extreme, and may occasion some apprehension that the members of a family will be raised to greater independence than is consistent with good order, and with a proper domestic subordination. As, in every country, the laws enforced by the magistrate are in a great measure confined to the rules of justice, it is evident that further precautions are necessary to guard the morals of the inhabitants, and that, for this purpose, the authority of parents ought to be such as may enable them to direct the education of their children, to restrain the irregularities of youth, and to instil those principles which will render them useful members of society.

* Travels of the Jesuits, compiled from their letters, translated by Lockman, vol. 1, p.448.

CHAPTER III

The authority of a Chief over the members of a tribe or village

SECTION I

The origin of a chief, and the degrees of influence which he is enabled to acquire

Having considered the primitive state of a family during the life of the father, we may now examine the changes which happen in their situation, upon the death of this original governor, and the different species of authority to which they are then commonly subjected.

When the members of a family become too numerous to be all maintained and lodged in the same house, some of them are under the necessity of leaving it, and providing themselves with a new habitation. The sons, having arrived at the age of manhood, and being disposed to marry, are led by degrees to have a separate residence, where they may live in a more comfortable manner. They build their huts very near one to another, and each of them forms a distinct family; of which he assumes the direction, and which he endeavours to supply with the means of subsistence. Thus the original society is gradually enlarged into a village or tribe; and according as it is placed in circumstances which favour population, and render its condition prosperous and flourishing, it becomes proportionably extensive, and is subdivided into a greater multiplicity of branches.

From the situation of this early community, it is natural to suppose that an uncommon degree of attachment will subsist between all the different persons of which it is composed. As the ordinary life of a savage renders him hardy and robust, so he is a stranger to all those considerations of utility, by which, in a polished nation, men are commonly induced to restrain their appetites, and to abstain from violating the possessions of each other. Different clans or tribes of barbarians are therefore disposed to rob and plunder one another, as often as they have an opportunity of doing it with success; and the reciprocal inroads and hostilities in which they are engaged become the source of continual animosities and quarrels, which are prosecuted with a degree of fury and rancour suited to the temper and dispositions of the people. Thus the members of every single clan are frequently at variance with all their neighbours around them. This makes it necessary that they should

244

be constantly upon their guard, in order to repel the numerous attacks to which they are exposed, and to avoid that barbarous treatment, which they have reason to expect, were they ever to fall under the power of their enemies. As they are divided from the rest of the world, so they are linked together by a sense of their common danger, and by a regard to their common interest. They are united in all their pastimes and amusements, as well as in their serious occupations; and when they go out upon a military enterprise, they are no less prompted to show their friendship for one another, than to gratify their common passions of enmity and resentment. As they have been brought up together from their infancy, and have little intercourse with those of a different community, their affections are raised to a greater height, in proportion to the narrowness of that circle to which they are confined. As the uniformity of their life supplies them with few occurrences, and as they have no opportunity of acquiring any great variety of knowledge, their thoughts are the more fixed upon those particular objects which have once excited their attention; they retain more steadily whatever impressions they have received, and become the more devoted to those entertainments and practices with which they have been acquainted.

Hence it is, that a savage is never without difficulty prevailed upon to abandon his family and friends, and to relinquish the sight of those objects to which he has been long familiar. To be banished from them is accounted the greatest of all misfortunes. His cottage, his fields, the faces and conversation of his kindred and companions, recur incessantly to his memory, and prevent him from relishing any situation where these are wanting. He clings to those well-known objects, and dwells upon all those favourite enjoyments which he has lost. The poorer the country in which he has lived, the more wretched the manner of life to which he has been accustomed, the loss of it appears to him the more insupportable. That very poverty and wretchedness, which contracted the sphere of his amusements, is the chief circumstance that confirms his attachment to those few gratifications which it afforded, and renders him the more a slave to those particular habits which he has acquired. Not all the allurements of European luxury could bribe a Hottentot to resign that coarse manner of life which was become habitual to him; and we may remark, that the 'maladie du pays,' which has been supposed peculiar to the inhabitants of Switzerland, is more or less felt by the inhabitants of all countries, according as they approach nearer to the ages of rudeness and simplicity.*

* Mr Kolben relates, that one of the Dutch governors at the Cape of Good Hope brought up a Hottentot according to the fashions and customs of the Europeans, teaching him several languages, and instructing him fully in the principles of the Christian religion, at the same

Those tribes that inhabit the more uncultivated parts of the earth being almost continually at war with their neighbours, and finding it necessary to be always in a posture of defence, have constant occasion for a leader to conduct them in their various military enterprises.

Wherever a number of people meet together in order to execute any measures of common concern, it is convenient that some person should be appointed to direct their proceedings, and prevent them from running into confusion. It accordingly appears to be a regulation, uniformly adopted in all countries, that every public assembly should have a president, invested with a degree of authority suitable to the nature of the business committed to their care. But in no case is a regulation of this kind so necessary as in the conduct of a military expedition. There is no situation in which a body of men are so apt to run into disorder, as in war; where it is impossible that they should co-operate, and preserve the least regularity, unless they are united under a single person, impowered to direct their movements, and to superintend and control their several operations.

The members of a family having been usually conducted by the father in all their excursions of moment, are naturally disposed, even when their society becomes larger, to continue in that course of action to which they have been accustomed; and after they are deprived of this common parent, to fall under the guidance of some other person, who appears next to him in rank, and has obtained the second place in their esteem and confidence.

Superiority in strength, courage, and other personal accomplishments, is the first circumstance by which any single person is raised to be the leader of a tribe, and by which he is enabled to maintain his authority.

In that rude period, when men live by hunting and fishing, they have no opportunity of acquiring any considerable property; and there are

time clothing him handsomely, and treating him in all respects as a person for whom he had an high esteem, and whom he designed for some beneficial and honourable employment. The governor afterwards sent him to Batavia where he was employed under the commissary for some time, till that gentleman died; and then he returned to the Cape of Good Hope. But having paid a visit to the Hottentots of his acquaintance, he threw off all his fine clothes, bundled them up, laid them at the governor's feet and desired he might be allowed to renounce his Christianity, and to live and die in the religion and customs of his ancestors; only requesting that he might be permitted to keep the hanger and collar which he wore, in token of his regard to his benefactor. While the governor was deliberating upon this, scarce believing the fellow to be in earnest, the young Hottentot took the opportunity of running away, and never afterwards came near the Cape, thinking himself happy that he had exchanged his European dress for a sheep-skin, and that he had abandoned the hopes of preferment for the society of his relations and countrymen.

The English East-India Company made the like experiment upon two young Hottentots, but with no better success.

no distinctions in the rank of individuals, but those which arise from their personal qualities, either of mind or body.

′ The strongest man in a village, the man who excels in running, in wrestling, or in handling those weapons which are made use of in war, is, in every contest, possessed of an evident advantage, which cannot fail to render him conspicuous, and to command respect and deference. In their games and exercises, being generally victorious, he gains an ascendency over his companions, which disposes them to yield him pre-eminence, and to rest fully satisfied of his superior abilities. When they go out to battle, he is placed at their head, and permitted to occupy that station where his behaviour is most likely to be distinguished and applauded. His exploits and feats of activity are regarded by his followers with pleasure and admiration; and he becomes their boast and champion in every strife or competition with their neighbours. The more they have been accustomed to follow his banner, they contract a stronger attachment to his person, are more afraid of incurring his displeasure, and discover more readiness to execute those measures which he thinks proper to suggest. Instead of being mortified by his greatness, they imagine that it reflects honour upon the society to which he belongs, and are even disposed to magnify his prowess with that fond partiality which they entertain in favour of themselves.

In many savage tribes the captain of an expedition is commonly chosen from the number of wounds he has received in battle. The Indians of Chili are said, in the choice of a leader to regard only his superior strength, and to determine this point according to the burden which he is able to carry.*

† Montaigne gives an account of three West Indian savages, who came to Rouen when Charles IX was there.

The king [says he] discoursed a long time with them. They were shown our manner of living, our pomp, and the several beauties of that great city. Some time after, a gentleman asked what it was that struck them most among the various objects they had seen. They answered, three things. First, They thought it very strange that so many tall men, wearing beards, and standing round the king (these in all probability were his Swiss guards) should submit

* 'Whenever they went to war, and a captain had to be elected among them, they took a large beam and put it on their shoulders one by one, and the one who carried it for the longest time was made their commander. Many of them carried it for 4, 5, and 6 hours; but one of them finally carried it for 24 hours; and that one was recognized as their leader.' Voyage d'Olivier de Noort. Recueil de voy. qui ont servi a l'etab. de la comp. Dans les Indes Orient. des Pais Bas.

† [Lifted out of footnote into text.]

voluntarily to a child; and that they did not rather choose to be governed by one of themselves.*

But when a people have begun to make improvements in their manner of fighting, they are soon led to introduce a variety of stratagems, in order to deceive their enemy, and are often no less indebted to the art and address which they employ, than to the strength or courage which they have occasion to exert. Thus, military skill and conduct are raised to higher degrees of estimation; and the experience of a Nestor, or the cunning of a Ulysses, being found more useful than the brutal force of an Ajax, is frequently the source of greater influence and authority.

This, as has been formerly observed, is the foundation of that respect and reverence which among early nations is commonly paid to old men. From this cause also it happens, that the leader of a barbarous tribe is often a person somewhat advanced in years, who retaining still his bodily strength, has had time to acquire experience in the art of war, and to obtain a distinguished reputation by his achievements.

The effect of these circumstances, to raise and support the authority of a leader or chief, is sufficiently obvious, and is fully illustrated, not only from the uniform history of mankind in a barbarous state, but also from a variety of particulars which may be observed in the intercourse of polished society.

And the people and princes of Gilead said one to another, What man is he that will begin to fight against the children of Ammon? He shall be head over all the inhabitants of Gilead.

Now Jephthah the Gileadite was a mighty man of valour, and he was the son of an harlot, and Gilead begat Jephthah.

And Gilead's wife bare him sons; and his wife's sons grew up, and they thrust out Jephthah, and said unto him, Thou shalt not inherit in our father's house; for thou art the son of a strange woman.

---

* Montaigne's essays, p. 169. Paris 1604, 8vo.

It has been remarked, that all animals which live in herds or flocks are apt to fall under the authority of a single leader of superior strength or courage. Of this a curious instance is mentioned by the author of Commodore Anson's voyage. 'The largest sea-lion,' says he, 'was the master of the flock; and, from the number of females he kept to himself, and his driving off the males, was styled by the seamen the bashaw. As they are of a very lethargic disposition, and are not easily awakened, it is observed, that each herd places some of their males at a distance in the manner of sentinels, who always give the alarm whenever any attempt is made either to molest or approach them, by making a loud grunting noise like a hog, or snorting like a horse in full vigour. The males had often furious battles with each other, chiefly about the females; and the bashaw just mentioned, who was commonly surrounded by his females, to which no other male dared to approach, had acquired that distinguished pre-eminence by many bloody contests, as was evident from the numerous scars visible in all parts of his body.'

In a herd of deer, the authority of the master-buck, founded upon his superior strength, is not less conspicuous.

Then Jephthah fled from his brethren, and dwelt in the land of Tob; and there were gathered vain men to Jephthah, and went out with him.

And it came to pass, in process of time, that the children of Ammon made war against Israel.

And it was so, that when the children of Ammon made war against Israel, the elders of Gilead went to fetch Jephthah out of the land of Tob.

And they said unto Jephthah, Come, and be our captain, that we may fight with the children of Ammon.

And Jephthah said unto the elders of Gilead, Did ye not hate me, and expel me out of my father's house? and why are ye come unto me now, when ye are in distress?

And the elders of Gilead said unto Jephthah, Therefore we turn to thee now, that thou mayest go with us, and fight against the children of Ammon, and be our head over all the inhabitants of Gilead.

And Jephthah said unto the elders of Gilead, If ye bring me home again to fight against the children of Ammon, and the Lord deliver them before me, shall I be your head?

And the elders of Gilead said unto Jephthah, The Lord be witness between us, if we do not so, according to thy words.

Then Jephthah went with the elders of Gilead; and the people made him head and captain over them: and Jephthah uttered all his words before the Lord in Mizpeh.*

When Saul was afterwards appointed king over the Jewish nation, we find that the prophet Samuel recommends him to the people, merely upon account of his superior stature, and the advantages of his person.

And when he stood among the people, he was higher than any of the people from his shoulders and upward.

And Samuel said to all the people, See ye him whom the Lord hath chosen, that there is none like him among all the people? And all the people shouted, and said, God save the king.†

In like manner, when the family of this prince was deprived of the crown, the minds of the people were prepared for that revolution by the opinion which they entertained of the superior valour and military accomplishments of his successor.

And it came to pass, when David was returned from the slaughter of the Phillistine, that the women came out of all the cities of Israel, singing and dancing, to meet king Saul, with tabrets, with joy, and with instruments of music.

And the women answered one another as they played, and said, Saul hath slain his thousands, and David his ten thousands.‡

---

* Judges, chap. x, ver. 18 chap. xi, ver. 1, etc.   † 1 Samuel, chap. x, ver. 23, 24.
‡ 1 Samuel, chap. xviii, ver. 6, 7.

After mankind have fallen upon the expedient of taming and pasturing cattle, in order to render their situation more comfortable, there arises another source of influence and authority which was formerly unknown to them. In their herds and flocks they frequently enjoy considerable wealth, which is distributed in various proportions, according to the industry or good fortune of different individuals; and those who are poor become dependent upon the rich, who are capable of relieving their necessities, and affording them subsistence. As the pre-eminence and superior abilities of the chief are naturally exerted in the acquisition of that wealth which is then introduced, he becomes of course the richest man in the society; and his influence is rendered proportionably more extensive. According to the estate which he has accumulated, he is exalted to a higher rank, lives in greater magnificence, and keeps a more numerous train of servants and retainers, who, in return for that maintenance and protection which they receive from him, are accustomed in all cases to support his power and dignity.*

The authority derived from wealth, is not only greater than that which arises from mere personal accomplishments, but also more stable and permanent. Extraordinary endowments, either of mind or body, can operate only during the life of the possessor, and are seldom continued for any length of time in the same family. But a man usually transmits his fortune to his posterity, and along with it all the means of creating dependence which he enjoyed. Thus the son, who inherits the estate of his father, is enabled to maintain an equal rank, at the same time that he preserves all the influence acquired by the former proprietor, which is daily augmented by the power of habit, and becomes more considerable as it passes from one generation to another.

Hence that regard to genealogy and descent which we often meet with among those who have remained long in a pastoral state. From the simplicity of their manners, they are not apt to squander or alienate their possessions; and the representative of an ancient family is naturally disposed to be ostentatious of a circumstance which contributes so much to increase his power and authority. ªAll the Tartars, of whatever country or religion, have an exact knowledge of the tribe from which they are descended, and are at great pains to ascertain the several branches into which it divided.

For the same reason the dignity of the chief, which in a former period was frequently elective, is, among shepherds, more commonly transmitted from father to son by hereditary succession. As the chief possesses

---

* The admiration and respect derived from the possession of superior fortune, is very fully and beautifully illustrated by the eloquent and ingenious author of the *Theory of Moral Sentiments*.

the largest estate, so he represents the most powerful family in the tribe; a family from which all the rest are vain of being descended, and the superiority of which they have been uniformly accustomed to acknowledge. He enjoys not only that rank and consequence which is derived from his own opulence, but seems entitled to the continuance of that respect and submission which has been paid to his ancestors; and it rarely happens that any other person, though of superior abilities, is capable of supplanting him, or of diverting the course of that influence which has flowed so long in the same channel.

The acquisition of wealth in herds and flocks, does not immediately give rise to the idea of property in land. The different families of a tribe are accustomed to feed their cattle promiscuously, and have no separate possession or enjoyment of the ground employed for that purpose. Having exhausted one field of pasture, they proceed to another; and when at length they find it convenient to move their tents, and change the place of their residence, it is of no consequence who shall succeed them, and occupy the spot which they have relinquished.

'Is not the whole land before thee?' says Abraham to Lot his kinsman; 'Separate thyself, I pray thee, from me: if thou wilt take the left hand, then I will go to the right; or if thou depart to the right hand, then I will go to the left.'*

ªThe wild Arabs, who inhabit a barren country, are accustomed to change their residence every fortnight, or at least every month. The same wandering life is led by the Tartars; though, from the greater fertility of their soil, their migrations are perhaps less frequent.

If people in this situation, during their temporary abode in any one part of a country, should cultivate a piece of ground, this also, like that which is employed in pasture, will naturally be possessed in common. The management of it is regarded as an extraordinary and difficult work, in which it is necessary that they should unite and assist one another; and therefore, as each individual is intitled to the fruit of his own labour, the crop, which has been raised by the joint labour of all, is deemed the property of the whole society.†

Thus among the natives of the island of Borneo, it is customary, in time of harvest, that every family of a tribe should reap so much grain as is sufficient for their maintenance; and the remainder is laid up by

---

* Genesis, chap. xii, ver. 9.—We read, however, of Abraham's buying a field for the particular purpose of a burying place, and of his having weighed, as the price, four hundred shekels of silver, current money with the merchant.

† That land is appropriated by tribes before it becomes the property of individuals, has been observed by Dr Stuart, in his acute dissertation concerning the antiquity of the English constitution.

the public, as a provision for any future demand. Similar practices have probably taken place in most countries, when the inhabitants first applied themselves to the cultivation of the earth.

* The Suevi [according to Caesar] are by far the greatest and most warlike of the German tribes. They are said to possess an hundred villages; from each of which a thousand armed men are annually led forth to war. The rest of the people remain at home; and cultivate the ground for both. These the following year take arms, and the former, in their turn, remain at home. Thus neither agriculture, nor the knowledge and practice of the military art is neglected. But they have no separate landed possessions belonging to individuals, and are not allowed to reside longer than a year in one place. They make little use of grain; but live chiefly upon milk and the flesh of their cattle, and are much addicted to hunting.†

But the settlement of a village in some particular place, with a view to the further improvement of agriculture, has a tendency to abolish this ancient community of goods, and to produce a separate appropriation of landed estates. When mankind have made some proficiency in the various branches of husbandry, they have no longer occasion to exercise them by the united deliberation and counsel of a whole society. They grow weary of those joint measures, by which they are subjected to continual disputes concerning the distribution and management of their common property, while every one is desirous of employing his labour for his own advantage, and of having a separate possession, which he may enjoy according to his own inclination. Thus, by a sort of tacit agreement, the different families of a village are led to cultivate different portions of land apart from one another, and thereby acquire a right to the respective produce arising from the labour that each of them has bestowed. In ‡ order to reap what they have sown, it is necessary that they should have the management of the subject upon which it is produced; so that from having a right to the crop, they appear of course entitled to the exclusive possession of the ground itself. This possession, however, from the imperfect state of early cultivation, is at first continued only from the seed-time to the harvest; and during the rest of the year, the lands of a whole village are used in common for pasturing their cattle. Traces of this ancient community of pasture-grounds, during the winter season, may still be discovered in several parts of Scotland. But after a person has long cultivated the same field, his possession becomes gradually more and more complete; it is continued during the whole year without interruption; and when by his industry and

* [Lifted out of footnote in Latin.] † Caesar, de bell. Gall. lib. 4, cap. 1.
‡ [From here to p. 257, '. . . for extending his authority', completely rewritten and greatly expanded.]

labour he seems justly entitled, not only to the immediate crop that is raised, but to all the future advantages arising from the melioration of the soil.

The additional influence which the captain of a tribe or village is enabled to derive from this alteration of circumstances, may be easily imagined. As the land employed in tillage is at first possessed in common the different branches of husbandry are at first carried on, and even the distribution of the produce is made, under the inspection of their leader who claims the superintendence of all their public concerns.

Among the negroes upon the banks of the river Gambia, the seed-time is a period of much festivity. Those who belong to the same village unite in cultivating the ground, and the chief appears at their head, armed as if he were going out to battle, and surrounded by a band of musicians, resembling the bards of the Celtic nations, who, by singing and playing upon musical instruments, endeavour to encourage the labourers. The chief frequently joins in the music; and the workmen accompany their labour with a variety of ridiculous gestures and grimaces, according to the different tunes with which they are entertained.

Upon the Gold Coast each individual must obtain the consent of the chief before he has liberty to cultivate so much ground as is necessary for his subsistence. At the same time when a person has been allowed to cultivate a particular spot, it should seem that he has the exclusive privilege of reaping the crop. This may be considered as one step towards the appropriation of land.

When men are disposed to separate and divide their landed possessions, every family, according as it is numerous and powerful, will be in a condition to occupy and appropriate a suitable extent of territory. For this reason the chief, from his superior wealth in cattle, and the number of his domestics, as well as from his dignity and personal abilities, can hardly fail to acquire a much larger estate, than any other member of the community. His retainers must of consequence be increased in proportion to the enlargement of his domain, and as these are either maintained in his family, or live upon his ground in the situation of tenants at will, they depend entirely upon him for subsistence. They become therefore, necessarily subservient to his interest, and may at pleasure be obliged either to labour or to fight upon his account. The number of dependents whom he is thus capable of maintaining will be so much greater, as, from the simplicity of his manners, he has no occasion to purchase many articles of luxury, and almost his whole fortune is consumed in supplying the bare necessaries of life.

The estate which is acquired by a chief, after the appropriation of land, is not only more extensive than what he formerly possessed in herds and flocks, but at the same time is less liable to be destroyed or impaired by accidents; so that the authority which is founded upon it becomes more permanent, and is apt to receive a continued accumulation of strength by remaining for ages in the same family.

SECTION II

The powers with which the chief of a rude tribe is commonly invested

The powers which belong to this early magistrate, who is thus exalted to the head of a rude society, are such as might be expected from the nature of his office, and from the circumstances of the people over whom he is placed.

He is at first the commander of their forces, and has merely the direction of their measures during the time of an engagement. But having acted for some time in this capacity, he finds encouragement to exert his authority on other occasions, and is entrusted with various branches of public administration.

From his peculiar situation, he is more immediately led to attend to the defence of the society, to suggest such precautions as may be necessary for that purpose, and to point out those enterprises which he thinks it would be expedient for them to undertake. By degrees they are accustomed to follow his opinion, in planning as well as in conducting their several expeditions. Warmly attached to his person, and zealous to promote his interest, they are disposed to accompany him for his own sake, and to espouse his quarrel upon every occasion. 'The Germans,' says Tacitus, 'esteem it an inviolable duty to defend their chief, to maintain his dignity, and to yield him the glory of all their exploits. The chiefs fight for victory: the attendants only for the chief.'* As the leader of a tribe affords protection and security to all its members, so he expects that they should make a proper return for these good offices by serving him in war. To refuse this service would not only expose them to his resentment, but be regarded as a mark of infidelity or cowardice that would disgrace them for ever in the opinion of all their kindred. When on the other hand, they are willing to fulfil their duty, by appearing in the field as often as they are summoned, and by discharging with honour the trust that is reposed in them, they are admitted to be the friends and companions of the chief; they are enter-

---

* Tacitus, de mor. Germ.

tained at his table, and partake in all his amusements; and after the improvement of agriculture has given rise to the appropriation of land, they obtain the possession of landed estates, proportioned to their merit, and suited to their rank and circumstances.

As the chief is, by his office, engaged in protecting and securing the members of his tribe from the hostile attacks of their neighbours, so he endeavours to prevent those disorders and quarrels which may sometimes arise among themselves, and which tend to weaken and disturb the society. When a dispute or controversy happens among those who belong to different families, he readily interposes by his good offices, in order to bring about a reconciliation between the parties; who at the same time, if they choose to avoid an open rupture, may probably be willing to terminate their difference by referring it to his judgment. To render his decisions effectual he is, at first, under the necessity of employing persuasion and intreaty, and of calling to his assistance the several heads of families in the tribe. When his authority is better established, he ventures to execute his sentences by force; in which, from considerations of expediency, he is naturally supported by every impartial and unprejudiced member of the society. Having been accustomed to determine causes in consequence of a reference, and finding that persons, accused of injustice, are frequently averse to such determination, he is at length induced, when complaints are made, to summon parties before him, and to judge of their differences independent of their consent. Thus he acquires a regular jurisdiction both in civil and criminal cases; in the exercise of which particular officers of court are gradually set apart to enforce his commands: and when lawsuits become numerous, a deputy-judge is appointed, from whom the people may expect more attention to the dispatch of business than the chief is usually inclined to bestow.

Of this gradual progress in the judicial power of a magistrate, from the period when he is merely an arbiter, to that when he is enabled to execute his decrees, and to call parties before him, several vestiges are still to be found even in the laws of polished nations. Among the Romans, the civil judge had no power to determine a law-suit, unless the parties had previously referred the cause to his decision, by a contract which was called *litis-contestatio*. In England, at this day, no criminal trial can proceed, until the culprit, by his *pleading*, has acknowledged the authority of the court. But while these practices were retained, from a superstitious regard to ancient usage, a ridiculous circuit was made, to avoid the inconveniences of which they were manifestly productive. At Rome, the plaintiff, after having desired the defendant to come voluntarily into court, was, upon his refusal, permitted to drag him by the throat;* and by the English law, the defendant, who *stands mute*, is subjected to the *peine fort et dure*, a species of torture intended to overcome the obstinacy of such as are accused of atrocious crimes.

According to the systems of religion which have prevailed in the unenlightened parts of the world, mankind have imagined that the Supreme Being is endowed with passions and sentiments resembling their own,† and that he views the extraordinary talents and abilities of their leader with such approbation and esteem as these qualities never fail to excite in themselves. The same person whom they look upon as the first of mortals, is naturally believed to be the peculiar favourite of Heaven, and is therefore regarded as the most capable to intercede in their behalf, to explain the will of the Deity, and to point out the most effectual means to avert his anger, or to procure his favour.

The admiration of a military leader in rude countries, has frequently proceeded so far as to produce a belief of his being sprung from a heavenly original, and to render him the object of that adoration which is due to the Supreme Being.

In some of the American tribes, the chiefs carry the name of the sun, from whom they are supposed to be descended, and whom they are understood to represent upon earth.‡ The Incas of Peru derived themselves, in like manner, from the sun. In the kingdom of Loango, the prince is worshipped as a god by his subjects. They give him the name or title usually bestowed upon the Deity; and they address him with the utmost solemnity for rain or fruitful seasons.

The superstition of the early Greeks, in this particular, is well known; which was carried to such a height, as enabled almost every family of distinction to count kindred with some one or other of the celestial deities. It is in conformity to this ancient mythology that Racine has put the following beautiful address into the mouth of Phedra.

> Noble et brillant auteur d'une triste famille,
> Toi, dont ma mère osoit se vanter d'être fille,
> Qui peut-être rougis du trouble où tu me vois,
> Soleil, je te viens voir pour la dernière fois!

The same principle has disposed men to deify those heroes who have rendered themselves illustrious by their public spirit, and their eminent abilities; to imagine that in another state of existence they retain their former patriotic sentiments, and being possessed of superior power,

---

* Obtorto collo.   † [Note anthropomorphic conception.]

‡ This is particularly the case among the Hurons and Natchez. Journal historique d'un voyage de l'Amerique, par Charlevoix, let. 30. Nouveaux voyages aux Indes orientales, tom. I, p. 42.

continue, with unremitting vigilance, to ward off the misfortunes, and to promote the happiness of their people.

When such are the prevailing dispositions of a people, the chief of a barbarous tribe is naturally raised to be their high priest; or if he does not himself exercise that office, he obtains at least the direction and superintendence of their religious concerns. For some time after the building of Rome, the leader of each *curia* or tribe, is said to have been their chief ecclesiastical officer. A similar police in this respect appears to have been originally established in the cities of Greece, and has probably taken place among the primitive inhabitants of most countries. It may easily be conceived that in ignorant nations, guided by omens and dreams, and subject to all the terrors of gross superstition, this branch of power, when added to the conduct of war, and the distribution of justice, will be an engine of great consequence to the magistrate, for carrying through his measures, and for extending his authority.

As, in conducting the affairs of a community, in the management of what relates to peace or war, and in the administration of justice, various abuses are apt to be committed, and many more may still be apprehended, the people are gradually led, by experience and observation, to introduce particular statutes or laws, in order to correct or ascertain their practice for the future. Even this legislative power, by which all the other branches of government are controlled and directed, is naturally assumed by the chief, after he has acquired considerable influence and authority. When the members of his tribe have become in a great measure dependent upon him with regard to their property, they are in no condition to dispute his commands, or to refuse obedience to those ordinances which he issues at pleasure, in order to model or establish the constitution of the society.

From these observations we may form an idea of that constitution of government which is naturally introduced among the members of a rude tribe or village. Each of the different families of which it is composed is under the jurisdiction of the father, and the whole community is subjected to a chief or leader, who enjoys a degree of influence and authority according to the superior abilities with which he is endowed, or the wealth which he has been enabled to acquire.

The rudest form of this government may be discovered among the Indians of America. As these people subsist, for the most part, by hunting or fishing, they have no means of obtaining so much wealth as will raise any one person greatly above his companions. They are divided into small independent villages, in each of which there is a chief, who is their principal leader in war. He bears the name of that particular tribe over which he presides; and in their public meetings he is known by no other. His authority, though greater in some villages than in others, does not appear in any of them to be very considerable. If he is never disobeyed, it is because he knows how to set bounds to his commands. Every family has a right to name an assistant to the chief; and the several heads of families compose an assembly, or 'council of the elders', which is accustomed to deliberate upon all matters of public importance.*

Each individual is allowed, in ordinary cases, to 'take up the hatchet', as it is called, or make war upon those who have offended him. Enterprises of moment, however, are seldom undertaken without the concurrence of the assembly. Each family has a jurisdiction over its own members. But the members of different families are at liberty to settle their differences in what manner they please; and the chief, or council, interfere only as mediators, or as arbiters; unless upon the commission of those enormous and extraordinary crimes which excite the general indignation, and which, from a sudden impulse of resentment, are instantly punished with severity.†

* 'The authority of the Chiefs properly extends only over those members of their tribe whom they look upon as their children. . . . Their power does not appear to have an absolute character, and they do not seem to have any way of compelling obedience in case of resistance. Nevertheless obedience is rendered them, and they command with authority, [even though] their commands have the force merely of requests, and the obedience rendered them appears entirely voluntary. . . . Although the Chiefs—except in a few particular instances—bear no outward marks of distinction or of superiority,—so much so that one cannot distinguish them from the people by any honours one needs to render them,—there is yet no lack of a certain respect paid them. It is, however, on public occasions, above all, that their dignity is exalted. The councils assemble on their orders, the meetings being held in their [the Chiefs'] homes (cabanes) unless there is available a public hall, like our City Halls, specially set aside for council meetings; business is conducted in their name; they preside at all kinds of meetings; they have a considerable part in festive occasions and in the general distributions. . . . For fear that the Chiefs might usurp too much authority, and try to take on unlimited powers, they are 'bridled' as it were, by the assignment to them of coadjutants (Adjoints) who share with them the sovereignty over the land; and these are called Agoianders by them. . . . Next in authority to the Agoianders is the Senate, composed of senior members of the community of Elders, called in their language Agokstenha: the number of these senators is not a fixed one— anyone has the right to enter this council to give it his vote.' [Millar should have continued the quotation to include, 'whenever he has achieved the maturity of years, understanding and knowledge of affairs that would make him deserving of this privilege, etc.'] P. Jos. Fr. Lafitau, Moeurs des sauvages Ameriquains, 4to à Paris, 1724, tom. i, pp. 472–475 [4 vol. ed., also Paris, 1724, tom. ii, pp. 173–6].

† 'Responsibility for dealing with criminal affairs belongs immediately to those of the kin-group [cabane] of the guilty parties, with respect to [out of regard for?] the guilty themselves, when anyone has killed a fellow member of his own kin-group. As it is assumed that the right over life and death belongs to the parties mutually involved, the village appears not to be concerned with the disorder which has arisen. . . . The matter takes on an entirely different character, however, when murder has been committed involving a member of another cabane, of another tribe or village, or even more, of a foreign nation; for then this death by violence becomes the concern of the entire community. Everyone takes sides with the deceased, and this contributes, in a manner, toward the restitution of the spirit—such is their

From the accounts which have been given of the wandering tribes of shepherds in different parts of the world, it would seem that their government is of the same nature, though the power of their leader is further advanced, according to the degrees of wealth which they enjoy. In proportion to the extent of his herds and flocks, the chief is exalted above all the other members of the tribe, and has more influence in directing their military operations, in establishing their forms of judicial procedure, and in regulating the several branches of their public administration. Thus the captain or leader of a tribe among the Hottentots, who have made but small progress in the pastoral life, and among the wild Arabs, who have seldom acquired considerable property, appears to have little more authority than among the savages of America.* The great riches, on the other hand, which are frequently acquired by those numerous bands of shepherds inhabiting the vast country of Tartary, have rendered the influence of the chief proportionably extensive, and have bestowed upon him an almost unlimited power, which commonly remains in the same family, and is transmitted from father to son like a private inheritance.

† The ancient German nations, described by Caesar and Tacitus, may be ranked in a middle situation between these extremes; having probably had more wealth than the Hottentots, or most of the wild Arabs, and less than the greater part of the Tartars. While they remained

expression—to the relatives aggrieved by the loss which they have sustained. All are at the same time interested in saving the life of the offender and in protecting his relatives from the vengeance of the others, which would not fail to break out sooner or later if one had failed to make the proper satisfaction prescribed for such cases by their laws and by their customs. There are, however, occasions where the crime is considered so heinous that one is no longer concerned with the protection of the murderer, and the Council, using its supreme authority, takes pains to effect his punishment.' Ibid. pp. 486 f., 490, 495 [respectively II, pp. 185 f., 189, 193.] Also, tom. 2, p. 167 [III, pp. 154 f.] [Translations my own. Ed.]

See also the view which is given of the state of government among the Americans, by P. Charlevoix, Journal historique d'un voyage de l'Amerique, let. 13, 18.

* ᵃ 'The Arabian tribes, though they have been for many ages under the Turkish yoke, are rarely interrupted, either in what may concern the course of justice, or in the succession to those few offices and dignities that belong properly to themselves.—Every *Dou-war* (i.e. village or encampment) therefore may be looked upon as a little principality, over which it is usual for that particular family, which is of the greatest name, substance, and reputation, to preside. However, this honour does not always lineally descend from father to son; but, as it was among their predecessors the Numidians, when the heir is too young, or subject to any infirmity, then they make choice of the uncle, or some other relation, who, for prudence and wisdom, is judged to be the fittest for that employ. Yet, notwithstanding the despotic power which is lodged in this person, all grievances and disputes are accommodated in as amicable a manner as possible, by calling to his assistance one person or two out of each tent: and as the offender is considered as a brother, the sentence is always given on the favourable side; and even in the most enormous crimes, rarely any other punishment is inflicted than banishment.' Shaw's Travels, chap. 4, p. 310.

† [Here to end of the chapter completely rewritten. Slight revision already in 2nd edition.]

in their own country, they were not altogether strangers to the cultivation of the ground; but they all led a wandering life, and seem to have had no idea of property in land; a sufficient proof that they drew their subsistence chiefly from their cattle, and regarded agriculture as only a secondary employment. Their chiefs appear to have been either hereditary, or elected from those families who had been longest in the possession of opulent fortunes; but their military expeditions were frequently conducted by such inferior leaders, as happened to offer their service, and could persuade their companions to follow them. In time of peace, justice was administered by the respective chiefs, or leading men, of the different villages.*

But when those barbarians had sallied forth from their native forests, and invaded the provinces of the Roman empire, they were soon led to a great improvement in their circumstances. The countries which they conquered had been cultivated and civilized under the Roman dominion; and the inhabitants, though generally in a declining state, were still acquainted with husbandry and a variety of arts. It was to be expected, therefore, that, while the Gothic invaders, during a long course of bloody wars, defaced the monuments of ancient literature, and wherever they came planted their own barbarous customs, they should, on the other hand, suddenly catch a degree of knowledge from the conquered people; and make a quicker progress in agriculture, and some of the coarser handicrafts connected with it, than they could have

---

* 'They take their kings on the ground of birth, their generals on the basis of courage: the authority of their kings is not unlimited or arbitrary; their generals control them by example rather than command, and by means of admiration which attends upon energy and a conspicuous place in front of the line.' Tacitus, de mor. Germ. § 7.

'On small matters the chiefs consult; on larger questions, the community; but with this limitation, that even the subjects, the decision of which rests with the people, are first handled by the chiefs. . . . When the crowd is pleased to begin they take their seats carrying arms. Silence is called for by the priests, who thenceforward have power also to coerce: then a king or a chief is listened to, in order of age, birth, glory in war, or eloquence, with the prestige which belongs to their counsel rather than with any prescribed right to command.' Ibid. § 11.

'At this assembly it is also permissible to lay accusations and to bring capital charges. The nature of the death penalty differs according to the offence: traitors and deserters are hung from trees; cowards and poor fighters and notorious evil-livers are plunged into the mud of marshes with a hurdle on their heads. . . . At the same gatherings are selected chiefs, who administer law through the cantons and villages: each of them has one hundred assessors from the people to be his responsible advisers.' Ibid. § 12.

'On the declaration of war a high command is set up and invested with powers over life and death; but in peace-time there is no central government. Justice is administered and disputes settled by various local chiefs. . . . When a chieftain formally proclaims his intention of leading a raid, he calls for volunteers: those who approve the project and trust the man himself stand up and promise their support amid loud applause from the whole assembly. Any one who goes back on that promise is considered a deserter and a traitor, and no one ever trusts him again.' Caesar, de bell. Gall. lib. 6, § 23.

done in the natural course of things, had they been left to their own experience and observation. By their repeated victories, different heads of families, or *barons*, were enabled to seize great landed estates. They also acquired many captives in war, whom they reduced into servitude, and by whom they were put into a condition for managing their extensive possessions.

After the settlement of those nations was completed, the members of every large family came to be composed of two sorts of people; the slaves, acquired for the most part by conquest; and the free men, descended from a common ancestor, and maintained out of his estate. The former were employed chiefly in cultivating their masters' grounds: the latter supported the interest and dignity of their leader, and in their turn were protected by him.

The authority of the baron was extremely absolute over all the members of his family; because they entirely depended upon him for subsistence. He obliged his slaves to labour at pleasure, and allowed them such recompense only as he thought proper. His kindred were under the necessity of following his banner in all his military expeditions. He exercised over both a supreme jurisdiction, in punishing their offences, as well as in deciding their differences; and he subjected them to such regulations as he judged convenient, for removing disorders, or preventing future disputes.

These barons, though in a great measure independent, were early united in a larger society, under circumstances which gave rise to a very peculiar set of institutions. The effect of that union, whence proceeded the system of feudal government in Europe, will fall to be considered in a subsequent part of this discourse.

CHAPTER IV

The authority of a Sovereign, and of subordinate officers, over a society composed of different tribes or villages

SECTION I

The constitution of government arising from the union of different tribes or villages

The improvement of agriculture, as it increases the quantity of provisions, and renders particular tribes more numerous and flourishing, so it obliges them at length to send out colonies to a distance, who occupy new seats wherever they can find a convenient situation, and are formed into separate villages, after the model of those with which they are acquainted. Thus, in proportion as a country is better cultivated, it comes to be inhabited by a greater number of distinct societies, whether derived from the same or from a different original, agreeing in their manners, and resembling each other in their institutions and customs.

These different communities being frequently at war, and being exposed to continual invasions from their neighbours, are in many cases determined, by the consideration of their mutual interest, to unite against their common enemies, and to form a variety of combinations, which, from the influence of particular circumstances, are more or less permanent. Having found the advantage of joining their forces in one expedition, they are naturally disposed to continue the like association in another, and by degrees are encouraged to enter into a general alliance. The intercourse which people, in such a situation, have maintained in war will not be entirely dissolved even in time of peace; and though the different villages should be originally strangers to each other, yet, having many opportunities of assembling in their military enterprises, they cannot fail to contract an acquaintance, which will become an inducement to their future correspondence. They have frequent opportunities of meeting in their common sports and diversions; the leading men entertain one another with rustic hospitality and magnificence: intermarriages begin to take place between their respective families; and the various connexions of society are gradually multiplied and extended.

[n]An alliance for mutual defence and security is a measure suggested

by such obvious views of expediency that it must frequently take place, not only among tribes of husbandmen, but also among those of shepherds, and even of mere savages. Many instances of it are, accordingly, to be found in Tartary, upon the coast of Guinea, in the history of the ancient Germans, and among the Indians of America. But such alliances are not likely to produce a permanent union, until the populousness of a country has been increased by agriculture, and the inhabitants, in consequence of that employment, have taken up a fixed residence in the same neighbourhood.

From a confederacy of this kind, a very simple form of government is commonly established. As every village, or separate community, is subjected to its own leader, their joint measures fall naturally under the direction of all those distinguished personages; whose frequent meeting and deliberation gives rise, in a short time, to a regular council, or senate, invested with a degree of power and authority corresponding to what each of its members has acquired over his own particular domestics and retainers.

The same considerations however which determine the individuals of a single tribe to be guided by a particular person in their smaller expeditions, must recommend a similar expedient in conducting a numerous army, composed of different clans, often disagreeing in their views, and little connected with each other. While every chief has the conduct of his own dependents, it is found convenient that some one leader should be instructed with the supreme command of their united forces; and as that dignity is commonly bestowed upon the person who, by his opulence, is most capable of supporting it, he is frequently enabled to maintain it during life, and even in many cases to render it hereditary. In this manner a great chief, or *king*, is placed at the head of a nation, and is permitted to assume the inspection and superintendence of what relates to its defence and security.

* But, notwithstanding the rank and pre-eminence enjoyed by this primitive sovereign, it may easily be conceived that his authority will not be very considerable. His advancement can hardly fail to excite the jealousy of chiefs unaccustomed to subordination, who will be disposed to take every opportunity of curbing his pretensions, and to allow him no higher prerogatives than are sufficient to answer the purposes for which he was created. His interpositions, in matters of public concern, will depend very much upon times and circumstances, and being directed by no previous rules, will be frequently made in an irregular and desultory manner. In a day of battle, when placed at the head of his army, he may venture, perhaps, to rule with a high hand, and it may

* [Revised, enlarged.]

be dangerous for any of his followers to disobey his orders; but upon other occasions his power is usually confined within a narrower compass, and frequently extends no further than to the members of his own clan. After the conclusion of a military enterprise, when the other tribes have retired to their separate places of abode, they are in a great measure withdrawn from his influence, and are placed under the immediate jurisdiction and authority of the respective chiefs by whom they are protected. As it is necessary that these leading men should give their consent to every public measure of importance, they are usually convened for that purpose by the king; who at the same time is accustomed to preside in all their deliberations.

Such, as far as can be collected from the scattered hints delivered by travellers, is the state of government in many rude kingdoms, both upon the coast of Africa, or in those parts of Asia, where a number of distinct tribes or villages have been recently and imperfectly united.

In the Odyssey, Alcinous, king of the Pheacians, says expressly, 'There are twelve chiefs who share dominion in the kingdom, and I am the thirteenth.'* He is accordingly obliged to call a council of his nobles, before he can venture to furnish Ulysses with a single ship, in order to transport him to his native country.

† In the island of Ithaca, the power of the chiefs, who usually deliberated in council upon the affairs of the nation, is equally conspicuous.

> 'Twas silence all, at last Aegyptius spoke;
> Aegyptius, by his age and sorrows broke:—
> Since great Ulysses sought the Phrygian plains,
> Within these walls inglorious silence reigns.
> Say then, ye Peers! by whose commands we meet?
> Why here once more in solemn council sit?
> Ye young, ye old, the weighty cause disclose:
> Arrives some message of invading foes?
> Or say, does high necessity of state
> Inspire some patriot, and demand debate?
> The present synod speaks its author wise;
> Assist him, Jove! thou regent of the skies!‡

From the early history of all the Greek states, we have reason to believe that their government was of a similar nature. The country of Attica, in particular, is said to have been peopled by colonies which were brought, under different leaders, from Egypt and some of the neighbouring countries, and which formed a number of distinct tribes or villages,

---

* Odyss. lib. 8, v. 390.   † [Lifted out of footnote.]   ‡ Pope's Odyss. book 2, l. 19.

independent of one another. The first association among these little societies happened in the time of Cecrops, the founder of Athens, who became their general, and who made a considerable reformation in their police and manners. They were afterwards more intimately united in the reign of Theseus, when the nobility, or principal inhabitants of the several towns or villages, were persuaded to settle at Athens, and composed a senate, or national council, which exercised an authority over the whole country, and obtained the chief direction of religious matters, together with the privilege of electing magistrates, and of teaching and dispensing the laws.

The resemblance between this and the ancient Roman constitution is sufficiently obvious. The foundation of that mighty empire was laid by a few tribes of barbarians, originally distinct from one another, who at first inhabited different quarters of the city, and who appear to have lived under the jurisdiction of their respective chiefs.* This was, in all probability, the origin of that connexion between the poor and the rich, which remained in after ages, and which has been commonly ascribed to the policy of Romulus. People of the lower class at Rome were all attached to some particular patron of rank and distinction; and every patrician had a number of clients, who, besides owing him respect and submission, were bound to portion his daughters, to pay his debts, and to ransom his person from captivity; as, on the other hand, they were entitled to his advice and protection. Of these leading men, who had an extensive influence over the populace, was formed the primitive senate, or council of the sovereign; which appears to have had the absolute determination of peace and war; and which, in the first instance, had not only the privilege of deliberating upon all public regulations, but also, upon the death of a king, that of naming a successor to the royal dignity.

† It must not be overlooked, however, that in the Roman, as well as in many of the Greek governments, there was originally a considerable mixture of democracy, arising from the peculiar circumstances of the people. The different tribes, or families, united in the formation of Rome, or of the independent cities which arose in Peloponnesus and some of the neighbouring countries, had very little property, either in moveables or in land; and their poverty must have prevented the growth of authority in their respective leaders. The influence of a chief, in each

---

* See the account which is given of the *forum originis*, by the author of the historical law-tracts [Kames]; whose acute and original genius has been employed in uniting law with philosophy, and in extending the views of a gainful profession to the liberal pursuits of rational entertainment. Historical law-tracts, chap. of courts.

† [Here to p. 272 'Kingdoms in Europe' new, replacing two pages (161-3) in original.]

of those petty states, depended, in all probability, upon the personal attachment of his followers, and their admiration of his abilities, more than upon his superiority in wealth; and the power which that influence enabled him to assume was, therefore, far from being absolute. For this reason, under the kingly government of Rome, the authority of the senate, composed of all the chiefs, was not alone sufficient for making general laws, or transacting business where dissension might be apprehended, but its decrees, in such cases, were usually confirmed by an assembly consisting of the whole people. The same practice obtained in Athens and Sparta, and probably in most of the other states of Greece.

The particulars related by Caesar concerning the inhabitants of ancient Gaul may be considered as affording the most authentic evidence of the state of government in any rude country. We learn from this author that the whole of that country was divided into a number of separate states, independent of each other, and differing considerably in the degrees of their power, as well as in the extent of their territories. In the several towns, villages, or families, belonging to each nation, there were certain leading persons, possessed of great influence and authority, by whom their respective followers were governed and protected. The affairs of a whole nation were conducted by a king, or chief magistrate, assisted by a national council; and when different nations were engaged in a common enterprise, they made choice of a general to command their united forces.*

The German nations who about the fifth century, over-ran and subdued the provinces of the Western empire, were in a different situation from any other people with whose history we are acquainted. While they remained in their own country, those nations had made considerable advances in the pastoral state, and had thereby acquired a good deal of wealth in herds and flocks. By their settlement in the Roman provinces, they had an opportunity, as has been already observed, of acquiring large estates in land, which tended to augment the authority of different leaders in proportion to their riches.

The inhabitants of a large tract of country were, at the same time,

---

* 'In every Gallic tribe, in every subdivision of the tribe, and almost, one might say, in every household, there are rival factions controlled by men who are popularly supposed to be most influential with the group, and who therefore enjoy the last word in determining all questions of policy. This ancient practice seems to have originated in a desire to give the common folk protection against powerful individuals; for no leader will tolerate the oppression or defrauding of his supporters: if he does, his authority is gone. The same principle holds good for Gaul as a whole; for all the tribes are grouped in two factions or parties.' Caesar, de bell. Gall. lib. 6, §11. See Treasurie of auncient and moderne Times, pub. 1619.

associated for their mutual defence, and in their common expeditions, were conducted by a great chief, or king, whose rank and dignity, like that of every subordinate leader, was supported by his own private estate. There were two circumstances which rendered the associations made upon this occasion much more extensive than they commonly are among nations equally barbarous.

As each of the nations who settled in the Western empire, though seldom large, was, by the rapid progress of its arms, and by a sudden improvement in agriculture, enabled to occupy a prodigious quantity of land, the different proprietors, among whom that land was divided, were placed at a great distance from one another, and spread over a wide country. But many of these proprietors consisting of kindred or acquaintance, and all of them having been accustomed to act under one commander, they were still inclined, how remote soever their situation, to maintain a correspondence, and to unite in their military enterprises.

The state of the Roman provinces was another circumstance which promoted an extensive association among the conquerors. Each province of the Roman empire constituted, in some measure, a separate government, the several parts of which had all a dependence upon one another. The inhabitants, not to mention their ancient national attachment, had usually a set of laws and customs peculiar to themselves, and were governed by the same officers civil and military. They were accustomed on public occasions to act in concert, and to consider themselves as having a common interest. The capital, which was the seat of the governor, became the centre of government, to which the gentry of the province resorted in expectation of preferment, or with a view of sharing in the pleasures of a court; and from thence, to the most distant parts of the country, innumerable channels of communication were opened, through the principal towns, where trade was carried on, where taxes were levied, or where justice was administered.

The connexions, which had thus subsisted for ages between the several districts of large territory, were not entirely destroyed when it came under the dominion of the barbarians. As the ancient inhabitants were no where extirpated, but either by submitting to servitude, or by entering into various treaties of alliance, were incorporated and blended with the conquerors, the habits of intercourse, and the system of political union which remained with the former, was, in some degree, communicated to the latter. When different tribes, therefore, though strangers to each other, had settled in the same province, they were easily reduced under one sovereign; and the boundaries of a modern kingdom, came frequently, in the western part of Europe, to be

nearly of the same extent with the dominions which had been formerly
subject to a Roman governor.

In proportion to the number of tribes, or separate families, united in
one kingdom, and to the wideness of the country over which they were
scattered, the union between them was loose and feeble. Every proprietor
of land maintained a sort of independence, and notwithstanding the
confederacy of which he was a member, assumed the privilege of
engaging in private wars at pleasure. From the violent disposition to
theft and rapine which prevailed in that age, neighbouring proprietors,
when not occupied in a joint expedition, were tempted to commit
depredations upon each other; and mutual injuries between the same
individuals being often repeated, became the source of family quarrels,
which were prosecuted with implacable animosity and rancour. There
was no sufficient authority in the public for repressing these disorders.
If, upon great provocation, the king had been excited to humble and
punish an opulent baron, he found in many cases that the whole force
of the crown was requisite for that purpose, and by the hazard and
difficulty of the attempt, was commonly taught to be cautious, for the
future, of involving himself in such disputes.

As individuals therefore, in those times of violence and confusion,
were continually exposed to injustice and oppression, and received little
or no protection from government, they found it necessary to be constantly attentive to their own safety. It behooved every baron, not
only to support his own personal dignity, and to maintain his own
rights against the attacks of all his neighbours, but also to protect his
retainers and dependents; and he was led, upon that account, to
regulate the state of his barony in such a manner, as to preserve the
union of all its members, to secure their fidelity and service, and to
keep them always in a posture of defence. With this view, when his
relations, who had hitherto lived about his house, were gradually
permitted to have families of their own, he did not bestow upon them
separate estates, which would have rendered them independent; but
he assigned them such portions of land as were thought sufficient for
their maintenance, to be held upon condition, that whenever they were
called upon, they should be ready to serve him in war, and that, in all
their controversies, they should submit to his jurisdiction. These grants
were made for no limited time, but might be resumed at pleasure; so
that though the master was not likely without some extraordinary
offence, to deprive his kinsmen of their possessions, yet his power in
this respect being indisputable, it could hardly fail to keep them in awe,
and to produce an implicit obedience to his commands.

The military tenants, supported in this manner, were denominated *vassals*; and the land held by any person upon such terms has been called a *fief*; though many writers, in order to distinguish it from what afterwards went under the same name, have termed it a *benefice*.

When the estate of a baron became extensive, the slaves, by whom it was cultivated, were likewise sent to a distance from the house of their master, and were placed in separate families, each of which obtained the management of a particular farm; but that they might, in those disorderly times, be more easily protected by the owner, and might be in a condition to defend and assist one another, a number of them were usually collected together, and composed a little village. Hence they received the appellation of *villani*, or villains.

The whole of a kingdom was thus divided into a number of baronies, of greater or smaller extent, and regulated nearly in the same manner. The king was at the head of a barony similar in every respect to those of his subjects, though commonly larger, and therefore capable of maintaining a greater number of vassals and dependents. But the land which belonged to the barons, was held in the same independent manner with that which belonged to the king. As each of those warlike chiefs had purchased his demesnes by his own activity and valour, he claimed the absolute enjoyment and disposal of them together with the privilege of transmitting them to his posterity; and as he had not been indebted to the crown for his original possession, neither was he obliged to secure the continuance of it, by serving the king in war, or by submitting to his jurisdiction. Their property, therefore, was such as has been called *allodial*, in contradiction to that feudal tenure enjoyed by their respective military tenants.*

---

* Different authors have entertained very different opinions concerning the primitive state of landed property, and the origin of feudal tenures, in the modern nations of Europe. The antiquaries who first turned their attention to researches on this subject, those of France in particular, living under an absolute monarchy, appear to have been strongly prepossessed by the form of government established in their own times, and their conjectures, with regard to the early state of the feudal institutions, were for a long time almost implicitly followed by later writers. They suppose that, when any of the German nations settled in a Roman province, the king seized upon all the conquered lands: that, retaining in his own possession what was sufficient to maintain the dignity of the crown, he distributed the remainder among the principal officers of his army, to be held precariously upon condition of their attending him in war: and that these officers afterwards bestowed part of their estates upon their dependents or followers, under similar conditions of military service.

This account seems liable to great objections. First, it may be asked how the king came to possess so much power as would enable him, at once, to acquire the entire property of the conquered lands? For it must be remembered that the conquest extended over the ancient inhabitants of the country, not over his own followers; and with respect to these last, the accounts given by Caesar and Tacitus of the German nations represent their princes as possessing a very limited authority.

2dly, Upon the supposition that all the conquered lands were originally held of the king during pleasure, his authority, immediately upon the settlement of these nations, must

These peculiarities, in the state of the kingdoms which were formed upon the ruins of the Roman empire, had a visible effect upon their constitution of government. According to the authority possessed by the barons, each over his own barony, and their independence with respect to each other, and with respect to the king, was their joint power and influence over that great community of which they were members. The supreme powers of government in every kingdom were, therefore, exercised by an assembly composed of all those proprietors, and commonly summoned by the king on every great emergency.

Two meetings of this great council appear to have been regularly held in a year, for the ordinary dispatch of business; the first, after the seed-time, to determine their military operations during the summer; the second, before the harvest, in order to divide the booty. In those meetings it was customary also to rectify abuses by introducing new regulations, and to decide those law-suits which had arisen between independent proprietors of land. Such was the business of the early parliaments in France, of the Cortes in Spain, of the Wittenagemote in England; and in each of the feudal kingdoms, we discover evident marks of a national council, constituted in the same manner, and invested with similar privileges.*

have been rendered altogether despotical. If the king had a power of dispossessing all his subjects of their landed estates, he must have been more absolute than any monarch at present upon the face of the earth. But the early history of the modern European nations gives an account of their government very different from this, and informs us that the nobility of each kingdom enjoyed great independence, and a degree of opulence, in many cases, little inferior to that of the monarch.

The idea that the king became originally proprietor of all the conquered lands seems now, upon a fuller examination of facts, to be in a great measure relinquished; and several writers of late have made it at least extremely probable that the land in the conquered provinces was at first occupied, according to circumstances, by different individuals, or distributed by lot among the warriors of each victorious tribe; and that each possessor became the full proprietor of that portion of land which had fallen to his share. See Le droit publique de France, eclairci par les monumens de l'antiquité. Par M. Bouquet. See also Observations sur l'histoire de France. Par M. L'Abbé de Mably.

It is true that, in the Modern kingdoms of Europe, the proprietors of lands were early understood to be under an obligation of going out to war as often as the public interest required it. But this was a duty which they owed to the community as citizens, not to the kings as vassals; and their attendance was required, not by an order of the monarch, but in consequence of a determination of the national assembly, of which they themselves were the constituent members.

* In France, under the Merovingian kings, all deeds of any importance, issuing from the crown, usually contained some such expression as these: *Una cum nostris optimatibus pertractavimus. De consensu fidelium nostrorum. In nostra et procerum nostrorum praesentia.* Obser. par M. de Mably. And there is good reason to believe that what is called the Salique Law was laid before the national assembly and received their approbation. 'Dictaverunt Salicam legem Proceres ipsius gentis, qui tunc temporis apud eam erant rectores.' Praef. leg. Sal. See lettres historiques sur les fonctions essentielles du parlement. Boulainvilliers, let. sur le parl. de France.

These observations may serve to show the general aspect and complexion of that political constitution which results from the first union of rude tribes, or small independent societies. The government resulting from that union is apt to be of a mixed nature, in which there is a nobility distinguished from the people, and a king exalted above the nobles. But though, according to that system, the peculiar situation of different nations may have produced some variety in the powers belonging to these different orders, yet, unless in very poor states, the influence acquired by the nobles has commonly been such as to occasion a remarkable prevalence of aristocracy.

SECTION II
The natural progress of government in a rude kingdom

The continued union of rude tribes, or small societies, has a tendency to produce a great alteration in the political system of a people. The same circumstances, by which, in a single tribe, a chief is gradually advanced over the different heads of families, contribute, in a kingdom, to exalt the sovereign above the chiefs, and to extend his authority throughout the whole of his dominions.

As the king is placed at the head of the nation, and acts the most conspicuous part in all their public measures, his high rank and station reflect upon him a degree of splendour, which is apt to obscure the lustre of every inferior chief; and the longer he has remained in a situation where he excites the admiration and respect of the people, it is to be supposed that their habits of submission to him will be the more confirmed.

From the opulence, too, of the sovereign, which is generally much greater than that of any other member of the community, as well as from the nature of his office, he has more power to reward and protect his friends, and to punish or depress those who have become the objects of his resentment or displeasure. The consideration of this must operate powerfully upon individuals, as a motive to court his favour, and, of consequence, to support his interest. It is therefore to be concluded that, from the natural course of things, the immediate followers and dependents of the king will be constantly increasing, and those of every inferior leader will be diminishing in the same proportion.

In a government so constituted as to introduce a continual jealousy between the crown and the nobles, it must frequently happen that the latter, instead of prosecuting a uniform plan for aggrandizing their own order, should be occupied with private quarrels and dissensions among themselves; so that the king, who is ready to improve every conjuncture for extending his power, may often employ and assist the great lords in destroying each other, or take advantage of those occasions when they have been weakened by their continued struggles, and are in no condition to oppose his demands.

According as the real influence and authority of the crown are extended, its prerogatives are gradually augmented. When the king finds that the original chiefs have become in a great measure dependent upon him, he is not solicitous about consulting them in the management of public affairs; and the meetings of the national council, being seldom called, or being attended only by such members as are entirely devoted to the crown, dwindle away from time to time, and are at last laid aside altogether. The judicial power of the heads of different tribes is gradually subjected to similar encroachments; and that jurisdiction, which they at first held in virtue of their own authority, is rendered subordinate to the tribunal of the monarch, who, after having established the right of appeal from their courts to his own court, is led to appoint the judges in each particular district. The power of making laws, as well as that of determining peace and war, and of summoning all his subjects to the field, may come in like manner to be exercised at the discretion of the prince.

This progress of government, towards monarchy, though it seems to hold universally, is likely to be accompanied with some diversity of appearances in different countries; and, in particular, is commonly more rapid in a small state than in a large one; in which point of view the ancient Greeks and Romans are most remarkably distinguished from the greater part of the feudal kingdoms in Europe.

The Roman and Greek states were originally of small extent, and the people belonging to each of them being, for the most part, collected in one city, were led in a short time to cultivate an acquaintance. The police which was easily established in such a limited territory, put a stop to the divisions so prevalent among neighbouring tribes of barbarians. Those who belonged to different families were soon restrained from injuring one another, and lived in security under the protection of the government. By conversing together almost every day, their ancient prejudices were eradicated; and their animosities, being no longer cherished by reciprocal acts of hostility, were allowed to subside, and left no traces behind. The whole people, being early engaged in violent struggles with the petty states around them, were obliged to hold an intimate correspondence, and acquired an high sense of public interest. In proportion as they were thus incorporated in a larger community, they lost all inferior distinctions. The members of each particular tribe had no reason to maintain their peculiar connexions, or to preserve their primitive attachment to their respective chiefs. The power of the nobility, therefore, which depended upon those circumstances, was quickly destroyed; and the monarch, who remained at the head of the nation without a rival to counterbalance his influence, had no difficulty in extending his influence over the whole of his dominions.

* For this reason, the ancient jurisdiction and authority of the chiefs is not very distinctly marked in the early history of those nations, among whom it was in a great measure destroyed before they were possessed of historical records. At Rome, so early as the reign of Servius Tullius, the practice of convening the people according to their tribes, or *curiae*, was almost entirely laid aside; and the public assemblies were held in such a manner, that every individual was classed according to his wealth.

† The great extent, on the other hand, of those modern kingdoms which, upon the downfall of the Roman empire, were erected in the western part of Europe, was formerly mentioned; and the political consequences, which appear to have been immediately derived from that circumstance, were likewise taken notice of. The numerous tribes, or separate families, that were associated under a sovereign, far from being collected in a single town, were spread over a large territory, and living at a distance from each other, were for a long time prevented from having much intercourse, or from acquiring the habits of polished society. Strangers to regular government, and little restrained by the authority of the public magistrate, they were devoted to their several chiefs, by whom they were encouraged to rob and plunder their neighbours, and protected from the punishment due to their offences. Mutual depredations became the source of perpetual animosity and discord among neighbouring barons, who, from jealousy, from an inter-ference of interest, or from resentment of injuries, were, for the most part, either engaged in actual hostilities, or lying in wait for a favourable opportunity to oppress and destroy one another. Thus every kingdom was composed of a great variety of parts, loosely combined together, and for several centuries may be regarded as a collection of small indepen-dent societies, rather than as one great political community. The slow advances which were afterwards made by the people towards a more complete union, appear to have been productive of that feudal subor-dination which has been the subject of so much investigation and controversy.

In those times of license and disorder, the proprietors of small estates were necessarily exposed to many hardships and calamities. Sur-rounded by wealthier and more powerful neighbours, by whom they

* [Lifted out of footnote.]   † [Revised and enlarged.]

were invaded from every quarter, and held in constant terror, they could seldom indulge the hope of maintaining their possessions, or of transmitting them to their posterity. Conscious therefore of their weakness, they endeavoured to provide for their future safety, by soliciting the aid of some opulent chief, who appeared most capable of defending them; and, in order to obtain that protection which he afforded to his ancient retainers or vassals, they were obliged to render themselves equally subservient to his interest; to relinquish their pretensions to independence, to acknowledge him as their leader, and to yield him that homage and fealty which belonged to a feudal superior.

The nature of these important transactions, the solemnities with which they were accompanied, and the views and motives from which they were usually concluded, are sufficiently explained from the copies or forms of those deeds which have been collected and handed down to us. The vassal promised in a solemn manner to submit to the jurisdiction of the superior, to reside within his domain, and to serve him in war, whether he should be engaged in prosecuting his own quarrels, or in the common cause of the nation. The superior, on the other hand, engaged to exert all his power and influence, in protecting the vassal, in defending his possessions, or in avenging his death, in case he should be assassinated. In consequence of these mutual engagements, the vassal, by certain symbols expressive of the agreement, resigned his property, of which he again received the investiture from the hands of the superior.* †

It is probable, however, that the extension of particular baronies, by the voluntary submission of allodial proprietors, contributed to ascertain the right of the vassal, and to limit that property with which the superior was originally invested. The ancient military tenants, who were the kindred and relations of the superior, and who had received their lands as a pure gratuity, never thought of demanding to be secured in the future possession; and while they continued to support the interest of the family, which they looked upon as inseparable from their own interest, they had no apprehension that they should ever be deprived of their estates. Thus, according to the more accurate ideas of

---

* Fidelis Deo propitio ille, ad nostram veniens praesentiam suggessit nobis, eo quod propter simplicitatem suam, causas suas minime possit prosequi, vel admallare, clementiae regni nostri petiit, ut illustris vir ille omnes causas suas in vice ipsius, tam in pago, quam in palatio nostro admallandum prosequendumque recipere deberet, quod in praesenti per fistucam eas eidem visus est commendasse. Propterea jubemus, ut dum taliter utriusque decrevit voluntas, memoratus ille vir omnes causas lui, ubicumque prosequi vel admallare deberet, ut unicuique pro ipso, vel hominibus suis, reputatis conditionibus, et directum faciat, et ab aliis similiter in veritate recipiat. Sic tamen quamdiu amborum decrevit voluntas. *Formul. Marculfi* 21.—Vid. Ibid. Formul. 13.

See also L'Esprit de Loix, liv. 31, chap. 8.

† [Two paragraphs dropped here.]

later times, they were merely tenants at will;[a] though from the affection of their master, and from their inviolable fidelity to him, they were commonly permitted to enjoy their lands during life; and in ordinary cases the same indulgence was even shown to their posterity.

But it was not to be expected that those who submitted to a foreign superior, and who gave up their allodial property as an equivalent for the protection which was promised them, would repose so much confidence in a person with whom they had no natural connexion, or be willing to hold their lands by the same precarious tenure. They endeavoured, by express stipulations, to prevent the arbitrary conduct of the master; and, according as they found themselves in a condition to insist for more favourable terms, they obtained a grant of their estates, for a certain limited time, for life, or to their heirs. By these grants the right of property, instead of being totally vested in the superior, came to be, in some measure, divided between him and his vassals.

* When a superior had entered into such transactions with his new retainers, he could not well refuse a similar security to such of his ancient vassals as, from any casual suspicion, thought proper to demand it; so that from the influence of example, joined to uninterrupted possession in a series of heirs, the same privileges were, either by an express bargain, or by a sort of tacit agreement, communicated, at length, to all his military tenants.

This alteration gave rise to what were called the *incidents* of the feudal tenures. The ancient military tenants, who were the kindred of the superior, might be removed by him at pleasure, or subjected to what burdens he thought proper to impose upon them; and there was no occasion to specify the services that might be required of them, or the grounds upon which they might forfeit their possessions. But when the vassal had obtained a permanent right to his estate, it became necessary to ascertain the extent of the obligations which he came under, and the penalty to which he was subjected upon his neglecting to fulfil them; so that, from the nature of the feudal connexion, he in some cases incurred a forfeiture, or total loss of the fief, and in others was liable for the payment of certain duties, which produced an occasional profit to the superior.

1. Thus when the vassal died without heirs; when he violated his duty by the commision of a crime, or by neglecting to perform the usual service; in either of these cases his lands returned to the superior. The emolument arising from this forfeiture, or termination of the fief, was called *an escheat.*

* [Here to p. 277, '. . . in a former period,' added; most of it in 2nd edition already in a footnote, pp. 213–15.]

2. When a person was admitted to hold a fief, he engaged by an oath to fulfil the duties of *homage* and *fealty* to the superior. Even after fief became hereditary, this ceremony was repeated upon every transmission of the feudal right by succession; so that while the heir of a vassal neglected to renew the engagement, he was not intitled to obtain possession, and the superior, in the mean time, drew the rent of the lands. Hence the incident of *non-entry*.

3. Though the heir of a vassal might claim a renewal of the feudal investiture, this was understood to be granted in consideration of his performing military service. When by his nonage, therefore, the heir was incapable of fulfilling that condition, the superior himself retained the possession of the lands; at the same time that he was accustomed, in that case, to protect and maintain his future vassal. This produced the incident of *wardship*.

4. Upon the death of a vassal, it was usual for the representative of his family to make a present to the superior, in order to obtain a ready admittance into the possession of the lands. When fiefs became hereditary, it was still found expedient to procure by means of a bribe, what could not easily be extorted by force; and the original arbitrary payment was converted into a regular duty, under the name of *relief*.

5. From the original nature of the feudal grants, the vassal could have no title to sell, or give away to any other person, the lands which he held merely as a tenant, in consideration of the service which he was bound to perform. But when fiefs had been granted to heirs, and when of consequence the right of the vassal approached somewhat nearer to that of property, it became customary to compound with the superior for the privilege of alienating the estate, upon payment of a sum of money. This gave rise to a perquisite, called the *fine of alienation*.

6. From the disorders which prevailed in the feudal times, when different families were so frequently at war, it was of great consequence that the vassals should not contract an alliance with the enemy of their Liege Lord; which might have a tendency to corrupt their fidelity. When fiefs therefore came to be granted for life, or to heirs, it was still held a sufficient ground of forfeiture that the vassal married without the superior's consent. This forfeiture was afterwards converted into a pecuniary penalty, called the incident of *marriage*.

7. According to the usual policy of the feudal nations, the superior levied no taxes from his retainers, but was maintained from the rent of his own estate. In particular cases however, when his ordinary revenue was insufficient, his vassals were accustomed to supply him by a voluntary contribution. When fiefs were precarious, what was given on those occasions depended upon the will of the superior, who might

even seize upon the whole estate of his tenants. But when the vassal had obtained a more permanent right, it became necessary to settle the cases when those contributions were to be made, as well as the quantity that might be demanded; and in this manner, *aid* or *benevolence* came to be enumerated among the duties payable to a superior.

The conversion of allodial into feudal property, by a voluntary resignation, as it proceeded from the general manners and situation of the people, continued to be a frequent practice, while those manners and that situation remained. The smaller barons were thus, at different times, subjected to their opulent neighbours; the number of independent proprietors was gradually diminished; their estates were united and blended together in one barony; and large districts were brought under the dominion of a few great lords, who daily extended their influence and authority, by increasing the number of their vassals.

These changes, by exalting a small part of the nobility over the great body of the people, had, for some time, a tendency to abridge, instead of enlarging the power of the crown, and to render the government more aristocratical. Whenever an independent proprietor had resigned his allodial property, and agreed to hold his land by a feudal tenure, he was no longer entitled to a voice in the national assembly, but was bound to follow the direction of the person to whom he had become liable in homage and fealty. This appears to be the reason of what is observed in France, that the national assembly was originally much more numerous than it came to be afterwards, when its constituent members were all persons of high rank and great opulence.* It would seem also that in England, under the later princes of the Saxon line, the great affairs of the nation were transacted in a meeting composed of a few great barons; and we discover no marks of those numerous assemblies which are taken notice of in a former period.†

But the same circumstances, by which the estates of different small proprietors were united in one barony, contributed afterwards to incorporate these larger districts, and to unite all the inhabitants of a kingdom in the same feudal dependency. As the barons were diminished in number, and increased in power and opulence, they became more immediate rivals to each other. In their different quarrels, which were prosecuted with various success, the weaker party was often obliged to have recourse to the king, who alone was able to screen him from the

---

* 'All the Franks continued without discrimination to have the right of entrance [into the national assembly]; but subsequently, their number having increased, and the distinction between Gauls and Franks having become gradually erased, each canton assembled separately; and scarcely any but those who held a certain rank in the state were admitted to the general assembly any more.' Let. hist. sur les parl.

† In early times the Wittenagemote is called 'infinita fidelium multitudo.'

fury of his enemy; and, in order to procure that succour and protection which his situation required, he became willing to surrender his property, and to hold his estate upon condition of his yielding that obedience, and performing that service, which a superior was accustomed to demand from his vassals. From the various disputes which arose, and the accidental combinations that were formed among the great families, the nobles were all, in their turns, reduced to difficulties from which they were forced to extricate themselves by the like compliances; and the sovereign, who laid hold of every opportunity to extend his influence, established his superiority over the barons by the same means which they themselves had formerly employed for subjecting the proprietors of smaller estates.

Thus, by degrees, the feudal system was completed in most of the countries of Europe. The whole of a kingdom came to be united in one great fief, of which the king was the superior, or lord paramount, having in some measure the property of all the land within his dominions. The great barons became his immediate vassals, and, according to the tenure by which they held their estates, were subject to his jurisdiction, and liable to him in services of the same nature with those which they exacted from their own retainers or inferior military tenants.

The precise period when this revolution was finally accomplished, as in most other gradual changes which happen in a country, is involved in doubt and uncertainty. From a comparison of the opinions of different authors who have written upon this subject, and of the facts which they bring in support of their several conjectures, it appears most reasonable to conclude, that in France the great barons continued their allodial possessions during the kings of the first and second race, and about the beginning of the Capetian line were, for the most part, reduced into a state of feudal subjection to the monarch.*

* Many of the French antiquaries and historians have believed that the feudal system was completed under their kings of the first race. (See Mezeray, hist. de France.—Loyseau, traité des seigneuries.—Salvaing, de l'usage des fiefs.—) Others have supposed that military tenures were unknown during this early period, and were introduced, either about the time of Charlemagne, or towards the end of the second race of kings, or about the time of Hugh Capet. (See Boulainvilliers, lettres sur les parlemens de France.—Chantereau de Fevre, traité des fiefs.—Henault, abr. de l'hist. de France.—Bouquet, droit publique de France, etc.) These various opinions appear to have arisen from a different view of the facts relating to the subject; and here, as in most other disputes, the truth probably lies in a middle between the opposite extremes. To those authors who observed that, soon after the settlement of the Franks in Gaul, the king and the great lords had a considerable number of vassals dependent upon them for protection, and liable in military service, it seemed a natural inference that the whole land in the country was held by military tenure. Those on the contrary who discovered that, under the kings of the first and second race, the great lords were in possession of allodial estates, and who observed, that, after the reign of Hugh Capet, many of the perquisites incident to the feudal tenures were established, thought they had reason from thence to conclude that the feudal system was not introduced before this period.

In England it would seem that, in like manner, the nobles maintained their independence during the time of the Saxon princes, and were reduced to be the vassals of the crown in the reign of William the Conqueror.*

This opinion is confirmed by observing the changes which, from those two periods, began to take place in the government of these kingdoms. From the reign of Hugh Capet, the dominions of France, appear more firmly united; they were no longer split upon the death of the sovereign, and shared among his children; the monarch was from this period capable of acting with more vigour, and continued to extend his prerogative till the reign of Lewis XI, who exercised the power of imposing taxes, as well as of making laws independent of the convention of estates. The same progress, though with some accidental interruptions may be traced in England, from the Norman conquest to the accession of the Tudor family, under which the powers and prerogatives of the crown were exalted to a height that seemed equally incompatible with the rights of the nobility and the freedom of the people.

---

* From similar circumstances it has been a subject of controversy, whether the feudal system took place in England under the government of the Saxon monarchs, or whether it was not first introduced in the reign of William the Conqueror. See *Wright's Introduction to the law of tenures*, chap. 2. and the authorities quoted by him upon both sides of the question.

ᵃ Sir Henry Spelman having said in his Glossary, v. *feodum*, that fiefs were brought into England by William the Conqueror, and the judges of Ireland, in their argument in the case of *defective titles*, having pointed out that opinion as erroneous, this industrious antiquary was thence excited to write a treatise upon the subject, in which he explains his meaning to be nothing more but that in England, fiefs were not rendered *hereditary* before the Norman conquest. Thus, after having stated the question, in the beginning of his treatise, he goes on as follows: 'A FEUD is said to be *usufructus quidam rei immobilis sub conditione fidei*. But this definition is of too large extent for such kind of *feuds* as our question must consist upon: for it includeth two members of species greatly differing the one from the other; the one *temporary* and *revocable* (as those at will or for years, life or lives); the other *hereditary* and *perpetual*. As for *temporary feuds*, which (like wild fig-trees) could yield none of the feudal fruits of *wardship, marriage, relief*, etc. unto their lords, they belong nothing unto our argument.' —And a little after he adds, 'But this kind of *feud* (we speak of) and no other, is that only whereof our law taketh notice, though time hath somewhat varied it from the first institution, by drawing the property of the soil from the lord unto the tenant. And I both conceive and affirm under correction, That this our kind of feuds being perpetual and hereditary, and subject to wardship, marriage, and relief, and other feodal services were not in use among our Saxons, nor our law of tenures (whereon they depend) once known unto them.' (Spelman's treat. on feuds and tenures by knight-service, chap. 1. The same author, in another part of his treatise, proceeds to shew that, in England among the Saxons, the estates of the nobility were denominated *Boc-land*, and were held in full property, but that *Folc-land*, or the land of the lower people, was held under condition of customary services, at the will of their lord the Thane. Ibid. chap. 5.

It is hoped the above remark will appear not improper; because the authority of Spelman upon this point, has been considered as of much weight; and also because some writers appear to have mistaken his opinion by consulting the passage in his glossary, without attending to the subsequent treatise, published among his posthumous works by Dr Gibson.

* The authors, who have written upon the feudal law, seem to have generally considered that sytem as peculiar to the modern nations of Europe; and from what has been observed above, it appears evident that the circumstances of the Gothic nations, who settled in the western provinces of Rome, rendered such a set of regulations more especially useful for the defence and security of the people. It is highly probable that, from those parts of Europe where the feudal law was first established, it was in some degree communicated, by the intercourse of the inhabitants and the force of example, to some of the neighbouring countries. But it merits particular attention that the same sort of policy, though not brought to the same perfection as in Europe, is to be found in many distant parts of the world, where it never could be derived from imitation; and perhaps there is reason to think that similar institutions, by which small bodies of men are incorporated in larger societies under a single leader, and afterwards linked together in one great community, have been suggested in every extensive kingdom, founded upon the original association of many rude tribes or families.

The kingdom of Congo, upon the southern coast of Africa, is divided into many large districts or provinces, the inhabitants of which appear to have made some progress in agriculture. Each of these districts comprehends a multitude of small lordships, which are said to have been formerly independent, but which are now united together, and reduced under a single chief or governor, who exercises absolute authority over them. The great lords, or governors of provinces, are in like manner dependent upon the king, and owe him the payment of certain annual duties. This monarch is understood to have an unlimited power over the goods of all his subjects; he is the proprietor of all the lands in the kingdom, which return to the crown upon the death of the possessors; and, according to the arbitrary will of the prince, are either continued in the same, or bestowed upon a different family. All the inhabitants are bound to appear in the field whenever they are required by the sovereign who is able in a short time to raise a prodigious army upon any sudden emergency. Every governor has a judicial power in his own district, and from his sentences there lies an appeal to the king, who is the supreme judge of the nation. Similar accounts are given of the constitution in the neighbouring kingdoms of Angola, Loango, and Benin.

The same form of government may be discovered in several parts of the East Indies, where many great lords, who have acquired extensive dominions, are often reduced into a sort of feudal dependence upon a single person.

† Among the natives of Indostan, there are a great number of families

* [Revised and enlarged.]   † [Added, already in 2nd edition.]

who have been immemorially trained up to arms, and who enjoy a superior rank to most of the other inhabitants. They form a militia capable of enduring much hardship, and wanting nothing to make good soldiers but order and discipline. These hereditary warriors are subject to the authority of chiefs, or Rajahs, from whom they receive lands, upon condition of their performing military service. It would seem that those different families were originally independent of each other. By degrees however many of the poorer sort have become subordinate to their opulent neighbours, and are obliged to serve them in war in order to obtain a livelihood. In like manner the leaders of more wealthy families have been gradually subdued by a certain Rajah, who mounted the throne, and whose influence became more and more extensive. This in all probability gave rise to the political constitution at present established in that country. The Rajahs, or nobility, are now for the most part retained by the Great Mogul in a situation resembling that of the crown vassals in Europe. At the same time there are some of those chiefs who still maintain an independency even in the heart of the empire. In the reign of Aureng-zebe, there were about an hundred, dispersed over the whole country, several of whom were capable of bringing into the field 25,000 horse, better troops than those of the monarch.

In the kingdom of Pegu, which was formerly an independent monarchy, the king is said to have been the sole heir of all the landed estates of his subjects. The nobility or chiefs had lands and towns assigned them, which they held of the crown, upon condition of their maintaining a certain number of troops in time of peace, and bringing them into the field in case of a war. Besides these military services, they were also bound to the performance of several kinds of work, which the sovereign rigorously exacted from them, in token of their subjection. This country is now annexed to the kingdom of Ava, in which, as well as in that of Laos and of Siam, the same regulations appear to be established.

* Travellers who make observations on the Malais [says the judicious M. Le Poivre] are astonished to find, in the centre of Asia, under the scorching climate of the line, the laws, the manners, the customs, and the prejudices of the ancient inhabitants of the north of Europe. The Malais are governed by feudal laws, that capricious system, conceived for the defence of the liberty of a few against the tyranny of one, while the multitude is subjected to slavery and oppression.

A chief, who has the title of king, or sultan, issues his commands to his great vassals, who obey when they think proper. These have inferiour vassals, who often act in the same manner with regard to them. A small

* [Five paragraphs added.]

part of the nation live independent, under the title of *Oramçay*, or *noble*, and sell their services to those who pay them best; while the body of the nation is composed of slaves, and lives in perpetual servitude.

With these laws, the Malais are restless, fond of navigation, war, plunder, emigrations, colonies, desperate enterprises, adventures, and gallantry. They talk incessantly of their honour, and their bravery, while they are universally regarded, by those with whom they have intercourse, as the most treacherous ferocious people on the face of the globe; and yet, what appeared to me extremely singular, they speak the softest language of Asia. What the Count de Forbin has said, in his Memoirs, is exactly true, and is the reigning characteristic of all the Malay nations. More attached to the absurd laws of their pretended honour, than to those of justice or humanity, you always observe, that among them, the strong oppress the weak: their treaties of peace and friendship never subsisting beyond that self-interest by which they were induced to make them. They are almost always armed, and either at war among themselves, or employed in pillaging their neighbours.*

The remains of this feudal policy are also to be found in Turkey. The Zaims and Timariots, in the Turkish empire, are a species of vassals, who possess landed estates upon condition of their upholding a certain number of soldiers for the service of the grand seignior. The Zaims have lands of greater value than the Timariots, and are obliged to maintain a greater number of soldiers. The estates of both, are, in some cases, held during pleasure, and in others hereditary. It was computed, in the last century, that the whole militia maintained in this manner, throughout the Turkish empire, amounted to an hundred thousand men.

In the history of the ancient Persians, during the wars which they carried on with the Roman emperors, we may also discover some traces of a similar constitution of government; for it is observed that this nation had no mercenary troops, but that the whole people might be called out to war by the king, and upon the conclusion of every expedition, were accustomed to return, with their booty, to their several places of residence.

When a great and polished nation begins to relapse into its primitive rudeness and barbarism, the dominions which belong to it are in danger of falling asunder; and the same institutions may become necessary for preventing the different parts of the kingdom from being separated, which had been formerly employed in order to unite the several members of an extensive society. This was the case among the Romans in the later periods of the empire. When the provinces became in a great measure independent, and the government was no longer able to protect them from the repeated invasions of the barbarians, the

* Les voyages d'une Philosophe.

inhabitants were obliged to shelter themselves under the dominion of particular great men in their neighbourhood, whom the emperor put in possession of large estates, upon condition of their maintaining a proper armed force to defend the country. Thus, in different provinces, there arose a number of chiefs, or leaders, who enjoyed estates in land, as a consideration for the military service which they performed to the sovereign. The Abbé Du Bos has thence been led to imagine that the feudal policy of the German nations was copied from those regulations already established in the countries which they subdued. But it ought to be considered, that the growth and decay of society have, in some respects, a resemblance to each other; which independent of imitation, is naturally productive of similar manners and customs.

CHAPTER V

The changes produced in the government of a people, by their progress in Arts, and in polished Manners*

SECTION I

Circumstances, in a polished nation, which tend to increase the power of the sovereign

The advancement of a people in the arts of life, is attended with various alterations in the state of individuals, and in the whole constitution of their government.

Mankind, in a rude age, are commonly in readiness to go out to war, as often as their circumstances require it. From their extreme idleness, a military expedition is seldom inconvenient for them; while the prospect of enriching themselves with plunder, and of procuring distinction by their valour, renders it always agreeable. The members of every clan are no less eager to follow their chief, and to revenge his quarrel, than he is desirous of their assistance. They look upon it as a privilege, rather than a burden, to attend upon him, and to share in the danger, as well as in the glory and profit of all his undertakings. By the numberless acts of hostility in which they are engaged, they are trained to the use of arms, and acquire experience in the military art, so far as it is then understood. Thus, without any trouble or expense, a powerful militia is constantly maintained, which, upon the slightest notice, can always be brought into the field, and employed in the defence of the country.

When Caesar made war upon the Helvetii they were able to muster against him no less than ninety-two thousand fighting men, amounting to a fourth part of all the inhabitants.

Hence those prodigious swarms which issued, at different times, from the ill cultivated regions of the north, and over-ran the several provinces of the Roman empire. Hence too, the poor but superstitious princes of Europe were enabled to muster such numerous forces under the banner of the cross, in order to attack the opulent nations of the east, and to deliver the holy sepulchre from the hands of the infidels.

The same observation will, in some measure, account for those immense armies which we read of in the early periods of history; or at

* [This chapter is part of ch. IV in the original, replacing pp. 178–91.]

least may incline us to consider the exaggerated relations of ancient authors, upon that subject, as not entirely destitute of real foundation.

These dispositions, arising from the frequent disorders incident to a rude society, are of course laid aside when good order and tranquillity begin to be established. When the government acquires so much authority as to protect individuals from oppression, and to put an end to the private wars which subsisted between different families, the people, who have no other military enterprises but those which are carried on in the public cause of the nation, become gradually less accustomed to fighting, and their martial ardour is proportionably abated.

The improvement of arts and manufactures, by introducing luxury, contributes yet more to enervate the minds of men, who, according as they enjoy more ease and pleasure at home, feel greater aversion to the hardships and dangers of a military life, and put a lower value upon that sort of reputation which it affords.* The increase of industry, at the same time, creates a number of lucrative employments which require a constant attention, and gives rise to a variety of tradesmen and artificers, who cannot afford to leave their business for the transient and uncertain advantages to be derived from the pillage of their enemies.

In these circumstances the bulk of a people become at length unable or unwilling to serve in war, and when summoned to appear in the field, according to the ancient usage, are induced to offer a sum of money instead of their personal attendance. A composition of this kind is readily accepted by the sovereign or chief magistrate, as it enables him to hire soldiers among those who have no better employment, or who have contracted a liking to that particular occupation. The forces which he has raised in this manner receiving constant pay, and having no other means of procuring a livelihood, are entirely under the direction of their leader, and are willing to remain in his service as long as he chooses to retain them. From this alteration of circumstances, he has an opportunity of establishing a proper subordination in the army, and according as it becomes fitter for action, and, in all its motions, capable of being guided and regulated with greater facility, he is encouraged to enter upon more difficult enterprises, as well as to meditate more distant schemes of ambition. His wars, which were formerly concluded in a few weeks, are now gradually protracted to a greater length of time, and occasioning a greater variety of operations, are productive of suitable improvements in the military art.

After a numerous body of troops have been levied at considerable

* [See further, *H.V.* vol. iv, pp. 184–201.]

expense, and have been prepared for war by a long course of discipline and experience, it appears highly expedient to the sovereign that, even in time of peace, some part of them, at least, should be kept in pay, to be in readiness whenever their service is required. Thus, the introduction of mercenary forces is soon followed by that of a regular standing army. The business of a soldier becomes a distinct profession, which is appropriated to a separate order of men; while the rest of the inhabitants, being devoted to their several employments, become wholly unaccustomed to arms; and the preservation of their lives and fortunes, is totally devolved upon those whom they are at the charge of maintaining for that purpose.

* This important revolution, with respect to the means of national defence, appears to have taken place in all the civilized and opulent nations of antiquity. In all the Greek states, even in that of Sparta, we find that the military service of the free citizens came, from a change of manners, to be regarded as burdensome, and the practice of employing mercenary troops was introduced. The Romans too, before the end of the republic, had found it necessary to maintain a regular standing army in each of their distant provinces.

In the modern nations of Europe, the disuse of the feudal militia was an immediate consequence of the progress of the people in arts and manufactures; after which the different sovereigns were forced to hire soldiers upon particular occasions, and at last to maintain a regular body of troops for the defence of their dominions. In France, during the reign of Lewis XIII, and in Germany, about the same period, the military system began to be established upon that footing, which it has since acquired in all the countries of Europe.

The tendency of a standing mercenary army to increase the power and prerogative of the crown, which has been the subject of much declamation, is sufficiently obvious. As the army is immediately under the conduct of the monarch; as the individuals of which it is composed depend entirely upon him for preferment; as, by forming a separate order of men they are apt to become indifferent about the rights of their fellow-citizens; it may be expected that, in most cases, they will be disposed to pay an implicit obedience to his commands, and that the same force which is maintained to suppress insurrections, and to repel invasions, may often be employed to subvert and destroy the liberties of the people.

The same improvements in society, which give rise to the mainten-

---

* [Here to end of chapter (p. 295) we have a complete rewriting and marked expansion of pp. 183-91 in original.] Six paragraphs are retained unaltered, much of the new material, also an extended quotation from Hume's *History*, already contained in 2nd edition.]

ance of standing forces, are usually attended with similar changes in the manner of distributing justice. It has been already observed that, in a large community, which has made but little progress in the arts, every chief or baron is the judge over his own tribe, and the king, with the assistance of his great council, exercises a jurisdiction over the members of different tribes or baronies. From the small number of law-suits which occur in the ages of poverty and rudeness, and from the rapidity with which they are usually determined among a warlike and ignorant people, the office of a judge demands little attention, and occasions no great interruption to those pursuits in which a man of rank and distinction is commonly engaged. The sovereign and the nobility, therefore, in such a situation, may continue to hold this office, though, in their several courts, they should appoint a deputy-judge to assist them in discharging the duties of it. But when the increase of opulence has given encouragement to a variety of tedious litigation, they become unwilling to bestow the necessary time in hearing causes, and are therefore induced to devolve the whole business upon inferior judges, who acquire by degrees the several branches of the judicial power, and are obliged to hold regular courts for the benefit of the inhabitants. Thus the exercise of jurisdiction becomes a separate employment, and is committed to an order of men, who require a particular education to qualify them for the duties of their office, and who, in return for their service, must therefore be enabled to earn a livelihood by their profession.

A provision for the maintenance of judges is apt, from the natural course of things, to grow out of their employment; as, in order to procure an indemnification for their attendance, they have an opportunity of exacting fees from the parties who come before them. This is analagous to what happens with respect to every sort of manufacture, in which an artificer is commonly paid by those who employ him. We find, accordingly, that this was the early practice in all the feudal courts of Europe, and that the perquisites drawn by the judges, in different tribunals, yielded a considerable revenue both to the king and the nobles. It is likely that similar customs, in this respect, have been adopted in most parts of the world, by nations in the same period of their advancement. The impropriety, however, of giving a permission to these exactions, which tend to influence the decisions of a judge, to render him active in stirring up law-suits, and in multiplying the forms of his procedure, in order to increase his perquisites; these pernicious consequences with which it is inseparably connected, could not fail to attract the notice of a polished people, and at length produced the more perfect plan of providing for the maintenance of judges by the appointment of a fixed salary in place of their former precarious emoluments.

It cannot be doubted that these establishments, of such mighty importance, and of so extensive a nature, must be the source of great expense to the public. In those early periods, when the inhabitants of a country are in a condition to defend themselves, and when their internal disputes are decided by judges who claim no reward for their interpositions, or at least no reward from government, few regulations are necessary with respect to the public revenue. The king is enabled to maintain his family, and to support his dignity, by the rents of his own estate; and, in ordinary cases, he has no farther demand. But when the disuse of the ancient militia has been succeeded by the practice of hiring troops, these original funds are no longer sufficient; and other resources must be provided in order to supply the deficiency. By the happy disposition of human events, the very circumstance that occasions this difficulty appears also to suggest the means of removing it. When the bulk of a people become unwilling to serve in war, they are naturally disposed to offer a composition in order to be excused from that ancient personal service which, from long custom, it is thought they are bound to perform. Compositions of this nature are levied at first, in consequence of an agreement with each individual: to avoid the trouble arising from a multiplicity of separate transactions, they are afterwards paid in common by the inhabitants of particular districts, and at length give rise to a general *assessment*, the first considerable taxation that is commonly introduced into a country.

If this tax could always be laid upon the people in proportion to their circumstances, it might easily be augmented in such a manner as to defray all the expenses of government. But the difficulty of ascertaining the wealth of individuals makes it impossible to push the assessment to a great height, without being guilty of oppression, and renders it proper that other methods of raising money should be employed to answer the increasing demands of the society. In return for the protection which is given to merchants in carrying their goods from one country to another, it is apprehended that some recompence is due to the government, and that certain duties may be levied upon the exportation and importation of commodities. The security enjoyed by tradesmen and manufacturers, from the care and vigilance of the magistrate, is held also to lay a foundation for similar exactions upon the retail of goods, and upon the inland trade of a nation. Thus the payment of *customs*, and of what, in a large sense, may be called *excise*, is introduced and gradually extended.

It is not proposed to enter into a comparison of these different taxes, or to consider the several advantages and disadvantages of each.

Their general effects in altering the political constitution of a state are more immediately the object of the present enquiry. With respect to this point, it merits attention that, as the sovereign claims a principal share at least, in the nomination of public officers, as he commonly obtains the chief direction in collecting and disposing of the revenue which is raised upon their account, he is enabled thereby to give subsistence to a great number of persons, who, in times of faction and disorder, will naturally adhere to his party, and whose interest, in ordinary cases, will be employed to support and to extend his authority. These circumstances contribute to strengthen the hands of the monarch, to undermine and destroy every opposite power, and to increase the general bias towards the absolute dominion of a single person.*

* [This paragraph introduces a theme greatly to be expanded in the *Historical View*, vol. IV, 88–99 and elsewhere.]

SECTION II

Other circumstances, which contribute to advance the privileges of the people

After viewing those effects of opulence and the progress of arts which favour the interest of the crown, let us turn our attention to other circumstances, proceeding from the same source, that have an opposite tendency, and are manifestly conducive to a popular form of government.

In that early period of agriculture when manufactures are unknown, persons who have no landed estate are usually incapable of procuring subsistence otherwise than by serving some opulent neighbour, by whom they are employed, according to their qualifications, either in military service, or in the several branches of husbandry. Men of great fortune find that the entertaining a multitude of servants, for either of these purposes, is highly conducive both to their dignity and their personal security; and in a rude age, when people are strangers to luxury, and are maintained from the simple productions of the earth, the number of retainers who may be supported upon any particular estate is proportionably great.

In this situation, persons of low rank, have no opportunity of acquiring an affluent fortune, or of raising themselves to superior stations; and remaining for ages in a state of dependence, they naturally contract such dispositions and habits are as suited to their circumstances. They acquire a sacred veneration for the person of their master, and are taught to pay an unbounded submission to his authority. They are proud of that servile obedience by which they seem to exalt his dignity, and consider it as their duty to sacrifice their lives and their possessions in order to promote his interest, or even to gratify his capricious humour.

But when the arts begin to be cultivated in a country, the labouring part of the inhabitants are enabled to procure subsistence in a different manner. They are led to make proficiency in particular trades and professions; and, instead of becoming servants to any body, they often find it more profitable to work at their own charges, and to vend the product of their labour. As in this situation their gain depends upon a variety of customers, they have little to fear from the displeasure of any single person; and, according to the good quality and cheapness of the commodity which they have to dispose of, they may commonly be assured of success in their business.

The farther a nation advances in opulence and refinement, it has occasion to employ a greater number of merchants, of tradesmen and artificers; and as the lower people, in general, become thereby more independent in their circumstances, they begin to exert those sentiments of liberty which are natural to the mind of man, and which necessity alone is able to subdue. In proportion as they have less need of the favour and patronage of the great, they are at less pains to procure it; and their application is more uniformly directed to acquire those talents which are useful in the exercise of their employments. The impressions which they received in their former state of servitude are therefore gradually obliterated, and give place to habits of a different nature. The long attention and perseverance, by which they become expert and skilful in their business, render them ignorant of those decorums and of that politeness which arises from the intercourse of society; and that vanity which was formerly discovered in magnifying the power of a chief, is now equally displayed in sullen indifference, or in contemptuous and insolent behaviour to persons of superior rank and station.

While, from these causes, people of low rank are gradually advancing towards a state of independence, the influence derived from wealth is diminished in the same proportion. From the improvement of arts and manufactures, the ancient simplicity of manners is in a great measure destroyed; and the proprietor of a landed estate, instead of consuming its produce in hiring retainers, is obliged to employ a great part of it in purchasing those comforts and conveniences which have become objects of attention, and which are thought suitable to his condition. Thus while fewer persons are under the necessity of depending upon him, he is daily rendered less capable of maintaining dependents; till at last his domestics and servants are reduced to such as are merely subservient to luxury and pageantry, but are of no use in supporting his authority.

From the usual effects of luxury and refinement, it may at the same time be expected that old families will often be reduced to poverty and beggary. In a refined and luxurious nation those who are born to great affluence, and who have been bred to no business, are excited, with mutual emulation, to surpass one another in the elegance and refinement of their living. According as they have the means of indulging themselves in pleasure, they become more addicted to the pursuit of it, and are sunk in a degree of indolence and dissipation which renders them incapable of any active employment. Thus the expense of the landed gentleman is apt to be continually increasing, without any proportional addition to his income. His estate therefore, being more and more incumbered with debts, is at length alienated, and brought into the possession of the frugal and industrious merchant, who, by success in trade, has been enabled to buy it, and who is desirous of obtaining that rank and consequence which landed property is capable of bestowing. The posterity, however, of this new proprietor, having adopted the manners of the landed gentry, are again led, in a few generations, to squander their estate, with a heedless extravagance equal to the parsimony and activity by which it was acquired.

This fluctuation of property, so observable in all commercial countries, and which no prohibitions are capable of preventing, must necessarily weaken the authority of those who are placed in the higher ranks of life. Persons who have lately attained to riches, have no opportunity of establishing that train of dependence which is maintained by those who have remained for ages at the head of a great estate. The hereditary influence of family is thus, in a great measure, destroyed; and the consideration derived from wealth is often limited to what the possessor can acquire during his own life. Even this too, for the reasons formerly mentioned, is greatly diminished. A man of great fortune having dismissed his retainers, and spending a great part of his income in the purchase of commodities produced by tradesmen and manufacturers, has no ground to expect that many persons will be willing either to fight for him, or to run any great hazard for promoting his interest. Whatever profit he means to obtain from the labour and assistance of others, he must give a full equivalent for it. He must buy those personal services which are no longer to be performed either from attachment or from peculiar connexions. Money, therefore, becomes more and more the only means of procuring honours and dignities; and the sordid pursuits of avarice are made subservient to the nobler purposes of ambition.

It cannot be doubted that these circumstances have a tendency to introduce a democratical government. As persons of inferior rank are placed in a situation which, in point of subsistence, renders them little dependent upon their superiors; as no one order of men continues in the exclusive possession of opulence; and as every man who is industrious may entertain the hope of gaining a fortune; it is to be expected that the prerogatives of the monarch and of the ancient nobility will be gradually undermined, that the privileges of the people will be extended in the same proportion, and that power, the usual attendant of wealth, will be in some measure diffused over all the members of the community.

SECTION III

Result of the opposition between these different principles

So widely different are the effects of opulence and refinement, which, at the same time that they furnish the king with a standing army, the great engine of tyranny and oppression, have also a tendency to inspire the people with notions of liberty and independence. It may thence be expected that a conflict will arise between these two opposite parties, in which a variety of accidents may contribute to cast the balance upon either side.

With respect to the issue of such a contest, it may be remarked that, in a small state, the people have been commonly successful in their efforts to establish a free constitution. When a state consists only of a small territory, and the bulk of the inhabitants live in one city, they have frequently occasion to converse together, and to communicate their sentiments upon every subject of importance. Their attention therefore is roused by every instance of oppression in the government; and as they easily take the alarm, so they are capable of quickly uniting their forces in order to demand redress of their grievances. By repeated experiments they become sensible of their strength, and are enabled by degrees to enlarge their privileges, and to assume a greater share of the public administration.

In large and extensive nations, the struggles between the sovereign and his people are, on the contrary, more likely to terminate in favour of despotism. In a wide country, the encroachments of the government are frequently over-looked; and, even when the indignation of the people has been roused by flagrant injustice, they find it difficult to combine in uniform and vigorous measures for the defence of their

292

rights. It is also difficult, in a great nation, to bring out the militia with that quickness which is requisite in case of a sudden invasion; and it becomes necessary, even before the country has been much civilized, to maintain such a body of mercenaries as is capable of supporting the regal authority.

It is farther to be considered that the revenue of the monarch is commonly a more powerful engine of authority in a great nation than in a small one. The influence of a sovereign seems to depend, not so much upon his absolute wealth, as upon the proportion which it bears to that of the other members of the community. So far as the estate of the king does not exceed that of the richest of his subjects, it is no more than sufficient to supply the ordinary expense of living, in a manner suitable to the splendour and dignity of the crown; and it is only the surplus of that estate which can be directly applied to the purposes of creating dependence. In this view the public revenue of the king will be productive of greater influence according to the extent and populousness of the country in which it is raised. Suppose in a country, like that of ancient Attica, containing about twenty thousand inhabitants, the people were, by assessment or otherwise, to pay at the rate of twenty shillings each person, this would produce only twenty thousand pounds; a revenue that would probably not exalt the chief magistrate above many private citizens. But in a kingdom, containing ten millions of people, the taxes, being paid in the same proportion, would in all probability render the estate of the monarch superior to the united wealth of many hundreds of the most opulent individuals. In these two cases therefore, the disproportion of the armies maintained in each kingdom should be greater than that of their respective revenues; and if in the one, the king was enabled to maintain two hundred and fifty thousand men, he would in the other, be incapable of supporting the expense of five hundred. It is obvious, however, that even five hundred regular and well disciplined troops will not strike the same terror into twenty thousand people, that will be created, by an army of two hundred and fifty thousand, over a nation composed of ten millions.

Most of the ancient republics, with which we are acquainted, appear to have owed their liberty to the narrowness of their territories. From the small number of people, and from the close intercourse among all the individuals in the same community, they imbibed a spirit of freedom even before they had made considerable progress in arts; and they found means to repress or abolish the power of their petty princes, before their effeminacy or industry had introduced the practice of maintaining mercenary troops.

The same observation is applicable to the modern states of Italy, who, after the decay of the western empire, began to flourish in trade, and among whom a republican form of government was early established.

In France, on the other hand, the introduction of a great mercenary army, during the administration of Cardinal Richelieu, which was necessary for the defence of the country, enabled the monarch to establish a despotical power. In the beginning of the reign of Lewis XIII was called the last convention of the states general which has ever been held in that country: and the monarch has, from that period, been accustomed to exercise almost all the different powers of government. Similar effects have arisen from the establishment of standing forces in most of the great kingdoms of Europe.

The fortunate situation of Great Britain, after the accession of James I, gave her little to fear from any foreign invasion, and superseded the necessity of maintaining a standing army, when the service of the feudal militia had gone into disuse. The weakness and bigotry of her monarchs, at that period, prevented them from employing the only expedient capable of securing an absolute authority. Charles I saw the power exercised, about his time, by the other princes of Europe; but he did not discover the means by which it was obtained. He seems to have been so much convinced of his divine indefeasible right as, at first, to think that no force was necessary, and afterwards, that every sort of duplicity was excuseable, in support of it. When at the point of a rupture with his parliament, he had no military force upon which he could depend; and he was therefore obliged to yield to the growing power of the commons.

The boldness and dexterity, joined to the want of public spirit, and the perfidy of Oliver Cromwell, rendered abortive the measures of that party, of which he obtained the direction; but the blood that had been shed, and the repeated efforts that were made by the people in defence of their privileges, cherished and spread the love of liberty, and at last produced a popular government, after the best model, perhaps, which is practicable in an extensive country.

Many writers appear to take pleasure in remarking that, as the love of liberty is natural to man, it is to be found in the greatest perfection among barbarians, and is apt to be impaired according as people make progress in civilization and in the arts of life.* That mankind, in the state of mere savages, are in great measure unacquainted with government, and unaccustomed to any sort of constraint, is sufficiently evident. But their independence, in that case, is owing to the wretchedness of their circumstances, which afford nothing that can tempt any one man to become subject to another. The moment they have quitted this

---

* [Referring no doubt chiefly to Rousseau. Cp. also above, p. 116 and below, p. 383.]

primitive situation, and, by endeavouring to supply their natural wants, have been led to accumulate property, they are presented with very different motives of action, and acquire a new set of habits and principles. In those rude ages when the inhabitants of the earth are divided into tribes of shepherds, or of husbandmen, the usual distribution of property renders the bulk of the people dependent upon a few chiefs, to whom fidelity and submission becomes the principal point of honour, and makes a distinguishing part of the national character. The ancient Germans, whose high notions of freedom have been the subject of many a well-turned period, were accustomed, as we learn from Tacitus, to stake their persons upon the issue of a game of hazard, and after an unlucky turn of fortune, to yield themselves up to a voluntary servitude. Where-ever men of inferior condition are enabled to live in affluence by their own industry, and, in procuring their livelihood, have little occasion to court the favour of their superiors, there we may expect that ideas of liberty will be universally diffused. This happy arrangement of things, is naturally produced by commerce and manufactures; but it would be as vain to look for it in the uncultivated parts of the world, as to look for the independent spirit of an English waggoner, among persons of low rank in the highlands of Scotland.

CHAPTER VI

The authority of a Master over his Servants*

SECTION I

The condition of servants in the primitive ages of the world

In the foregoing chapters we have surveyed the principal distinctions of rank which occur among the free inhabitants of a country, and have endeavoured to mark the progress of society, with regard to the power of the husband, the father, and the civil magistrate. It may now be proper to consider the state of the servants, and to observe the degrees of authority which the laws and customs of different nations have bestowed upon the master.

From the situation of mankind in rude and barbarous countries, we may easily conceive in what manner any one person is, at first, reduced to be the servant of another. Before the manners of men are civilized, and a regular government has been established, persons of small fortune are subject to great inconveniencies from the disorder and violence of the times, and are frequently obliged to solicit the assistance and protection of some powerful neighbour, by whom they are entertained in the station of vassals or military dependents. But those who, from their idleness, have acquired nothing, or who, by accident, have been deprived of their possessions, are necessarily exposed to much more severe calamities. They have no room or encouragement for the exercise of those beneficial trades and professions, the effects of luxury and refinement, by which, in a polished nation, a multitude of people are enabled to live in a comfortable manner. In many cases, therefore, they are under the necessity of serving some opulent person, who, upon account of their labour, is willing to maintain them; and as they are entirely dependent upon him for their subsistence, they are engaged, according to his circumstances, and according to the qualifications they possess, in all the mean and servile occupations which may be requisite for the convenience and support of his family.

In early ages, when neighbouring tribes or nations are almost continually engaged in mutual hostilities, it frequently happens that one of the parties, is totally reduced under the power of another. The

* [This is chapter v in original.]

use that is made of a victory, upon these occasions, is such as might be expected from a fierce and barbarous people, who have too little experience or reflection to discover the utility of carrying on the trade of war with some degree of humanity. The vanquished are often put to death, in order to gratify a spirit of revenge; or, if they are spared, it is only from the consideration that their future labour and service will be of more advantage to the conqueror. As in those times every individual goes out to battle at his own charges, so he claims a proportional share of the profits arising from the expedition; and of consequence obtains the absolute disposal of the captives whom he has procured by his valour, or who, in a division of the booty, are bestowed upon him as the reward of his merit.

* This ancient acquisition of servants by *captivity* gave rise, in subsequent periods, to another method of acquiring them, by the *sentence of a judge*. In the primitive state of society, the public was not invested with sufficient power to punish the crimes that were committed; and when a difference arose between individuals, the injured party had frequently no other way of procuring redress than by making war upon the offender, and reducing him into captivity. In more civilized ages, when the magistrate was enabled to restrain these disorders, he sometimes afforded the same redress by his own authority, and assigned the labour and service of the criminal as an indemnification to the sufferer for the loss he had sustained.

By these three† methods, by captivity, by the voluntary submission of the indigent, or by the sentence of a judge, many are reduced into a state of unlimited subjection, and become the servants of those who are opulent and prosperous. It may be questioned, in such a case, how far a person is intitled to make use of that power which fortune has put into his hands. It is difficult to ascertain the degree of authority which, from the principles of justice and humanity, we are, in any situation, permitted to assume over our fellow-creatures. But the fact admits of no question, that people have commonly been disposed to use their power in such a manner as appears most conducive to their interest, and most agreeable to their predominant passions. It is natural to suppose that the master would let no bounds to his prerogative over those unhappy persons who, from their circumstances, were under the necessity of yielding an implicit obedience to his commands. He forced them to labour as much, and gave them as little in return for it as possible. When he found them negligent of their employment, he bestowed upon them such correction as he thought proper; and, actuated by the boisterous dispositions of a savage, he was in some cases provoked to chastise them

* [Lifted out of footnote.]   † ['Two' in original, former footnote now included.]

with a degree of severity, by which they might even be deprived of their life. When he had no use for their work, or when a good opportunity was presented, he endeavoured by a sale to dispose of them to the highest advantage. When he chose to increase the number of his servants, he sometimes encouraged and directed their multiplication; and the same authority which he exercised over the parents was extended to their offspring, whom he had been at the trouble of rearing, and who were equally dependent upon him for their subsistence.

To be a servant, therefore, in those primitive times, was almost universally the same thing as to be a slave. The master assumed an unlimited jurisdiction over his servants, and the privilege of selling them at pleasure. He gave them no wages beside their maintenance; and he allowed them to have no property, but claimed to his own use whatever, by their labour or by any other means, they happened to acquire.

Thus the practice of domestic slavery appears to have been early established among the nations of antiquity; among the Egyptians, the Phoenicians, the Jews, the Babylonians, the Persians, the Greeks, and the Romans.

The same practice obtains at present among all those tribes of barbarians, in different parts of the world, with which we have any correspondence.

There are indeed but few slaves among the greater part of the savages of America; because, from the situation of that people, they have no opportunity of accumulating wealth for maintaining any number of servants. As, in ordinary cases, they find it burdensome to give subsistence to an enemy whom they have subdued, they are accustomed to indulge their natural ferocity by putting him to death, even in cold blood. If ever they behave with humanity to their captives, it is only when being greatly reduced by the calamities of war, or by uncommon accidents, they are under the immediate necessity of recruiting their strength; and as this rarely happens, the persons whose lives have been thus preserved, are not distinguished from the children of the family into which they are brought, but are formally adopted into the place of the deceased relations, whose loss they are intended to supply.*

The Tartars, on the other hand, who have great possessions in herds and flocks, find no difficulty in supporting a number of domestics. For this reason they commonly preserve their captives, with a view of reaping the benefit that may arise from their labour; and the servitude established among that people disposes them to treat their enemies with

---

* These captives are worse treated by some of the American nations than by others; but in fact they are always retained in the condition of slaves. See Lafitau, Moeurs de Sauvages Ameriquains, 4to. tom. 2, p. 308.

a degree of moderation, which otherwise could hardly be expected from their fierce and barbarous dispositions.

The same observation may be extended to the negroes upon the coast of Guinea, who, from their intercourse with the nations of Europe, derive yet greater advantages from sparing the lives of their enemies. At the same time it cannot be doubted, that, as the encounters of those barbarians have upon this account become less bloody, their wars have been rendered more frequent. From the great demand for slaves to supply the European market, they have the same motives to seize the person of their neighbours, which may excite the inhabitants of other countries to rob one another of their property.

SECTION II

The usual effects of opulence and civilized manners, with regard to the treatment of servants

These institutions and customs are such as might be expected from the limited experience, as well as from the rude manners of an early age. By reducing his servants into a state of slavery, the master appears, at first sight, to reap the highest advantage from their future labour and service. But when a people become civilized, and when they have made considerable progress in commerce and manufactures, one would imagine they should entertain more liberal views, and be influenced by more extensive considerations of utility.

A slave, who receives no wages in return for his labour, can never be supposed to exert much vigour or activity in the exercise of any employment. He obtains a livelihood at any rate; and by his utmost assiduity he is able to procure no more. As he works merely in consequence of the terror in which he is held, it may be imagined that he will be idle as often as he can with impunity. This circumstance may easily be overlooked in a country where the inhabitants are strangers to improvement. But when the arts begin to flourish, when the wonderful effects of industry and skill in cheapening commodities, and in bringing them to perfection, become more and more conspicuous, it must be evident that little profit can be drawn from the labour of a slave, who has neither been encouraged to acquire that dexterity, nor those habits of application, which are essentially requisite in the finer and more difficult branches of manufacture.

This may be illustrated from the price of labour in our **West-India** islands, where it will not be doubted that the inhabitants are at great pains to prevent the idleness of their slaves. In Jamaica, the yearly labour of a field-negro, when he is upheld to the master, is rated at no more than nine pounds, currency of that island. When a negro has been instructed in the trade of a carpenter, the value of his yearly labour will amount at the utmost to thirty-six pounds; whereas a free man is capable of earning seventy pounds yearly in the very same employment.*

It is further to be observed, that, in a polished nation, the acquisition of slaves is commonly much more expensive than among a simple and barbarous people.

After a regular government has been established, the inhabitants of a country are restrained from plundering one another; and, under the authority of the magistrate, individuals of the lowest rank are sufficiently secured from oppression and injustice. In proportion to the improvement of commerce and manufactures, the demand for labour is increased, and greater encouragement is given to industry. The poor have more resources for procuring a livelihood, by such employments as are productive of little subjection or dependence. By degrees, therefore, people of inferior condition are freed from the necessity of becoming slaves in order to obtain subsistence; and the ancient agreement by which a free person resigned his liberty, and was reduced under the power of a master, being rendered more and more unusual, is at length regarded as inconsistent with the natural rights of a citizen.

† Thus among the Romans, during the commonwealth, and even under the emperors, no free citizen was allowed, by contract, to become the slave of another.‡ It was consistent with the refined laws of that

---

* ᵃIn north America, where slaves are said to be much better treated than in the West-India islands, it is believed, the expense of a negro-slave, for common labour, is not much inferior to that of a free labourer. In the Jerseys, and in New York, the expense of a negro-slave may be stated as follows:

The original price, about 100 *l.* currency, for which double interest allowed, at 7 *per cent.*	£14
Yearly expence of clothing	6
For medicines, etc.	3
For maintenance	15
In all	£38 yearly.

A free labourer, in those provinces, when hired by the year, receives from 24 *l.* to 30 *l.* yearly; to which may be added 15 *l.* for maintenance. And in balancing this account we must take in the risk that the negro, when purchased, may not be fit for the purpose, and that his labour may be of little value.

† [Part lifted out of footnote; part new.]

‡ See Heineccius, Ant. Rom. lib. 1, tit. 5, § 6. This regulation, however, admitted of an exception, where a man fraudulently suffered himself to be sold in order to share in the price; in which case he became the slave of the person whom he had defrauded. L. 3. Dig. quib. ad. libert. proclam. non licet

people, which rescinded those unequal contracts where one party had gained an undue advantage, or even obtained an unreasonable profit at the expense of the other, to declare that a bargain by which a man surrendered all his rights to a master, and consequently received nothing in return, should have no support or encouragement from the civil magistrate.

As men begin to experience the happy effects of cultivating the arts of peace, and are less frequently employed in acts of hostility, they have less occasion to acquire any number of slaves by captivity. The influence of civilization upon the temper and dispositions of a people has at the same time a tendency to produce a total revolution in the manner of conducting their military operations. That ancient institution, by which every one who is able to bear arms is required to appear in the field at his own charges, becomes too heavy a burden upon those who are enervated with pleasure, or engaged in lucrative professions; and the custom of employing mercenary troops in defence of the country is therefore gradually established. As an army of this kind is maintained by the government; as the soldiers receive constant pay, which is understood to be a full equivalent for their service; they appear to have no title to the extraordinary emoluments arising from the spoil of the enemy; and therefore the captives, though reduced into servitude, are no longer held as belonging to those particular persons by whom they have been subdued, but to the public, at whose expense and hazard the war is supported.*

† We may take notice of a similar change in the acquisition of slaves by the sentence of a judge. In rude times, the chief aim of punishment was to gratify the resentment of the private party; and if a person accused of a crime had been found guilty, he was, for that reason, frequently delivered up as a slave to the plaintiff. But upon greater improvement of manners, the interpositions of the magistrate came to be influenced more by considerations of general utility; and as the crimes of individuals were principally considered in the light of offences against the society, it was agreeable to this idea that a criminal should become the slave of the public, and should either be employed in public works, or disposed of in the manner most advantageous to the revenue of the community.

The inhabitants of a civilized country, being thus in a great measure deprived of the primitive modes of acquisition, are obliged to acquire

* It is accordingly held, in the later Roman law, that a soldier is entitled to no part of the plunder acquired in war, unless from the special donation of the emperor. L. 20. § 1. Dig. de capt. et postl. l. 36. § 1. c. de donat.

† [Lifted out of footnote.]

the bulk of their slaves, either by a purchase from their poorer and more barbarous neighbours, or by propagating and rearing from the original stock which they possess. In such a situation, therefore, when we compute the expense attending the labour of a slave, not only the charge of his maintenance, but also the money laid out in the first acquisition, together with all the hazard to which his life is exposed, must necessarily be taken into the account.

When these circumstances are duly considered, it will be found that the work of a slave, who receives nothing but a bare subsistence, is really dearer than that of a free man, to whom constant wages are given in proportion to his industry.

Unhappily, men have seldom been in a condition to examine this point with proper attention, and with sufficient impartiality. The practice of slavery being introduced in an early age, is afterwards regarded with that blind prepossession which is commonly acquired in favour of ancient usages: its inconveniences are overlooked, and every innovation, with respect to it, is considered as a dangerous measure. The possession of power is too agreeable to be easily relinquished. Few people will venture upon a new experiment; and, amidst the general prejudices of a country, fewer still are capable of making it with fairness. We find, accordingly, that this institution, however inconsistent with the rights of humanity, however pernicious and contrary to the true interest of the master, has generally remained in those countries where it was once established, and has been handed down from one generation to another, during all the successive improvements of society, in knowledge, arts, and manufactures.

The advancement of a nation, in these particulars, is even frequently attended with greater severity in the treatment of the slaves. The simplicity of early ages admits of little distinction between the master and his servants, in their employments or manner of living; and though, from the impetuosity and violence of his temper, they may, on some occasions, be subjected to hardships, he enjoys no great superiority over them, in their dress, their lodging, or ordinary entertainment. By the introduction of wealth and luxury, this equality is gradually destroyed. The various refinements which tend to multiply the comforts and conveniencies of life; whatever contributes to ease, to pleasure, to ostentation, or to amusement, is in a great measure appropriated to the rich and the free, while those who remain in a state of servitude are retained in their primitive indigence. The slaves are no longer accustomed to sit at the same table with their master. They must look upon him as a being of superior order, whom they are seldom permitted to approach, and with whom they have hardly any thing in common;

who beholds with indifference the toil and drudgery to which they are subjected, and from whom they can with difficulty procure a scanty subsistence.

> *a* Ipse dominus dives operis, et laboris expers,
> Quodcunque homini accidit libêre, posse retur:
> Aequom esse putat: non reputat laboris quid sit:
> Nec, aequom anne iniquom imperet, cogitabit.*

What a painful and humbling comparison, what mortifying reflections does this afford to those wretches who are reduced into a state of bondage! reflections which cannot fail to sour their temper, to inspire them with malevolent dispositions, and to produce an untoward and stubborn behaviour; for† it is impossible that man, by any system of management, should be so inured to oppression as, like a beast of burden, to submit entirely to the yoke, and not, on some occasions, to feel and testify resentment against the oppressor. A more severe discipline is thus rendered necessary, to conquer the obstinacy of persons, unwilling to labour in their employments. Besides, from the number of slaves which are usually maintained in a wealthy and luxurious nation, they become formidable to the state; and it is requisite that they should be strictly watched, and kept in the utmost subjection, in order to prevent those desperate attempts to which they are frequently instigated in revenge of their sufferings. This is at least the pretence for that shocking barbarity to which the negroes in our colonies are frequently exposed, and which is exhibited even by persons of the weaker sex, in an age distinguished for humanity and politeness.

The prodigious wealth acquired by the Romans towards the end of the commonwealth, and after the establishment of despotism, gave rise to a degree of cruelty and oppression, in the management of their slaves, which had been unknown in former times.

> ‡ Hic frangit ferulas, rubet ille flagellis,
> Hic scutica: sunt quae tortoribus annua praestent.
> Verberat, atque obiter faciem linit, audit amicas,
> Aut latum pictae vestis considerat aurum,
> Et caedit, longi relegit transversa diurni
> Et caedit, donec lassis caedentibus, exi
> Intonet horrendum, jam cognitione peracta:
> Praefectura domus Sicula non mitior aula.§

* Plautus, Amphitr.   † [Rest of sentence added.]   ‡ [Lifted out of footnote.]
§ Juvenal, Sat. 6.

Vedius Pollio, a Roman citizen, is said to have fed the fishes in his fish-ponds with the flesh of his own slaves. Donat. ad Terentii Phorm. act 2, scen. 1.

With regard to the treatment of the Roman slaves, see Mr. Hume's learned essay on the populousness of ancient nations.

It was to be expected, however, that particular enormities of this kind would at length excite the attention of the public, and would be in some measure restrained by the gradual progress of government. Although the institution of slavery was permitted to remain, regulations came to be made, by which the master was prevented from such wanton exercise of his power as must have been highly prejudicial to his interest, and could only be regarded as an absurd abuse of his property.

In the Jewish law, we meet with some regulations for this purpose at an early period.

If a man smite his servant, or his maid, with a rod, and he die under his hand, he shall surely be punished.

Notwithstanding, if he continue a day or two, he shall not be punished: for he is his money.

And if a man smite the eye of his servant, or the eye of his maid, that it perish; he shall let him go free for his eye's sake.

And if he smite out his man-servant's tooth, or his maid-servant's tooth; he shall let him go free for his tooth's sake.*

At Athens, the slaves who had been barbarously treated by their master were allowed to fly for sanctuary to the temple of Theseus, and to commence a suit at law against their master, who, if their complaint appeared well founded, was laid under the necessity of selling them.

Various equitable laws, upon this subject, were made by the Roman emperors. At Rome, the absolute power of the master was first subjected to any limitation in the reign of Augustus, who appointed that the *Praefectus urbi* should afford redress to such of the slaves as had been treated with immoderate severity. In the reign of the emperor Claudius, it was enacted, that if a master abandoned the care of his slaves during their sickness, he should forfeit the property of them; and that if he put them to death, he should be held guilty of homicide. Soon after, the inhuman practice of obliging the slaves to fight with wild beasts, which was carried to a prodigious height, and which appears to have afforded a favourite entertainment to men of all ranks, was in some measure restrained. Other statutes were afterwards made, in the reigns of Adrian, or Antoninus Pius, and of Constantine, by which it was finally established, that the master who killed his own slave, by design, and not from the accidental excess of chastisement, should suffer the ordinary punishment of murder.

* Exodus, chap. xxi, ver. 20, 21, 26, 27. It has been a question whether the last quoted laws, in ver. 26 and 27, related to the slaves acquired from foreign nations, or only to such of the Israelites as had been reduced into a state of servitude. Grotius is of the latter opinion. Vide Grotius, com. ad cit. cap.

SECTION III

Causes of the freedom acquired by the labouring people in the modern nations of Europe

By what happy concurrence of events has the practice of slavery been so generally abolished in Europe? By what powerful motives were our forefathers induced to deviate from the maxims of other nations, and to abandon a custom so generally retained in other parts of the world?

The northern barbarians, who laid the foundation of the present European states, are said to have possessed a number of slaves, obtained either by captivity or by voluntary submission, and over whom the master enjoyed an unlimited authority *

When these nations invaded the Roman empire, and settled in the different provinces, they were enabled by their repeated victories to procure an immense number of captives, whom they reduced into servitude, and by whose assistance they occupied landed estates of proportionable extent From the simple manner of living to which those barbarians had been accustomed, their domestic business was usually performed by the members of each family; and their servants, for the most part, were employed in cultivating their lands.

† It appears that, upon the settlement of these invaders in the Roman empire, no immediate change was produced in their notions with respect to slavery, and that the slaves which they gradually acquired by the success of their arms were, at first, in the same condition with those which they had anciently possessed. The master exercised an

* The following account is given by Tacitus, concerning the state of the slaves among the ancient Germans. 'Gambling,' says he, speaking of that people, 'one may be surprised to find, they practice in all seriousness in their sober hours, with such recklessness in winning or losing that, when all else has failed, they stake personal liberty on the last and final throw: the loser faces voluntary slavery; though he be the younger and the stronger man, he suffers himself to be bound and sold; such is their persistence in wrong-doing, or in their good faith, as they themselves style it. Slaves so acquired they trade, in order to deliver themselves, as well as the slave, from the humiliation involved in such victory.

'Their other slaves are not organized in our fashion: that is, by a division of the services of life among them. Each of them remains master of his own house and home: the master requires from the slave as serf [colonus] a certain quantity of grain or cattle or clothing. The slave so far is subservient; but the other services of the household are discharged by the master's wife and children. To beat a slave and coerce him with hard labour and imprisonment is rare: if they are killed, it is not usually to preserve strict discipline, but in a fit of fury, like an enemy, except that there is no penalty to be paid.' Tacitus, de mor. Germ. § 24, 25.

† [Lifted out of footnote, slightly revised.]

unlimited power of chastising them, and might even put them to death with impunity. They were liable to be alienated, or impledged by the master at pleasure, and were incapable, either of marrying, or of entering into any other contract, without his consent. They were so much his property, that he might claim them from every possessor, by the ordinary action which was given for the recovery of his goods; and in consequence of this, it was held they could have no civil rights; so that whatever was acquired by their labour belonged to the master, from whom they usually received nothing but a precarious subsistence. In a public capacity, the people of this class were viewed in a light no less humiliating; they enjoyed none of the privileges of a citizen, and were seldom permitted to give evidence against a free man in a court of justice.*

The situation, however, of these bond-men, and the nature of the employment in which they were usually engaged, had a tendency to procure them a variety of privileges from their master, by which, in a course of ages, their condition was rendered more comfortable, and they were advanced to higher degrees of consideration and rank.

As the peasants belonging to a single person could not be conveniently maintained in his house, so in order to cultivate his lands to advantage, it was necessary that they should be sent to a distance, and have a fixed residence in different parts of his estate. Separate habitations were therefore assigned them; and particular farms were committed to the care of individuals, who from their residing in the neighbourhood of one another, and forming small villages or hamlets, received the appellation of 'villains'.

It may easily be imagined that, in those circumstances, the proprietor of a large estate could not oversee the behaviour of his servants, living in separate families, and scattered over the wide extent of his demesnes; and it was in vain to think of compelling them to labour by endeavouring to chastise them upon account of their idleness. A very little experience would show that no efforts of that kind could be effectual; and that the only means of exciting the industry of the peasants would be to offer them a reward for the work which they performed. Thus, beside the ordinary maintenance allotted to the slaves, they frequently obtained a small gratuity, which, by custom, was gradually converted into a regular hire; and, being allowed the enjoyment and disposal of that subject, they were at length understood to be capable of having separate property.

After the master came to reside at a distance from the bulk of his

---

* Potgiesserus, de statu servorum, lib. 2 cap. 1. 3, 4, 5. 9 Ibid. cap. 10, § 3. 7, 8. Ibid. lib. 3, § 1. 3.

servants, and had embraced the salutary policy of bribing them, instead of using compulsion, in order to render them active in their employment, he was less apt to be provoked by their negligence; and as he had seldom occasion to treat them with severity, the ancient dominion which he exercised over their lives was at length entirely lost by disuse.

When a slave had been for a long time engaged in a particular farm, and had become acquainted with that particular culture which it required, he was so much the better qualified to continue in the management of it for the future; and it was contrary to the interest of the master that he should be removed to another place, or employed in labour of a different kind. By degrees, therefore, the peasants were regarded as belonging to the stock upon the ground, and came to be uniformly disposed of as a part of the estate which they had been accustomed to cultivate.

* As these changes were gradual, it is difficult to ascertain the precise period at which they were completed. The continual disorders which prevailed in the western part of Europe, for ages after it was first over-run by the German nations, prevented for a long time the progress of arts among the new inhabitants. It was about the twelfth century that a spirit of improvement, in several European countries, became somewhat conspicuous; and it may be considered as a mark of that improvement, with respect to agriculture, that about this time, the villains had obtained considerable privileges; that the master's power over their life was then understood to be extinguished; that the chastisement to which they had been formerly subjected was become more moderate; and that they were generally permitted to acquire separate property.†

The effect of the foregoing circumstances is even observable in the history of the Greeks and Romans, among whom the peasants were raised to a better condition than the rest of their slaves. They were indeed bound to serve the proprietor during life, and might have been sold along with the ground upon which they were employed; but their persons were not subject to the absolute jurisdiction of their master; they had the privilege of marrying without his consent; they received wages in return for their labour, and were understood to have a full

---

* [Lifted out of footnote and rewritten.]

† Potgiesserus, de statu serv. lib. 2, cap. 1, § 24. A singular proof of the moderation of the masters in correcting their slaves, about this period, is mentioned by the same author, as follows:

'The punishment was, however, lenient in this way, that slaves might not be beaten with a stick wider and thicker than one *veru* (thickness of an arrow) as I remember having seen in the ancient parchment codex of Werdinensis.' Ibid.

right of property in whatever goods their industry had enabled them to accumulate.

It should seem, however, that the limited territory possessed by these ancient nations prevented the farther extension of the privileges bestowed upon their peasants: seven acres were originally the utmost extent of landed property which a Roman citizen was permitted to enjoy; a portion which he was able to cultivate with his own hands, or with no other assistance but that of his own family; and there is reason to believe that, for several centuries, no individual acquired such an estate as gave occasion to his retaining many servants for the management of it, or could render the inspection and government of those whom he employed a matter of great trouble or difficulty.*

But after the wide and populous countries under the Roman dominion were subdued and laid waste by the small tribes of the Germans, very extensive landed estates, together with an adequate number of slaves, were immediately acquired by particular persons. As the people retained their primitive simplicity of manners, and were in a great measure strangers to commerce, these large possessions remained for ages without being dismembered. And thus, during all the successive improvements of agriculture, the proprietor of an estate, embarrassed with the multitude of his villains, was obliged to repose a confidence in them, and came by degrees to discover more clearly the utility of exciting them to industry by the prospect of their own private advantage.

The same motives, by which the master was induced to reward his slaves for their labour, determined him afterwards to increase his bounty in proportion to the work which they performed. Having no opportunity of looking narrowly into their management, he was commonly led to estimate their diligence according to their success; and therefore, when they brought him a good crop, he made an addition to their wages, at the same time that he allowed them to expect a suitable compensation for their future labour and economy. This at length gave rise to an express stipulation, that their profits should depend upon the fertility of their different farms, and that, in all cases, they should be permitted to retain a certain share of the produce, in consideration of their labour.

An expedient so obvious and well calculated for promoting the industry of the peasants, could hardly fail to be generally embraced in all the countries of Europe, as soon as the inhabitants became attentive to the improvement of their estates. The remains of this practice are still to be found in Scotland, where, in some cases, the landlord is

* See Dr Wallace, on the numbers of mankind.

accustomed to stock the farm, and the tenant pays him a rent in kind, consisting of a certain proportion of the fruits.*

By this alteration, the villains entered into a sort of co-partnership with their master; and having always a prospect of gain, according to the vigour or talents which they exerted, they were enabled to earn a more comfortable subsistence, and were even gradually raised to affluence. The acquisition of wealth paved the way to a farther extension of their privileges. Those who had obtained something considerable found themselves in a condition to stock their own farms, and to offer a fixed rent to the master, upon condition of their being allowed to retain the surplus for their own emolument. An agreement of this kind, so advantageous to both parties, was concluded without any difficulty. As the tenant secured to himself the whole profit arising from his industry, the landlord was freed from the hazard of accidental losses, and obtained not only a certain, but frequently an additional revenue from his lands.

Thus, by degrees, the ancient villanage came to be entirely abolished. The peasants, who cultivated their farms at their own charges, and at their own hazard, were of course emancipated from the authority of their master, and could no longer be regarded as in the condition of servants. Their personal subjection was at an end. It was of no consequence to the landlord how they conducted themselves; and, provided they punctually paid his rent, nothing farther could be required of them. There was no reason to insist that they should remain in the farm longer than they pleased; for the profits it afforded made them, commonly, not more willing to leave it than the proprietor was to put them away. When agriculture became so beneficial a trade, when the state of those who followed that profession had been rendered so comfortable, no person had any difficulty to procure a sufficient number of tenants to labour his estate. It was, on the contrary, sometimes difficult for the farmer to obtain land sufficient for the exercise of his employment; and, after he had been at pains to improve the soil, he was in danger of being dispossessed by the proprietor, before he was indemnified for the trouble and expense which he had sustained. This made it necessary to stipulate that he should be allowed to remain for a certain time in the possession, and gave rise to leases, for a term of years, and even sometimes for life, or for a longer period, according to the circumstances or inclination of the parties.

The modern nations of Europe continued for a long time to be almost

---

* The stock which is delivered by the master to his tenant goes under the name of 'steel-bow goods' in the law of Scotland. At the end of the lease the tenant is bound to restore the same in quantity and quality to the master.

entirely unacquainted with manufactures; and, as they had no other slaves but those which were employed in agriculture, the privileges acquired by the villains had therefore a tendency to produce a total extinction of servitude. By degrees, however, as the people began to improve their circumstances, and to multiply the comforts and conveniencies of life, their attention was more and more diverted to other employments. At the same time that the villains were engaged in cultivating the ground, they were also bound to perform any other services which the master thought proper to require, and were often called to assist him in the practice of those few mechanical arts which were then understood. Particular persons acquiring a singular dexterity in these occupations, were distinguished upon that account, and came to be more frequently employed than their neighbours. In proportion to the liberty which they enjoyed as peasants, they were enabled with more advantage to prosecute this collateral business; and while they received a reward for the crop which they produced upon their farms, they were not restrained from working, for hire, in that peculiar trade or profession which they were qualified to exercise. As the progress of luxury and refinement multiplied these occupations, and rendered the profits which they afforded superior in many cases to those which were derived from agriculture, individuals were gradually led to quit the latter employment, and to attach themselves entirely to the former. In that state of the country, the children of farmers were frequently bred to manufactures; and a number of tradesmen and artificers, having arisen in different villages, were advanced to consideration and esteem, in proportion as their assistance became more essentially necessary in supplying the wants of mankind. According to the wealth which this new order of men had accumulated, they purchased immunities from their master; and, by permitting him to levy tolls and duties upon their commerce, they were enabled to secure his patronage and protection. Thus the privileges acquired by the peasants appear to have given rise to domestic freedom, which was communicated to the trading part of the inhabitants; while the employment of the latter became, on the other hand, the source of great opulence, and contributed, as has been formerly observed, to raise the people of inferior rank to political independence.

Other circumstances may be mentioned, which, in a subordinate manner, have, perhaps contributed something to this remarkable change of European manners.

The establishment of Christianity has been supposed by many to be the principal circumstance which rooted out the practice of slavery so universally permitted and encouraged among all the heathen nations. There is no doubt that the spirit of this religion, which considers all mankind as children of the same Father, and as all equally the objects of his paternal care and affection, should inspire them with compassion for the miseries of each other, and should teach the opulent and the proud to consider those who are depressed with labour and penury as creatures of the same species, to treat them with mildness and humanity, and to soften the rigours to which their severe and unequal fortune has unavoidably subjected them. But it does not seem to have been the intention of Christianity to alter the civil rights of mankind, or to abolish those distinctions of rank which were already established. There is no precept of the gospel by which the authority of the master is in any respect restrained or limited; but, on the contrary, there are several passages from which it may be inferred that slaves, even after they had embraced the Christian religion, were not absolved from any part of the duties formerly incumbent upon them.*

We accordingly find that slavery remained all over Europe for several centuries after Christianity became the established religion: not to mention that this institution is still retained in Russia, in Poland, in Hungry, and in several parts of Germany; and that it is at present admitted, without limitation, in the colonies which belong to the European nations, whether in Asia, Africa, or America. ᵃ The Quakers of Pennsylvania, are the first body of men in those countries, who have discovered any scruples upon that account, and who seem to have thought that the abolition of this practice is a duty they owe to religion and humanity.

It has likewise been imagined that the state of the clergy, their great influence and ambition, together with that opposition between the civil and ecclesiastical powers, which subsisted for a long time in most of the nations of Europe were favourable to the lower ranks of men, and contributed to limit and destroy the ancient practice of villanage. The learning, the ideas of policy, and, above all, the peaceable manners of ecclesiastics, naturally produced an aversion to the disorders incident to the feudal governments, and disposed them to shelter the weak and defenceless from the tyranny of their superiors.

In those dark and superstitious ages, the church was, at the same time, most successful in establishing her authority over the lowest and most

---

* Thus Onesimus, notwithstanding his conversion to Christianity, is understood by the apostle Paul to continue still the slave of Philemon; and it is not supposed that the master, who was also a Christian, was under an obligation to relinquish any part of his authority, far less to give liberty to his servant. See St Paul's epistle to Philemon. See also, to the same purpose, Rom. chap. xiii, ver. 1, etc.—Ephes. chap. vi, ver. 5.—Coloss. chap. iii, ver. 22.— 1 Tim. chap. vi, ver. 1, 2.—Tit. chap. ii, ver. 9, 10.—1 Pet. chap. ii, ver. 18.—1 Cor. chap. vii, ver. 21, 22.

ignorant of the people, and was therefore led, in a particular manner, to exert her power and abilities in protecting that order of men by which she was most firmly supported. As dying persons were frequently inclined to make considerable donations for pious uses, it was more immediately for the interest of churchmen, that people of inferior condition should be rendered capable of acquiring property, and should have the free disposal of what they had acquired.

* The progress of ecclesiastical rapacity seems at length to have produced a custom that villains, who obtained their liberty by the influence of the clergy, should reward their benefactors; and that the manumission should, for this reason, be confirmed by the church. In these circumstances, the ministers of religion did not fail to recommend the manumission of slaves, as an action highly proper to atone for the offences of a sinner; and ecclesiastical censures were, in some cases, inflicted upon the master, when he refused to allow his villains the liberty of alienating their goods by a testament. So much does this appear to have been an object of attention, that a bull was published by Pope Alexander III exhorting the Christian world to a general emancipation of the villains.

It was not, however, to be expected that, from such interested views, the clergy would be disposed to strike at the root of servitude, or to employ their casuistry in overthrowing an institution upon which so great a part of their own property depended. Like physicians, they were far from thinking it necessary to swallow that medicine which they had prescribed to the people; and while they appeared so extremely liberal with regard to the estates of the laity, they held a very different conduct with relation to the villains in their own possession. These being appropriated to pious uses, and being only held in usufruct, were not to be alienated by the present incumbent. Thus we meet with many ecclesiastical regulations, both in France and Germany, by which it is provided that no bishop, or priest, shall manumit a slave in the patrimony of the church, without purchasing two others of equal value to be put in his place.†

* [Two paragraphs considerably revised.]

† See the different decrees of councils referred to by Potgiesserus, *de stat. serv.* lib. 4, cap. 2, 4, 5.

In one of these it is enacted, 'Episcopus liberos ex familiis ecclesiae, ad condemnationem suam facere non praesumat. Impium enim est, ut qui res suas ecclesiae Christi non contulit, damnum inferat, et ejus ecclesiae rem alienare contendat. Tales igitur libertos successor episcopus revocabit, quia eos non aequitas, sed improbitas absolvit.' [Or, freely translated, 'A bishop presumes to his condemnation to emancipate slaves from among families of the church. For it would be an impiety that one who has not conferred his own property upon the church of Christ should incur a loss to His Church by attempting to alienate her property.

The Authority of a Master over his Servants

The state of the civil government, in most of the countries of Europe, may be regarded as another circumstance which had some influence in abolishing domestic slavery. From the aristocratical constitution established in these kingdoms, the sovereign was engaged in long and violent struggles with his barons; and being often incapable of carrying his measures by direct force, he was obliged to employ every artifice that his situation would admit, in order to humble his rivals, and reduce them under subjection. For this purpose he frequently exerted his authority in protecting the villains from the tyranny of the master; and thus endeavoured to undermine the power of the nobles, by withdrawing the submission of their immediate dependents.

* While the monarch was, upon this account, endeavouring to protect the villains possessed by his barons, and to raise them to such a condition as might render them less dependent upon their masters, he found means of deriving some revenue from the people of that class, upon pretence of confirming, by royal authority, the privileges that were bestowed upon them. Other reasons, in the mean time, induced the sovereign to give particular encouragement to the bond-men upon his own demesnes; as these, under the shelter of the crown, had been enabled to acquire a degree of opulence, not only by their advances in agriculture, but also by their application to trade and manufactures, and consequently were in a condition to purchase freedom and immunities by pecuniary compositions, or by submitting to regular duties for the support of government. From such political considerations, we find that repeated efforts were made, and many regulations were introduced by different princes of

Therefore the bishop who succeeds him, will recall such freedmen because they were wrongfully rather than justfully set free.']

In another it is said, 'Mancipia monachis donata ab abbate non liceat manumitti. Injustum est enim, ut monachis quotidianum rurale opus facientibus, servi eorum libertatis otio potiantur.' [Or in English, 'It is not permissible for an abbot to manumit slaves given to the monks. For it would be unjust that the slaves of monks should enjoy leisure in freedom while they themselves had to labour in the fields day after day.']

It is likely, however, that the clergy treated their slaves with greater lenity than was usual among the rest of the people. Mention is made of a bishop of Arles, who, in conformity to the Mosaical institution, never allowed above thirty-nine stripes to be given, at one time, to any of his servants—'Solebat sanctus vir id accurate observare, ut nemo ex istis qui ipsi parebant, sive illi servi essent, sive ingenui, si pro culpa flagellandi essent, amplius triginta novem ictibus ferirentur. Si quis vero in gravi culpa deprehensus esset, permittebat quidem ut post paucos dies iterum vapularet, sed paucis.' [Or, translated, 'This saintly man was always very careful to see that none of his subjects, whether slave or free, should be given more than thirty-nine stripes in punishment for any offence. If the offence was a very serious one, he might be given additional stripes after a few days, but only a few.'] Ciprianus, in *vita S. Caefarii*, Cit. Potgiess. lib. 2, cap. 1, § 6.

* [Three sections largely rewritten.]

313

Europe, for extending and securing the liberties and rights of the lower and more industrious part of their subjects.

In this manner domestic slavery, having gradually declined for ages, has at last been exploded from the greater part of Europe. In several European kingdoms, this has happened, from the natural progress of manners, and without any express interposition of the legislature. Thus in England, the peasants having, in consequence of their situation, acquired successive privileges, many of them were promoted to the rank of vassals or free-holders, while the rest, advancing more slowly, have remained in the condition of those who are called *copy-holders* at present. So late as the reign of Queen Elizabeth it appears that real bond-men were still to be found in many parts of the kingdom.*

In Scotland the slavery of the villains, which was probably of a similar nature to what obtained in the other countries of Europe, appear in like manner to have gone into disuse without any aid of statute; but the period when this change was effected has not been ascertained by lawyers or historians.

The remains of bondage which are still to be found in the case of colliers and salters in Scotland, and of those who work in the mines in some other parts of Europe, are sufficient to point out the chief circumstance, from which, in all other cases, the ancient institution has been so generally abolished. In a coal-work, as the different workmen are collected in one place, instead of being scattered, like the ordinary peasants, over an extensive territory, they were capable of being put under the care of an overseer, who might compel them to labour; and the master did not so immediately feel the necessity of resigning that authority over them with which he was invested.

After domestic liberty had been thus, in a great measure, established in those European nations which had made the greatest improvement in agriculture, America was discovered; the first settlers in which, from their distance, and from the little attention that was paid to them by the government of their mother countries, were under no necessity of conforming to the laws and customs of Europe. The acquisition of gold and silver was the great object by which the Spaniards were directed in their settlements upon that continent; and the native inhabitants, whom they had conquered, were reduced into slavery and put to work in the mines. But, these being either exhausted by the severity with which they were treated, or not being thought sufficiently robust for that kind of labour, negro-slaves were afterwards purchased for this purpose from the Portuguese settlements on the coast of Africa. When sugar-planta-

---

* See observations on the statutes, chiefly the more ancient: 1 Rich. II. A.D. 1377. Smith's Commonwealth of Eng. Bk. 3, chap. 10.

tions were erected, the same people were employed in these, and in most other kinds of work which came to be performed in that part of the world. Thus the practice of slavery was no sooner extinguished by the inhabitants in one quarter of the globe, than it was revived by the very same people in another, where it has remained ever since, without being much regarded by the public, or exciting any effectual regulations in order to suppress it.*

It merits particular attention, that the chief circumstance which contributed to procure freedom to the slaves in Europe, had no place in our American plantations. From the manner of working the mines, a number of slaves are usually collected together, and may therefore be placed under the command of a single person, who has it in his power to superintend their behaviour, and to punish their negligence. The same observation is applicable to the planting of sugar, and to the other occupations in our colonies, in which the negroes perform the same sort of work which in Europe is commonly performed by cattle, and in which, of consequence, many servants are kept upon the same plantation. As the slaves are continually under the lash of their master, he has not been forced to use the disagreeable expedient of rewarding their labour, and of improving their condition by those means which were found so necessary, and which were employed with so much emolument, to encourage the industry of the peasants in Europe.

SECTION IV
Political consequences of slavery

In the history of mankind, there is no revolution of greater importance to the happiness of society than this which we have now had occasion to contemplate. The laws and customs of the modern European nations have carried the advantages of liberty to a height which was never known in any other age or country. In the ancient states, so celebrated upon account of their free government, the bulk of their mechanics and labouring people were denied the common privileges of men, and treated upon the footing of inferior animals. In proportion to the opulence and refinement of those nations, the number of their slaves was increased, and the grievances to which they were subjected became the more intolerable.

* See [Adam] Anderson's history of commerce, vol. 1, p. 336.—The first importation of negro slaves into Hispaniola was in the year 1508. Ibid.

* The citizens of Athens, according to an enumeration of Demetrius Phalerius, are said to have amounted to 21,000, the strangers residing in that city to 10,000, and the slaves possessed by the whole people, to no less than 400,000. There is reason to believe, however, that, in this enumeration of the free men, none but the heads of families are included, and in that of the slaves, every individual is comprehended; for an account of the former would probably be taken with a view to the taxes imposed upon each head of a family, and the latter, it is most likely, would be numbered, like cattle, in order to ascertain the wealth of each proprietor. Thus, allowing five persons to each family, the Athenian slaves exceeded the free men in the proportion of between two and three to one.†

In the most flourishing periods of Rome, when luxury was carried to so amazing a pitch, the proportion of the inhabitants reduced into servitude was in all probability still greater. The number of slaves possessed by particular Roman citizens was prodigious. T. Minucius, a Roman knight, is said to have had 400. Pliny mentions one Caecilius, who bequeathed in his testament upwards of 4000 slaves. And Athenaeus takes notice, that the Roman slaves, belonging to individuals, often amounted to 10,000, or even to 20,000; and sometimes, to a greater number.

The negro-slaves in the West-Indies are commonly said to exceed the free people nearly as three to one; and it has been supposed that the disproportion between them is daily increasing.

It may in general be observed, that according as men have made greater progress in commerce and the arts, the establishment of domestic freedom is of greater importance; and that, in opulent and polished nations, its influence extends to the great body of the people, who form the principal part of a community, and whose comfortable situation ought never to be overlooked in the provisions that are made for national happiness and prosperity.

In whatever light we regard the institution of slavery, it appears equally inconvenient and pernicious. No conclusion seems more certain than this, that men will commonly exert more activity when they work for their own benefit, than when they are compelled to

* [Four paragraphs and footnote almost entirely new.]

† Mr Hume supposes that, in the above enumeration, none but heads of families, either of the slaves or free men, are included; from which it would follow that, throwing aside the strangers, the slaves exceeded the citizens nearly as twenty to one; and as this disproportion is highly incredible, he is of opinion that the number of slaves should be reduced to 40,000. But the precise reduction to this number is entirely arbitrary; and upon the supposition which I have made, there will be no reason to suspect the account either of exaggeration or inaccuracy.

labour for the benefit merely of another. The introduction of personal liberty has therefore an infallible tendency to render the inhabitants of a country more industrious; and, by producing greater plenty of provisions, must necessarily increase the populousness, as well as the strength and security of a nation.

Some persons have imagined that slavery is conducive to population, on account of the frugality with which the slaves are usually maintained, and on account of the attention which is given by the master to their multiplication.

With regard to the former circumstance, it ought to be considered, that the work of a labourer depends very much upon the subsistence which he receives. As by living in too great affluence he may occasion an useless consumption of provisions, so by obtaining too little he is rendered less fit for the exercise of those employments by which mankind are supported. To promote the populousness of a country, the mechanics and labouring people should be maintained in such a manner as will yield the highest profit from the work which they are capable of performing; and it is probable that they will more commonly procure the enjoyments of life according to this due medium, when they provide their own maintenance, than when it depends upon the arbitrary will of a master, who, from narrow and partial views, may imagine that he has an interest to diminish the expense of their living as much as possible. To those who have occasion to know the extreme parsimony with which the negro-slaves in our colonies are usually maintained, any illustration of this remark will appear superfluous.

With respect to the care of the master to encourage the multiplication of his slaves, it must be obvious that this is of little moment, unless it be accompanied with an increase of the means of their subsistence. If slavery be always unfavourable to industry, and tend to hinder the improvement of a country, the number of inhabitants will be proportionably limited, in spite of all the regulations that can be made, and of all the encouragement that can be given to the propagation of the species. It is impossible even to multiply cattle beyond a certain extent, without having previously enriched the pastures upon which they are fed.

But slavery is not more hurtful to the industry than to the good morals of a people. To cast a man out from the privileges of society, and to mark his condition with infamy, is to deprive him of the most powerful incitements to virtue; and, very often, to render him worthy of that contempt with which he is treated. What effects, on the other hand, may we not expect that this debasement of the servants will produce on the temper and disposition of the master? In how many different ways is it possible to abuse that absolute power with which he is invested? And what vicious habits may be contracted by a train of such abuses, unrestrained by the laws, and palliated by the influence of example? It would seem that nothing could exceed the dishonesty and profligacy of the Roman slaves, unless we except the inhumanity and the extravagant vices which prevailed among the rest of the inhabitants.

* Various statutes were made to restrain the manumission of slaves, and to prevent the dignity of a Roman citizen from being communicated to such infamous persons.

Such is the confusion of our times [says Dionysius of Halicarnassus,] so much has the Roman probity degenerated into shameful meanness, that some, having gathered money by robberies, prostitutions, and all kinds of wickedness, are enabled to procure their freedom, and to become Romans; others, associating with their masters, in poisonings, murders, and crimes committed both against the gods and the commonwealth, are rewarded in the same manner.†

‡ It has been alleged that, in one respect, the institution of slavery is beneficial to a nation, as it affords the most convenient provision for those who are become unable to maintain themselves. The maintenance of the poor, is doubtless, a very important object, and may be regarded as one of the most difficult branches in the police of a country. In the early periods of society, when family-attachments are widely extended, the rich are commonly willing to take care of their indigent relations; and from the dispositions of a people unacquainted with luxury, those persons who have no other resource may expect relief from the occasional charity of their neighbours. But in a commercial and populous nation in which the bulk of the people must work hard for their livelihood, many individuals are, by a variety of accidents, reduced to indigence; while at the same time, from their numbers, as well as from the prevailing spirit of the age, their misery is little regarded by their fellow creatures. The cunning impostor, in such a case, may sometimes carry on a profitable trade of begging; but the real object of distress is apt to be overlooked, and without some interposition of the public, would often perish from want. Poor-rates therefore, in some shape or other, must be established; and from the nature of such an establishment, it is usually attended with much expense, and liable to many abuses. In a country where slavery is practised, no such inconvenience is felt. As the master may be obliged, in all cases, to maintain his slaves, no assessment is necessary, no charges are incurred in collecting and distributing

* [Lifted out of footnote.]   † Dion. Hal. Antiq. Rom. Lib. 3.
‡ [Two paragraphs added. Already contained in 2nd edition, pp. 304–6.]

money, for the benefit of the poor: not to mention, that the nuisance of common begging is thus effectually removed.

᠎It must be owned that this is a frugal regulation; but that it will answer the purpose is far from being so evident. When the same person, who is subjected to a tax, is also entrusted with the application of the money, what security is there that he will ever apply it to the uses for which it is intended? When a master is ordered to support his slaves, after they have become unfit for labour, what measures can be taken to secure their obedience? As it is plainly his interest to get free of this burden, what reason have we to expect that he will submit to it longer than he thinks fit? In a matter of domestic economy, how is it possible for the public to watch over his conduct, or to observe one of a thousand instances in which he may neglect his decayed servants, or withhold from them the common necessaries of life? Instead of maintaining the poor therefore, this is only a method of starving them in the most expeditious, and perhaps, in the most private manner. In perusing the Roman history, with relation to this subject, we meet with enormities which fill the mind with horror. Among that people it appears that, notwithstanding all the laws that were made by emperors, of the best intentions and possessed of absolute power, the master did not even think it necessary to conceal his barbarity, or to show more regard to his slaves, than is usually shown to cattle which, from age or diseases, are no longer of service to the owner.

Considering the many advantages which a country derives from the freedom of the labouring people, it is to be regretted that any species of slavery should still remain in the dominions of Great Britain, in which liberty is generally so well understood, and so highly valued.

The situation of the colliers and salters in Scotland may seem of little consequence, as the number of persons engaged in that employment is not very great, and their servitude is not very grievous. The detriment, however, which arises from thence to the proprietor of such works is manifest. No man would choose to be a slave if he could earn nearly the same wages by living in a state of freedom. Each collier therefore must have an additional premium for his labour, upon account of the bondage into which he is reduced: otherwise he will endeavour to procure a livelihood by some other employment.*

Many of the coal masters begin to be sensible of this, and with that their workmen were [are] upon a different footing; although, with a timidity natural to those who have a great pecuniary interest at stake, they are averse from altering the former practice, until such alteration shall be rendered universal by an act of parliament. But whatever advantages

* [Extended note on current wage-rates om.]

might accrue to them from a general law abolishing the slavery of the colliers, it seems evident that these advantages would be reaped in a much higher degree by any single proprietor who should have the resolution to give liberty to his workmen, and renounce the privileges which the law bestows upon him, with respect to those who might afterwards engage in his service. If the slavery of the colliers tends to heighten their wages, surely any one master who should be freed from this inconvenience before the rest, would be in the same circumstances with a manufacturer who produces a commodity at less expense than his neighbours, and who is thereby enabled to undersell them in the market.*

The slavery established in our colonies is an object of greater importance, and is, perhaps, attended with difficulties which cannot be so easily removed. It has been thought, that the management of our plantations requires a labour in which free men would not be willing to engage, and which the white people are, from their constitution, incapable of performing. How far this opinion is well founded, according to the present manner of labouring in that part of the world, seems difficult to determine, as it has never been properly examined by those who are in a condition to ascertain the facts in question. But there is ground to believe that the institution of slavery is the chief circumstance that has prevented those contrivances to shorten and facilitate the more laborious employments of the people, which take place in other countries where freedom has been introduced.

ᵃ Notwithstanding the connexion between our colonies and the mother-country, the instruments proper for some of the most common branches of labour are little known in many parts of the West Indies. In Jamaica the digging of a grave gives full employment to two men for a whole day; as from the want of proper tools it is necessary to make a large hole no way adapted to the human figure. I am informed, that, unless it has been procured very lately, there is hardly a spade in the whole island. In procuring firewood for boiling sugar, etc., a work that takes up about five or six weeks yearly, no use is made of the saw, but the trees are cut with an axe into logs of about 30 inches in length. Instead of a flail the negroes make use of a single stick in threshing the Guinea-corn; so that in this and in winnowing, ten women are capable of doing no more work in a day, than, with our instruments and machinery, two men would perform in two hours. From the want of a scythe or sickle, they are obliged every night to cut with a knife, or

* By a late act of parliament such regulations have been made as, in a short time, will probably abolish the remains of that servitude to which this order of men have been so long subjected.

pull with their hands, a quantity of grass sufficient to serve their horses, mules, and black cattle.*

With regard to the planting of sugar, experiments have been made, in some of the islands, from which it appears that, in this species of cultivation, cattle might be employed with advantage, and that the number of slaves might be greatly diminished.† But these experiments have been little regarded, in opposition to the former usage, and in opposition to a lucrative branch of trade which this innovation would in a great measure destroy.

At any rate, the interest of our colonies seems to demand that the negroes should be better treated, and even that they should be raised to a better condition. The author of a late elegant account of our American settlements has proposed, that small wages should be given them as an encouragement to industry. If this measure were once begun, it is probable that it would gradually be pushed to a greater extent; as the master would soon find the advantage of proportioning the wages of the slaves to the work which they performed. It is astonishing that so little attention has hitherto been paid to any improvements of this nature, after the good effects of them have been so fully illustrated in the case of the villains in Europe. The *a* owner of a sugar or tobacco plantation, one would think, might easily estimate the average value of the crop which it had formerly yielded, and could run no hazard, whatever profit he might reap, by allowing the people employed in the cultivation to draw a share of any additional produce obtained by their labour and frugality.

It affords a curious spectacle to observe that the same people who talk in a high strain of political liberty, and who consider the privilege of imposing their own taxes as one of the unalienable rights of mankind, should make no scruple of reducing a great proportion of their fellow-creatures into circumstances by which they are not only deprived of property, but almost of every species of right. Fortune perhaps never produced a situation more calculated to ridicule a liberal hypothesis, or to show how little the conduct of men is at the bottom directed by any philosophical principles.‡

§ In those provinces, however, of North America, where few slaves have ever been maintained, and where slavery does not seem to be

* These observations were made about the year 1765, and relate more immediately to the parishes of Vere, Hanover, and St Thomas in the vale.

† See *American husbandry*, published in 1775.

‡ [It is worth noting that this paragraph already occurs as the final paragraph of the 1771 edition.]

§ [Remaining paragraphs added.]

recommended by the nature of those employments in which the people are usually engaged, there may be some ground to expect that its pernicious effects upon industry will soon be felt, and that the practice will of course be abandoned. It is said that some of the provincial assemblies in that country have lately resolved to prevent or discourage the importation of negroes; but from what motives this resolution has proceeded, it is difficult to determine.*

The advancement of commerce and the arts, together with the diffusion of knowledge, in the present age, has of late contributed to the removal of many prejudices, and been productive of enlarged opinions, both upon this and upon a variety of other subjects. It has long been held, in Britain, that a negro slave, imported into this country, obtained thereby many of the privileges of a free man. But by a late judgment in the court of king's-bench it was found that the master could not recover his power over the servant by sending him abroad at pleasure.†

By a still more recent decision of the chief court in Scotland, it was declared:

That the dominion assumed over this negro, under the law of Jamaica, being unjust, could not be supported in this country to any extent: that therefore the defender had no right to the negro's service for any space of time; nor to send him out of the country against his consent.‡

This last decision, which was given in 1778, is the more worthy of attention, as it condemns the slavery of the negroes in explicit terms, and, being the first opinion of that nature delivered by any court in the island, may be accounted an authentic testimony of the liberal sentiments entertained in the latter part of the eighteenth century.

* See a vindication of the address to the inhabitants of the British settlements on the slavery of the negroes in America, by a Pennsylvanian, printed at Philadelphia, 1773.

† In the case of Somerset, the negro, decided in 1772.

‡ Joseph Knight, a negro, against John Wedderburn, 15 January 1778.

PART IV

SELECTIONS FROM OTHER WRITINGS

INTRODUCTION

The selections that follow are in no way intended to convey any idea of the objectives, scope and character of Millar's *Historical View* as a history of the British constitution. They are aimed, rather, at illustrating select aspects of his social and political theory to which only minor attention is given in the *Ranks*; something more of his historical method; and his grasp of economic realities and of the broad trends of historical development, in social and political as well as in economic life. Selections II and IX in particular, and less directly also some of the others, are aimed also at showing how Millar's political theory and his more personal political tenets were brought to bear upon the very live issues on the political scene in his own day.

It will be noticed that much of the material presented is taken from Volumes III and IV of the *Historical View*, which were not prepared for the press by Millar himself, some of it, indeed, left by him in a rather unfinished state. For its presentation thus we offer no apology, since we are more interested in showing his mind at work than in viewing critically a finished product; and in seeing a few rough edges of genuine human interest that he might well have trimmed off, had he prepared the material for publication himself.

Since the individual selections are nearly all prefaced by a line or two each of orientation, no further introduction is necessary here. Any other needed background will be found elsewhere in this volume.

All footnotes contained in the original—and there are but few of them—are retained, unbracketed, unless otherwise indicated; the notes in brackets are the present editor's.

SELECTION I

MILLAR'S PHILOSOPHY OF ECONOMICS

This and the following essay (Selection II) from the posthumously published 'Dissertations connected with the history of the government', subjoined to the *Historical View*, are reprinted in their entirety as they, more perhaps than any other pieces that might have been selected, give Millar's views on these subjects in a reasonably systematic fashion. The first (*H.V.* vol. IV, pp. 102–

325

Selections from Other Writings

37) represents a historical view, with yet considerable resort to economic theory, of the development of the prevailing economic system of his own day. It is presented, of course, from the point of view indicated in the title.

The Advancement of Manufactures, Commerce, and the Arts, since the Reign of William III; and the Tendency of this Advancement to diffuse a Spirit of Liberty and Independence

The natural advantages of England, in the cultivation of wool, having promoted her woollen manufacture, it was to be expected that her industry, and her capital, derived from that source, would be communicated to other branches of labour, in which they might be employed with similar success. Her maritime situation, by extending the benefit of water-carriage over a great part of the island, and by rendering many of the inhabitants acquainted with navigation, was calculated to produce a similar extension of commerce, and to open a foreign market for such of her commodities as exceeded her internal consumption. The full establishment of a regular and free constitution was alone wanting to improve these favourable circumstances, by exciting that energy and vigour which political liberty, and the secure possession and enjoyment of property are wont to inspire. This was obtained by the memorable Revolution in 1688, which completed, and reduced into practice, a government of a more popular nature, and better fitted to secure the natural rights of mankind, than had ever taken place in a great nation. From this happy period, therefore, commerce and manufactures assumed a new aspect, and, continuing to advance with rapidity, produced innumerable changes in the state of society, and in the character and manners of the people.

It would be superfluous to observe, that these improvements have been attended with correspondent advances in agriculture, and in the arts connected with it. Commerce and manufactures, by increasing wealth and population, must enhance the demand for provisions; and consequently, by augmenting the profits of the farmer, cannot fail to stimulate his industry and activity. It will be found, accordingly, from the general history of the world, that, in all countries where there is no trade, the cultivation of the ground, if at all known, is performed in a rude and slovenly manner; and that a considerable progress of mercantile improvements has generally preceded an equal degree of skill and dexterity in the several branches of husbandry. The cultivation of the ground, as Dr Smith justly observes, can never, in any country, approach to perfection, until the price of butcher-meat has, from the diffusion of wealth, risen to such a pitch as will induce the farmer to

326

employ his best grounds, at least occasionally, in the pasturing of cattle; by which he may obtain a constant supply of manure, sufficient to repair that part of his land which has been exhausted by tillage. As England has been long in that situation, her best land is frequently retained for the sole purpose of feeding cattle, or in what is called *meadow*; while in Scotland, whose mercantile and agricultural improvements have been much later, there is no such general practice; and the appellation of *meadow*, is only given to those marshy grounds, which, for want of draining, are unfit for the plough.

The same circumstances, which thus promoted the internal trade of England, were no less favourable to her commercial intercourse with other nations. The encouragement of her foreign trade became a great object as far back as the reign of James I and of Elizabeth; when trading companies were erected by public authority, and colonies, under the protection of government, were formed in distant parts of the globe. Those great companies were, at the same time, invested with exclusive privileges, calculated to secure them in the monopoly of the several branches of trade for which they had been incorporated. In the infancy of commerce, such regulations were, perhaps, requisite for the encouragement of new and hazardous undertakings; and their apparent equity, inasmuch as they bestowed upon the adventurers the fruit of their own spirited activity, could hardly be disputed. But in a subsequent period, when the progress of commercial improvements had produced large capitals, and a numerous body of merchants, ready to engage in every enterprise which promised an adequate, though perhaps, a distant return of profit, it began to be perceived that these monopolies were in every view, inconvenient and pernicious. They contributed to check any competition among the workmen engaged in producing those commodities, which were the subject of the monopoly trade; and, consequently, tended to diminish the *quantity*, as well as to degrade the *quality*, of those commodities. They also prevented all competition in the sale of such commodities, and enabled the monopolists, by starving the market, to advance their price in proportion. Thus the community at large became a sufferer in two respects; first, by procuring goods of an inferior quality to what might otherwise have been expected; secondly, by being obliged to purchase them above their natural rate. Since the revolution, therefore, these exclusive trading companies have been gradually abolished; and their trade laid open to the whole nation. The monopoly of the East India company has alone been excepted, and continues to be enforced with the utmost rigour. Some authors have endeavoured, from the distance of the country, and from the extent and other peculiarities of the Indian trade, to justify this exception; but, after all, there is little room to doubt, that it has proceeded from political, more than from commercial considerations, and that the strength, not the weakness of this company, is the real ground of the support which it has of late received from government.

The system of imposing restrictions upon commerce has not been directed solely to the purpose of encouraging particular trading companies. Politicians have conceived that individuals, in prosecuting schemes of private interest, were it not for the watchful inspection and control of government, might be tempted to employ their labour, and their capitals, upon such branches of trade as are less beneficial to the public than others; and that they ought to be restrained and diverted from so doing by numerous regulations; by taxes, prohibitions, and bounties. In particular, the view of preserving a favourable balance of our trade with foreign nations, ought to drive us out of every market in which our imports exceed our exports. Our trade with every foreign country was regarded as profitable, if we sent to it more goods than we received, and, consequently, obtained a surplus in money. If the contrary, it was considered as unprofitable and hurtful. The maxim which runs through the older writers on trade, appears now to be almost universally exploded. When we give to our neighbours money for useful and marketable commodities, we obtain a real value, and an adequate mercantile profit, no less than when we give commodities for their money. To carry on the trade of our country with advantage, and to supply the wants of the inhabitants, it may often be requisite that we should purchase the goods of particular nations, who have not an equal demand for our manufactures; but this will be compensated by our trade with others, who are in opposite circumstances, and who give to us a surplus in money. If our consumption be not greater than our productions; that is, if we are an industrious people; the balance of our trade with all the world, taken complexly, whatever may be the case with particular nations, can never be against us: and, if we have commodities for which there is a general demand, we can seldom remain long without an opportunity of turning them into money.

The quantity of the current species upon the face of the globe is naturally, and without any artificial direction, adjusted to the extent of the circulation in each particular country; for its occasional scarcity, in any one quarter, would raise its value in that place, and make it constantly flow thither until the equilibrium should be restored.

Upon the whole, there is good reason to conclude, that the mercantile people are the best judges of their own interest, and that, by pursuing those lines of trade which they find most beneficial to themselves, they are likely to produce, in most cases, the greatest benefit to the public. The administrators of government can seldom, from their own knowledge, be sufficiently qualified to judge in matters of this kind: and they are likely to be directed by persons who have an interest to mislead them. They have, therefore, frequently contributed more to hurt, than to improve the commercial machine, by their tampering; and their interpositions, besides loading the public with immediate expense, from the bounties, bestowed upon the favourite branches of trade, have diverted the mercantile capitals of the nation into channels, very different from their natural course, in which they have been productive of less profit, than they would otherwise have yielded.

For inculcating this truth, and placing it in a great variety of lights, the world is much indebted to the philosophers of a neighbouring country; and still more to the ingenious and profound author of 'The Causes of the Wealth of Nations'; by whom the subject is explained and illustrated in a manner that affords the fullest conviction. The universal approbation which this new doctrine has met with in the higher classes of mercantile people, in opposition to a rooted prejudice, connected with the private interests of a numerous body of men, is, of itself, a decisive proof of the high advances of commercial improvement, and of the enlarged views of political economy, by which the present age has become so eminently distinguished.*

The great extension of those means, which have been devised to promote and facilitate the circulation of commodities, affords another satisfactory illustration of the great extent, and the rapid increase, of our commercial dealings.

The introduction of money was a necessary contrivance for producing an exchange between persons who had no reciprocal demand for the goods of each other. By this expedient, any person, provided with a sufficient quantity of the current species, was in a condition to purchase from every one who had goods to dispose of. But when, in the progress of commerce, merchants came to be engaged in a multiplicity of transactions, the quantity of money which they were obliged, at all times, to keep in their possession, for satisfying their occasional demands, became proportionably large; and the retaining so much dead stock, which yielded no profit, was an inconvenience, from which, we may easily suppose, they endeavoured, by every possible means, to relieve themselves. If they had the reputation of wealth, they might sometimes persuade a creditor to accept of their personal obligation in place of immediate payment; and their promissory note, properly authenticated, might even be regarded as nearly equivalent to ready money, and might

* [See, however, letter Millar to Hume, Appendix I below.]

therefore pass from hand to hand in the purchase of goods. From an extension of this practice proceeded the establishment of *banks*, or mercantile companies, possessed of sufficient wealth to ensure their good credit, who made it a regular business, upon receiving an equivalent, to issue promissory notes payable on demand; and even, upon a suitable premium, to advance money upon the personal obligation of others. These institutions were introduced into the mercantile countries of Europe from the interposition of public authority, by which the members of each banking company were incorporated, and exempted from being liable to their creditors beyond the extent of a certain specified capital. Upon this footing, the Bank of England was erected, soon after the accession of William III; and at a subsequent period, two smaller companies, of a similar nature, were established in the northern part of the island. But the advantages derived from this branch of trade, have since produced innumerable private adventurers over the country, who without any aid from government, and consequently becoming liable to the amount of their whole fortunes, have engaged in the banking business, and appear to have pushed all its branches to their utmost extent. By the assistance of these banks, whether public or private, the nation has obtained a variety of resources for procuring money upon a sudden demand, and for turning it to an immediate account as soon as the demand is over; so that the quantity of current specie, which must ever lie unemployed in the hands of an individual, has been rendered more and more insignificant.

The same effect has flowed indirectly from the establishment of the funds belonging to some great mercantile corporations, and of those created by the public for paying the interest of the national debt; the nature of which I shall have occasion hereafter to consider. As every one is permitted to buy or sell, at his conveniency, greater or smaller shares in those funds, he has thus the command of money for any lucrative undertaking, and may replace it with profit whenever it ceases to be better employed.

In these progressive improvements of our commercial policy, without entering farther into particulars, we cannot fail to recognize the appearances of a nation which has long enjoyed all the advantages of high prosperity in trade and manufactures; and it remains to inquire, how far the uninterrupted possession, and daily increase of these blessings, have contributed to inspire the people with higher notions of liberty, and more ardent zeal in defence of their privileges.

The spirit of liberty appears, in commercial countries, to depend chiefly upon two circumstances: first, the condition of the people relative to the distribution of property, and the means of subsistence:

secondly, the facility with which the several members of society are enabled to associate and to act in concert with one another.

1. With respect to the former circumstance, the whole property of such a country, and the subsistence of all the inhabitants, may, according to the phraseology of late writers upon political economy, be derived from three different sources; from the rent of land or water; from the profits of stock or capital; and from the wages of labour: and, in conformity to this arrangement, the inhabitants may be divided into landlords, capitalists, and labourers.

Of labourers, who form the lowest class, the situation and way of life must, in every country, render them in some degree dependent upon the person who gives them employment.* Having little or no property, and earning a bare subsistence by their daily labour, they are placed in a state of inferiority which commonly disposes them to feel some respect for their master; they have an interest to avoid any difference with him; and in the execution of their work, being constantly required to follow his directions, they are apt, in some degree, to acquire habits of submission to his will.

The relative condition of the labouring people, however, must vary considerably according to the differences which occur in the general state of society.† In rude countries, even where domestic slavery is excluded, the chief labourers are either menial servants, or such as cultivate the ground; and, as they generally continue for life in the service of the same person, his influence over them is naturally very great. But, in commercial countries, the bond of union between the workmen and their employer is gradually loosened. There, the most numerous class of labourers are those employed in subserviency to trade or manufactures; and they are so indiscriminately engaged in the service of different persons, that they feel but little the loss of a particular master, with whom they have formed but a slight connexion. When a country, at the same time, is rapidly advancing in trade, the demand for labourers is proportionably great; their wages are continually rising; instead of soliciting employment, they are courted to accept of it; and they enjoy a degree of affluence and of importance, which is frequently productive of insolence and licentiousness.

That the labouring people in Britain have, for some time, been raised to this enviable situation, is evident from a variety of circumstances; from the high price of labour, and the difficulty of procuring workmen; [from] the absurd attempts of the legislature to regulate their wages, and to prevent them from deserting particular employments; from the

* [Indirect reference, it would seem, to Harrington.]

† [See also *H.V.* vol. IV, pp. 151 ff.; vol I, 135 ff., 315 ff.; vol. III, 101 ff.]

zeal displayed by the lower orders in the vindication of their political, as well as of their private rights; and, above all, from the jealousy and alarm with which this disposition has, of late, so universally impressed their superiors.

When a labourer has acquired so much property as will enable him, without wages, to subsist until he has manufactured a particular commodity, he may then gain, upon the sale of it, a profit over and above the ordinary value of his labour. In proportion to the enlargement of his capital, his productions, by the employment of subordinate hands will be multiplied, and his profits, of course, extended. Thus, according as the business of producing and disposing of commodities becomes more extensive and complicated, it is gradually subdivided into various departments, and gives rise to the several classes, of manufacturers, tradesmen, and merchants.

To discover the different sources of mercantile profit, we may distinguish two sorts of stock, or capital, belonging to a manufacturer or merchant; the *circulating*, and the *permanent* * stock; the former comprehending the goods which he brings to market; the latter, the houses, the machinery, and the various accommodations which he requires for the manufacture or sale of his goods.

To a manufacturer, the circulating stock affords a profit, by enabling him to unite many different branches of labour upon the same commodity, and, consequently, to save that expense of carriage, which would be incurred if those branches were separately performed in different places, and the amount afterwards collected. If, for example, the several operations requisite in the woollen manufacture were to be performed separately, by workmen at a distance from each other, there would be an expense of carriage necessary to unite the effect of their several productions, which is totally avoided by collecting the different hands in the same neighbourhood, and accumulating their labour upon the same commodity. The manufacturer, therefore, draws a return for his capital, inasmuch as it has been the means of shortening the labour, and consequently of diminishing the expense of his manufacture.

It is unnecessary to observe, that by the saving of carriage there is also a saving of *time*, which is no less valuable; and the manufacturer obtains an additional profit, according as, with the same labour, he can sooner bring his goods to market.

As by collecting many hands in the same manufacture, the undertaker saves an actual expense, he also obtains a direct advantage by having it in his power to divide minutely, the several branches of labour among different workmen, so that each acquires more skill and

* [Millar's use of these terms does not appear to us altogether satisfactory.]

dexterity in the single branch allotted to him, and is prevented from idling and losing time, as commonly happens in passing from one branch to another. The prodigious effect of this division of labour, by increasing the quantity of work done in a given time, as well as by improving its quality, becomes also, like every other circumstance tending to facilitate labour, a separate source of profit to the manufacturer.*

To the merchant, or tradesman, the circulating stock is the source of profit upon similar principles. It enables him to save the purchasers from the trouble and expense of bespeaking the goods before they stand in need of them, and of providing themselves at once with more than they immediately want; while the quantity which he has collected, and the number of his customers, ensure to him the disposal of the whole within a reasonable time. The larger the stock of the merchant, provided it does not exceed the general demand, the saving which he thus procures to his customers, without loss to himself, will be the more complete and certain.

With respect to *permanent* mercantile stock, consisting of the machinery, the houses, and the various accommodations employed by manufacturers or traders, in the course of their business, it is intended for the sole purpose of assisting and promoting the operations upon *circulating* stock; and having therefore, still further a tendency to shorten and facilitate labour, it must, upon that account, be also productive of a suitable profit.

It should seem, therefore, an evident conclusion from these observations, that the benefit resulting from every species of trade or manufacture, is ultimately derived from *labour*; and that the profit arising from every branch of mercantile stock, whether permanent or circulating, is derived from its enabling the merchant, or manufacturer, to produce the same effect with less labour, and consequently with less expense than would otherwise have been required.

It merits attention, however, that the whole revenue drawn by a merchant or manufacturer, though in a loose way commonly called his profit, does not with propriety come under this description. Besides the value of his capital, from its effect in shortening, facilitating, and super-

* A part of the profit of a manufacturer may also be drawn from the workman, who, however, will have a full equivalent for what he thus resigns. By working to a master he is sure of constant employment, is saved the trouble of seeking out those who may have occasion for his labour, and avoids the anxiety arising from the danger of being thrown occasionally idle. In return for these advantages, he willingly relinquishes to his master some part of what he can earn while employed. Accordingly in Scotland, where it is still very common for good housewives to manufacture linens for the use of their families, the weavers whom they employ, usually demand wages somewhat higher than the ordinary rates paid by the manufacturers.

seding labour, he draws an adequate compensation for his own efforts in putting that capital in motion, for his attention and skill in conducting the several parts of the business, and for the inconvenience he may sustain in waiting a distant, and in some degree, an uncertain return. The former is properly the *rent* of capital: the latter may be called the *wages* of mercantile exertion. These two branches of revenue are frequently separated, inasmuch as the merchant, or manufacturer, borrows a part of the capital with which he trades, and pays for it a regular *interest*, or as the acting partners of the commercial company draw salaries for their personal attendance.

Those who obtain a revenue from capital, therefore, are either monied men who live upon the interest of their money, or mercantile adventurers, who draw, either a profit from their own capital, or a sort of wages from trading with the capital of others. Both of these orders are much more independent in their circumstances than the common labourer: but the former according to the extent of his revenue, is more independent than the latter. The mercantile adventurer draws his revenue from a multiplicity of customers, with whom he is commonly upon equal terms of affluence, and to each of whom he is but little obliged; but the monied man lives entirely upon his property, and is obliged to nobody for any part of his maintenance.*

When we consider the changes in this respect, which have taken place in Britain since the period of the revolution; in what proportion both of these orders of capitalists have been multiplied; when we observe the number of common labourers who are daily converted into artificers, frequently vending their own productions; what crowds of people are continually rising from the lower ranks, and disposed of in the various branches of trade; how many have acquired, and how many more are in the high road of acquiring opulent fortunes; how universally mutual emulation, and mutual intercourse, have diffused habits of industry, have banished idleness, which is the parent of indigence, and have put it into the power of almost every individual, by the exertion of his own talents, to earn a comfortable subsistence; when, I say, we attend to the extent of these improvements, which affect the whole mercantile part of the inhabitants, we cannot entertain a doubt of their powerful efficacy to propagate corresponding sentiments, of personal independence, and to instil higher notions of general liberty.

The observations which have been made, with respect to the trader and capitalist, are, in a great measure, applicable to the cultivator and proprietor of land. The farmer, who by his labour and skill, and by the employment of Stock, draws a revenue from the cultivation of land, is in

* [See above, p. 128.]

circumstances similar to those of the manufacturer. From his cattle, from his tools and instruments of husbandry, and from the money expended in the management of his farm, he derives a profit suitable to their effect, in shortening and facilitating his labour; and the ground itself may be regarded as a part of his permanent stock, contributing, like a loom, or other piece of machinery, to the result of his operations. But as the ground has greater stability, as it appears of much greater importance than all the remaining stock of the farmer, and as in many cases it belongs to a different person, the profit arising from it, which is regularly payable to the landlord, has been commonly distinguished under the name of *rent*, while that which arises from the other part of agricultural stock, is viewed in the same light with mercantile profit. There is, however, no essential difference between those two branches of revenue; they both depend upon the same principles, and bear a regular proportion to the value of the respective funds from which they are drawn.

There is, indeed, one particular in which they require to be distinguished; I mean, with respect to the degree of independence which, in different situations, they bestow upon the possessor. In poor countries, where agriculture is in a low state, the great value of land, compared with the other parts of agricultural stock, renders the employment of the latter in a great measure subordinate to that of the former; and reduces the people who cultivate the ground to be a sort of servants or dependents of the proprietor. But the improvement of husbandry gives more dignity to this useful profession, and raises the condition of those who exercise it. As the operations of the farmer become extensive, his capital must be enlarged; and as he lays out greater expense in improvement, he must obtain a longer lease to afford him the prospect of a return from the lands. He is thus totally emancipated from his former dependence; becomes more enterprising in proportion to his opulence; and upon the expiration of his lease, he finds that it is not more his object to obtain a good farm, than it is the interest of every landlord to obtain a good tenant. This has, for some time, been the general condition of the farmers in England; and to this independent state they are quickly advancing in the more improvable parts of Scotland.

Such are the changes which, in the course of the present century, have taken place, and are still rapidly advancing in Britain, with relation to the different branches of revenue, arising from the wages of labour, and from the employment of stock, either in trade, or in the cultivation of the earth; and with relation to the condition of the respective orders of men by whom those branches of revenue are enjoyed. The tendency of improvement in all the arts of life, and in every trade or profession, has been uniformly the same; to enable mankind more easily to gain a livelihood by the exercise of their talents, without being subject to the caprice, or caring for the displeasure of others; that is, to render the lower classes of the people less dependent upon their superiors.

It must not, however, be imagined, that this independent situation of mankind, with respect to the means of subsistence, will always prevent such inequalities of fortune, as may create in some of the members of society an influence over others. The unequal distribution of property, is a necessary consequence of the different degrees of application or abilities, co-operating with numberless accidents, which retard or promote the pecuniary pursuits of individuals; and the poor will often find their account in courting the favour of the rich. Any attempt, upon the part of the public, to limit the free accumulation of wealth, would be fatal to that industry or exertion which is the foundation of national prosperity. Sound policy requires that every man should feel a continual spur to his activity from the prospect of enjoying at pleasure, and disposing of the fruits of his labour. But the circumstances of a country, highly advanced in commerce and manufactures, are such as, naturally, and without any interposition of government, have a tendency to moderate those great differences of fortune, which, in a rude age, are usually the source of tyranny and oppression. Where a multitude of people are engaged in lucrative trades and professions, it must commonly happen that numbers of competitors, placed in similar circumstances, will meet with nearly equal success; and that their several acquisitions will counterbalance each other, so as to prevent, in any one quarter, the growth of an influence that might be dangerous to the community. The same spirit, being universally, and in some measure equally diffused, and being subject to no obstruction, either from the state of society, or from the injudicious regulations of the public, is likely to form such a gradation of opulence, as leaving no chasm from the top to the bottom of the scale, will occasion a continual approximation of the different ranks, and will frequently enable the inferior orders to press upon the superior. 'The toe of the peasant comes so near the heel of the courtier, that it galls his kibe.' *

The effect of superiority in wealth, as I had occasion to show in a former part of this discourse, is further diminished in commercial countries, by the frequent alienation of estates. As persons of low rank are incited by their situation to better their circumstances, and commonly acquire such habits of industry and frugality, as enable them to accumulate; those who are born to great fortunes, are apt, on the other

* [Quoted from Shakespeare's *Hamlet*, Act v, scene i, l. 153.]

hand, to become idle and dissipated, and living in all the expense which opulence renders fashionable, are frequently tempted to squander their estates. Hence, opulent families are quickly reduced to indigence; and their place is supplied by professional people from the lower orders; who, by the purchase of land, endeavour to procure that distinction which was the end of their labours. The descendants of these upstarts, in a generation or two, usually go the same round of luxury and extravagance, and finally experience the same reverse of fortune. Property is thus commonly subjected to a constant rotation, which prevents it from conferring upon the owner the habitual respect and consideration, derived from a long continued intercourse between the poor and the rich.

To preserve old families from this destruction became a great object in Britain, and in the other countries of Europe, as soon as commerce began to threaten the dissolution of estates. Entails were invented to arrest and secure the estate; titles of nobility, to preserve the personal dignity of the possessors. But these contrivances were of little avail. When such restrictions became inconsistent with the manners of the age, they could no longer be enforced. In England the fetters of an entail were, by the ingenuity of lawyers, gradually lightened, and at length easily struck off; though in Scotland, a country in which aristocratic government was more firmly rooted, they still remain in full force. The rank of nobility being connected with political distinction, has hitherto maintained its ground, and continues to be the object of ambition; but when separated from the estate which gave it support, so far from being of service to the owner, it operates as an exclusion from almost all the paths of industry, and seems to confer a mock-dignity upon real and hopeless indigence and servility.

The opulence of Britain, in the present century, it is evident, has greatly surpassed that of the preceding ages, in facilitating to the poor the means of accumulation, in multiplying to the rich those artificial wants which produce a rapid circulation of estates, and consequently, in subverting that permanent state of property which is the foundation of all hereditary influence.

2. As the advancement of commerce and manufactures in Britain has produced a state of property highly favourable to liberty, so it has contributed to collect and arrange the inhabitants in a manner which enables them, with great facility, to combine in asserting their privileges.

When government has been so far established as to maintain the general tranquillity, and to introduce peaceable manners; and when a set of magistrates, and rulers, are invested with an authority, confirmed by ancient usage, and supported, perhaps, by an armed force, it cannot be expected that the people, single and unconnected, will be able to resist the oppression of their governors; and their power of combining for this purpose, must depend very much upon their peculiar circumstances. In small states, consisting merely of a capital city, with a narrow adjacent country, like those of ancient Greece and Rome, the inhabitants were necessarily led to an intimate union and correspondence; which appears to have been the chief cause of their being able, at an early period, to expel their petty princes, and establish a popular government. But in large kingdoms, the people being dispersed over a wide country, have seldom been capable of such vigorous exertions. Living in petty villages, at a distance from one another, and having very imperfect means of communication, they are often but little affected by the hardships which many of their countrymen may sustain from the tyranny of government; and a rebellion may be quelled in one quarter before it has time to break out in another. The efforts, which are occasionally made, in different parts of the country, to limit the prerogative, being without union or concert, are commonly unsuccessful; and therefore, instead of producing the effect intended, usually terminate in the exaltation of the crown. The unlucky insurgents are obliged to make their peace with the sovereign, by submitting to new encroachments; and to wipe off their former demerits by assisting to reduce their fellow-citizens to obedience. To this want of concert in the members of a wide country, we may ascribe the rise of the greater part of rude monarchies; and more especially those of the great Asiatic nations.

From the progress, however, of trade and manufactures, the state of a country, in this respect, is gradually changed. As the inhabitants multiply from the facility of procuring subsistence, they are collected in large bodies for the convenient exercise of their employments. Villages are enlarged into towns; and these are often swelled into populous cities. In all those places of resort, there arise large bands of labourers or artificers, who by following the same employment, and by constant intercourse, are enabled, with great rapidity, to communicate all their sentiments and passions. Among these there spring up leaders, who give a tone and direction to their companions. The strong encourage the feeble; the bold animate the timid; the resolute confirm the wavering; and the movements of the whole mass proceed with the uniformity of a machine, and with a force that is often irresistible.

In this situation, a great proportion of the people are easily roused by every popular discontent, and can unite with no less facility in demanding a redress of grievances. The least ground of complaint, in a town, becomes the occasion of a riot; and the flames of sedition spreading from one city to another, are blown up into a general insurrection.*

Neither does this union arise merely from local situations; nor is it confined to the lower class of those who are subservient to commerce and manufactures. By a constant attention to professional objects, the superior orders of mercantile people become quick-sighted in discerning their common interest, and, at all times, indefatigable in pursuing it. While the farmer, employed in the separate cultivation of his land, considers only his own individual profit; while the landed gentleman seeks only to procure a revenue sufficient for the supply of his wants, and is often unmindful of his own interest as well as of every other; the merchant, though he never overlooks his private advantage, is accustomed to connect his own gain with that of his brethren, and is, therefore, always ready to join with those of the same profession, in soliciting the aid of government, and in promoting general measures for the benefit of their trade.

The prevalence of this great mercantile association in Britain, has, in the course of the present century, become gradually more and more conspicuous. The clamour and tumultuary proceedings of the populace in the great towns are capable of penetrating the inmost recesses of administration, of intimidating the boldest minister, and of displacing the most presumptuous favourite of the back-stairs. The voice of the mercantile interest never fails to command the attention of government, and when firm and unanimous, is even able to control and direct the deliberations of the national councils. The methods which are sometimes practised by the ministry to divide this mercantile interest, and to divert its opposition to the measures of the crown, will fall more properly to be considered hereafter.

So much with regard to the progress of trade and manufactures in Britain since the period of the revolution, and its consequences in rendering the people opulent, as well as independent in their circumstances. I shall now proceed to examine the tendency of this independence and opulence, to promote the cultivation of the liberal arts and sciences, to extend knowledge and literature over the great body of the people, and to introduce opinions and sentiments which may affect the nature of government.†

* [Would seem to be referring chiefly to the contemporary scene, though perhaps also drawing upon historical experience elsewhere.]

† [Carried out largely in Essay IV, only in small part reproduced in Selection VI below.]

THE PRINCIPLES OF LAW AND GOVERNMENT

The title of this selection, which is Essay VII in vol. iv, pp. 266–310 of the *Historical View*, is adequately descriptive of its content.

The Progress of Science Relative to Law and Government *

As the advancement of commerce and civilization tends to promote the virtue of strict justice, it of course disposes mankind to cultivate and improve the science of law. By attention and experience, and by a gradual refinement of their feelings, men attain a nicer discrimination in matters of right and wrong, and acquire more skill and dexterity in settling the claims and disputes of individuals, or in proportioning punishments to the various offences which may invade the peace of society.

There is this remarkable difference between justice and the other virtues, that the former can be reduced under general rules, capable, in some degree, of accuracy and precision; while the latter, more uncertain and variable in their limits, can frequently be no otherwise determined than from a complex view of their circumstances, and must, in each particular case, be submitted to the immediate decision of taste and sentiment. Justice requires no more than that I should abstain from hurting my neighbour, in his person, his property, or his reputation; that I should pay the debts, or perform the services, which by my contracts, or by the course of my behaviour, I have given him reason to expect from me; and that, if I have ever transgressed in any of these particulars, I should make a suitable compensation and reinstate him, as far as possible, in those advantages of which I have unwarrantably deprived him. The line of duty suggested by this mere negative virtue, can be clearly marked, and its boundaries distinctly ascertained. It resembles a matter of calculation, and may, in some sort, be regulated by the square and the compass.

But the other virtues, those more especially which lead us to promote the positive happiness of our neighbours, admit of a greater variety of aspects, and are of a more delicate nature. What is the precise behaviour consistent with the most perfect friendship, generosity, gratitude, or

* [Compare with this essay portions of *Wealth of Nations*, Bk. v, Pt. ii.]

other benevolent affections, may often be a difficult question; and the situations which give rise to the complete exercise of those virtues are so diversified by a multiplicity of minute circumstances, that there seldom occur two instances altogether alike; and there is no room for determining any number of cases according to the same general view.

Though mankind, therefore, have in all ages given a very universal attention to morality, though their constant aim and endeavour has been to recommend themselves, one to another, by practising, or by seeming to practise, those virtues which procure esteem, or affection and confidence—they have made, after all, but slender advances in digesting their knowledge upon the subject, and in reducing it to a regular system. Philosophers have been able to do little more than to exhibit a description or picture, more or less animated, of the principal virtues and vices, together with their various combinations in the characters of individuals, and at the same time to suggest considerations and views, which, from the condition of human nature, are likely to produce an admiration and love of virtue, as well as a detestation and abhorrence of vice.

The first moralists, among an ignorant and simple people, were contented with giving general advices, for the benefit of such as were destitute of experience, to guard against the temptations to vice, and the irregular influence of the passions. Parents, desirous of promoting the welfare of their children, men of sagacity, who, in the course of a long life, had surveyed the vicissitudes of human affairs, were induced to communicate the fruits of their experience, and to inculcate such observations and maxims, as might correct the errors and imprudences to which mankind are peculiarly liable. Hence the numerous proverbs which have been circulated in all nations, containing such moral and prudential maxims, as, from an apparent shrewdness of remark, from strength or felicity of allusion, or from any peculiar point of expression, were thought worthy of attention, and frequently repeated. Of a similar nature, but uniting, in some cases, a train of reflection upon the same subject, are those observations, and advices, relating to the conduct of life, which have been collected by early writers, or delivered by ancient sages of high reputation; such as, the proverbs of Solomon, the words of Agur, the wisdom of the son of Sirah, a part of the writings of Hesiod, and the sayings of those who are denominated the wise men of Greece.

Succeeding writers endeavoured to explain and enforce these observations and maxims by historical events, real or fictitious; and to illustrate their truth, by allegorical representations, taken from the brute creation, or from those different parts of nature in which we may trace any resemblance to human actions and passions. Of this latter sort are the parables of Scripture, the fables known to us by the name of Pilpay, which appear to have enjoyed a very ancient and extensive reputation in the eastern world; and those of equal celebrity in Europe, which are ascribed to Æsop, and which have been translated, paraphrased, and embellished by such a multitude of eminent authors. Even after those early observations, from the general diffusion of knowledge, have ceased to convey much instruction, the apologue or fable, has continued, with several men of genius, to be a favourite mode of composition, on account of the delicate strokes with which it is capable of exhibiting the follies and foibles of human life.

When men had been accustomed to consider in detail the several branches of human conduct, they were led by degrees to more connected views, and extensive reasonings. They were led to enumerate and arrange the principal virtues and vices, and to distribute them into different classes, according to the various feelings or passions, from which they proceed, or the different ends to which they are directed. The celebrated and well known division of the virtues into four great classes, usually denominated the four cardinal virtues, which has been handed down to us by the Greek and Roman writers, and which is reported to have been brought by Pythagoras from the east, appears to be a very ancient, and at the same time, a successful attempt of this nature.

The arrangement and classification of the several virtues, could hardly fail to occasion inquiries and discussions concerning the peculiar character of each; and more especially to suggest an examination of the circumstances by which all the virtues are distinguished from the opposite vices. This gave rise to the far-famed question, *Wherein consists virtue?*

The great distinction between virtue and vice appears to consist in the different sentiments which they excite in the beholders, and in their opposite tendency, to produce *happiness* or *misery* to mankind.

There is in virtue a native beauty and excellence, which is felt and acknowledged by all the world; which from the immediate contemplation of it, and without regard to its consequences, is the genuine source of pleasure and satisfaction; and which procures to the person in whom it is discovered, universal love and esteem, with various modifications of benevolence. The natural deformity of vice; the disgust and aversion with which it is regarded; and the contempt and abhorrence, or the indignation and resentment which it excites, are no less conspicuous. That these feelings exist in the human mind is indisputable; but whether they are simple and original feelings, intended by nature for this purpose alone; or whether they are excited from different views and reasonings, and consequently, are capable of explanation and analysis, has been the subject of much philosophical disquisition; a disquisition highly curious and interesting to the lovers of metaphysical knowledge; though, in relation to practical morality, of little or no importance.

The tendency of all virtuous actions to produce happiness, either to the person who performs them or to others, and the contrary tendency of all vicious actions, are considerations, which, to the bulk of mankind, will appear of still greater magnitude, in creating a preference of the former to the latter. In this view, those virtuous actions which promote a man's own good, are agreeable to a spectator, from those benevolent feelings which render him pleased with the happiness of the person who performs them; while those actions which promote the good of others, gratify the selfish feelings of the spectator, and call forth a sort of gratitude from every person who conceives himself within the sphere of their beneficial influence. We need not be surprised, therefore, that men should universally bestow much higher applause upon the benevolent, than upon the selfish virtues; or that some eminent philosophers have considered the latter in the light merely of useful qualities, which are not the proper objects of moral approbation. The person who performs a benevolent action appears in the light of a benefactor; and, as we readily suppose ourselves to be the objects of his beneficence, we feel, upon that account, a disposition to make a suitable return of good offices; we look upon him as peculiarly worthy of our good-will and affection; and are thence led to form a notion of his meriting a reward.

From considering the beneficial tendency of all the virtues, philosophers proceeded to a more general inquiry, concerning the supreme good or happiness of mankind, and the circumstances by which it is produced; whether it be produced by virtue alone, or by what is called pleasure, or from the union and co-operation of both?

Such appear to be the principal steps by which men have advanced in cultivating the general science of morality, which have undoubtedly been of great utility in presenting such views and considerations as were fitted to awaken the noblest and best affections of the heart; but which often terminating in vague reflection, or speculative disquisition afford no specific information, no precise land-marks for the regulation of our conduct. If we do not miss our way in the journey of life, it is more from our general knowledge of the compass, than from any directions we receive concerning the several windings and turnings of the road.

But in relation to strict justice, the attention of mankind has been excited and directed in a different manner, and has produced an examination of particulars much more minute and accurate. As individuals who have much intercourse, are likely, on many occasions, to experience an opposition of interest, and if they are independent of each other, must be liable to numerous disputes in matters of right, they have in the infancy of society, no other method of terminating any difference which cannot be amicably adjusted than either by fighting, or by referring it to the decision of a common arbiter; and this latter mode of accommodation, which flatters the sanguine expectations of either party, and which, by preventing a quarrel, must commonly be agreeable to their private friends, as well as to the friends of good order and public tranquillity, is likely to be more frequently adopted in proportion as, by the habits of living in society, people become less quarrelsome in their temper, and more under the guidance of prudence and discretion.

The arbiters most frequently chosen on those occasions, will probably be persons who from their eminent reputation for wisdom and integrity, possess the confidence of both parties, and by their high station, and superior influence, are capable of giving weight to their decisions. The longer these men have officiated in the same employment, provided they have acted with tolerable propriety, the respect paid to their opinions will be the greater, and the disposition to treat them with deference and submission, will become the more habitual. Their own efforts to render their sentences effectual will also, from considerations of expediency, be supported by the general voice of the community; till at length, by the assignment of an armed force to assist them in enforcing obedience, they are invested with power to determine law-suits independent of any reference to parties, and thus, in the natural progress of things, are converted into regular and permanent judges.

Corresponding to the advices and prudential maxims which are circulated by men of experience and observation, in the primitive cultivation of morality, are the decisions of arbiters and judges, which constitute the foundation of the science of law. From the various disputes of individuals, and from the various claims that are successively decided and enforced, there is formed a set of practical rules of justice, which are gradually multiplied, and according to the different situations and relations of mankind in society, gradually extended and diversified.

The disputes among mankind are innumerable: but as one dispute is often very like another, it is apt to be decided in a similar manner; and when a number of cases have been determined upon the same grounds, there is introduced a general rule, which from the influence of habit and of analogy, is extended, even without examination to other cases of the same kind. Though this procedure originates in a propensity natural to all mankind, it is doubtless recommended and confirmed by its utility.

The general rules of law are of signal service, by enabling every person to simplify his transactions, as well as to ascertain the tenor of conduct which he is bound to maintain, and by proving at the same time, a check to the partiality of judges, who must be ashamed or afraid to deviate from that beaten path, which is universally known and easily distinguished.

The advantages, however, arising from the general rules of justice, are not without limitations. When a great number of claims are decided from the consideration of those outlines in which they all agree, the smaller circumstances in which they happen to differ must of course be overlooked; and the decision may, therefore, in some instances be productive of injustice. This is the foundation of that old complaint, which in every country, has been made against the *extremity of the law*. It is necessary, for this reason, to forego in many cases, the benefit of that uniformity and certainty derived from the strict observance of a general rule, and by introducing an exception from the consideration of what is equitable in particular circumstances, to avoid the hardship which would otherwise fall upon individuals. We must on this as on many other occasions, compare and balance the inconveniencies which present themselves on opposite sides, and be contented with submitting to those which are of the least importance.

The interpositions of equity, which are made in detached and singular circumstances, are at first regarded as extraordinary deviations from that legal maxim, which, however just and expedient in other cases, is found in some particular instance, to be hard and oppressive. But when these interpositions have been often repeated in similar situations, they become familiar and habitual; and such of them as depend upon a common principle, are reduced into the same class, the boundaries of which are precisely determined.

In this manner, by the successive litigation of individuals, and by the continued experience and observation of judges, the science of law grows up in society, and advances more and more to a regular system. Particular decisions become the foundation of general rules, which are afterwards limited by particular exceptions; and these exceptions being also generalized, and reduced into different classes, are again subjected to future limitations. From a few parent stems, there issue various branches; and these are succeeded by subordinate ramifications; diminishing gradually in size, while they increase in number; separated from each other by endless divisions and subdivisions; exhibiting a great multiplicity and variety of parts, uniformly and regularly adjusted; and which may, therefore, be easily and readily traced through all their different connexions.

But though the rules of justice derive their origin from the business of the world, and are introduced by the actual decisions of judges, their extensive utility is likely to attract the notice of speculative reasoners, and to render them the subject of criticism and philosophical discussion. As from various causes the practical system of law in any country is apt, in many respects to deviate from that standard of perfection which nature holds up to the speculative mind, the detecting of its errors and imperfections, and the display of its peculiar advantages, become an agreeable exercise to men of ingenuity and reflection; and from such disquisitions, it is reasonable to expect that the knowledge of mankind will be extended, their prejudices corrected, and useful improvements suggested.

In speculating upon the system of law in any country, it is natural to compare it with other systems, and by examining and contrasting the respective advantages or disadvantages of each, to explain and illustrate the nature and tendency of different regulations. From these comparisons, pursued extensively, and accompanied by such reflections as they must naturally suggest, philosophers at length conceived the idea of delivering a system of law, free from the defects which occur in every practical establishment, and which might correspond in some measure, with our views of absolute perfection; a noble idea, which does not appear to have entered into the imagination of any Roman or Greek writer, and which may be regarded as one of the chief improvements in the philosophy of modern Europe. Hence the systems of *jurisprudence*, which, after the revival of letters, have occurred in such multitudes, and which have been dressed in different shapes, and with different degrees of accuracy by Grotius and other speculative lawyers.

It must be acknowledged, that the execution of those works has not equalled the merit of the attempt. Although they profess to deliver the rules of justice, abstracted from the imperfections of every particular establishment, they appear, for the most part to follow implicitly, at least in several particulars, the ancient Roman system, which, notwithstanding the consideration and celebrity it has very deservedly attained, is in many of its doctrines erroneous, and in some of its principles narrow and illiberal.

A more material defect in most of the writers on jurisprudence is their not marking sufficiently the boundaries between strict law and mere morality. They seem to consider, what a good man, from the utmost propriety of feelings and scruples of conscience, would be disposed to do, rather than what an upright judge would compel him to perform; and are thus led frequently to confound what is properly called justice (which requires that we should avoid hurting our neighbours) with generosity or benevolence, which prompts us to increase their positive happiness.

The attempts to delineate systems of jurisprudence, which have been so often repeated with more or less perspicuity or conciseness, but with little variation in substance, opened at length a new source of speculation, by suggesting an inquiry into the circumstances which have occasioned various and opposite imperfections in the law of different countries, and which have prevented the practical systems, in any, from attaining that improvement which we find no difficulty in conceiving. In the prosecution of this inquiry, more especially by President Montesquieu, by Lord Kames, and by Dr Smith, the attention of speculative lawyers has been directed to examine the first formation and subsequent advancement of civil society; the rise, the gradual development, and cultivation of arts and sciences; the acquisition and extension of property in all its different modifications, and the combined influence of these and other political causes upon the manners and customs, the institutions and laws of any people. By tracing in this manner the natural history of legal establishments, we may be enabled to account for the different aspect which they assume in different ages and countries, to discover the peculiarity of situation which has, in any case, retarded or promoted their improvement, and to obtain, at the same time, satisfactory evidence of the uniformity of those internal principles which are productive of such various and apparently inconsistent operations.

The system of law, in every country is divided into that part which regulates the powers of the state, considered as a corporation or body politic; and that which regulates the conduct of the several members of which this corporation is composed. The former is the government, the law which *constitutes*; the latter, the law which is *constituted*. The former may with propriety, though not in the common acceptation be called the *public*; the latter the *private* law.

To government belongs the province of appointing judges for the determination of law-suits; of establishing an armed force, to secure internal tranquillity as well as for defence against foreign enemies; and also, in cases where the dictates of justice are silent, that of superadding to the private law such positive regulations or statutes, as peculiar conjunctures may render necessary or expedient. It is evident, therefore, that the state of the private law in any country must be entirely subordinate to the nature of its government; and that according to the merit or demerit of the latter, will be the excellence or deficiency of the former. The origin and progress of different public institutions, and the manner in which they have arisen, and been variously modified, from the circumstances of mankind, and from the different improvements in

347

society, are on this account, objects of great curiosity, which present an important and leading speculation in the natural history of law.

All government appears to be ultimately derived from two great principles. The first which I shall call *authority*, is the immediate effect of the peculiar qualities or circumstances, by which any one member of society may be exalted above another. The second is the consideration of the advantages to be derived from any political establishment.

1. Superior bodily qualities, agility, strength, dexterity of hand, especially in using the weapons employed in fighting—as well as uncommon mental endowments, wisdom, knowledge, fidelity, generosity, courage, are the natural sources of admiration and respect, and consequently of deference and submission. A school-boy, superior to his companions in courage and feats of activity, becomes often a leader of the school, and acquires a very despotic authority. The strongest man of a parish assumes a pre-eminence in their common diversions, and is held up as their champion in every match or contest with their neighbours. The patriarchal government in the primitive ages of the world, and the authority possessed by the leaders of barbarous tribes in those periods which preceded the accumulation of property, are known to have arisen from similar circumstances. The heroes and demi-gods of antiquity, were indebted solely to their valour, and their wonderful exploits, for that enthusiastic admiration which they excited, and for that sovereign power to which they were frequently exalted.

The acquisition of property, whether derived from occupancy and labour in conformity to the rules of justice, or from robbery and oppression, in defiance of every law, human and divine, became another and a more extensive source of authority. Wealth, however improperly in the eye of a strict moralist, seldom fails to procure a degree of admiration and respect. The poor are attracted and dazzled by the apparent happiness and splendour of the rich; and they regard a man of large fortune with a sort of wonder, and partial prepossession, which disposes them to magnify and over-rate all his advantages. If they are so far beneath him as not to be soured by the malignity of envy, they behold with pleasure and satisfaction the sumptuousness of his table, the magnificence of his equipage, the facility and quickness with which he is whirled from place to place, the number of his attendants, the readiness with which they observe all his movements, and run to promote his wishes. Delighted with a situation which appears to them so agreeable, and catching from each other the contagion of sympathetic feelings, they are often prompted by an enthusiastic fervour, to exalt his dignity, to promote his enjoyments, and to favour his pursuits. Without distinguishing the objects which figure in their imagination, they transfer to his person that superiority which belongs properly to his condition, and are struck with those accomplishments, and modes of behaviour, which his education has taught him to acquire, and which his rank and circumstances have rendered habitual to him. They are of course embarrassed in his presence by impressions of awe and reverence, and, losing sometimes the exercise of their natural powers, are sunk in abasement and stupidity.*

The authority, however, of the rich over the poor is, doubtless, chiefly supported by selfish considerations. As in spending a great fortune, the owner gives employment, and consequently subsistence, to many individuals, all those who, in this manner, obtain or expect any advantage, have more or less an interest in paying him respect and submission. The influence which may be traced from this origin, operates in such various directions, is distributed in such different proportions, and so diffused through every corner of society, that it appears in its degree and extent to be incalculable. Uncommon personal talents occur but seldom; and the sphere of their activity, so to speak, is often very limited. But the inequalities in the division of wealth are varied without end; and though their effect is greater in some situations of mankind than in others, they never cease, in any, to introduce a correspondent gradation and subordination of ranks.

These original circumstances, from which authority is derived, are gradually confirmed and strengthened by their having long continued to flow in the same channel. The force of habit, the great controller and governor of our actions, is in nothing more remarkable than in promoting the respect and submission claimed by our superiors. By living in a state of inferiority and dependence, the mind is inured to subjection; and the ascendant which has been once gained is gradually rendered more complete and powerful.

But the force of habit is much more effectual in confirming the authority derived from wealth, than that which is founded on personal qualities. The superior endowments, either of the body or of the mind, can seldom operate very long in the same direction. The son of an eminent general, or poet, or statesman, is most commonly remarkable for none of the splendid abilities by which the father was distinguished; at the same time, that we behold him in a contrasted light, which deepens the shade of his deficiency. The case is different with relation to wealth, which, in the ordinary course of things, is transmitted, by lineal succession, from father to son, and remains for many generations in the same family. The possessor of that estate, therefore, who bears the name, and who exercises the powers which belonged to his ancestors,

* Theory of Moral Sentiments.

obtains not only the original means of creating dependence which they enjoyed, but seems to inherit, in some degree, that consideration and respect, that influence or attachment, which, by their high station, and by the distribution of their favours during a long period, they were able to accumulate. This is the origin of what is called *birth*, as the foundation of authority, which creates a popular prepossession for the representative of an ancient family, giving him the preference to an upstart, though the latter should possess greater abilities and virtues.

From the operation of these different circumstances; from the accidental superiority of personal qualities; and from the unequal distribution of wealth, aided and confirmed by the force of habit, systems of government have grown up, and been variously modified, without exciting any inquiry into their consequences, and without leading the people to examine the grounds of their submission to the constituted authorities.

2. But when, in the course of political transactions, particular persons grossly abuse their powers, or when competitions arise among individuals possessing influence and authority, and of consequence parties are formed, who espouse the interest of the respective leaders, the public attention is roused to scrutinize the pretensions of the several candidates, to compare the different modes of government which they may propose to introduce, and to examine their title to demand obedience from the rest of the community.

In such inquiries, it is hardly possible to avoid suggesting another principle, more satisfactory than that of mere authority; the general *utility* of government; or rather its absolute necessity, for preventing the disorders incident to human society. Without a subordination of ranks, without a power, vested in some men, to control and direct the behaviour of others, and calculated to produce a system of uniform and consistent operations, it is impossible that a multitude of persons, living together, should be induced to resign their own private interest, to subdue their opposite and jarring passions, and regularly to promote the general happiness.

There are natural rights, which belong to mankind antecedent to the formation of civil society. We may easily conceive that, in a state of nature, we should be entitled to maintain our personal safety, to exercise our natural liberty, so far as it does not encroach upon the rights of others; and even to maintain a property in those things which we have come to possess, by original occupancy, or by our labour in producing them. These rights are not lost, though they may be differently modified when we enter into society. A part of them, doubtless, must be resigned for the sake of those advantages to be derived from the social state. We must resign, for example, the privilege of avenging injuries, for the advantage of being protected by courts of justice. We must give up a part of our property, that the public may be enabled to afford that protection. We must yield obedience to the legislative power, that we may enjoy that good order and tranquillity to be expected from its cool and dispassionate regulations. But the rights which we resign, ought, in all these cases, to be compensated by the advantages obtained; and the restraints, of burdens imposed, ought neither to be greater, nor more numerous, than are necessary for the general prosperity and happiness.

Were we to examine, according to this criterion, the various political systems which take place in the world, how many might be weighed in the balance and found wanting? Some are defective by too great strictness of regulation, confining and hampering natural liberty by minute and trivial restraints; more have deviated widely from the purpose by too great laxity, admitting an excessive license to the various modifications of knavery and violence; but the greatest number have almost totally failed in producing happiness and security from the tyranny of individuals, or of particular orders and ranks, who, by the accidental concurrence of circumstances, acquiring exorbitant power, have reduced their fellow-citizens into a state of servile subjection. It is a mortifying reflection, to observe, that, while many other branches of knowledge have attained a high degree of maturity, the master-piece of science, the guardian of rights, and of every thing valuable, should, in many enlightened parts of the world, still remain in a state of gross imperfection. Even in countries where the people have made vigorous efforts to meliorate their government, how often has the collision of parties, the opposite attractions of public and private interest, the fermentation of numberless discordant elements, produced nothing at last but a residue of despotism.

It may here be remarked, that, when a political constitution is happily constructed, it not only excites approbation from the ultimate view of its beneficial tendency, but, like a complex machine, in which various wheels and springs are nicely adjusted, it affords additional pleasure, from our sense of order and beautiful arrangement. If we are pleased with the survey of a well-regulated farm or workhouse, in which there is nothing slovenly or misplaced, nothing lost or superfluous, but in which every operation, and every article of expense, is directed to the best advantage, how much greater satisfaction must we receive, in beholding the same regular disposition of parts, the same happy adjustment of means to a beneficial purpose, exhibited in a system so complicated and extensive, as to comprehend the moral and political movements of a great nation?

In England, where the attention of the inhabitants has been long directed to speculations of this nature, the two original principles of government, which I have mentioned, were distinguished by political writers as far back, at least, as the commencement of the contest between the king and the people, upon the accession of the House of Stewart,* and were then respectively patronized and adopted by the two great parties into which the nation was divided. The principle of *authority* was that of the tories; by which they endeavoured to justify the pretensions of the sovereign to absolute power. As the dignity of the monarch excited universal respect and reverence, and as it was not conferred by election, but had been immemorially possessed by a hereditary title, it was understood to be derived from the author of our nature, who has implanted in mankind the seeds of loyalty and allegiance. The monarch is, therefore, not accountable to his subjects, but only to the Deity, by whom he is appointed; and consequently his power, so far as we are concerned, is absolute; requiring, on our part, an unlimited passive obedience. If guilty of tyranny and oppression, he may be called to an account in the next world, for transgressing the laws of his Maker; but in this life, he is totally exempted from all restraint or punishment; and the people, whom heaven in its anger has visited with this affliction, have no other resource than prayers and supplications.

The whigs, on the other hand, founded the power of a sovereign, and of all inferior magistrates and rulers, upon the principle of *utility*. They maintained, that as all government is intended for defending the natural rights of mankind, and for promoting the happiness of human society, every exertion of power in governors, inconsistent with that end, is illegal and criminal; and it is the height of absurdity to suppose, that, when an illegal and unwarrantable power is usurped, the people have no right to resist the exercise of it by punishing the usurper. The power of a king is no otherwise of Divine appointment than any other event which happens in the dispositions of Providence; and, in the share of government which is devolved upon him, he is no more the vicegerent of God Almighty than any inferior officer, to whom the smallest or meanest branch of administration is committed.

* [The reference is no doubt chiefly to Harrington and Hobbes, Milton and Sir Edward Coke, and later Locke and Filmer; but Millar no doubt also had in mind such authors as Thomas Smith (*de republica Anglorum* or *Commonwealth*) and Bacon on one side, and King James I, *The Trew Law of Free Monarchies*, and William Barclay, *de regno et regale potestate* (1600) on the other.]

At the same time that the whigs considered the good of society as the foundation of our submission to government, they attempted to modify and confirm that principle by the additional principle of *consent*. As the union of mankind in society is a matter of choice, the particular form of government introduced into any country depends, in like manner, upon the inclination of the inhabitants. According to the general current of popular opinion, they adopt certain political arrangements, and submit to different rulers and magistrates, either by positive regulation and express contracts, or by acting in such a manner as gives room to infer a tacit agreement. As government, therefore, arose from a contract, or rather a number of contracts, either expressed or implied, among the different members of society, the terms of submission between the governors and the governed, as well as the right of punishing either party, upon a violation of those original agreements, may thence be easily and clearly ascertained.

With respect to this origin of the duty of allegiance, which has been much insisted on by the principal writers in this country, and which has of late been dressed and presented in different shapes by politicians on the continent, it seems rather to be a peculiar explanation and view of the former principle of utility, than any new or separate ground of our submission to government; and, even when considered in this light, it must be admitted with such precautions and limitations, that very little advantage is gained by it.

The obligation of a contract is liable, in all cases, to be controlled and modified by considerations of general utility; and a promise inconsistent with any great interest of society is not productive of moral obligation. In reality, men, when they come into society, are bound to preserve the natural rights of one another; and, consequently, to establish a government conducive to that end. Good government is necessary to prevent robbery, murder, and oppression; and if a man be supposed to have promised, that he would support or obey a government of an opposite tendency, it would be his duty to break such an illegal compact, and to reform such an unjust constitution.

The addition of a promise, at the same time, appears but little to increase the weight of that previous obligation. The obligation to abstain from murder, receives but little additional strength by our giving a promise to that effect.

It seems, indeed, to be a maxim universally admitted, that every nation is entitled to regulate its own government; but this proceeds upon the presumption that every nation is the best judge of what is expedient in its peculiar circumstances, and is likely to receive most benefit from that peculiar constitution which is introduced by the voice of the majority. The maxim, therefore, must be understood with exception of such political arrangements as are evidently tyrannical, and is applicable to such forms of government only, as in point of expediency admit of different opinions.

It is understood, on the other hand, that no foreign state is entitled to control or restrain its neighbours, in modelling and establishing their own political system; because, whatever pretences for such interference may be assumed, it never is dictated by a benevolent purpose, but commonly proceeds from selfish and sinister motives.* As different states have always a separate, and very frequently an opposite, interest, it must be expected that each will invariably pursue its own; and that, in seeking to aggrandize itself, the constant object of its policy, whether professed or concealed, will be to limit the power, and prevent the aggrandizement of its neighbours. There could not, therefore, exist a more fatal calamity to any country, than that its administration and government should be settled under the direction of its neighbours.

There occur, at the same time, a variety of circumstances, in which it should seem, that the inhabitants of a country, by living under the protection of its laws, give no good reason to infer a tacit promise of submission to its government.

It would be absurd to suppose, that the inhabitants of Turkey have given a free consent to support that government under which they live. Even in other countries, less benumbed with ignorance and stupidity, or sunk in the lethargy of despotism, a great part of the inhabitants feel themselves under a sort of necessity to remain where the language and habits of life are familiar to them, where they enjoy the comfortable intercourse of their friends, and where they have already secured the regular means of subsistence.† Their submission to the government is, therefore, extorted by the prospect of those inconveniencies which would attend their emigration; and, if it were at all to be regarded in the light of a promise, would be such a one as ought to be set aside from equitable considerations.

When we examine historically the extent of the tory and of the whig principle, it seems evident, that from the progress of arts and commerce, the former has been continually diminishing, and the latter gaining ground in the same proportion. In England, so late as the year 1688:

> 'The right divine of kings to govern ill,'

was a doctrine still embraced in general by the landed gentry, by the church, and by a great part of the nation; and had it not been for the

---

* [A reference, clearly, to France and Pitt's war policy against France. See *Letters of Crito, passim.*]

† [Cp. Hume's essay, 'Of the Original Contract'.]

terror of popery, the revolution at that time would not have taken place. Since that period, however, there has been a gradual progress of opinions. Philosophy has been constantly advancing in all the departments of science; has been employed in reducing all the works of art, all the appearances of nature, to their principles; and has not neglected to push her researches into political, as well as other branches of speculation. The mysteries of government have been more and more unveiled; and the circumstances which contribute to the perfection of the social order have been laid open. The degrees of power committed to individuals have been placed on their proper basis; and the chief magistrate, when stripped of his artificial trappings, and when the mist of prepossession which had surrounded him is dispelled, appears naked, and without disguise, the real servant of the people, appointed for the important purpose of superintending, and putting in motion the great political machine. The blind respect and reverence paid to ancient institutions has given place to a desire of examining their uses, of criticising their defects, and of appreciating their true merits. The fashion of scrutinizing public measures, according to the standard of their utility, has now become very universal; it pervades the literary circles, together with a great part of the middling ranks, and is visibly descending to the lower orders of the people.*

During the rebellion in 1745, a gentleman of some eminence, who had embarked in that ridiculous project, is said to have distinguished himself, by defending the measure upon what were called whig principles. This was at that time regarded as a novelty, and was far from being well received by his associates; but so great has been the progress of opinion since that period, that the more liberal part of the tories have now caught universally the mode of reasoning employed by their adversaries, and are accustomed to justify the degree of monarchical power which they wish to establish, not by asserting that it is the inherent birthright of the sovereign, but by maintaining that it is necessary for the suppression of tumult and disorder.

Even that hardy race, who formerly issued from their mountains to attack him whom they considered as the usurper of the throne, are long

* [Cf. his observation apropos of the alleged alarm of the European autocrats over developments in France:

'Their authority was obviously founded upon opinion; and that opinion rested upon old custom and prejudice. If the people should once be led to *think* upon the subject of government, they must immediately see the absurdity of sacrificing their lives, and everything they hold valuable, to the private interest, to the avarice and ambition, to the whim and caprice of a single individual. They must immediately see that government is intended, by the wise and good Author of nature, for the benefit of the whole community; and that every power, inconsistent with this great principle, assumed by any person, under whatever title, of prince king, or emperor, is manifestly unjust and tyrannical.' *Letters of Crito*, p. 9.]

since fully reconciled to the beneficial government of a German elector, raised by an act of parliament to the sovereignty of a free people.*

The whigs themselves have not been exempted from the progressive operation of the same circumstances, which have gradually exalted their speculative principles, and occasioned a proportional change in their practical system. It cannot be overlooked, that the disposition to pry into the abuses of government is likely to suggest limitations in the power of rulers; and when a people at large employ themselves in discussing the advantages arising from different political arrangements, they must feel a bias in favour of that system, which tends to the equalization of ranks, and the diffusion of popular privileges.†

The despotism, which had long been deeply rooted upon the neighbouring continent, checked the progress of political speculation, and taught the people, not only to suffer, but even to exult in their fetters. Philosophy, however, triumphed at length over ancient customs; and the light of science, which had long been diffused in every other department, discovered the rights of man, and the true principles of government. The nation awoke, as from a dream of horror and distress. Their enthusiasm in correcting abuses, and in propagating the new system, rose to a height proportioned to the danger which they had escaped, and the obstacles which they had to surmount. It bore down all opposition; it swept away those corrupt institutions which had been the work of ages; it levelled with the dust those bulwarks which avarice and ambition had erected for maintaining their encroachments; but unhappily, in the general wreck of opinions, it overthrew those banks and landmarks, which, while they defended the civil rights of the inhabitants, might have contributed to direct and regulate the new establishment.

It seems worthy of remark, that when the new system in France appeared likely to spread over the rest of Europe, the alarm and panic which it struck among the inhabitants of this country, was chiefly

---

* See Addison's verses to Sir Godfrey Kneller.

† Hence the distinction between the *old* and the *new* whigs, by which a famous political character endeavoured lately to cover the desertion of his former tenets; and hence too a pretty general suspicion, that many nominal adherents of that party have become secret admirers of democracy. [Millar had been an ardent admirer of Burke's. In a letter addressed to him as of 13 November, 1785, Millar writes:

'For my own part I must look upon it as one of the most fortunate circumstances of my life that brought me into your acquaintance by connecting me with you as a member of the same society [the University of Glasgow, where Burke was then Rector], a connection which I cannot bring myself to think of relinquishing.'

But in his remarks here, and in his much sharper language in the *Letters of Crito* (pp. 32 f.), he has become critical of Burke, perhaps unable to forgive him his unkindly break with Fox, whom Millar continued to follow. Ed.]

excited by a prospect of the dangers with which they were threatened, and the arguments employed in opposing and combating that system, were drawn entirely from the anarchy and confusion, the destruction of all rights and liberties, religious and civil, with which it would be attended; and the chief alarmists were taken from that class of men who had been denominated whigs.*

Upon the whole, it is evident that the diffusion of knowledge tends more and more to encourage and bring forward the principle of utility in all political discussions; but we must not thence conclude that the influence of mere authority, operating without reflection is entirely useless. From the dispositions of mankind to pay respect and submission to superior personal qualities, and still more to a superiority of rank and station, together with that propensity which every one feels to continue in those modes of action to which he has long been accustomed, the great body of the people, who have commonly neither leisure nor capacity to weigh the advantages of public regulations, are prevented from indulging their unruly passions, and retained in subjection to the magistrate. The same dispositions contribute in some degree to restrain those rash and visionary projects, which proceed from the ambition of statesmen, or the wanton desire of innovation, and by which nations are exposed to the most dreadful calamities. Those feelings of the human mind, which give rise to authority, may be regarded as the wise provision of nature for supporting the order and government of society; and they are only to be regretted and censured, when, by exceeding their proper bounds, they no longer act in subordination to the good of mankind, but are made, as happens, indeed, very often, the instruments of tyranny and oppression.†

* [A reference, undoubtedly, also to Burke. This whole passage confirms, of course, what was said above (in chapter VII) on Millar's attitude toward the French Revolution. This was presumably written or revised at least late in the 90's.]

† [It need hardly be remarked, that this whole essay is remarkably revealing not only of Millar's political theory, but also of his personal political philosophy—which was a many-sided one.]

SELECTION III

THREE STUDIES IN HISTORICAL CAUSATION

In all three of these selections we see Millar addressing himself to some outstanding political, religious or social and economic event or movement in English history and attempting to explain or otherwise interpret it, in his own characteristic manner, by reference to various economic, environmental, political or other historical factors, not to the denial, but to the minimizing of any ideal elements or personal leadership roles.

A. HOW AND WHY THE GREAT CHARTERS OF ENGLISH LIBERTIES CAME TO BE GRANTED

The passage reproduced here follows a brief account of the granting of the Magna Charta by King John in 1215, the Charter of the Forest by Henry III in 1217, and their confirmation or reaffirmation by Edward I in 1297, with passing reference also to the charters earlier granted by Henry I and Henry II (1154–89). The reference is *Historical View*, vol. II, ch. I, pp. 74–82. See also pp. 58–74.

1. When we take a view of these great transactions, and endeavour to estimate the degree of attention which they merit, their number, their similarity, and the long intervals of time at which they were procured, are circumstances which cannot be overlooked. Had one charter only been granted by the sovereign, on a singular occasion, it might well be supposed to have arisen from a concourse of accidents, and from partial views. Instead of expressing the opinions entertained by the king and his people, concerning the rights of either, it might, in that case, have been the effect of a mere casual advantage, which the one party had gained over the other; and, so far from displaying the ordinary state of the government at that period, it might have exhibited the triumph and injustice of a temporary usurpation. But those important stipulations, not to mention the confirmations of them in a later period, were begun and repeated under the reigns of six different monarchs, comprehending a course of about two hundred years; they were made with princes of extremely different characters, and in very opposite situations; and though, by the insertion of different articles, those deeds were gradually expanded, and accommodated to the circumstances of the

times, yet their main object continued invariably the same; to limit those abuses of prerogative, which, from the nature of the monarchy, were most likely to be committed. Taking those charters, therefore, in connexion with one another, they seem to declare, in a clear and un-equivocal manner, the general and permanent sense of the nation, with respect to the rights of the crown; and they ascertain, by express and positive agreement between the king and his subjects, those terms of submission to the chief magistrate, which, in most other governments, are no otherwise explained than by long usage, and which have there-fore remained in a state of uncertainty and fluctuation.

2. It seems to be a common opinion, that, by these charters, the crown was deprived of many of those powers which had been assumed by William the Conqueror, or by his son William Rufus, and the constitution was brought nearer to that equal balance, which it had maintained under the direction of the Saxon princes. In particular, by the charter of king John (for the preceding charters have been fre-quently overlooked) it has always been supposed that the bounds of the prerogative were greatly limited. But upon examination it will be found, that this opinion is contrary to the real state of the fact. During the whole period which we are now considering; that is, from the Norman conquest to the time of Edward the First; while the barons were exerting themselves, with so much vigour, and with so much apparent success, in restraining the powers of the crown, those powers were, notwithstanding, continually advancing; and the repeated concessions, made by the sovereign, had no farther effect than to prevent his authority from increasing so rapidly as it might otherwise have done. For a proof of this we can appeal to no better authority than that of the charters themselves; from which, if examined according to their dates, it will appear, that the nobility were daily becoming more moderate in their claims; and that they submitted, in reality, to a gradual extension of the prerogative; though, by more numerous regulations, they endeavoured to avoid the wanton abuses of it. Thus, by the great charter of Henry the Third, the powers of the crown are less limited than by the charter of king John; and by this last the crown-vassals abandoned some important privileges with which they were invested by the charter of Henry the First.

In the charter of Henry the First, *the incident of wardship*, the severest and most oppressive of all the feudal incidents, is relinquished by the sovereign; and, according to the same charter, the *incident of marriage* extended no farther than to prevent the vassals of the crown from marrying any woman with whose family the superior was at variance. But, in the reign of king John, the incident of wardship had taken such root, that the crown vassals no longer thought of disputing the continuance of it; and that of marriage had been so much enlarged, as to imply a right in the superior to prohibit his vassals from marrying without his consent, and even to require that they should marry any woman whom he presented to them. In the charter of this monarch, therefore, the former incident is understood to be completely established and some regulations are made to prevent abuses in making it effectual. With regard to the latter, it is provided that the heirs of a vassal shall be married without *disparagement*, that is, they shall not be required to contract unsuitable alliances; and, to secure them from imposition or undue influence, in a matter of this kind, it is farther stipulated, that before they contract any marriage their nearest relations shall be informed of it.*

The charter of king John may, on the other hand, be compared with that of Henry the Third, in relation to *aids* and *scutages*, a sort of indirect taxes, from which a considerable part of the crown-revenue was derived. By the charter of John, the exclusive power of imposing those duties is committed to parliament; but that of Henry the Third is entirely silent upon this point; and leaves the monarch under no restraint in imposing such burdens by virtue of his own prerogative. It is true, that the former limitation upon this part of the prerogative was afterwards renewed in the reign of Edward the First.†

What I have observed, concerning the variations in the series of great charters, does not seem applicable to the laws of the forest. The violations of private property, committed in this respect by William the First, and his successors, were too notorious to be seriously defended; and therefore, notwithstanding the general progress of monarchy, it was thought necessary to remove these abuses, and to guard against them for the future.

3. Whoever enquires into the circumstances in which these great charters were procured, and into the general state of the country at that time, will easily see that the parties concerned in them were not actuated by the most liberal principles; and that it was not so much their intention to secure the liberties of the people at large, as to establish the privileges of a few individuals. A great tyrant on the one side, and a set of petty tyrants on the other, seem to have divided the kingdom; and the great body of the people, disregarded and oppressed on all hands, were beholden for any privileges bestowed upon them, to the jealousy of their masters; who, by limiting the authority of each other over their dependants, produced a reciprocal diminution of their

* [Text followed here is that of the first edition.]
† 34 Edw. I, stat. 4, cap. i.—Also 25 Edw. I. 2, 5, 6.

power.* But though the freedom of the common people was not intended in those charters, it was eventually secured to them; for when the peasantry, and other persons of low rank, were afterwards enabled, by their industry, and by the progress of arts, to emerge from their inferior and servile condition, and to acquire opulence, they were gradually admitted to the exercise of the same privileges which had been claimed by men of independent fortunes; and found themselves entitled, of course, to the benefit of that free government which was already established. The limitations of arbitrary power, which had been calculated chiefly to promote the interest of the nobles, were thus, by a change of circumstances, rendered equally advantageous to the whole community as if they had originally proceeded from the most exalted spirit of patriotism.

When the commons, in a later period, were disposed to make further exertions, for securing their natural rights, and for extending the blessings of civil liberty, they found it a singular advantage to have an ancient written record, which had received the sanction of past ages, and to which they could appeal for ascertaining the boundaries of the prerogative. This gave weight and authority to their measures; afforded a clue to direct them in the mazes of political speculation; and encouraged them to proceed with boldness in completing a plan, the utility of which had already been put to the test of experience. The regulations, indeed, of this old canon, agreeable to the simplicity of the times, were often too vague and general to answer the purposes of regular government; but, as their aim and tendency were sufficiently apparent, it was not difficult, by a proper commentary, to bestow upon them such expansion and accommodation as might render them applicable to the circumstances of an opulent and polished nation.

B. CAUSES OF THE REFORMATION UNDER HENRY VIII

This passage comes from vol. II of the *Historical View*, pp. 427–37.

The most remarkable event, in the reign of Henry the Eighth, was the sudden downfall of the great system of ecclesiastical tyranny, which,

---

* [Note this comparable observation on another 'pillar of the British constitution':
' The effect of this maxim, in supporting the democratical part of the government, is now universally admitted; but that it was dictated by a regard to the interest of the people, or from the view of increasing their weight in the exertions of the legislature, there is no reason to believe. . . . not the fruit of any preconceived system of policy, nor the result of any claim of right, . . . ; it arose merely from the nature of the business under consideration, which was most conveniently brought to an issue in that manner. . . .' (*H.V.* vol. II, pp. 260 f.)]

during the course of many centuries, the policy of the Roman pontiff had been continually extending. To this religious reformation, the minds of men, in other European countries as well as in England, were predisposed and excited by the changes which had lately occurred in the general state of society.

1. The Christian religion, by teaching mankind to believe in the unity of the Deity, presented to their minds the contemplation of the astonishing attributes displayed in the government of the universe. While the professors of Christianity thus agreed in the main article of their belief, their disposition to speculate upon other points was promoted by their differences of opinion, by the controversies with one another in which they were unavoidably engaged, and by the variety of sects into which they were at length divided. The church, however, assumed the power of determining the orthodox faith; and by degrees availed herself of the prevailing superstition, in order to propagate such opinions as were most subservient to her interest. Hence the doctrines relating to purgatory, to the imposition of penances, to auricular confession, to the power of granting a remission of sins, or a dispensation from particular observances, with such other tenets and practices as contributed to increase the influence of the clergy, were introduced and established. Not contented with requiring an implicit belief in those particular opinions, the church proceeded so far as to exclude entirely the exercise of private judgment in matters of religion; and, in order to prevent all dispute or enquiry upon that subject, even denied to the people the perusal of the sacred scriptures, which had been intended to direct the faith and manners of Christians. A system of such unnatural restraint, which nothing but extreme ignorance and superstition could have supported, it was to be expected that the first advances of literature would be sufficient to overturn. Upon the revival of letters, accordingly, in the fourteenth and fifteenth centuries, it was no longer possible to prevent mankind from indulging their natural propensity in the pursuit of knowledge, and from examining those fundamental tenets of Christianity which had been so anxiously withheld from their view. They were even prompted, so much the more, to pry into the mysteries of religion, because it was prohibited. To discover the absurdity of many of those doctrines, to which an implicit assent had been required, was not difficult. But the mere examination of them was to reject the decrees of the church, and to merit the censure of contumacy.

2. While the advancement of knowledge disposed men to exert their own judgment in matters of religion, the progress of arts, and of luxury, contributed to diminish the personal influence of the clergy. 'In

the province of arts, manufactures, and commerce,' says the ingenious and profound author of the Inquiry into the Nature and Causes of the Wealth of Nations:*

the clergy, like the great barons, found something for which they could exchange their rude produce, and thereby discovered the means of spending their whole revenue upon their own persons, without giving any considerable share of them to other people. Their charity became gradually less extensive, their hospitality less liberal, or less profuse. Their retainers became consequently less numerous, and by degrees dwindled away altogether. The clergy, too, like the great barons, wished to get a better rent from their landed estates, in order to spend it, in the same manner, upon the gratification of their own private vanity and folly. But this increase of rent could be got only by granting leases to their tenants, who thereby became, in a great measure, independent of them. The ties of interest, which bound the inferior ranks of people to the clergy, were, in this manner, gradually broken and dissolved.—The inferior ranks of people no longer looked upon that order, as they had done before, as the comforters of their distress, and the relievers of their indigence. On the contrary, they were provoked and disgusted by the vanity, luxury, and expense of the richer clergy, who appeared to spend upon their own pleasures what had always before been regarded as the patrimony of the poor.

3. The improvement of arts, which obliged the dignified clergy, as well as the great barons, to dismiss their retainers, enabled this inferior class of men to procure subsistence in a different manner, by the exercise of particular trades and professions. By this way of life, they were placed in a condition which rendered them less dependent upon their superiors, and by which they were disposed to resist every species of tyranny, whether ecclesiastical or civil. That spirit of liberty, however, which, from these circumstances, was gradually infused into the great body of the people, began sooner to appear in opposing the usurpations of the church, than in restraining the encroachments of the king's prerogative. In pulling down the fabric of ecclesiastical powe., and in stripping the clergy of their wealth, all who had any prospect of sharing in the spoil might be expected to give their concurrence. But in limiting the power of the crown, the efforts of the people were counteracted by the whole weight of the civil authority. Thus, in England, the reformation was introduced more than a century before the commencement of the struggle between Charles the First and his parliament; although the

* I am happy to acknowledge the obligations I feel myself under to this illustrious philosopher, by having, at an early period of life, had the benefit of hearing his lectures on the *History of Civil Society* [emphasis ours.—Ed.], and of enjoying his unreserved conversation on the same subject.—The great Montesquieu pointed out the road. He was the Lord Bacon in this branch of Philosophy. Dr Smith is the Newton.

same principle which produced the latter of these events, was evidently the chief cause of the former.

But whence has it happened, that the circumstances above-mentioned have operated more effectually in some parts of Europe than in others? What has enabled the pope to retain in obedience one half of his dominions, while the other has rejected his authority? That this was owing, in some measure, to accident, it seems impossible to deny. The existence of such a person as Luther in Germany, the dispute that arose in England between Henry the Eighth and his wife, the policy of particular princes, which led them to promote or to oppose the interest of his holiness; these, and other such casual occurrences, during the course of this great religious controversy, had undoubtedly a considerable influence in determining its fate. We may take notice, however, of certain fixed causes, which contributed more to the progress of the reformation in some of the European countries than in others.

1. The Roman pontiff found it easier to maintain his authority in the neighbourhood of his capital than in countries at a greater distance. The superstition of the people was not, indeed, greater in the neighbourhood of Rome than in the distant parts of Europe. The contrary is well known to have been the case. But Rome was the centre of ecclesiastical preferment, and the residence, as well as the occasional resort, of great numbers of the most opulent churchmen, whose influence over the people was proportionably extensive. Here the pope was a temporal, as well as an ecclesiastical sovereign; and could employ the arm of flesh, as well as the arm of the spirit. Besides, he had here a better opportunity, than in remoter countries, of observing and managing the dispositions and humours of the inhabitants; and, being at hand to discover the seeds of any disorder, was enabled to crush a rebellion in the bud. This circumstance tended to prevent, or to check, the reformation in Italy, or in France, more than in Sweden, in Denmark, in Germany, in England, or in Scotland.

2. Independent of accidental circumstances, it was to be expected that those countries, which made the quickest progress in trade and manufactures, would be the first to dispute and reject the papal authority. The improvement of arts, and the consequent diffusion of knowledge, contributed, on the one hand, to dispel the mist of superstition, and, on the other, to place the bulk of a people in situations which inspired them with sentiments of liberty. That principle, in short, which is to be regarded as the general cause of the reformation, produced the most powerful effects in those countries where it existed the soonest, and met with the greatest encouragement.

This alone will account for the banishment of the Romish religion from the independent towns of Germany, from the Dutch provinces, and from England; those parts of Europe which were soon possessed of an extensive commerce. In the ten provinces of the Netherlands, the advancement of trade and manufactures was productive of similar effects. The inhabitants acquired an attachment to the doctrines of the reformation; and maintained them with a degree of courage and firmness which nothing less than the whole power of the Spanish monarchy was able to subdue. In France too the same spirit became early conspicuous, in that part of the inhabitants which had made the greatest improvement in arts; and, had it not been for the most vigorous efforts of the crown, accompanied with the most infamous perfidy and barbarity, and assisted by the celebrated league of the Catholic powers, it is probable that Calvinism would have obtained the dominion of the Gallican church. The tendency of mercantile improvements to introduce an abhorrence of the Catholic superstition, and of papal domination, is thus equally illustrated from the history of those kingdoms where it prevailed, as of those where, by the concurrence of casual events, it was obstructed and counteracted.

3. In those countries where the smallness of a state had given rise to a republican constitution, the same notions of liberty were easily extended from civil to ecclesiastical government. The people, in those governments, were not only disposed to reject the authority of the pope, as they did that of a temporal sovereign; but were even disgusted with the hierarchy, no less than with that subordination which is required in a monarchy. Hence that high-toned species of reformation, which began in Geneva, and in some of the Swiss cantons; and which, from the weakness and imprudent opposition of the crown, was introduced by the populace into Scotland.

The small states of Italy, indeed, although they fell under a republican government, and some of them were distinguished by their early advancement in commerce, have remained in the Catholic church. In some of the cantons of Switzerland, notwithstanding their very limited extent, and their popular government, the reformation has likewise been unsuccessful. The vicinity of the pope's residence, and of his temporal dominions, appear, in spite of the circumstances which had so plainly an opposite tendency, to have retained them under his jurisdiction. It may deserve, however, to be remarked, that the Venetians, the principal traders of Italy, and who formed the most eminent republic, though they did not establish the doctrines of any sect of the reformers, effected what is perhaps more difficult, and had more the appearance of moderation: they diminished the authority of the pope, without rejecting it altogether; and, though they did not attempt to root out the ancient system, they lopped off such parts of it as they deemed inconsistent with their civil constitution.

C. CONCURRENCE OF EVENTS PRODUCING THE COMMERCIAL AND INDUSTRIAL REVOLUTIONS OF THE ELIZABETHAN AGE

This passage (taken from *H.V.* vol. II, ch. VIII, pp. 375–85) shows with remarkable clarity Millar's appreciation of the impact of a number of key events in early modern history on the economic transformation of England.

Towards the end of the sixteenth, and the beginning of the seventeenth century, three great events concurred to produce a remarkable revolution upon the state of trade and manufactures in general, and that of Europe in particular.

1. The first of these was the invention of the mariner's compass; which changed the whole system of navigation, by enabling navigators to find their way with certainty in the wide ocean, to undertake more distant expeditions, and to complete them with much greater quickness. When this discovery had been properly ascertained, and reduced to practice, those who inhabited the coast of a narrow sea had no longer that superiority, with respect to commerce, which they formerly possessed; for, whatever advantages they might have in a small coasting navigation, these were overbalanced by the inconveniencies of their situation, whenever they had occasion to sail beyond those adjacent capes or promontories by which they were limited and circumscribed. The harbours, which became then most favourable to commerce, were such as had formerly been least so; those which were the farthest removed from straits, or dangerous shores, and, by their distance from opposite lands, admitted the freest passage to every quarter of the globe.

2. The discovery of America, and the opening of a passage to the East-Indies by the Cape of Good Hope, which may be regarded as a consequence of the preceding improvement in navigation, contributed still farther to change the course of European trade. By these discoveries a set of new and magnificent objects of commerce was presented, and Europe began to entertain the prospect of forming settlements in distant countries; of trading with nations in various climates, producing a proportional variety of commodities; and of maintaining an easy correspondence between the remotest parts of the world. The merchants of Italy, and of the Northern parts of Germany, were naturally left behind, in the prosecution of these magnificent views. Their situation,

hemmed in by the coast of the Baltic, or of the Mediterranean, was particularly unfavourable for that new species of trade. They had, besides, a reluctance, we may suppose, to abandon their old habits, and to relinquish that settled traffic in which they had been long engaged, for the new and hazardous adventures which were then pointed out to them. Adhering, therefore, to their former course, they found their profits decrease according as the new commerce became considerable; and their commercial importance was at length, in a great measure, sunk and annihilated.

3. The violent shock given, by the Spanish government, to the trading towns of the Netherlands, occasioned, about this period, a change in the manufactures of Europe, no less remarkable than the two foregoing circumstances produced in its commerce. Philip the Second of Spain embraced the narrow and cruel policy of his father Charles the Fifth, in attempting to extirpate the doctrines of Luther throughout his dominions; at the same time that he added a bigotry peculiar to himself, which led him to seek the accomplishment of his purpose by measures yet more imprudent and sanguinary. The doctrines of the reformation had been spread very universally in the Netherlands; and had been adopted with a zeal not inferior to that which appeared in any other part of Europe. Philip employed the whole force of the Spanish monarchy in order to subdue that spirit of religious innovation; and, after a long and obstinate struggle, he at last prevailed; but it was by extirpating a great part of the inhabitants, and ruining the manufactures of the country. The most independent and spirited, that is, the most active and skilful part of the manufacturers, disdaining to submit to a tyranny by which they were oppressed in their most valuable rights, fled from their native country; and, finding a refuge in other European nations, carried along with them that knowledge and dexterity in manufactures, and those habits of industry, which they possessed in so eminent a degree.

Of all the European nations, Great Britain was in a condition to reap the most immediate profit from these important changes in the state of commerce and manufactures.

England has long enjoyed the peculiar advantage of rearing a greater number of sheep, and producing larger quantities of wool, fit for manufacture, than most other parts of the world. This is probably derived from the flatness of the country, by which a great part of it is plentifully supplied with moisture, and from the moderate temperature of its climate; both of which circumstances appear favourable to the production of pasture, and to the proper cultivation of sheep. But, whatever be the causes of it, the fact is certain, that, Spain excepted, no other country can, in this particular, be brought in competition with England. Particular mention is made of the English wool, even when Britain was a Roman province; and, in the early periods of our history, the exportation of that commodity was a considerable article of commerce. What is remarkable, the English wool of former times appears to have been of a finer quality than the present; and there is even reason to believe that it was held superior to the Spanish.* Of this extraordinary fact it seems difficult to give any satisfactory account. I am credibly informed, that the improvements, made of late years, in the pasture-grounds of England, have greatly debased the quality of the wool; though, by the increase of the quantity, they have sufficiently indemnified the proprietors.

By possessing the raw material in great plenty, the English appear to have been incited, at an early period, to make some attempts toward the fabrication of it. The woollen cloth of England is taken notice of while the country was under the dominion of the Romans. The disorders which followed while the Saxons were subduing the country, and during the subsequent ravages of the Danes, gave great interruption to manufactures; but, soon after the Norman conquest, and particularly in the reigns of Henry the Third and Edward the First, that of woollen cloth appears to have become an object of attention.

The flourishing reign of Edward the Third was extremely favourable to improvements; and that enterprising monarch, notwithstanding his ardour in the pursuit of military glory, was attentive to reform the internal policy of the kingdom, and gave particular encouragement to the woollen manufacture. He invited and protected foreign manufacturers; and, in his reign, a number of Walloon weavers, with their families, came and settled in England. An act of parliament was made, which prohibited the wearing of foreign cloth; and another, by which the exportation of wool was declared to be felony. These regulations, however narrow the principles upon which they were built, were certainly framed with the best intentions; but they could have little or no effect, as the English, at that time, were neither capable of manufacturing the whole of their wool, nor even of supplying their own demand for woollen cloth. The crown, therefore, in virtue of its dispensing power, was accustomed to relieve the raisers of wool, by granting occasionally, to individuals, a licence for exportation; and, as a dispensation in this case was absolutely necessary to procure a market for the commodity, it became the source of a revenue to the sovereign, who obtained a price for every licence which he bestowed.

* See Observations upon National Industry, by James Anderson, and the authorities to which he refers.

The woollen trade of England made considerable advances in the reign of Henry the Seventh, when, after a long course of civil dissension, the people began to enjoy tranquillity under a prince who favoured and protected the arts of peace. About this time were set on foot the coarse woollen manufactures of Yorkshire; particularly at Wakefield, Leeds, and Halifax; places remarkably well adapted to that species of work, from the plenty of coal, and the numerous springs of water with which they are supplied.

The extension of manufactures, about this period, became so considerable as to produce an alteration in the whole face of the country; and in particular, gave rise to remarkable improvements in husbandry, and in the different arts connected with it. The enlargement of towns and villages, composed of tradesmen and merchants, could not fail to increase the demand for provisions in the neighbourhood, and, by enhancing the value of every article raised by the farmers, to advance the profits of their employment. From this improvement of their circumstances, the tenants were soon enabled, by offering an additional rent, to procure leases for a term of years; and the master, whose daily expenses were increased by the progress of trade and luxury, was content to receive a pecuniary compensation, for the loss of that authority over his dependants, which he was obliged to relinquish. Thus the freedom and independence, which the mercantile and manufacturing people derived from the nature of their employment, was, in some measure, communicated to the peasantry; who, instead of remaining tenants at will, were secured for a limited term in the possession of their farms.

In consequence of these changes, the number of villains in England was greatly diminished, in the reign of Henry the Seventh; and before the accession of James the First, that class of men had entirely disappeared. Without any public law upon the subject, their condition was gradually improved by particular bargains with their master; and, according as their opulence enabled them to purchase higher privileges, they acquired longer leases, or were converted into *copyholders*, or *freeholders*.

As, from this time, the English continued, with unremitting ardour, to prosecute their improvements, and were continually advancing in opulence, as well as in skill and dexterity, and in the habits of industry, it was to be expected that, in the long run, the possession of the rude material of the woollen manufacture would give them a manifest superiority in that branch of business, and put it in their power to undersell other nations who had not the same advantage.

In the reign of queen Elizabeth, that severe blow, which I formerly mentioned, was given to the trade of the Low Countries; by which every

branch of manufacture was greatly impaired, and that of woollen
cloth was totally destroyed. Thus the destruction of the woollen trade of
the Netherlands happened at the very critical period, when the English
were come to be in a condition of turning that event to their own
emolument. The manufacturers who had been driven from their
native land found a welcome refuge from queen Elizabeth; and the
greater part of them took up their residence in England; so that the
inhabitants of the former country became, in the highest degree, in-
strumental in promoting the trade of the latter; instead of retarding or
depressing it, by that superiority of industry and skill, and that uninterrupted possession of the market which they had long maintained.*

SELECTION IV

RELIGIOUS OPINION AND CHURCH
PARTIES AND POLITICS

Of a number of possible selections on religion, the church and ecclesiastical
policy, in their social and political implications, between which we had to
choose, we present this one in which Millar characterizes the tenets and
tendencies of the major religious groups in England and Scotland in their
bearings upon the great political struggles of the Cromwellian period.
(*H.V.* vol. III, pp. 128–45, with omissions. Cp. also, vol. I, chs. v and XIII
and pp. 361 ff. above.)†

Two great religious parties, at this time, divided the whole nation; the
Protestants and the Roman Catholics: the former, who, by undaunted
resolution and fortitude, and with various success encountering severe
trials and bloody persecutions, had at length obtained a decided
superiority; the latter, who, though defeated, were not broken; and
who, though they had quitted the open field, were still powerful in
number, connections, and resources, and were only lying in wait for
the first favourable opportunity to retrieve their fortune. These two
parties were animated by mutual hatred and resentments. The oppression to which the Protestants had been subjected, and the barbarities
which at the instigation of the church, they had suffered from the
secular arm, were still fresh in their memory; while they dreaded the
machinations of a party, with whose unrelenting dispositions they were
well acquainted, and whose activity and power, seconded by the papal

---

* [Conclusion of the argument (pp. 385–90) decline of Spanish competition, development
of maritime and naval enterprise, and political stabilization, omitted for reasons of space.—Ed.]

† See also *Wealth of Nations*, Bk. V, ch. I, Pt. III, Art. 3.

influence and authority over a great part of Europe, were still very formidable. The Roman Catholics, on the other hand, could not easily forget the mortifying degradation which they had suffered; the complete overthrow of their faith and worship; the loss of their splendid and lucrative establishment; the insolence and contempt of heretics, irritated by former bad usage; and the hardships which they had reason to expect from adversaries, now triumphant, and supported by the civil magistrate. . . .

The presbyterians, who had gained the ascendancy in Scotland, were in England, about this period, the most numerous body of sectaries. Their system appears to have arisen from a natural progression of the same views and opinions by which the religious reformation had been originally suggested. They proposed to correct the abuses of the Roman Catholic church, and to guard against the undue influence and domination of the clergy, by the abolition of ecclesiastical dignities, by establishing a perfect parity among churchmen, by restricting them to very moderate livings, and by rejecting that pomp and pageantry of worship which is manifestly calculated to promote superstition, and to create in the people a blind veneration for their spiritual directors.

[The Independents, on the other hand] considered all ecclesiastical establishments as incompatible with religious freedom. To this description of religionists, the interference of government in favour of any one sect, by maintaining its clergy at the public expense, appeared a kind of persecution of every other, and an encroachment upon the rights of private judgement. . . .

These four religious parties, the Roman Catholic, the Church of England, the Presbyterian, the Independent, which comprehended nearly the whole nation, were led to embrace different political systems, and became allied to different parties in the State. The two first, in a political view, exhibited characters diametrically opposite to those of the last two; and though differing in some respects from each other, their leading features were similar.

The Roman catholic religion may be regarded as a deep-laid system of superstition, which took a firmer hold of the human mind than any other that has appeared in the world. It was founded upon a more complicated and rational theology than the rude systems of a former period; and gave rise to a multiplicity of interesting opinions and tenets, which exercised and frequently perplexed the pious believer, so as to lay him under the necessity of resorting to the aid of a religious instructor for the regulation and direction of his faith. It represented the Deity as an omnipotent, but an austere and vindictive being, capable of anger and resentment against those who transgress his laws, and intending this world, not for the present comfort and satisfaction of his creatures, but as a place of preparation for a future state of eternal happiness or misery. As all men must be conscious of great weakness and frailty, of not only deviating from the standard of perfect virtue, but of being frequently stained with numberless vices, and even atrocious crimes, which excite self-condemnation and remorse, they could not fail, upon conceiving themselves in the all-seeing eye of this impartial and severe Judge, to be covered with shame and confusion, and overwhelmed with consternation and terror. Under the impression of these feelings, it was natural that they should endeavour to procure consolation from the intercourse of some ghostly father whom they should call upon to supplicate the offended Deity in their behalf, and whose advice and direction they should eagerly solicit in attempting to atone for their transgressions, by submitting to voluntary penances or mortifications, and by every expression or demonstration of humility and abasement, of sorrow and repentance. These dispositions and circumstances of the people had produced a clergy, opulent and powerful beyond example, who had laboured to promote and regulate that superstition which was the original foundation of their authority; and who, in their advancement to riches and dominion, had, like the officers of a regular army, fallen into a subordination of power and rank. The doctrines and the practical conduct inculcated by this clergy, were such as might contribute most effectually to their own aggrandizement. The people were taught to believe in mysteries which their pastors alone pretended to explain, to approach and worship the Supreme Being by superstitious rites and ceremonies, in which the clergy presided, to discover to their spiritual instructor all their secret thoughts and actions, and, upon submitting to the discipline prescribed by the church in such cases, to receive from him absolution and pardon for their sins. In a word, the clergy were understood to have in their possession the keys of heaven; in consequence of which, the treasures of the earth, and the hearts of mankind, were laid open to them.

In the exercise and extension of their power, they were supported, not only by their ecclesiastical leader, the Roman pontiff, but also by their temporal sovereign, who, though on some occasions he might quarrel with them for their encroachments upon his prerogative, had commonly an interest to promote their influence over the people; as they, on the other hand, from his having a great share in the disposal of their livings, were induced to employ that influence in promoting and maintaining his authority. Thus, between the great power of the crown and that of the church, both of which were the offspring of ignorance and prejudice, there arose a sort of family compact, which being consolidated by length of time and by mutual habits, proved no less advantageous to either party than it was inimical to the interest of the whole community.

Of all the systems of religion established at the time of the reformation, the church of England approached the nearest to that Roman catholic stock upon which it was engrafted. It rejected, indeed, many absurd opinions adopted by the church of Rome, and, from the greater diffusion of knowledge, it acquired a more limited influence over the minds of the people. But so far as its authority extended, its character and tendency were the same. Though its features were a little softened, it presented the same aspect of superstition, the same pomp and parade of worship, the same dignitaries invested with jurisdiction and authority, the same opulence and splendour in the higher clergy, which tended to procure them consideration and respect, the same train of subordination in the ranks and orders of churchmen, which united them in one compact body, and enabled them, in promoting their common interest, to act with unanimity and vigour.

The constitution of the church of England had even a stronger tendency than that of Rome to render its clergy devoted to the interest of the crown. They were more uniformly dependent upon the sovereign, who, by the annihilation of the papal supremacy, became, without a rival, the acknowledged head of the church, and obtained the entire disposal of the higher ecclesiastical dignities.

The presbyterian and independent systems were of a different spirit and complexion. The adherents of the former, in correcting the errors and abuses of the church of Rome, had acquired a degree of ardour and enthusiasm, which led them, in their acts of public worship, to reject with indignation all forms and ceremonious observances, and to consider their approaches to the Deity, by prayer and supplication, as a mere sentimental intercourse, calculated to demonstrate and improve those feelings of the heart which were due to their Creator. They regarded the functions of a clergyman, therefore, as of no further importance than to preserve good order in the public exercise of religious worship, to inspect the behaviour of the people under his care, and to instruct them in the great duties of morality and religion. It was consistent with this moderate and rational estimation of the clerical character, that the clergy should be moderately provided in livings, that they should not be exalted one above another by any scale of dignities or jurisdiction, and that their authority, upon the whole, should be inconsiderable. By their activity, indeed, and by their attention to the duties of their profession, they were capable of gaining great influence and respect; but in order to do this, it was necessary that they should recommend themselves to the people rather than cultivate the patronage of men in power. They could, therefore, be of little service to the sovereign in supporting his prerogative, and, of consequence, had little to expect from his favour. On the contrary, as their interest and habits connected them with the populace, they entered with alacrity into the popular feelings and views, beheld with jealousy and apprehension the lofty pretensions of the crown, and sounded throughout the kingdom the alarm of regal usurpation.

As the system of the independents proceeded a step further than that of the presbyterians, by declaring against all ecclesiastical establishments, and rendering the provision of every religious instructor perfectly precarious, their clergy becoming still more dependent upon their employers, were proportionably more interested in courting popular favour, and in struggling for the extension of popular privileges.

The presbyterians, as they approved of a permanent clergy, appointed and paid by the public, and possessed of a certain jurisdiction, so, in their political system, they had no aversion to a hereditary monarch, invested with permanent civil powers, and superintending all the ordinary branches of executive government. But the independents, who held that the appointment of the clergy should be left to the discretion of those who thought proper to employ them, were led, in consistency with this doctrine, to maintain that every civil officer, whether supreme or subordinate, should likewise be elected by the community. The presbyterians, therefore, were the friends of limited monarchy. The independents preferred a democratical constitution. The connexion, however, between these religious and civil plans of government, though sufficiently obvious, was not acknowledged, nor perhaps discovered all at once; but was gradually developed and brought to light, during the course of the long contest between the king and the commons. For some time after the establishment of the reformation, the Roman Catholics continued to be the object of hatred and resentment to all denominations of protestants; but their disposition to support the prerogative did not escape the two first princes of the house of Stuart, who secretly favoured their interest, as much as they hated the presbyterians and independents. Upon pretence of lenity to tender consciences, these two princes assumed the power of dispensing with the penal statutes against *nonconformists*; but the real purpose of those dispensations was apparent to all, and the nation felt equal alarm and indignation from considering those exertions of the prerogative as no less direct and palpable violations of the constitution, than they were decided marks of predilection for a party, the apprehension of whose return into power still continued to fill the nation with terror. . . . .

. . . How inconsistent soever it may seem with the genuine principles of religious reformation, the primitive reformers, of every denomination, were no less destitute than the Roman Catholics, of that liberality of sentiment which teaches men to indulge their neighbours in the same freedom of opinion which they claim to themselves. They were, all of them, so highly impregnated with the spirit of bigotry and fanaticism as to regard any remarkable deviation from their own tenets in the light of a damnable error, which ought, by every possible means, to be corrected or suppressed; and for the attainment of this object, they were easily excited to brave every danger, and to submit to any inconvenience or hardship. Their interference, therefore, was always formidable to the civil power, and became frequently the chief cause of revolutions in government. At a subsequent period, the harshness and asperity attending the first exuberant growth of religious differences, have been gradually mellowed and softened in their progress to maturity; and the prejudices contracted in the dawn of philosophy, have been dissipated by the fuller light of science and literature, and by that cool and dispassionate inquiry which is the natural fruit of leisure, tranquillity and affluence. It may, perhaps, be considered as the strongest proof of those intellectual improvements which mankind have attained in the present age, that we have [beheld] the most astonishing political changes, to which religion has in no respect contributed, and which have been regarded by the ministers of the altar in no other light but that of pecuniary interest.

SELECTION V

SOCIAL AND POLITICAL DEVELOPMENTS UNDER THE TUDORS AND STUARTS

In this selection the emphasis is strongly on the social emancipation of the former 'lower classes' and the rise of a middle class at the expense of the nobility. It will serve also as another example of Millar's 'economic' interpretation of history. The source is *H.V.* vol. III, ch. II, pp. 101–9, 117 f.)

By the progress of these improvements [in the arts and crafts] a greater proportion of the inhabitants, instead of living as retainers or servants of the rich, became engaged in various mechanical employments, or in different branches of traffic, from which they could earn a livelihood without the necessity of courting the favour of their superiors. An artificer, whose labour is enhanced by the general demand for it, or a tradesman who sells his goods in a common market, considers himself as his own master. He says that he is obliged to his employers, or his customers; and he treats them with civility; but he does not feel himself greatly dependent upon them. His subsistence, and his profits, are derived not from one, but from a number of persons; he knows, besides, that their employment or their custom proceeds not commonly from personal favour, but from a regard to their own interest; and consequently that, while he serves them equally well, he has no reason to apprehend the decline of his business.* Rising more and more to this independent situation, artificers and tradesmen were led by degrees to shake off their ancient slavish habits, to gratify their own inclinations or humours, and to indulge that love of liberty, so congenial to the mind of man, which nothing but imperious necessity is able to subdue.

The independence and the influence of this order of people was farther promoted by the circumstance of their being collected in towns, whence they derived an extreme facility in communicating their sentiments and opinions. In a populous city, not only the discoveries and knowledge, but the feelings and passions of each individual are quickly and readily propagated over the whole. If an injury is committed, if an act of oppression is complained of, it immediately spreads an alarm, becomes the subject of clamour and censure, and excites the general indignation and resentment. Everyone roused by the example of those around him, loses the sense of his own danger in the ardour and impetuosity of his companions. Some bold and enterprising leader acquires an ascendancy over their common movements; and while their first impressions are yet warm, finds no difficulty in uniting them to defend their privileges, or to demand redress for their wrongs.

While the tradesmen, manufacturers, and merchants of England, were thus rapidly increasing in number, and advancing to such comfortable situations, many individuals in those classes were, by successful industry in the more lucrative branches of trade, and by a rigid and persevering economy, the natural effect of their habits, enabled to acquire splendid fortunes, and to reflect a degree of lustre upon the profession to which they belonged. In this, as in all other cases, property became the source of consideration and respect; and, in proportion as the trading part of the nation became opulent they obtained more weight in the community.

The progressive advancement to freedom and independence of the manufacturing and mercantile people was followed, in the natural course of things, by that of the peasantry or farmers, the other great

* [Note similarity to statements by Adam Smith on same subjects.]

class of the commonalty. From the multiplication of the trading towns, and their increasing population and riches, the consumption of all the necessaries of life was promoted, and the market for every species of provisions proportionably extended. The price of every article produced by the land was therefore enhanced by a greater competition of purchasers; and the labour of those persons employed in agriculture was called forth and rewarded by an augmentation of profits; not to mention, that the activity and enterprising genius of merchants, arising from their large capitals, their extensive dealings, and their mutual intercourse, were naturally communicated to the neighbouring farmers; who, from the limited nature of their undertakings, and from their dispersed and solitary residence, trusting to the slow experience and detached observations of each individual, were likely, independent of this additional excitement, to proceed with great caution and timidity, and therefore to advance very slowly in the knowledge of their profession. In proportion to the general improvement of agriculture, it was expected that farmers should undertake more expensive operations in manuring and meliorating their grounds; and to encourage these undertakings, the master found it necessary to give them a reasonable prospect of indemnity, by securing them for an adequate length of time in the possession of their farms. By the extension of leases of land, which became more and more universal, the farmers of England not only were emancipated from their primitive dependence, but acquired a degree of rank and importance unknown in most other countries.

The same causes which exalted the common people, diminished the influence of the nobility, or of such as were born to great fortunes. The improvement of arts, the diffusion of all those accommodations which are the natural consequence of that improvement, were accompanied with a change of manners; the ancient plainness and simplicity giving place by degrees to a relish for pleasure and to a taste of luxury and refinement, which were productive of greater expense in all the articles of living. Men of high rank, who found themselves, without any exertion of their own possessed of great wealth, were not prompted by their situation to acquire habits either of industry or of economy. To live upon their estates, to pass their time in idleness, or to follow their amusement, was regarded as their birth-right. Gaining nothing, therefore, by their industry, and exposed by the growing luxury of the times to the daily temptation of increasing their expenses, they were, of course, involved in difficulties, were obliged to devise expedients for raising money, and reduced to the necessity of purchasing an additional rent, by granting long leases, or even more permanent rights to their tenants. The ancient retainers, whom every feudal baron had been accustomed to maintain upon his estate for the purpose of defending him against all his enemies, were unavoidably dismissed; and the military services, which had been formerly exacted from the vassals, were converted into stated pecuniary payments. These conversions, indeed, were at the same time recommended from the change of manners and the alterations in the state of the country; as, by the suppression of private feuds among the great lords, and the general establishment of peace and tranquillity, the maintainence of such retainers, on account of personal defence, had become superfluous.

The nobility, or great barons, were thus deprived of that armed force, and of that multitude of adherents and dependents by which they had formerly supported their authority and dignity. Many individuals among them, from the progress of dissipation and extravagance, were at length obliged, upon the failure of other resources, to contract debts, to mortgage, and to squander away their estates. The frugal and industrious merchant, who had acquired a fortune by trade, was enabled, in such a case, to purchase what the idle and extravagant proprietor found it necessary to sell. Property in land, originally the great source of influence, was in this manner transferred from the higher to the lower classes; the character of the trader and that of the landed gentleman were in some measure confounded; and the consideration and rank of the latter were, by a change of circumstances, communicated to the former.

These gradual changes in the state of the country could not fail to affect the condition of the monarch, as well as the authority of parliament, and, in particular, the relative weight of the two houses.

The improvement of arts, and the progress of luxury and refinement, which increased the rate of living to every nobleman, or private gentleman, had necessarily the same effect upon that of the sovereign. The additional accommodations and pleasures, the various modes of elegance or ostentation, which the fashion of the times was daily introducing, occasioned a proportional addition to the expense requisite for supporting the king's household, and maintaining the dignity of the crown. The different officers and servants employed in all the branches of public business, finding their subsistence more expensive than formerly, required of course an augmentation of salaries or emoluments. From the advancement of society in civilization, from the greater accumulation of property in the hands of individuals, and from a correspondent extension of the connections and pursuits of mankind, a more complicated set of regulations became necessary for maintaining good order and tranquillity; and the number of different officers and servants in the various departments of administration was unavoidably

378

augmented. Upon all these accounts, the king, who found his ancient revenue more and more inadequate to his expenses, was laid under greater difficulties in supporting the machine of government, and obliged more frequently to solicit the aid of parliament for obtaining additional supplies. . . .

In England, as well as in other European countries which had made considerable progress in arts and manufactures, we may discover the operation of two principles which had an opposite political tendency; the independence and opulence acquired by the lower classes of the people, which tended to produce a popular government; and the introduction of mercenary armies for the purpose of national defence, which contributed to extend and support the power of the crown. This gave rise, unavoidably, to a contest between the king and the people; while the former was endeavouring to extend his prerogative, and the latter to maintain or augment their privileges.

SELECTION VI

SOCIAL CONSEQUENCES OF THE DIVISION OF LABOUR

In this selection we lift out of the essay on the influence of industrialization on 'the extension and diffusion of knowledge and literature' only those portions which bear directly on the effects of the division of labour in the factory system on the working classes, and the challenge this presents to educational policy. The picture presented is characterized by 'an habitual vacancy of thought', becoming 'like machines actuated by a regular weight', 'a tendency to render them ignorant and stupid' and 'degraded from the rank which they held in the scale of society', wrapped in a 'thicker cloud of ignorance and prejudice'. The passage comes from *H.V.*, IV, Essay, iv, pp. 143–6; 153–6; 159–61.*

There can be no doubt that this division in the labours, both of art and of science, is calculated for promoting their improvement. From the limited powers both of the mind and the body, the exertions of an individual are likely to be more vigorous and successful when confined to a particular channel, than when diffused over a boundless expanse. The athlete who limited his application to one of the gymnastic

---

* [Compare Adam Smith's *Wealth of Nations*, Bk. V, ch. I, Pt. III, Art. 2, toward the end, and *Lectures*, pp. 253–9.]

exercises, was commonly enabled to practice it with more dexterity than he who studied to become proficient in them all.

But though the separation of different trades and professions, together with the consequent division of labour and application in the exercise of them, has a tendency to improve every art or science, it has frequently an opposite effect upon the personal qualities of those individuals who are engaged in such employments. In the sciences, indeed, and even in the liberal arts, the application of those who follow particular professions can seldom be so much limited as to prove destructive to general knowledge. . . . But the mechanical arts admit such minute divisions of labour, that the workmen belonging to a manufacture are each of them employed, for the most part, in a single manual operation, and have no concern in the result of their several productions. It is hardly possible that these mechanics should acquire extensive information or intelligence. In proportion as the operation which they perform is narrow, it will supply them with few ideas; and according as the necessity of obtaining a livelihood obliges them to double their industry, they have the less opportunity or leisure to procure the means of observation, or to find topics of reflection from other quarters. As their employment requires constant attention to an object which can afford no variety of occupation to their minds, they are apt to acquire an habitual vacancy of thought, unenlivened by any prospects, but such as are derived from the future wages of their labour, or from the grateful returns of bodily repose and sleep. They become, like machines, actuated by a regular weight, and performing certain movements with great celerity and exactness, but of small compass, and unfitted for any other use. In the intervals of their work, they can draw but little improvement from the society of companions, bred to similar employments, with whom, if they have much intercourse, they are most likely to seek amusement in drinking and dissipation. . . .

Even in the same country there is a sensible difference between different professions; and, according as every separate employment gives rise to a greater subdivision of workmen and artificers, it has a greater tendency to withdraw from them the means of intellectual improvement. The business of agriculture, for example, is less capable of a minute subdivision of labour than the greater part of mechanical employments. The same workman has often occasion to plough, to sow, and to reap; to cultivate the ground for different purposes, and to prepare its various productions for the market. He is obliged alternately to handle very opposite tools and instruments; to repair, and even sometimes, to make them for his own use; and always to accommodate the different parts of his labour to the change of the seasons and to the variations of the weather. He is employed, in the management and rearing of cattle, becomes frequently a grazier and a corn-merchant, and is unavoidably initiated in the mysteries of the horse-jockey. What an extent of knowledge, therefore, must he possess! What a diversity of talents must he exercise, in comparison with the mechanic, who employs his whole labour in sharpening the point, or in putting on the head of a pin? How different the education of those two persons! The pin-maker, who commonly lives in a town, will have more of the fashionable improvements of society than the peasant; he will undoubtedly be better dressed; he will, in all probability, have more book-learning, as well as less coarseness in the tone of his voice, and less uncouthness in his appearance and deportment. . . . But in a bargain, he would, assuredly, be no match for his rival. He would be greatly inferior in real intelligence and acuteness; much less qualified to converse with his superiors, to take advantage of their foibles, to give a plausible account of his measures, or to adapt his behaviour to any peculiar and unexpected emergency.*

The circumstance now mentioned affords a view not very pleasant in the history of human society. It were to be wished that wealth and knowledge should go hand in hand, and that the acquisition of the former should lead to the possession of the latter. Considering the state of nations at large, it will, perhaps, be found that opulence and intellectual improvements are pretty well balanced, and that the same progress in commerce and manufactures which occasions an increase of the one, creates a proportional accession of the other. But, among individuals, this distribution of things is far from being so uniformly established; and, in the lower orders of the people, it appears to be completely reversed. The class of mechanics and labourers, by far the most numerous in a commercial nation, are apt, according as they attain more affluent and independent circumstances, to be more withdrawn and debarred from extensive information; and are likely, in proportion as the rest of the community advance in knowledge and literature, to be involved in a thicker cloud of ignorance and prejudice. Is there not reason to apprehend, that the common people, instead of sharing the advantages of national prosperity, are thus in danger of losing their importance, of becoming the dupes of their superiors, and of being degraded from the rank which they held in the scale of society? . . .

. . . The doctrine maintained by some politicians, that the ignorance of the labouring people is of advantage, by securing their patience and submission under the yoke which their unequal fortune has imposed

* [Note the social turn he gives to Adam Smith's illustration.]

upon them,* is no less absurd, than it is revolting to all the feelings of humanity. The security derived from so mean a source is temporary and fallacious. It is liable to be undermined by the intrigues of any plausible projector, or suddenly overthrown by the casual breath of popular opinion.

As the circumstances of commercial society are unfavourable to the mental improvements of the populace, it ought to be the great aim of the public to counteract, in this respect, the natural tendency of mechanical employments, and by the institution of schools and seminaries of education, to communicate, as far as possible, to the most useful, but humble class of citizens, that knowledge which their way of life has, in some degree, prevented them from acquiring. It is needless to observe how imperfect such institutions have hitherto been. The principal schools and colleges of Europe have been intended for the benefit merely of the higher orders; and even for this purpose, the greater part of them are not very judiciously modelled. But men of rank and fortune, and in general those who are exempted from bodily labour, have little occasion, in this respect, for the aid of the public, and perhaps would be better supplied, if left, in a great measure, to their own exertions. The execution, however, of a liberal plan for the instruction of the lower orders, would be a valuable addition to those efforts for the maintenance of the poor, for the relief of the diseased and infirm, and for the correction of the malefactor, which have proceeded from the humanity and public spirit of the present age. The parish schools in Scotland, are the only extensive provisions of that nature hitherto known in the island; and though it must be confessed that they are but ill calculated for the purposes of general education, the advantages resulting from them, even in their present state, have been distinctly felt, and very universally acknowledged.

* [Note for example Mandeville, *Fable of the Bees*.]

THE RELATIONSHIP BETWEEN MORALITY AND ECONOMICS

From the lengthy and profuse essay on the effects of commerce on morals, in three sections: 'Of Courage and Fortitude', 'Of Sobriety and Temperance', and 'Of Justice and Generosity', we offer here only a few brief selections, chiefly from the section on 'Justice and Generosity'. The whole is rich in observations and illustrative materials, both from history and from the contemporary scene, and the author attempts to maintain strict objectivity rather than to moralize on the subject; but the essay can hardly be said to add greatly to what he has said elsewhere on the theory of 'economic determinism'. A few of his generalizations and interpretations, as for example those on the decline of the military spirit, might be considered of somewhat doubtful validity. The influence of Smith's 'Moral Sentiments' is clearly in evidence in this whole essay. (See also *Lectures*, pp. 253–9.) The passage is from *H.V.*, vol. IV, pp. 174 f.; 236–41; 245–9.

The Effects of Commerce and Manufactures, and of Opulence and Civilization, upon the Morals of a People: Of Justice and Generosity.

That the dispositions and behaviour of man are liable to be influenced by the circumstances in which he is placed, and by his peculiar education and habits of life, is a proposition which few persons will be inclined to controvert. But how far this influence reaches, and what differences are to be found between the morals of rude and of civilized nations, it is not so easy to determine. The fact, I believe, has been seldom examined with that impartiality and deliberation which its importance requires. Moral and religious writers have usually thought proper to treat the subject in the style of satire and invective, and in declaiming against the vices of their own times, have been led to exalt the merit of distant ages. A late celebrated author,* possessed of uncommon powers of eloquence, has gone so far as to maintain, first in a popular discourse, and afterwards in a long serious dissertation,† that the rude and savage life is the parent of all the virtues, the vices of mankind being the proper and peculiar offspring of opulence and civilization.

Instead of combating, or of criticising such paradoxical opinions, it is proposed to examine the effects of poverty and riches, of simplicity and

* Rousseau. † [Meaning presumably the *Social Contract*.]

refinement, upon practical morality; and to compare the predominant virtues and vices of the different periods of society. We shall thence be enabled to discover the influence which the commercial improvements of Great Britain have had upon the moral character of the nation, and how far this influence has affected the political state of the people. . . .

That the advancement of arts, manufactures, and commerce, has a tendency to improve the virtue of justice in all its branches, appears indisputable.

Mankind are induced to abstain from injustice by the feelings of humanity, which dispose them to avoid hurting their neighbours, as well as by the consideration that such a conduct will be highly conducive to their own interest; and both of these principles operate with peculiar force from the circumstances in which a commercial people is placed. By commerce and manufactures, the contracts and transactions of a country are multiplied almost without end; and the possessions of individuals are extended and varied in proportion; whence the injuries arising from the breach of promise, from dishonesty and fraud, or from any violation of property, are more sensibly felt, and productive of more sympathy and regret. The advantages, at the same time, which every individual derives from a strict observance of the rules of justice, become also proportionably greater and more manifest. According as the intercourse of society is extended, it requires more and more a mutual trust and confidence, which cannot be maintained without the uniform profession and rigid practice of honesty and fair-dealing. Whoever is unable in this respect, to maintain a fair character, finds himself universally reprobated, is of course disqualified for the exercise of any lucrative profession, and becomes a sort of outcast, who, like the stricken deer, is carefully avoided by the whole herd. Compared with so dreadful a misfortune, the gain which is likely to accrue from the most artful knavery is a mere trifle.

In such a situation it becomes the object of early education to recommend and inculcate the rules of justice. Children are deterred from any failure in this respect by timely correction, and by the disgrace which attends it. At a more advanced period of life, the principles of honour, dictated by the general sentiments of mankind, and communicated through the different ranks and orders of society, confirm the same doctrine. In addition to these considerations, religion bestows her aid, by representing what is infamous among men, as offensive to the Deity, and as incurring the effects of his displeasure; while the sanctions of civil government are employed in repressing such disorders, by the salutary example of human punishments.

These principles and habits which characterize a mercantile age and country, are apt to appear most conspicuous in that part of the inhabitants who are actually engaged in trade; because they feel most powerfully the influence of the various motives which have been mentioned. In the most commercial nations of Europe, it is not, indeed, considered as inconsistent with the rules of fair trade, to lay hold of an accidental scarcity for enhancing the price of any commodity; but a merchant of credit is accustomed to deal at a word, and to take no advantage of the ignorance of his customer. Among the rest of the inhabitants, who traffic occasionally, the same scrupulous punctuality is not required; and it is not unusual to chaffer, or even to over-reach in a bargain. This is particularly the case in the sale of commodities, which have, in some degree, an arbitrary value; as of horses, where even the country gentleman is frequently not ashamed to become a species of horse-jockey.

The manners of rude nations are, in the present view, diametrically opposite to those of a commercial people. Barbarians, whatever may be their other virtues, are but little acquainted with the rules of justice; they have seldom any regard to their promises, and are commonly addicted to theft and rapine. This is evident from the history of all early nations. In Captain Cook's first voyage to Otaheite the inhabitants of that island were so far from being ashamed of their thefts, that upon being challenged, they held up the stolen goods in triumph at their success. In Kamtschatka, it is said, that a young women has difficulty to procure a husband, until she has given proof of her dexterity in filching.* Among the ancient Egyptians there was no punishment for theft;† nor among the Gauls, when the crime was committed between the members of different tribes.‡

In the highlands of Scotland, stealing of cattle was denominated *lifting*; a term to which no blame appears to have been attached; and it is a well-known fact, that an inhabitant of that country, who, upon the suppression of the rebellion, 1745, had the Pretender under his protection, and who had not been tempted to deliver him up by the great premium offered by government, was at a subsequent period tried at Inverness, and condemned to a capital punishment for horse-stealing.

As in countries highly advanced in trade and manufactures, the trading part of the inhabitants are the fairest and most punctual in their dealings, they are, in the infancy of commerce, the most knavish and dishonest.

In a rude and military age, mechanics and tradesmen, who follow

---

* See the accounts of the Russian emissaries.   † Aul. Gell. Noct. Att. lib. 11. 58.
‡ Caesar, de bell. Gall. lib. 6. 5. 23.

sedentary professions, are despised on account of their unwarlike dispositions, and from the low estimation in which they are held, become degraded in their own eyes, and regardless of their character and behaviour. The first merchants, who are a sort of pedlars, wandering from place to place, and frequently reduced to the necessity of begging their bread and their lodging among strangers, are even in a meaner condition than artificers, or labourers, who enjoy a fixed residence in the midst of their kindred and acquaintance. When Ulysses in Homer, is twitted with being a wandering merchant, the patient hero is unable to bear this unmerited reproach; and though he had before determined to conceal his rank, he starts up immediately to wipe off the aspersion, by distinguishing himself in the athletic exercises. . . .

But the circumstances of a nation which has been enriched by trade are not more friendly to justice, than unfavourable to generosity, and to the higher exertions of benevolence.

That a man should be induced to a constant observance of the rules of justice, nothing further is commonly requisite than to understand his own pecuniary interest; but before he can become eminently generous or benevolent, he must resolve to sacrifice that interest to the good of others. Justice is the result of a deliberate purpose to reject an incidental advantage for obtaining an ultimate, and much greater profit. Generosity is the fruit of a violent impulse, which overlooks all private and selfish considerations. The careful and penurious tradesman, the industrious and active manufacturer, or merchant, can have little temptation to desert the one, but in the course of his professional views, he meets with as little incitement to practise the other. To be just, is to breathe his natural element; to require that he should be generous, is to invert his ordinary functions, and to make him subsist by organs to which he has not been accustomed.

In a commercial country, the mercantile spirit is not confined to tradesmen or merchants; from a similarity of situation it pervades, in some degree, all orders and ranks, and by the influence of habit and example, it is communicated, more or less, to every member of the community. Individuals form their notions of propriety according to a general standard, and fashion their morals in conformity to the prevailing taste of the times. By living much in society, and maintaining an intimate correspondence, they are led also to a frequent and ready communication of their thoughts and sentiments. They learn by experience to do this, without hurting the feelings of one another; to conceal their own selfishness or contempt of others; to assume a tone of moderation, deference, and respect; and, without apparent restraint or effort, to accommodate their behaviour to the disposition and temper of their company. While in this manner, they improve in the arts of civility and politeness, they can hardly fail to cultivate their social feelings, by participating in the pleasures and pains of each other, and by mutual endeavours to promote the former, and to relieve or soften the latter. But this intercourse is often little more than a petty traffic, which aims merely at the purchase of reciprocal good offices; or when it proceeds from better motives, it is the offspring of a subordinate, and in some measure a speculative humanity, which in the case of any serious distress, contents itself with weeping and lamenting over the afflicted, but never thinks of sacrificing any great interest to afford him relief.

Even this tinsel reciprocation of small benefits, which people are apt to value more than it deserves, but which, in reality, is of signal utility in removing the inconveniencies, and improving the comforts which attend our journey of human life, is frequently interrupted by those opposite and jarring passions which arise amid the active pursuits of a commercial nation. In a rude age, where there is little industry, or desire of accumulation, neighbouring independent societies are apt to rob and plunder each other; but the members of the same society are attracted by a common interest, and are often strongly united in the bands of friendship and affection, by mutual exertions of benevolence, or by accidental habits of sympathy. But in a country where nobody is idle, and where every person is eager to augment his fortune, or to improve his circumstances, there occur innumerable competitions and rivalships, which contract the heart, and set mankind at variance. In proportion as every man is attentive to his own advancement, he is vexed and tormented by every obstacle to his prosperity, and prompted to regard his competitors with envy, resentment, and other malignant passions.

The pursuit of riches becomes a scramble, in which the hand of every man is against every other. Hence the dissensions among persons of the same trade or profession, which are more conspicuous according as the opposition of interest is more direct and pointed. The physicians, the apothecaries, and the lawyers of a small town are commonly not in speaking terms; they are not more instigated to advance their own success than to thwart and oppose that of each other; and even the customers of each party are frequently involved in the quarrel. The same principles exhibit themselves with less indecorum, perhaps, or violence, but not less invariably, through the whole commercial world. That there is no friendship in trade is an established maxim among traders. Every man for himself, and God Almighty for us all, is their fundamental doctrine.

SELECTION VIII

LEISURE, THE FINE ARTS AND SOCIETY

Millar, following Adam Smith in this perhaps, is known to have given considerable attention to belles lettres, music and the fine arts generally. Until we can be certain of his authorship of the 'M' articles in the *Analytical Review* (see App. II), the following brief excerpts from his fragment on this subject, 'The Gradual Advancement of the Fine Arts—Their Influence on Government', Essay VIII in vol. IV of the *Historical View* (pp. 311–17, 322 f.), must serve to illustrate this interest of his. (Cp. also *Ranks*, above, pp. 212–18.)

The diversions and amusements of any people are usually conformable to the progress they have made in the common arts of life. Barbarians, who are much employed in fighting, are obliged to procure subsistence, as well as to defend their acquisitions, by vigorous corporeal exertions, amuse themselves with mock fights, and with such contentions as display their strength, agility and courage. Long after mankind have made such advances in rearing cattle, and in agriculture, as to derive their principal maintenance from those arts, they continue to follow hunting and fishing, with all the varieties of rural sport, as their chief recreation and pastime. But when, in consequence of their improvement in useful arts, the bulk of a people are engaged in peaceable professions, and from their advancement in opulence and civilization, have become averse from hazardous exertions, and desirous of repose and tranquility, it may be expected that a suitable variation will take place in the style of their amusements. Instead of engaging in the athletic exercises, they will hire others to exhibit spectacles of that nature, and will become sedentary spectators of the struggle. Or if they have attained a higher degree of refinement, they will invent games which admit the display of mental address and ingenuity; and will at length introduce entertainments calculated to gratify the taste of whatever is beautiful in the compass of art or of nature. In some countries, no doubt, accidental circumstances have retarded the improvement of these elegant pleasures, and preserved, in the midst of opulence and civilization, an uncommon attachment to the primitive amusements of a rude age. The Romans, in consequence of early and deep impressions which they had received from their long and constant employment in war, were disgraced, even at the most exalted period of their philosophy and literature, by the fondness which they retained for the barbarous exhibitions of the amphitheatre. The inhabitants of this island, among whom the lower orders have considerable influence in directing the fashions, have incurred the ridicule of their neighbours, for their strong partiality to the inelegant amusements of the cock-pit and the bear-garden. But whatever exceptions may occur in particular cases, it is commonly observed, that the refinements of taste, and the cultivation of the elegant arts, among a people, are in proportion to those improvements which multiply the comforts and conveniencies of life, and give rise to extensive influence and luxury. . . .

In examining, therefore, the improvements which have taken place in this country, since the revolution, it would be improper to overlook that progressive culture of the fine arts which has been so conspicuous, and from which the inhabitants of the higher, and even middling ranks, derive so great a share of their amusement. . . .

A song contains the rudiments of poetry and music, two arts, which, in a state of extreme simplicity, are commonly united. But when the musician, on the one hand, has invented a rich and varied melody, and the poet, on the other hand, has acquired so much experience and knowledge as to introduce a long and intricate series of thoughts, it is no longer possible to enjoy at once the result of their different improvements, and it becomes necessary that the two arts should be separated. The consequence of that separation is the superior cultivation and improvement of each, with regard to all those effects which they are separately capable of producing. As music is thus gradually rendered more intricate, and of more difficult execution, the mechanical part of it requires a longer and more intense application for acquiring a proficiency in the performance, and surpassing more and more the patience and perseverance of the ordinary gentleman performer, is at length abandoned in a great measure to the mere artist, who follows that profession for hire; while poetry, of which the mechanism is more simple and easy, and in which the powers of imagination are less confined in the trammels of art, becomes not so much a professional object as the occasional exercise of all those persons to whom inclination or genius happens to recommend that species of amusement. . . .

The same character of sublimity [referring to paragraphs omitted here] may be recognised in those relics of Celtic poetry, ascribed to Ossian; which no credulity can believe to be an entire forgery of the publisher; but from which we may easily suppose that he has removed a great part of their original imperfections.

That the sublime genius of Homer was greatly indebted to the character of the age in which he lived, will readily be admitted; but the difficulty lies in conceiving, by what means, in so rude an age, he could acquire that correctness of taste and judgement for which he is so conspicuous. What an astonishing phenomenon is the Iliad, if we survey the extensive and regular plan upon which it is composed, the skill and experience with which it is executed, together with the purity of expression, and the harmony of numbers, which everywhere prevail in that immortal work; and if, at the same time, we consider that the author must have lived before the return of the Heraclidae into Peloponnesus, otherwise he would undoubtedly have made some allusion to that event of so much importance to all Greece; that is, he must have lived within eighty years of the Trojan war, when the art of writing was hardly known to the Greeks, and more than three hundred years before their oldest prose-writer, of whom we have any accounts! How much more advanced was the state of arts and sciences in England during the life of Spenser, than in Greece during the period when Homer is understood to have lived; but how obsolete is the language of the former compared with that of the latter?* . . .

SELECTION IX

THE NEED FOR PARLIAMENTARY REFORM

Our last selection, taken, not like the others from the *Historical View*, but from one of the *Letters of Crito*, is our only selection of a strictly political, that is a 'pamphleteering' character. It represents, like various passages in the *Historical View* (esp. vol. IV, Essay II. See also above, pp. 75 f.), a strong attack on the increase of the royal prerogative and of ministerial power, and on the patronage system; it boldly attacks the government in power, as do all of these letters, and is perhaps his strongest published statement on the need, as he saw it, for parliamentary reform. The reference is *Letters of Crito*, Letter xv in part, pp. 100–10. (Cp. also the whole of Letter III.)

It is evident that not only a change of Ministry, but a total change of *measures*, has become indispensably requisite for the preservation of our liberties.

Whoever is acquainted with the principles of our Constitution, and considers the nature of the Revolution-settlement, in 1688, will easily perceive that, from the course of public events, and from the change in the state of society, great alterations have, since that period, occurred

* [Other examples, illustrations and discussions of epic poetry, and then of dramatic poetry, follow.]

in our political system. By that great transaction, the boundaries of the prerogative were ascertained and fixed, in such a manner as precluded all hazard from any of those encroachments against which the nation, from past experience, had been taught to provide. From this time forward, a new order of things was introduced. The House of Commons, no longer jealous of the Crown, became hearty and liberal in granting supplies; and the expensive wars in which the nation was involved, occasioned a rapid increase of taxes. Ministers, taking advantage of the national spirit, became proportionably daring and rapacious; and when the expense of their projects could not be defrayed within the year, they ventured to borrow a capital, providing only a sum for the annual discharge of the interest. Thus the system of *funding*, which from small beginnings was gradually extended, and has risen to such a monstrous pitch, taught the nation to engage in military undertakings beyond their strength, and rendered her familiar with an endless accumulation of public burthens.

It is unnecessary to observe, that this augmentation of the public revenue, by creating a correspondent increase of patronage, has produced an extension of *influence*, pervading all the different branches of administration, and advancing without end, like the sources from which it is derived. . . . it must be acknowledged that, by the immense patronage arising from the disposal of so much money; not to mention the church livings in the gift of the Crown, the appointments of the East India Company, under the control and direction of ministry, with many other offices and places of emolument in their nomination, none of which are included in the foregoing calculation of the public revenue, there is produced an universal ascendency in all the departments of government, which often lulls asleep and palsies our sense of duty, holds in derision all pretences to public spirit, and seems at length to overbear and destroy all opposition. With what propriety the different powers of government are distributed and balanced, how beautiful the political machine may appear in theory, and with what apparent nicety its various parts are adjusted to one another, is of little importance, if our ministers shall be possessed of a magical instrument, by which they may secretly tamper with all its operations, and control or direct all its movements!

It was this view of our political state which, in the course of the American war, extorted the memorable declaration from the House of Commons, 'that the influence the Crown had, was increasing and ought to be diminished'. It was the same view which, upon the conclusion of that war, produced, among men of all ranks, a very general attention to a circumstance of great importance in the government, (though formerly it had excited little concern or uneasiness) the unequal representation of the community in the House of Commons. While the secret influence of ministry, from the limited state of the revenue, was inconsiderable, this deviation from the original principles of our government, which, in a course of time, had proceeded from various causes, was attended, perhaps, with no great inconvenience; but, in consequence of the vast extension of ministerial patronage, it came necessarily to be regarded as a defect, of the utmost magnitude, in the constitution of the legislature.

Notwithstanding the prodigious progress of Ministerial influence and corruption, there still remained one check upon the conduct of every Administration, which had always been considered as the great safe-guard of our liberties. Though the doctrine of absolute confidence in Ministers had been exalted to a wonderful pitch, and though their measures could, in ordinary cases, be carried into execution with nearly the same facility as in the most despotical government, it was always expected, that, upon extraordinary occasions, when those measures had become extremely unpopular, the interposition of the House of Commons, by a petition to the Crown, would infallibly produce a change of Ministry, and a consequent change of system. This ultimate control, it was thought, might prove a terror to evil doers, and might prevent the executive power from shutting its ears to the loud voice of the nation. But the transactions in the year 1784 put an end to that expectation, and demonstrated, that if ever the Crown, from a singular concurrence of accidents, should lose a majority in that House, its Ministers might safely venture upon a dissolution of Parliament as an infallible expedient for supporting their interest. A great majority of the Commons being, in the present state of the representation, returned by the interest of a small number of individuals, a dissolution of Parliament, as far as related to that House, was not, in reality, an appeal to the nation at large, but, in a great measure, an appeal to such of the nobility and gentry as had acquired the direction of *rotten boroughs*, or of certain political districts. After this leading experiment, it became now evident to all the world, that a reform in the mode of electing the national representatives was indispensably requisite, for counteracting the effects of that great influence acquired by Ministers, and for maintaining the free exercise of those powers established at the Revolution.

It was by expressing great zeal in the pursuit of this object, and by professing various opinions of a similar tendency, together with the possession of a pompous and plausible eloquence, that our Prime Minister had acquired such popularity as rendered him, at the time alluded to, a necessary ally to that collection of the adherents of prerogative which came to be placed at the helm. He continued, when in office, to make some feeble and awkward attempts for promoting a parliamentary reform, but soon acquiesced in the negative which was given to that measure, chiefly by his ministerial friends. How far he had been in earnest in those attempts became evident in 1792, when a motion for the same purpose was brought, from another quarter, under the consideration of Parliament, and countenanced by a society of gentlemen, whose rank and character afforded a sufficient pledge of their good intentions; upon which occasion, this versatile statesman not only opposed the measure with all the weight of ministerial interest, but endeavoured to hold it up to the public as calculated to promote the designs of republicans and levellers.* It was, in fact, to disappoint the measures proposed at that time, as I formerly observed, that the war with France was undertaken. Had a temperate reform been then carried into execution, the system of alarm, which has been so artificially spread over the kingdom, would have been superseded; this ruinous war, with all its dreadful consequences, would have been prevented; and the national prosperity would have risen to a height without example in any former period.

But if it was, at that time, a measure of supreme necessity to counter-act the tendency of ministerial influence, by correcting the inequality of the national representation, how much more so must it appear at present; when, in consequence of the war, that influence has been so wonderfully extended; and when the terrors which were excited, and the malignant suspicions which were instilled into the minds of men, have contributed to arm our ministers with such new and unprecedented powers? What an implicit faith in those Ministers has been inculcated? With what an absolute dominion over all ranks and orders of men have they been invested? What discretionary powers have been committed to them on pretence of guarding the public safety, though at the expense of personal liberty; and what abuses have been made of these powers by the prosecution and oppressive treatment of innocent persons? What restraints have been imposed upon the liberty of the press, that necessary instrument for checking the encroachments of prerogative? What restraints, what prohibitions have been laid upon meetings of the people for the defence of their privileges? In a mixed government like ours, is it not the privilege of every British subject to petition the Sovereign; to petition Parliament, whenever he conceives his rights to be invaded? Is not this privilege secured expressly by the *Bill of Rights*, that sacred and fundamental law of the kingdom? But how are men to know when encroachments are made upon their rights; and how are they to

* [Cf. *Crito*, pp. 17 f.]

petition with any effect for redress, if they are not allowed to meet and converse together upon political subjects? And with what sort of freedom can they communicate their thoughts, and procure mutual information, if they are liable to be silenced, imprisoned, and punished, at the discretion of an officer, appointed by that very executive power of whose oppression they may have occasion to complain?

When a parliamentary reform was proposed, immediately before the commencement of the war, the chief objection, which any person chose to avow, was founded upon a suspicion that the people would not be contented with an amendment of the defects particularly specified, but, in imitation of the French, were, in reality, desirous of a total revolution. It is hoped the experience we have had, since that period, of the temper and moderation of the people in all parts of the island, will be sufficient entirely to remove this objection, and to satisfy us that the lower orders are in general firmly attached to the British Constitution. They have undergone a severe scrutiny. Their conduct has been strictly watched. No political offences, however trivial, have been overlooked. No pains have been spared to convict offenders; and the law has not withheld her utmost severity from such as were convicted. Nor has the conduct of Administration, with respect to the populace, been of a conciliating nature. But notwithstanding the mortifying suspicions which have been cast upon them, notwithstanding the neglect which their humble petitions on behalf of their favourite object have constantly met with, notwithstanding the invidious distinctions which have unnecessarily and injudiciously been held up between them and the superior ranks, they have never been betrayed into violent or unconstitutional measures; they have never testified any marks of resentment against the ruling powers; and, under the pressure of uncommon difficulties, even in procuring their daily bread, they have waited with patience the issue of a war which they could not approve of, and against which they had in vain remonstrated. Of the many who were capitally prosecuted for political offences, all have been acquitted by the verdict of a jury, except two obscure persons in Scotland, of whom the principal was a noted spy, that had received a bribe upon the part of the Executive Government.

SELECTED LETTERS BY MILLAR

I have knowledge of thirteen letters written by Millar, and except for the last listed below, preserved in the original. These are, in the order of their dating so far as known, the following, all dated at Glasgow except no. 12:

1. To David Erskine, Earl of Buchan. 8 November 1763, *re* conferring of a degree. Edinburgh University Library (Laing manuscripts, II, 588.)

2. To Adam Smith. 2 February 1764, *re* successor to his chair. University of Glasgow Library manuscripts. Bannerman Papers. Also Scott, *Adam Smith as Student and Professor*, p. 257.

3. To William Craig, Esq., later Lord Craig of Court of Session, etc. 4 February 1776, *re* membership in Literary Society. National Library manuscripts (MS. 124, p. 92.)

4. To the Seventh Earl of Lauderdale. 16 May 1777, *re* vocational promise of his son, the future eighth Earl of Lauderdale. Possession Lauderdale Estate, Thirlstane Castle, Lauder, Berwickshire.

5. To David Hume (the philosopher, or his nephew?). n.d. except 'Sunday', presumably mid-1776, *re Wealth of Nations*. Hume collection, Royal Society, Edinburgh. Also J. H. Burton, *Letters of Eminent Persons Addressed to David Hume* (Edinburgh and London, 1849), vol. II, pp. 479 f.

6. To Alexander Carlyle. 8 August 1782, *re* professorial appointment. Edinburgh University Library manuscripts. (D.c. 4.41. 108.)

7–11. Five letters addressed to Edmund Burke as Rector of the University: 16 August 1784 (original in Lamport Hall Burke collection); 15 November 1784; 19 January 1785; 17 April 1785 and 13 November 1785, respectively, *re* University matters. Fitzwilliam-Burke manuscripts, Sheffield City Library.

12. To David Douglas, cousin of Adam Smith and his executor, recently a 'resident student' with Millar. Milheugh, 10 August 1790, *re* Adam Smith's manuscripts. University of Glasgow Library manuscripts, Bannerman Papers. Also Scott, *op. cit.* p. 311.

13. Communication to Dugald Stewart, probably early 1791. Biographical data on Adam Smith, in Stewart's *Account of the Life and Writings of Adam Smith*, early 1793. See also letter Millar to Douglas, below. Original probably not preserved.

Appendix I

Letters 1, 4, 6 and four of the Burke letters are not reproduced here. The latter deal with matters purely internal to the University, revolving about difficulties with Professor Anderson (see above p. 46). The one reproduced here has a more general interest, as do also excerpts quoted on pp. 71 f. above. The letter to Lord Craig is of interest both for its references to the Literary Society and for its humorous and only slightly veiled political references to the difficulties with the American colonies. The reproduction here of the letters to Smith, Hume, Lord Reston and Stewart should hardly call for any justification even though they are to be found in print elsewhere.

MILLAR TO ADAM SMITH,
RE SELECTION OF SUCCESSOR TO LATTER

Glasgow,
February 2d, 1764

Dear Sir,

I write this to you with the concurrence of Dr Black, to acquaint you of the state of your office since you left us. Dr Reid at Aberdeen has been strongly recommended by Lord Kames. He is also recommended to Dr Trail by Lord Deskford. There is great reason to believe that interest will be used from all these different quarters with Mr McKenzie. Possibly, too, the Duke of Queensberry and Lord Hopeton will be engaged in his behalf, the consequence of which in the present state of things is altogether uncertain.

Black and I think that Young [Thomas Young, whom Smith had engaged to finish out his year] is by far the best man, who has appeared; for Morehead refuses to accept. We earnestly beg that, if you can do anything in counter-working these extraneous operations, you will exert yourself. I cannot but say that we join also in wishing that, if you know any place where your opinion of Young would be of service, you would take an opportunity of giving it. I can assure you he needs that assistance. There is now a strong circumstance in his favour which we could not know formerly. He has taught the class hitherto with great and universal applause; and by all accounts discovers an ease and fluency in speaking, which, I own, I scarce expected. No body knows of my writing this but Black.

Yours sincerely,
John Millar

Selected Letters by Millar

MILLAR TO WILLIAM CRAIG, ESQ.
(LATER LORD CRAIG), EDINBURGH

Glasgow, 4 Feb^{ry}, 1776

My Dear Sir,

I have been commissioned by our Literary Society to acquaint you that you are elected a member of their body. And I have to beg your pardon for having from mere forgetfulness neglected to execute this commission till a week or two after the thing really happened. You will perhaps be surprised to find that a step of so much consequence to your *status civilis* has been taken without consulting you and procuring your previous consent. To this I answer that this is agreeable to the *constitution*. It is now an established point that a man ought to be *taxed* without his consent—and you will admit that the greater power comprehends the less. Besides, tho' you had, strictly speaking, no representative on this occasion, yet as the transaction passed in presence of persons belonging to the same country and profession with yourself, it is reasonable to presume they would take care of your interest. It is therefore hoped you will not show yourself so much an enemy to the good order as to make any opposition to this measure, and that you will take the first opportunity of sending a faithful and loyal address to this effect. You may depend upon it that a contrary behaviour will be viewed, by the impartial world, that is, by every person that wishes your compliance, in the same light with the opposition of colonies to the just demands of their mother country.*—If you signify your acceptance of this dignity, which I hope to have the honour of presenting, it might also be a popular measure that you should mention the time when you propose to give a discourse, as well as the *subject-matter*. You know that there is a penalty in case of negligency in such cases, at the same time you will undoubtedly be of opinion that it is the duty of a good citizen to obey the law, and that a man does not fulfil this duty merely by submitting to the punishment attending disobedience.

[Paragraph on some more personal matters omitted.]

Yours ever,
John Millar

* [It is known that Millar considered the claims of the colonies just, and, during the war, feared for the consequences to British liberties of their suppression by military force. Note date of letter.—Ed.]

MILLAR TO DAVID HUME
RE SMITH'S 'WEALTH OF NATIONS'

Glasgow, Sunday, n.d.
[Mid 1776?]

My Dear Sir,

I am afraid your criticisms on Smith's style are not altogether without foundation—though I think you rather severe. There is something in Smith's style that appears as *original*, as there is in the thought; and the one is exceedingly well adapted to the other. I own, however, that, notwithstanding all the pains he has taken, there are many of his positions which I have great difficulty in admitting—and some where I am not sure in what latitude he means to establish them. In particular, his great leading opinion concerning the unbounded freedom of trade. I have but a vague notion how far it is true, or how far he means to say that it ought to be carried. I should be glad to know what is your view of this point. I admit that government should be cautious of regulating trade; because those who direct the administration are commonly but bad judges of those matters; so that when we talk of the wisdom of the nation, we often make use of a very violent figure of speech. I also admit that regulations with respect to trade are not easily enforced, and the attempt to enforce them is generally attended with much expense. But still, notwithstanding these two considerations, may there not be cases where a regulation of trade is proper? I imagine the point must be determined in the affirmative or negative according as we find that the interest of every merchant and manufacturer coincides in all cases with that of the public or otherwise. We may suppose that mercantile people will generally understand their own interest: and if their private interest always coincides with that of the public, they may be safely left to trade as they please. But I doubt whether there be not some branches of trade, very profitable to the merchant, which are hurtful to the public, or at least, among different branches equally profitable to the private undertaker, there be not some much more beneficial to the public than others. If this be true, then a regulation of trade must often be highly expedient.

I shall [presume (?)] one case. The question occurs, whether a trade of importing wines be more beneficial than another for importing raw material. The respective merchants in these branches will consider that their own profits may be greater in the wine trade than in the other— though [the latter (?)] seems more beneficial to the public. In this case, therefore, the good trade will be given up for a bad one, unless the government should interfere. Perhaps the instance I have pitched upon is not so good as some others that might be mentioned. You will observe that I am at present setting aside the case of infant manufacturers, which Smith makes an exception to his general rule.

I find that I have got no time for the [law (?)*] question which you put, which I shall answer soon.

Yours,

J. Millar

MILLAR TO THE RIGHT HONOURABLE EDMUND BURKE, THEN LORD RECTOR OF THE UNIVERSITY OF GLASGOW †

Glasgow, 15 November, 1784

Dear Sir,

It is with great pleasure I have to inform you that you were this day re-elected Lord Rector of this University by the unanimous voice of all the four nations. By the same post with this you will receive an official letter to that purpose from our Principal. I trouble you just now in order to acquaint you that your re-election was by no means a mere matter of form, proceeding from the tacit rule of continuing the same Rector for two years, but that it was supported by the Professors with the warmest cordiality and zeal. In short if there are *divisions* among us, there has been no appearance of them on this occasion. Give me leave, Dear Sir, to express to you my earnest desire that you will again accept of the office; in doing which I set aside all opinions or affections peculiar to myself and any particular friends. What appears to me of most consequence is the character of our University, which I think must suffer by your declining in the present circumstances to be once more our first magistrate. It will probably be thought and said by those who do not wish well to us, that you refused the office from a knowledge of our sentiments, and that we paid a respect to the ministerial place of last year, which we now wish to withdraw when you are out of it. It will even have the aspect of our being more desperate in our expectations of a change upon that subject than I hope there is any occasion for.

I have only time to assure you that I am, Dear Sir,

Your Most faithful

Obed^t. Servt.

John Millar

* [The script is blurred here as in several other places, by the breaking of the seal. If 'law' is the correct reading, it suggests, as do also other circumstances, that this letter may have been addressed not to the philosopher, who must already have been quite ill by this time, but to his nephew, who had recently been a 'resident student' in Millar's home. See above p. 39. The elder Hume wrote to Smith 1 April 1776, congratulating him on *The Wealth of Nations*; he died 25 August. He and Millar were not infrequently in correspondence.]

† With permission.

Appendix I

Milheugh
10 Aug^t, 1790

My Dear Sir,

I am much obliged to you for the particulars of which you give me an account, both with respect to our late worthy friend, and to yourself. I could easily have supposed it was not an object with Mr Smith to make money, but if he had not been remarkably inattentive to that article, as he was a man of no personal expense, he must have made much more than he has done. As it is, I sincerely think you have enough for any good purpose. You have little enough to excite you to activity in business, and what is abundantly sufficient to enable you to carry it on with proper frugality. I mean without encroaching upon the library, which you certainly will be disposed to retain undiminished. I should think your best scheme would be, upon your putting on the gown,* to buy a small house, for which you have already more furniture than will be sufficient, and to procure an elderly female servant for your house-keeper. In this way you may live very comfortably, and as frugally as you please You will easily perceive that I have it in view to eat a bit of toasted cheese with you of an evening These are the only entertain-ments you should give for many years to come, unless it be a dinner to a favourite *writer*, or rather a writer who makes a favourite of you.

I regret the fate of the MSS. though I am not suprised at it. If they were unfinished, it was judicious to prevent their coming before the public, because an author who has acquired a high reputation has much to lose, but little to gain by any new publication. If a man has written one book of merit, everyone thinks that it requires nothing but industry to write another. But if he falls off, the first was a lucky hit. It would have been happy for John Hume, that he had never written any thing but 'Douglas'. I am far from imagining, however, that Mr Smith's MSS. would have conveyed any such idea. Indeed I *know* the contrary. They would have conveyed the same marks of genius, a genius of the highest order, perhaps with less correctness, or at least with some inequality in the composition.

It will give me the greatest pleasure to contribute any hints to Mr

---

* [See notes to letter in Scott, *op. cit.* pp. 311–13; also letters and notes, pp. 306–10; and above, p. 36. Smith had died 17 July. Douglas was made executor of Smith's estate. He 'passed advocate' the next year; was made a Lord of the Court of Session in 1813; Lord of Justiciary in 1816.]

Stuart with regard to Mr Smith's professorial talents, or any other particular you mention, while he remained at Glasgow—with this proviso, that Mr Stuart shall use the utmost freedom with every article and make the whole entirely his own, as far as he makes use of it. I shall expect to hear soon from you or Mr Stuart, at what time I should be ready.

I am glad to hear that a part of Mr Smith's writings are likely to see the light—for I hope you and your privy council will use all the latitude you can upon that side of the question. Of the discourses which he intended upon the imitative arts, he read two to our society at Glasgow, but the third was not then finished. I wish it may be finished now. Of all his writings, I have most curiosity about the metaphysical work you mention. I should like to see his powers of illustration employed upon the true old Humean philosophy. You have not, I hope, given up thought of a visit to us this summer. I can easily imagine* . . . you have felt for some time must have . . . to your studies with much effect. That, however, is a circumstance of little moment. Perhaps it may be as well to admit a little further dissipation before you buckle to for the winter. You have been so regular hitherto that you need not be afraid of yourself. I have been constantly at home, and shall, in all probability, continue for the rest of the summer. Everybody here desires to be remembered to you.

I am ever, My Dear Friend, Yours sincerely,

John Millar

MILLAR TO DUGALD STEWART, RE ADAM SMITH†

In the Professorship of Logic, to which Mr Smith was appointed on his first introduction into this University, he soon saw the necessity of departing widely from the plan that had been followed by his predecessors, and of directing the attention of his pupils to studies of a more interesting and useful nature than the Logic and Metaphysics of the schools. Accordingly, after exhibiting a general view of the powers of the mind, and explaining so much of the ancient logic as was requisite, to gratify curiosity with respect to an artificial method of reasoning, which had once occupied the universal attention of the learned, he dedicated all the rest of his time to the delivery of a system of Rhetoric

* [Omissions due to breaking of seal.]

† [Excerpts from a letter or 'notes' supplied by Millar to Dugald Stewart for his Account of the Life and Writings of Adam Smith—written, apparently, soon after the above letter to David Douglas dated 10 August 1790. The memoir was read 21 January and 18 March 1793.]

and Belles-lettres. The best method of explaining and illustrating the various powers of the human mind, the most useful part of metaphysics, arises from an examination of the several ways of communicating our thoughts by speech, and from an attention to the principles of those literary compositions which contribute to persuasion or entertainment. By these arts, everything that we perceive or feel, every operation of our mind, is expressed and delineated in such a manner, that it may be clearly distinguished and remembered. There is, at the same time, no branch of literature more suited to youth at their first entrance upon philosophy than this, which lays hold of their taste and their feelings.

It is much to be regretted, that the manuscript containing Mr Smith's lectures on this subject was destroyed before his death. The first part, in point of composition, was highly finished; and the whole discovered strong marks of taste and original genius. From the permission given to students of taking notes many observations and opinions contained in these lectures have either been detailed in separate dissertations, or engrossed in general collections, which have since been given to the public. But these, as might be expected, have lost the air of originality and the distinctive character which they received from their first author, and are often obscured by that multiplicity of commonplace matter in which they are sunk and involved.

About a year after his appointment to the Professorship of Logic, Mr Smith was elected to the Chair of Moral Philosophy. His course of lectures on this subject was divided into four parts. The first contained Natural Theology; in which he considered the proofs of the being and attributes of God, and those principles of the human mind upon which religion is founded. The second comprehended Ethics, strictly so called, and consisted chiefly of the doctrines which he afterwards published in his *Theory of Moral Sentiments*. In the third part, he treated at more length of that branch of Morality which relates to Justice, and which, being susceptible of precise and accurate rules, is for that reason capable of a full and particular explanation.

Upon this subject he followed the plan that seems to be suggested by Montesquieu; endeavouring to trace the gradual progress of jurisprudence, both public and private, from the rudest to the most refined ages, and to point out the effects of those arts which contribute to subsistence, and to the accumulation of property, in producing correspondent improvements or alterations in law and government. This important branch of his labours he also intended to give to the public; but this intention, which is mentioned in the conclusion of the *Theory of Moral Sentiments*, he did not live to fulfil.

In the last part of his lectures, he examined those political regulations which are founded, not upon the principle of *justice*, but that of *expediency*, and which are calculated to increase the riches, the power, and the prosperity of a State. Under this view, he considered the political institutions relating to commerce, to finances, to ecclesiastical and military establishments. What he delivered on these subjects contained the substance of the work he afterwards published under the title of *An Inquiry into the Nature and Causes of the Wealth of Nations.*

There was no situation in which the abilities of Mr Smith appeared to greater advantage than as a Professor. In delivering his lectures, he trusted almost entirely to extemporary elocution. His manner, though not graceful, was plain and unaffected; and, as he seemed to be always interested in the subject, he never failed to interest his hearers. Each discourse consisted commonly of several distinct propositions, which he successively endeavoured to prove and illustrate. These propositions, when announced in general terms, had, from their extent, not unfrequently something of the air of a paradox. In his attempts to explain them, he often appeared, at first, not to be sufficiently possessed of the subject, and spoke with some hesitation. As he advanced, however, the matter seemed to crowd upon him, his manner became warm and animated, and his expression easy and fluent. In points susceptible of controversy, you could easily discern, that he secretly conceived an opposition to his opinions, and that he was led upon this account to support them with greater energy and vehemence. By the fulness and variety of his illustrations, the subject gradually swelled in his hands, and acquired a dimension which, without a tedious repetition of the same views, was calculated to seize the attention of his audience, and to afford them pleasure, as well as instruction, in following the same object, through all the diversity of shades and aspects in which it was presented, and afterwards in tracing it backwards to that original proposition or general truth from which this beautiful train of speculation had proceeded.

His reputation as a Professor was accordingly raised very high, and a multitude of students from a great distance resorted to the University, merely upon his account. Those branches of science which he taught became fashionable at this place, and his opinions were the chief topics of discussion in clubs and literary societies. Even the small peculiarities in his pronunciation or manner of speaking, became frequently the objects of imitation.

PROBABLE ANONYMOUS WRITINGS

The question of anonymous authorship, as relating to Millar, involves four, or possibly five pieces.

Concerning his authorship of the *Letters of Crito*, which have been briefly discussed elsewhere, there is scarcely any room for doubt, even though he himself never publicly acknowledged their authorship. These shall, therefore, further concern us here only as they may have bearing on the other pieces.

That the *Letters of Sidney* (sometimes Sydney), ten of the eighteen first published serially in the same *Scots Chronicle* closely following the Crito letters (in fact with a slight overlap in time) were also from Millar's pen, has nowhere, to my knowledge, been suggested in print, unless it be in Craig's phrase, 'one or two anonymous pamphlets'; but there is strong internal evidence to support such a claim.

'There is no circumstance,' the series begins, 'which can so seriously affect the morals, government and general welfare of a nation as the state of property. The influence which it possesses over manners, opinions and actions is highly important; . . . opulence is attended with such weight and authority as will always render complete equality unattainable.' This sounds most like Millar. That the author repeatedly refers to his ideas as merely reflecting the ideas 'introduced by Professor Millar of Glasgow in his lectures on civil law' it would seem not unfair to interpret as a 'camouflage'; and the allegation that these in turn but reflect chiefly the ideas of Adam Smith would be much more likely to be made by Millar than by anyone else. Who but a man like Millar would be quoting Harrington in 1796; and who else in Scotland would be likely to know of a law on testaments just passed in France, of which he had not yet seen 'the specific regulations'!

The letters constitute an attack on the dangerously increasing inequality in the distribution of property, with yet disapproval of anything that might be called 'levelling', at the very time Millar is known to have been losing faith in the 'union of talent and rank' in propertied families. They defend ideas like Millar's against the distortions and misrepresentations of them by the Tories, and like the Crito letters they charge those in power with 'propping their own corrupt power by means which threaten the ruin of the country', and of turning the war with France into a Holy War to preserve the *status quo* at home. In the pamphlet form they are dedicated to one of Millar's closest friends, the Earl of Lauderdale, who was of the same mind with Millar politically, and one of the promoters and a financial supporter of this new anti-Tory journalistic venture.* There is much more that suggests Millar's authorship, and nothing that speaks clearly against it.

In an early number of the same periodical reference is made to a letter of carping criticism, on some matters of grammar and style, addressed to the editor by a member of the Glasgow College and signed 'A Schoolmaster'. This letter is countered by another signed, 'A Scholar', praising 'the quality, choice and arrangement of your matter'. The author of the latter would in all probability be Millar. And this suggests in the third place, that he may also have been the 'Citizen of Glasgow' who addressed some five letters to the editor in late 1796 and early 1797 on the matter of an adult educational movement that appears to have taken on considerable proportions in the Glasgow area and South-west Scotland at this time. The author appears to be active in the organization of 'reading societies' and local libraries among working men. Many of the ideas expressed are strongly reminiscent of Millar's known interest and position in this matter, and also of Adam Smith's position (see Pt. IV, Selection VI; also, *Wealth of Nations*, Bk. V, ch. I, Pt. IV). Millar's authorship remains, however, rather conjectural.

Much more likely is his authorship of the 'M' review-articles, previously referred to, in the *Analytical Review* from 1788 to 1792 or 1793. This problem is too complicated for discussion within the limits of this note, and, moreover, calls for further technical study, style-analysis, etc. We can here only state a few facts in the case and leave the rest to some other occasion.

Millar is known to have contributed 'a few articles' to this review at about this time. Some fifty reviews, some medium length, some long, some mere notes of but a few lines, bear the signature 'M'; no other initials or other symbols used would fit Millar's name. Most of the reviews are well in line with Millar's known avocational interests and political tenets, some very distinctly so; few if any seem impossibly Millar's. The founder and early editor of this avowedly 'objective' but actually whiggish review was a Scot, Thomas Christie, who had paid a visit to Glasgow, where he found Millar and Reid particularly congenial to his mind, before going down to London.† Whether its publisher J. Johnson, near St Pauls, was in any way connected, or even to be identified with the John Johnstone, 'late of the Oracle in London' who

---

* W. J. Couper, *The Edinburgh Periodical Press* (Stirling, 1908), vol. II, pp. 212–18.

† John Nichols, *Literary Anecdotes of the Eighteenth Century* (9 vols. London, 1812–15), vol. ix, p. 376. Letter of, July 24 1787.

was business manager of the *Scots Chronicle*, we do not know; it suggests the possibility of an interesting sidelight. The rest is, for the present, a matter of 'combinations', conclusions and conjecture.

Our fifth item is the suggestion that has been made that the author of the student-notes on Adam Smith's 'Lectures', published by Cannan, might have been the same as the author of the notes descriptive of these lectures, and of other matters regarding Smith, as published by Dugald Stewart—which was of course Millar (see App. I). A note in Cannan's introduction to the *Lectures* (pp. xix f.) would seem to rule out this possibility. In the absence of further evidence, it must be considered too conjectural for further consideration here.

APPENDIX III

STUDENT-NOTES ON MILLAR'S LECTURES

Students took notes on their professors' lectures in Millar's time as they do now. Often, of course, but certainly not in Millar's case, 'prelections' took the very form, still apparently implied in that designation, of dictations intended to be written down verbatim by the students, and only supplemented by oral digressions and running commentary. Such note-taking may have served genuinely educational purposes; its chief purpose appears, however, to have been that of facilitating preparation for examinations on the lectures, or on the subjects, generally, lectured upon.

Sometimes these notes were little more than mere jottings as memory-jogs; more often they were made, with the aid of an individually devised 'shorthand', to reflect reasonably well the main ideas of the lectures; often, though, as we know from contemporary testimony and from the testimony of surviving notes themselves, they were taken down in a regular shorthand and might, therefore, so fully reflect the content of the lectures as in their transcription and circulation sometimes to embarrass the professor or force him to publish his lectures to prevent plagiarization or careless distortion. A younger contemporary of Millar's complains that the student's attention is often so fully taken up in a mere mechanical 'transferring of the words of the lecture into his notebook' that 'the mind of the student received scarcely any ideas connected with the subject under discussion', or any rational exercise—with the result that 'when he leaves college . . . his portfolio contains the chief part of the instruction he carries away'.*

At any rate, we are fortunate in Millar's case in having—chiefly through the efforts of David Murray (see above, pp. 7., 57 n.—an abundance of notes taken down by students in his classes for his various courses of lectures. Some are very sketchy; others offer at least a reasonably adequate account of the general content of his lectures; one set, at least, is so full and so grammar-perfect, in the transcription of what must have been shorthand notes, on the Lectures on Government that they appear to reflect in very considerable part—style of lecturing, and most digressions and supplementary remarks apart, of course—the

* Jardine (see p. 33 n. above), p. 278.

actual wording of the lectures, and would bear publication with only slight editing. One set (recently acquired by the National Library) is so largely in shorthand and shorthand interlarding as to be almost completely illegible except for the lecture-heads and occasionally other portions.

It cannot be the purpose of this note to offer either a catalogue of these various sets of notes or even the briefest synopsis of their content. We can only call attention to their existence and availability, attempt to characterize them most briefly and to indicate lines of their further study and utilization—as could not well be done in the text above.

There are from two to—in the case of the 'Institutes'—six sets of such notes on each of the various courses of lectures delivered by Millar, except for the 'English Law' lectures, for which only one set has been located. Their dates run from 1776 to 1794, with the last mentioned copy, however, bearing the date of 1800–1, the very last year in which he lectured. Two or three sets are broken or incomplete. There is thus a complete set on 'Government', and a broken one on civil law (Institutes and 'Jurisprudence'), by his own son James; and a complete set on civil law, another on 'Government', and a partial one on the Pandects, by David Boyle, one of his most distinguished former students.

Most of these notes are in the Murray collection in the University Library, Glasgow; two copies on civil law and one on 'Government' in the National Library; and one, inscribed by George Bell, in the Edinburgh University Library. Except for the last mentioned, and for some sets also inscribed by William Galbraith Millar as collector-owner, we assume the name inscribed to be that of the first owner, though one or two, at least, appear to be little more than copies of other available ones.

'Lecture-heads' or course-outlines have also been preserved for all, or nearly all the courses, variously dated and a number of them in print, announcing the topics of each of the forty-five to fifty lectures, usually, to be given in the session indicated.

The 'Lectures on Government' notes, in particular, but also those on 'jurisprudence', and to a much lesser extent those in the other fields, permit comparison at many points with his published works, especially with the *Historical View*, and it is possible that their closer analysis would throw further light on the development of Millar's thought, as present knowledge of them already does on other aspects of his mind. Part III offers a more systematic account of the British constitution, or 'The Present State of the English Government' than is to be found anywhere in his published works. These latter lecture-notes are perhaps a fair equivalent of Millar's own manuscript on the same subject which has unfortunately been lost or destroyed. They would seem to represent one of the earliest, if not the very earliest instance on record of an entire course or at least a very extensive series of lectures on the British constitution ever to be delivered in a British university—or anywhere else, for that matter. Blackstone's Viner lectures at Oxford, begun only a few years earlier, are only a partial exception to this statement. The lectures on jurisprudence in the Moral Philosophy courses from Hutcheson to Smith, Beattie and Ferguson were either statements of principles only, or they were too limited in scope to bear fair comparison.

Many of these lecture-notes provide materials on the history of law that are but slightly in evidence in Millar's published works; others, again, provide at least brief surveys of ethical and psychological theory that are even less in evidence there.

Some of them provide echoes of the classroom and of actual teaching procedure—suggestions as to methods of study and review for examinations, suggestions for further reading, etc. 'The examination will force you to a second reading of the textbook [Heineccius] which will help you to fix the matter of fact in your head.' 'Finnius is both large and often dry, but he is by far the best with regard to matters of fact.' 'Upon disputed points I would advise you to turn to a corpus and exercise your own judgement on it.' 'Those who have less time should keep to the textbook and make themselves master of it, at the same time reading some good author on general jurisprudence.' (Grotius especially recommended.)

The notes bring us illustrative materials (see above, pp. 33 f.), small details on legal relationships, asides on contemporary political events and issues, and occasionally bits of humour or sarcasm, even invective, that he considered either too trivial for, or beneath the dignity of the printed page for the critical reader.

On the whole, these notes deserve further study, and some of them possibly publication.

THE MILLARS OF MILHEUGH

Beside Craig's *Life*, Murray's *Memories* and Gray's *Autobiography* previously cited, the following sources may be consulted on Milheugh and the Millars of Milheugh:

Stewart Wright, *The Annals of Blantyre* (Glasgow, 1885).

William Grossart, *Historic Notices and Domestic History of the Parish of Shotts*, (Glasgow, 1880).

D. Ure, *The History of Rutherglen and East Kilbride* (Glasgow, 1793), (only passing reference to the Millars and inclusion of several of them in list of subscribers).

The Old Country Houses of the Old Glasgow Gentry [J. G. Smith, ed.?] (Glasgow, 1870; 2nd ed. 1878), Exhibition LXXI. (Contains cut of Milheugh as of about 1870.)

One Hundred Glasgow Men: Memories and Portraits of Glasgow (Glasgow, 1886), vol. I.

The Memorial Catalogue of the Old Glasgow Exhibit: 1894 (Glasgow, 1894).

Fasti Ecclesiae Scoticanae, H. Scott, D.D., ed. (new ed., Edinburgh, 1920), vol. III, *s.v.* Shotts, Hamilton, James Millar, Alexander Hutchison, James Baillie.

J. A. Wilson, *A Contribution to the History of Lanarkshire* (2 vols., Glasgow, 1936), vol. I, pp. 129–49, especially 146–8; vol. II, page opposite p. 72.

Robert Wodrow, *Analecta* (4 vols., Glasgow, 1842–43), vol. II, pp. 63–4, 105; vol. IV, pp. 10–15 (x–xv?).

Henry Moncreiff Wellwood, *Life and Writings of John Erskine* (Edinburgh, 1818), pp. 128–36 and Notes.

Matriculation Album of the University of Glasgow (Glasgow, 1913).

Parish Records in the Register House, Edinburgh: under Glasgow, Shotts, Blantyre.

James Templeton of Barnhill, High Blantyre, is in possession of various antiquarian details on Milheugh, some of which have appeared in print in the local press.

The history of the 'mylne' of Mylnheugh—the mill in a glen with steep over-hanging braes—has been traced back practically to the days of Robert the Bruce and Bannockburn, and the Millar title to it at least well into the fifteenth century, with a fresh title in 1602. In 1556–7 a 'John Myllar of Mylnehwycht' is on record as a witness to some official document; in 1564 a 'John Myllar of Mylneheuch' as a participant in some financial transaction (see J. A. Wilson, *op. cit.* above).

From Professor Millar's grandfather John, Milheugh passed to his uncle John, and from him, in the absence of issue, to his brother's eldest and only surviving son, the professor. From him—his eldest son John predeceased him without issue—it passed to his second son, James, and from him—his only son, John, having also died earlier and without issue—to his daughter Margaret, through whose marriage to Andrew Bannatyne (1828), the distinguished Dean of the Glasgow Faculty of Procurators, it passed into the Bannatyne line of descendants where it remains to this day.

Millar's father, it is interesting to note, led the opposition, in the Glasgow Synod, against the itinerant evangelistic tactics of Whitefield, active in Scotland about 1742–8 with the near-by Cambuslang as a centre. Many felt that his tactics and following were making inroads into the stability of local congregational life, (see Wellwood, *John Erskine*).

Millar's eldest sister Margaret (b. January 1739) appears to have died young. Of his only brother, Archibald, we know only the date of his birth and baptism (5 and 13 November 1748) and the fact of his death without issue in 1776. His sister Anne's (b. 7 May 1744) marriage to Alexander Hutchison, who succeeded his father-in-law first in the Second, and then in the First Church at Hamilton, we have spoken of before.

The names and birth-dates of Professor and Mrs Millar's thirteen children, gleaned—all but the eldest—from the scattered baptismal records in the files of the Register House, are as follows:

1.	John	b. 27 . 7 . 60; bpt. ?
2.	James	b. 10 . 6 . 62; „ 14 . 6 . 62
3.	Mary*	b. 8 . 5 . 63; „ 18 . 5 . 63
4.	Ann	b. 15 . 6 . 64; „ 23 . 6 . 64
5.	William	b. 24 . 5 . 65; „ 3 . 6 . 65
6.	Mary	b. 11 . 4 . 66; „ 24 . 4 . 66
7.	Archibald	b. 26 . 4 . 67; „ 9 . 5 . 67
8.	Agnes	b. 12 . 4 . 68; „ 27 . 4 . 68
9.	Gabriel*	b. 11 . 6 . 69; „ 19 . 6 . 69
10.	Margaret	b. 29 . 4 . 71; „ 11 . 5 . 71
11.	Janet	b. 21 . 11 . 75; „ 1 . 12 . 75
12.	Helen	b. 17 . 10 . 76; „ 26 . 10 . 76
13.	Jean	b. 29 . 4 . 78; bpt. 13 . 5 . 78

The matriculation numbers and years of the Millars' four sons, as recorded in the Matriculation Album, are, in the order of their birth: 3403 (1774), 3536 (1775), 3996 (1779), and 4044 (1780). Those of

* Gabriel and the first Mary died in infancy.

411

their grandson John M. by their son James, 9412 (1815); of their three grandsons James, John Millar and William Mylne, by their daughter Agnes, 9123 (1814), 10,451 (1820), and 10,490 (1820), respectively. Those of his nephew James Hutchison are 5549 (1794), and of her nephew John Craig, 3883 (1778). These Album entries contain, in many cases, considerable biographical information of interest.

Another grandson, Allen Thomson, was briefly mentioned above (p. 27). We do not know whether there were other grandchildren by Agnes. Some information on James Millar's family will be found on his gravestone in the Old Churchyard. For descendants in the Bannatyne family see *The Old Country Houses of the Old Glasgow Gentry* and *One Hundred Glasgow Men.*

Young John Millar's emigration to America ('the back-country of Pennsylvania') in 1794 was clearly induced by his discouragement over the 'witch-hunt' of the time in which he was involved to the extent of fearing his future as a 'rising young lawyer' seriously jeopardized, though his father pleaded with him to bide the storm, which would soon blow over. Failing health also entered into the calculation. He had previously published a highly regarded work on *Elements of the Law Relating to Insurances* (Edinburgh, 1787).

This emigration had not only the tragic consequence of his untimely death from 'sun-stroke' while he was improving his farm in an unaccustomed climate It had also this historically interesting consequence that his widow, returned to Scotland, befriended the young Frances Wright, and with the Mylnes counselled with her in her plans to visit America. The 'friend in England' to whom her charming letters published as *Views of Society and Manners in America* by 'An English Woman' (London, 1821) were addressed, was none other than this Robina Millar, daughter-in-law of the Professor.* The Mylnes, the Thomsons, if not also the Bannatynes, into which families the Millar daughters married, were like his own children apparently all loyal to the Millar tradition of political liberalism.

In her *Autobiography*, Mrs Fletcher, widow of Archibald Fletcher, a distinguished member of the liberal Edinburgh 'Reform' group, speaks in terms of the highest praise of both the daughter-in-law (Robina

---

* See A[lice] J. G. Perkins, and Theresa Wolfson, *Frances Wright: Free Enquirer* (New York and London, 1939), especially pp. 20–3, 31–6, 40–6, 54, 90 and 175. Also Wm. R. Waterman, *Frances Wright* (New York, Columbia University Press, 1924), pp. 19, 56, 58. The twelve letters addressed by the widowed Robina Craig Millar to her friend, the distinguished Dr Benjamin Rush at Philadelphia, whom she addresses as 'dear father', between March 1798 and April 1812, are revealing both in the facts given and in the opinions expressed. From them we learn that their sizeable farm was located in 'Penstown, Northumberland County' some 40–45 miles north-north-east of the present Harrisburg. (25 Rush MSS: 84–97, Library Company of Philadelphia.)

Cullen Millar) and of the daughters of Professor Millar, whose friendship she enjoyed. Of her own daughter she remarks that 'her visits at
Milheugh to the daughters of the celebrated Professor Millar . . . increased her ardour and love of knowledge, and excited her to a degree
she had never before experienced. She used to speak of the visit at
Milheugh as the acme of her intellectual existence' greatly quickening
her interest in 'subjects of taste, politics and morals'.*

In the Blantyre parish records for July 1795 and May 1801, respectively, we note these trivial but yet sentimentally interesting items:

> 'For Mrs Millar's mort-cloth £oo 6sh. ood.'
> 'For Professor Millar's mort-cloth, £oo 6sh. ood.'

The left half of the table-stone over the Millar grave in the Old
Churchyard bears this tribute of affection: 'To the memory of Margaret
Craig, the respected and beloved wife of John Millar of Milheugh; the
affectionate and happy mother of thirteen children, ten of whom with
her husband survived her to mourn the irreparable loss of their best
benefactor, their dearest friend. She died 5 July 1795, aged 60 years.'

These burial-ground references may serve as a reminder to us that
neither Shotts nor Hamilton nor Blantyre were far removed from
Bothwell Bridge of Covenanter days (1679). Many of the scenes of
Scott's *Old Mortality* still recalled vivid memories to the older Millars.

Downstream hardly more than a hundred paces from the site of the
stately Milheugh mansion a restored bridge and the barely visible
foundations of the old mill mark the spot, approximately, where on the
fateful 13 May 1586 Mary Queen of the Scots crossed the 'rowten
Cawther' on her way to Langside.

A fifteen or twenty minutes' walk would take us to the birth-place of
David Livingstone where a Livingstone and Blantyre Mills museum are
still maintained.

The last regular occupants of Milheugh—that 'sweetest little retirement that could be desired', the house that the editor of *Old Country
Houses* considered one of the finest in the environs of Glasgow—were
Andrew Millar Bannatyne, of the law firm of Bannatyne, Kirkwood,
France and Co., and his family. After they vacated it in 1944, the house
fell into such sad disrepair, through its occupancy by irresponsible
'squatters' in the post-war housing shortage, that a year or two ago it
had to be razed to the ground.†

---

* *Autobiography of Mrs [Elizabeth Dawson] Fletcher, with Letters and other Family Memorials.*
Edited by her daughter, Lady M. Richardson (Boston, 1876), pp. 64 f., 344 f. Also pp. 129,
349–53. (First published Carlisle, 1874.)

† Information supplied by Mr Templeton.

The old Whitemoss farm, at the edge of the village of East Kilbride, where the Millars spent their summers before 1785, and which is now occupied by the Graham family, is also being threatened by a new industrial development in this today thriving community.

We take our leave of Milheugh, however, on a more pleasant note, by quoting these lines from the verse addressed to one of the Millar daughters by a friendly neighbour, the once renowned Scottish poet and dramatist, Joanna Baillie, and inscribed on a wooden plaque* on the wall of a little bower by the side of the Calder:

> Here the hammer's active din
> Blends with sound of roaring lin,
> As brawling Calder hastens through
> The shady holms of sweet Milheugh.
> Here from planed board the shavings rise,
> And like sunn'd mists the sawdust flies.
> But scarce a lady of the land
> May own a smaller, fairer hand,
> Than she, who 'neath this roof's cool shade
> Plies fitfully her chosen trade.
> With skilful sleight and eager eye,
> A female Amateur of Carpentry.

* This plaque containing twenty lines of verse—a replica presumably of the original—remained in the arbour-like bower until the latter was torn down only some five years ago. The plaque itself was rescued and placed in safe-keeping by Mr Templeton.

GENERAL BIBLIOGRAPHY

For the general historical background of our study the following will prove most helpful. They all contain materials on intellectual as well as on social, economic and political history.

H. G. Graham, *The Social Life of Scotland in the Eighteenth Century* (London, 1899, and later editions). Also his *Scottish Men of Letters in the Eighteenth Century* (London, 1901). Especially chapters I, IV–VII.

P. Hume Brown, *History of Scotland*. 3 vols. (Cambridge, 1911), vol. III.

W. L. Mathieson, *The Awakening of Scotland: A History from 1747 to 1797*, (Glasgow, 1910).

On the contemporary economic and political backgrounds, respectively:

H. Hamilton, *The Industrial Revolution in Scotland* (Oxford, 1932).

H. W. Meikle, *Scotland and the French Revolution* (Glasgow, 1912).

For atmosphere and personal side-lights of various kinds:

Alexander Carlyle, *Autobiography* (1722–1805), (Edinburgh and London, 1860, and later editions).

Thomas Somerville, *My Own Life and Times* (Edinburgh, 1861).

Alexander F. Tytler (Woodhouselee), *Memoirs of the Life and Writings of the Hon. Henry Home of Kames* (Edinburgh, 1807).

John Ramsay of Ochtertyre (A. Allardyce, ed.), *Scotland and the Scotsmen in the Eighteenth Century*. 2 vols. (Edinburgh, 1888).

H. Cockburn, *Memorials of his Time* (Edinburgh, 1856). (Edinburgh, 1909 ed. used.)

For the University history and background the following proved most helpful:

David Murray, *Memories of the Old College of Glasgow* (Glasgow, 1927).

James Coutts, *A History of the University of Glasgow: From its Foundation in 1451 to 1949* (Glasgow, 1909).

J. D. Mackie, *The University of Glasgow: 1451–1951* (Glasgow, 1954).

Inaugural Addresses by the Lords Rectors of the University of Glasgow (with 'An Historical Sketch and Account of the Present State of the University' and notes to same). John B. Hay, ed. (Glasgow, 1839).

'Statistical Account of the University of Glasgow.' Anonymously by Professor Reid, in Sir John Sinclair, *Statistical Account of Scotland* (21 vols, 1791–9). vol. xxi, App., pp. 1–50. Also Reid, *Works* (Hamilton), pp. 721–39.

Minutes of the Meetings of the Senate and of the Faculty of the University for the period covered. Cited in notes as University Manuscripts by volume, disregarding distinction between Senate or University and Faculty or College minutes.

John Rae, *Life of Adam Smith* (London, 1895).

W. R. Scott, *Adam Smith as Student and Professor* (Glasgow, 1937).

BIBLIOGRAPHY OF MILLAR'S WORKS

The following are all the editions, reprints and translations of Millar's works known to me.

Disputatio Juridica ad Tit. 3 Lib. xxvi, Pand. De confirmando tutore vel curatore: etc. [Bar examination] Edinburgh, 1760. (Edinburgh University Library, P.1022/8.)

Observations Concerning the Distinction of Ranks in Society. 4to. (London: John Murray, 1771.)

The same. 8vo. (Dublin: Ewing, pirated ? 1771.)

The same. 2nd ed., greatly enlarged. 8vo. (London: Murray, 1773.)

The Origin of the Distinction of Ranks: or, An Enquiry into the Circumstances which Give Rise to Influence and Authority in the Different Members of Society. '3rd. ed.' (of the above), 'corrected and enlarged.' 8vo. (London: Murray, 1779.)

The same. Another printing (London: Murray, 1781).

The Same. 8vo. (Basel: Turneisen, pirated ?, 1793.)

The same, 4th ed., 'corrected' [unchanged]. 'To which is pre-fixed An Account of the Life and Writings of the Author, by John Craig, Esq.' 8vo. (Edinburgh: Blackwood; and London: Longmans, 1806.)

Translations of the above:

Bemerkungen ueber den Unterschied der Staende in der buergerlichen Gesellschaft. Aus dem Englischen uebersetzt. 8vo. (Leipzig: Schwickert, 1772.)

Observations sur les commencemens de la societe. Traduit de l'anglais d'après la seconde edition. 12mo. (Amsterdam: Arkstee et Meerkus, 1773.)

Aufklärungen über den Ursprung und Fortschritte des Unterschieds der Stände und des Ranges, in Hinsicht auf Kultur und Sitten bei den vorzüglichsten Nationen. Aus dem Englischen [3rd ed.]. 8vo. (Leipzig: Weygand, 1798.)

(Note: *Biographie Universelle Ancienne et Moderne* (Michaud), nouvelle ed, Paris, vol. xxviii, s.v. Millar, mentions an Italian translation I am unable to confirm. Sombart (above, p. 133 n.) hints at other German translations, without giving details.)

An Historical View of the English Government: From the Settlement of the Saxons in Britain to the Accession of the House of Stewart. 4to. (London: Strahan and Cadell, and J. Murray, 1787.)

The same. 8vo. (Dublin: Graeber and M'Allister, pirated? 1789. ? also 1787.)

The Same. 2nd ed. [very little altered] 4to. (London: Strahan and Cadell, 1790.)

An Historical View of the English Government: From the Settlement of the Saxons in Britain to the Revolution in 1688; to which are Subjoined some Dissertations Connected with the History of the Government from the Revolution to the Present Time. 4 vols. 8vo. Edited by John Craig and James Mylne. Vols I and II are a reprinting without alterations of the two books of the 2nd ed. (London: Mawman, 1803.)

The same, reprinted with corrections of some errors. (London: Mawman, 1812.)

The same, reprinted without alterations, except '4th ed.' imprinted on the title-page. (London: Mawman, 1818.)

Translation of above:

Historische Entwicklung der englischen Staatsverfassung. Aus dem Englischen von Dr K[arl] E[rnst] S[chmid]. 3 vols. (vol. IV is not translated). 8vo. (Jena: Schmid, 1819, 1820, 1821.)

(Under the pseudonym of 'Crito'.) Letters of Crito: On the Causes, Objects and Consequences of the Present War. (15 letters serially published in *Scots Chronicle*, Edinburgh, May to September, 1796. Only known copy in files of Edinburgh Public Library.)

The same in 12mo. pamphlet form, x + 109 pp., dedicated to Charles Fox. (Edinburgh: Johnstone; and London: Debrett, 1796.)

(Authorship probable, but not clearly established.) Letters of Sidney. [Sydney] to the editor of the *Scots Chronicle* on Inequality of Property. Ten letters published serially in *Scots Chronicle*, August to October 1796. (Edinburgh Public Library.)

The same, with 8 additional letters, reprinted in 12mo. pamphlet form. Dedicated to the Earl of Lauderdale. (Edinburgh, 1796.)

INDEX

M. — Professor Millar. Footnotes in Part III are not indexed.

Index

Index

Index

McCulloch, J. R., 104 n., 116, 146.
MacFie, A. L., 91 n., 104 n.
MacIver, R. M., Foreword, xiv.
Mackenzie, George, 96, 114.
Mackenzie, Fordon, 91 n.
Mackenzie, Henry, 91 n.
Mackenzie, Peter, 70 n., 150.
Mackie, J. D., 28 n., 45 n., 120, 127, 415.
Mackintosh, Sir James, 2 n., 120, 147, 150, 160.
McLennan, J. F., 146, 153, 161 n.
Madison, James, 153 f.
Magistrates in early society, 246, 255, 257.
Magna Charta, 65, 358 ff.
Malabar, 199, 202 n.
Malays, 281 n., 282.
Male authority, domination, 193 f., 200, 247 f., 248 n.
Mandelbaum, M. H., 98 n.
Manufactures, 326, 332, 367, 369; see also Commerce and industry.
Manumission, 312, 313 n., 318.
Mariner's compass, 366.
Marital fidelity, infidelity, 188, 227.
Marriage, 137, 184 ff., 187, 198, 206, 227 f., 244, 276, 359 f.
Marx, Karl, 157 f., 159.
Massagetae, 188, 190 f.
Master-servant relations, 76, 140, 233 f., 296, 300 f.
Matriarchy, 198 ff., 203.
Mathieson, W. L., 148 n., 415.
Matrilocal residence, 200.
Mechanical arts, see Trades and professions.
Mechanist interpretations, 94, 122 f.
Medes, 202.
Meek, R., 91 n., 151 n., 159 n.
Meikle, H., 10 n., 54 n., 71 n., 415.
Melbourne, 2nd and 3rd Viscounts (W. and F. Lamb), 23 n., 37 n., 42 n., 82 n., 149.
Men of learning, Scottish, 2, 95.
Mendelssohn, M., 155.
Mercantile adventurers, 334.
Mercantile arts and liberty, 74, 290 ff.
Mercantile spirit, 129, 386 f.
Mercantilism, 328 f.
Mercenary armies, soldiers, 282, 285 ff., 292 f., 301, 378 f.
Mercenary spirit, 207, 387.
Merchants, merchandizing, 366, 376 ff., 386, 398.
Mickle, W. J., 119 f.
Merovingian kings, 270 n.
Milheugh, 8 f., 10 f., 27, 29, 61 n., 82, 84, 410 ff., 414.
Military arts, leadership, 138, 246 f., 256.
Military establishments, policy, 130, 138, 247, 256, 264, 284 ff., 292, 294, 301, 347.
Military spirit, virtues, 210 f., 215, 246 f.
Military tenants, 268 f., 274 f.
Mill, James, 11, 15, 60 n., 151 f., 158, 160.
Mill, John Stuart, 112 n., 152, 159, 161 f.
Millar, James (father), 10, 410.

Millar, James (son), 26, 125 n., 411 f.
Millar, Prof. John
biographical highlights, 10, 12, 16 f., 19 f., 25, 26, 28, 29 f., 39, 46 ff., 50 f., 52 f., 72, 85, 410 ff.;
influence: on future leaders, statesmen, 1, 34 ff., 149 f., 151; on legal profession, 24, 28, 36, 69; on social and political thought at home, 151 f.; on social and political thought abroad, 153 ff.; on students, see Students;
law practice, limited, 18, 24 ff.
lectures characterized, 31 ff., 57 f., 408 f.;
neglect of writings, xi, 145 ff.;
personal characterization, 17, 30 ff., 53 f., 63 f., 67 f., 81 ff., 85;
writings characterized, reviewed, 55 f., 58 ff., 122 f.
Millar, John (son), 26, 73, 81, 412.
Millar, John (others), 10, 27, 411.
Millar, John H., 153.
Millar, Robina Cullen, 154 n., 412 f.
Millar, Thomas, Lord Advocate, 18.
Ministers, ministry, Christian, 11, 40 f., 93.
Ministerial government, powers, 73, 390 ff.
Minstrelsy, 215.
Mistresses, kept, 228.
Mobility, social, 138, 334, 336
Moderatism, 9, 95, 148
Modesty, sex, 190, 192.
Monarchy, 66, 72, 269 n., 272, 289, 338, 352, 374.
Monboddo, Lord (Burnet), 95, 100.
Moncreiff, J., 111 n., 149.
Money, 196, 251 n., 291, 328 f., 334.
Monied men, 128, 334.
Monopolies, 327.
Montaigne, 248 n.
Montesquieu, 3, 104, 107, 108, 111, 120, 123, 150 f., 156, 179 n., 274 n., 347, 402.
Moor, Prof. J., 15, 45, 53 n.
Moore, J., 28.
Morality and religion, 118, 228, 373 f., 383.
Morality and society, 105, 124, 383 ff.
Morals, science, theories of, 93, 105, 124, 341 ff.
Morgan, Alexander, 77 n.
Morgan, L. H., 133 n., 161.
Moses, Mosaic law, 194 f., 231, 235, 304, 313 n.; see also Bible, O.T.
Mother-right, 129, 153, 156 f., 198 ff., 203.
Moxos, 200.
Mueller, Adam, 157 n.
Muir, Thomas, 37 n., 53 n., 70, 73, 150.
Mungo, St, 12.
Murray, David, 1 n., 7, 14 n., 19 n., 22 n., 33 n., 36 n., 57 n., 78 n.
Music, M.'s interest in, 84, 388 f.
Mylne, James, 26, 45, 412, 417 (Bibl.).

N

Nakedness and morals, 191 f.
Nation, nationalism, 271, 330, 353.

National debt, funding of, 330, 391.
National defence, 286, 288, 379.
Natural aristocracy, 67.
'Natural history', 58, 93, 95, 99, 107, 122, 127, 167, 180, 282 f., 347 f.
Natural law (physical), 3, 93, 141, 142.
Natural law (moral), rights, 3, 45, 326, 350.
Natural philosophy, 25, 45, 94, 95.
'Natural progress', 59, 123, 176 f., 203, 228, 271, 314, 344, 371.
Natural religion, theology, 3, 93, 402.
Nature, naturalism, 3, 91 ff., 95.
Nature and nurture, culture, 118, 142, 190.
Nature, state of, 119, 134.
Navigation, 325 f., 366.
Negroes, 76, 193, 320, 322.
Netherlands, 245, 365, 367, 369, 370.
Newcastle, 320.
Newton, I., 93, 363 n.
Niebuhr, B. G., 156.
Nineteenth century, reaction to 18th, 162.
Nobles, nobility: decline of, 271, 292, 337, 377 f.; struggles with Crown, see Crown and nobility.
Nomadism, 129, 251, 259.
Nonconformists, 374.
Notes, promissory, 330.
Notices of lectures, 23.

O

Oath of office, M.'s, 20 n.
Offices held by M., 46 n.
Old Testament, see Bible.
Opinion, basis of government, 66, 142, 156, 355 n.
Opulence, 217, 268, 271, 289 f., 292 f., 296, 334, 339, 376; and see Wealth, Luxury.
Ossian, 119, 206 f., 231, 389.
Otaheiti (Tahiti), 119, 190, 385.

P

Paine, T., 80, 116.
Papacy, pope, Roman pontiff, 362, 364, 370, 372.
Parents, parent-child relations, 234 ff., 240 ff., 258, 298.
Parliament (British), 3, 38, 57, 66, 391, 393.
Parliamentary Reform, 3, 10, 26, 38, 70, 72 f., 74, 148 n., 149, 390 ff.; Tory opposition to, 68, 71 f., 148 n., 393 f.; radicalism denied, 67, 394.
Parliaments, parliamentary government, 135, 270, 378.
Parricide, 232, 241; and see Aged, Infanticide.
Pascal, R., 155 n., 159 n.
Pastoral economy, 203, 206 ff., 266; social and political consequences of, 203, 205, 250 f., 259; combined with agriculture, 259 f.; conquest, migration and, 260 f.
Pasturing cattle, 205 f., 239, 250, 327.
Paternal authority, jurisdiction, 69, 229-38,

239 ff., 243; limited by law, 240 ff.; moderation of, 235, 238 ff.; see also *Patria Potestas*.
Paton, G. C. H., 39 n.
Patria Potestas, 129, 236 ff.; limitation, moderation of, 238-43.
Patriarchal authority, 231, 257 f., 348, 352.
Patronage, 66, 74, 75, 391.
Peasants, peasantry, 139 f., 306 f., 308, 376.
Pegu, 189.
Pekin, 242.
Peloponnesus, 265, 390.
Perfectibility, 67, 100, 107.
Periclean Age, 4.
Pericles, 221.
Persia (Persians), 242, 282, 298.
Peru, 200, 256.
Petition, right of, denied, 393 f.
Phoenicians, 298.
Pitt, William, Pitt Government, 26, 38, 56, 74 n., 354 n., 390 ff.
Plantations, 315, 320 f.
Playfair, John, 156.
Pliny, 316.
Plutarch, 189.
Poetry, 40, 83, 216, 389 f.
Political activities, M.'s, 68, 71 ff.
Political economy, 39, 60 n., 97 f., 127 f., 325 ff., 329.
Political tenets, M.'s, 34 f., 39, 60, 64 ff., 71 f., 72 f., 148, 325, 390 ff.
Political theory, 97, 124 ff., 325, 347-57; see also Government.
'Politicking', 76.
'Poisoning' young minds, 39, 68 f.
Polybius, 102, 119.
Polyandry, 202.
Polygamy, 34, 129, 202, 225 f., 228, 242.
Polynesians, 120.
Poor, the (indigent), 318 f.
Poor-law, -rates, 318 f.
Pope, Alexander, 191 n.
Popery, popish, see Papacy, Roman Catholicism.
Popular government, 67, 326.
Population: numbers, increase of, 176, 244, 303, 316 f., 377; commerce and, 326; slavery and, 76, 317.
Portuguese, 119, 120, 315.
Power-relations, xii, 127, 132, 137, 140, 143, 293 f., 403.
Prerogative, royal, 58, 64, 66, 74 f., 124, 127, 143, 271, 288, 292, 379, 393.
Presbyterian, Presbyterianism, 14, 44, 65, 94, 137, 371, 373 f.
Pretender, the Young, 385.
Price, prices, 127, 326.
'Pride of family', 183, 213.
Priests, priestly, 257; and see Clergy.
Primitive society, see 'Rudeness, 'rude' society.
Primogeniture, 136.
Professions, division of labour in, 380 f.

property among, 183, 198, 246, 251, 257; warfare, 192, 387, 388; evolutionary implications, 125, 129, 224; general, 119 f., 200, 383.

Rules of conduct, 175, 243.

Rural isolation and conservatism, 9, 72, 124, 134, 377.

Rural-urban contrasts, interdependencies, 65, 128, 134, 369, 377, 378.

Russia, Russian, 37 n., 157 n., 235, 311, 385 n.

Russian students, professors, 37 n.

S

Sacred scriptures, 342, 362.

Sacred-secular, 92 n.

St Mungo, Chronicles of, 12.

Salique law, 213 n.

Salomon, Albert, 106 n.

Samoyedes, 184 n.

Sanctity of personality, 84, 143.

Savages, 93 n., 176, 183 f., 198, 230, 297, 302; and see 'Rudeness'.

Savigny, F. C., 156.

Saxon, Saxons, 59, 127, 277, 279, 368.

Say, J. B., 157.

Schiller, F., 155.

Scientific interests, M.'s, 60, 83.

Scots Chronicle, 56, 404, 406.

Scots law, see Law, Scots.

Scots Magazine, 29.

Scott, Sir Walter, xi, 13, 29 n., 37 n., 101, 413.

Scott, W. R., 51 n., 61 n., 95 n., 395, 400 n., 416 n.

Scottish awakening: intellectual, xi, 3, 9, 65, 91, 117, 148 n.; educational, 1, 14, 65 f., 77 f., 382; political, 9 f., 66, 68; economic, 9, 116 f.; Mathieson on, 415.

Scottish-English contrasts: economic and political, 65, 327, 333 n., 335; educational, 14, 78, 117; juridical, 34, 57 f., 65, 96, 116 f., 186, 337; general, 31, 34, 180, 186, 295.

Scottish men of learning, general, 2, 53 n., 95.

Scottish modes of thought, xii, 61 f., 78, 92 ff., 94, 104, 112.

Scythia, 202.

Secularization, 35, 91, 92, 93, 124, 160.

Serfs, serfdom, 64, 65.

Servility, 65, 217, 296, 361; see also Villein-age.

Servitude, 58, 64 f., 290, 295, 298, 302, 305 f., 312, 319; see also Slaves.

Settlement, agricultural, consequences of, 130, 250 f.

Sex: passion of, 141, 192, 196, 198; attitudes, mores of, 130; psychology of, 130; role in society, 193.

Sex-communism, limited, 189 f., 201.

Sex-promiscuity denied, 188.

Sex-ratio, 34.

Sexes: the commerce, intercourse of, 58, 129, 183, 188 f., 190, 198, 208, 210, 218, 225; roles of, 202; status of, 203.

Shaftesbury, Earl of, (philosopher), 93, 95, 113.

Shelburne, Lord, 15 n.

Shepherds, 129, 263; see Pastoral economy.

Shepperson, George, 120 n.

Shotts, parish; Kirk o' Shotts, 10, 11, 410, 413.

Siam, 189, 281.

Sicily, 207.

Sidney (Sydney), *Letters of*, 56, 60, 404.

Signet, library of, xv, 25; writers to, 16 n., 26.

Simson, Robert, 15, 45, 53, 150.

Sinclair, Sir John, *Statistical Account*, 94, 416.

Sinecures, 75.

Sismondi, 157.

Size of states, influence of, 265 f., 271 f., 292 ff., 338.

Skene, D., letters of, 24 n., 93 n.

'Skeptical philosophy', 95.

Slaves, slavery: general, 76, 197, 296–322; status defined, 298 f., 305, 313 f.; origins of, 296 f., 301; prevalence, severity of, 303 f., 316; gradual abolition of, 308 ff.; survivals of, 314, 319 f.; modern revival of, 314 ff.; dys-economy of, 302, 317 ff.; moral effects, 76, 317 f.; the church and, 311 f.

Slave Coast, 193.

Slave Trade, attack upon, 38, 50, 65, 72, 298 f., 304, 314 f.

Small, Albion, 106.

Smith, C. P., on James Wilson, 153, 154.

Smith, Adam
friend and colleague of M., 2, 17, 18, 28, 45;
influence on M., 4, 16 f., 114, 116, 127, 363, 383;
characterization by M., 401 ff.;
Theory of Moral Sentiments, 105, 115, 250, 349, 383, 402.
Wealth of Nations, 4, 97, 98, 105, 115, 155, 329, 363, 398, 403, 405;
lectures, 4, 16, 406;
historical interests of, 99, 147;
social psychologist, 105 f., 147;
general, xi, xiii, 8 n., 10, 11, 23 n., 51, 52, 53, 56, 91 n., 92, 93 n., 95, 101, 106 n., 114, 116 n., 119, 123, 128, 150, 153, 157, 158, 326, 346 f., 388, 395, 396, 399, 400 f., 404, 405.

Smith, C. P., on James Wilson, 153, 154 n.

Smith, Thomas, *Commonwealth*, 127 n., 196, 314 n.

'Social science', 152, 162.

Society: conception of, 134 ff.; nature and origin of, 104 ff., 122 f., 142 f., 176 f.; structural-functional, 135 ff.; dynamic view of, 59, 100, 129 f., 135, 296; civil and political, 134, 142, 350; and see Evolution, Progress, Ranks, 'State of society'.

Index